Commercial
Property
Risk Management
and
Insurance

Volume I

Commercial Property Risk Management and Insurance

Volume I

WILLIAM H. RODDA, CPCU
Consultant to Insurance Companies

JAMES S. TRIESCHMANN, D.B.A., CPCU, CLU
*Associate Dean, College of Business Administration
and Dudley L. Moore, Jr.,
Professor of Insurance*

ERIC A. WIENING, M.S., CPCU, ARM, AU
*Director of Curriculum Development
American Institute for Property
and Liability Underwriters*

BOB A. HEDGES, Ph.D., CPCU, CLU
*Professor and Chairman
Department of Risk Management and Insurance
Temple University*

Third Edition • 1988

AMERICAN INSTITUTE FOR
PROPERTY AND LIABILITY UNDERWRITERS
Providence and Sugartown Roads, Malvern, Pennsylvania 19355

Third Edition • *July 1988*

Library of Congress Catalog Number 88-70870
International Standard Book Number 0-89463-052-0

Printed in the United States of America

The revision of this text has been made possible through a generous grant provided by the family of the late William Gammon, Jr., an early pioneer in the CPCU professional movement.

Bill Gammon, Jr., demonstrated his life-long concern with high standards of competence in insurance at the very beginning of his career by earning the CPCU professional designation in 1948. Throughout his career, he personally maintained high standards of integrity and competence, thus exemplifying the professional ideals for which the CPCU designation stands.

His career served as an example of the true meaning of professionalism—a dedication to the service of others.

Foreword

Over the years, the American Institute for Property and Liability Underwriters and the Insurance Institute of America have responded to the educational needs of the property and liability insurance industry by developing courses and administering national examinations specifically for insurance personnel. These companion nonprofit educational organizations receive the support of the insurance industry in fulfilling this need.

The American Institute maintains and administers the program leading to the Chartered Property Casualty Underwriter (CPCU)® professional designation.

The Insurance Institute of America offers a wide range of associate designations and certificate programs in the following technical and managerial disciplines:

Accredited Adviser in Insurance (AAI)®
Associate in Claims (AIC)
Associate in Underwriting (AU)
Associate in Risk Management (ARM)
Associate in Loss Control Management (ALCM)®
Associate in Premium Auditing (APA)®
Associate in Management (AIM)
Associate in Research and Planning (ARP)®
Associate in Insurance Accounting and Finance (AIAF)
Associate in Automation Management (AAM)
Associate in Marine Insurance Management (AMIM)
Certificate in General Insurance
Certificate in Supervisory Management
Certificate in Introduction to Claims
Certificate in Introduction to Property and Liability Insurance

The first CPCU designations were conferred in 1943 to a class of six. Since then, over 22,000 have received this designation by passing ten national essay examinations, meeting an experience requirement, and agreeing to be bound by a Code of Professional Ethics. The American Institute publishes the textbooks and course guides for the CPCU national examinations. This is one of the texts in that series.

As with all Institute publications, this text has been extensively reviewed by a group of academic and industry experts, and they are recognized in the authors' preface. Throughout the development of this series of texts, it has been—and will continue to be—necessary to draw on the knowledge and skills of Institute personnel. These individuals will receive no royalties on texts sold; their writing responsibilities are seen as an integral part of their professional duties. We have proceeded in this way to avoid any possibility of conflict of interests.

We invite and welcome any and all criticisms of our publications. It is only with such comments that we can hope to provide high quality study materials. Comments should be directed to the Curriculum Department of the Institutes.

Norman A. Baglini, Ph.D., CPCU, CLU, AU
President

Preface

This text was designed for CPCU 3, one of the ten courses in the curriculum leading to the CPCU® (Chartered Property Casualty Underwriter) professional designation. Study aids for the course are provided in a companion volume—the CPCU 3 Course Guide. The Course Guide contains educational objectives, outlines of study material, key terms and concepts, review and discussion questions, and, where appropriate, updates and supplementary readings. The Course Guide also contains administrative information about the CPCU program and registration forms for the CPCU 3 national examination. Policies and forms are not included in this text, but are available in a Policy Kit. The Course Guide and the Policy Kit are revised annually. Current editions of the CPCU 3 Course Guide and of the Policy Kit may be purchased from the American Institute.

This text is devoted primarily to the identification, analysis, and treatment of the *property* exposures faced by modern business firms, governmental bodies, educational institutions, and charitable organizations. These are referred to as *commercial* property exposures to distinguish them from the property exposures faced by individuals and families, which are examined in another CPCU text.

The third edition differs markedly from the first two editions of this text, reflecting the fact that the most widely used commercial insurance policies have recently been revised. Other changes have been necessary to reflect general changes in the insurance environment. The net effect is that approximately two-thirds of the content of the previous edition has been replaced.

Changes have been in the works for several years. During 1984, Insurance Services Office (ISO) announced the details of its Commercial Lines Simplification Program, a simultaneous revision of coverage forms and rating rules for most commercial coverages. The initial forms bore November 1985 edition dates. Actual use of the revised forms, for most insurers, began during 1986 and 1987. As of July 1987, ISO ceased to provide support for the presimplified forms on which previous editions of this text were based. The ISO changes alone made it necessary to revise approximately half the text.

Such a large-scale introduction of new insurance coverage forms created special challenges for us as authors. Many insurance textbooks deal with long-standing policy provisions that have stood the test of time. In writing this edition, we found ourselves dealing with policies that had never yet been sold. Obviously, policy wording and coverage provisions introduced in the simplified forms had not yet had a chance to be tested and interpreted in the courts. We were often working from policy drafts, explanatory materials, and filing memoranda about which no other written commentary existed.

Despite the difficulty of dealing with brand new forms, policy simplification has made it easier to explain insurance coverages. Simplification has greatly reduced the number of forms we needed to cover. Simplification has also made it unnecessary to detail many minor variations among similar coverage forms, because most of those variations have been eliminated. In other cases, the new ISO forms have simply taken a more straightforward approach. Because we needed to devote less space to a plethora of forms, variations, and complexities, we have been able to devote more space to explanations that should lead to a deeper understanding. Yet, simplified or not, the reader is cautioned that one can never predict with certainty how the policies will be interpreted in the courts. The new forms are by no means perfect, but the simplification project has been a giant step forward for insurers, risk managers, and consumers—and also for insurance students and educators.

In this text, insurance is examined in a risk management context, because the usefulness and significance of any insurance coverage depend on its value as a risk management device. Chapter 1 presents an overall analysis of organizations' exposures to property loss. The risk management context is further developed in Chapter 2, which deals with measuring and controlling commercial property loss exposures. Various control measures are described, with emphasis on fire loss control.

Subsequent chapters deal primarily, but not exclusively, with insurance coverages. Also considered are (1) the nature of the loss exposure to which each coverage relates and (2) the risk management techniques other than insurance that can be used to deal with those exposures. Discussed first are the coverage categories that include standard ISO forms (although non-ISO forms are also discussed where appropriate). Most of the ISO forms discussed in these early chapters can be combined with one another in a commercial package policy. Thus, Chapters 3, 4, 5, and the first part of Chapter 6 concentrate on the ISO "commercial property" forms; the last part of Chapter 6 deals with boiler and machinery forms; Chapters 7 and 8 deal with crime insurance; and Chapters 9 and 10 with inland marine insurance.

Ocean marine exposures and insurance are examined in Chapters 11 and 12. Chapter 13 deals with businessowners policies, farm insurance, financial institution bonds, and related coverages. Chapter 14, "Miscellaneous Coverages," true to its title, covers such diverse topics as EDP floaters, flood insurance, difference in conditions coverage, and nuclear property and liability insurance. Chapter 15 examines the loss financing alternatives to insurance—noninsurance transfers and retention—and concludes with two case studies.

Many chapters of this text deal with coverages and copyrighted forms developed by Insurance Services Office, Inc. (ISO). Excerpts from ISO policies are used with permission.

Completion of this third edition would not have been possible without the teamwork and willing assistance of a great many dedicated professionals. It is no exaggeration to say that every single page of text bears the touch of several authors, editors, and reviewers.

We are especially grateful to the contributing authors, listed separately following this Preface, for writing, rewriting, or revising manuscripts upon which several chapters are based. Samuel L. Rosenthal, CPCU, ARM, an active insurance consultant, developed the original manuscript for Chapter 6. Among Sam's credits are his previous work as a contributing author to the CPCU 4 text. Donald S. Malecki, CPCU, also an active consultant, drafted Chapter 8. Don has been involved with CPCU study materials for more than a dozen years, and is a co-author of the texts currently used in CPCU 2 and CPCU 4.

Portions of Chapter 14 are based on manuscripts by Arthur L. Flitner, M.A., CPCU, Assistant Director of Curriculum of the American Institute for Property and Liability Underwriters and the Insurance Institute of America.

The following persons reviewed major portions of the text and provided constructive suggestions, comments, and edits that significantly improved the completeness, accuracy, and clarity of the presentation: John G. Earhart, CPCU, Manager, Commercial Property, American Association of Insurance Services; Thomas W. Mallin, J.D., CPCU, Vice President and General Counsel, Property Loss Research Bureau; John A. Reiner, CPCU, AU, Product Development Manager, Crum & Forster Commercial Insurance; and Lawton Swan III, CPCU, CLU, ARM, CSP, President, Interisk Corporation.

Reviewers who provided special expertise in more limited subject areas include: James F. Donahue, CPCU, CLU, Managing Director, Bowles, Troy, Donahue, Johnson; C. Raymond Ford, Director of Field Underwriting, The Hartford Steam Boiler Inspection and Insurance Co.; Patrick F. Genovese, CSP, Property Manager, Midwest Region

Loss Control, CNA Insurance; Jenny Law, CPCU, Assistant Vice President, Johnson and Higgins of Delaware Inc.; John F. McComb, CPCU, Vice President, Transco Syndicate #1, Ltd.; Robert Olausen, Sr., Rate Analyst, Surety Association of America; John L. O'Marra, J.D., Risk Management Director, GPU Service Corporation; Frances M. Pommer, CPCU, ARM, AAI, CIC, Regional Manager, Omaha Flood Insurance Programs; Burt C. Proom, CPCU, President and Chief Executive Officer, American Nuclear Insurers; Robin V. Weldy, Director-Legal, Surety Association of America; and James A. Zrebiec, CPCU, Assistant Vice President, Commercial Union Insurance Companies.

Domenick J. Yezzi, Jr., CPCU, Manager-Industry Relations, Insurance Services Office, coordinated the reviews of many chapters dealing with ISO forms and fielded many questions from the authors. We are grateful to the following ISO personnel for the special insights provided in their reviews: Janet T. Battistelli, Supervisor; Lawrence E. Brown, Assistant Manager; Joseph Mirra, Insurance Lines Specialist; Michael Podoshen, Manager, Individual Risk Rating and Corporate Insurance Division; and Maurice E. Southwell, CPCU, CLU, ChFC, ARM, Assistant Manager.

Others who provided valuable reviews of portions of the text include: James Giambalvo, CPCU, Vice President, IRM Insurance; David G. Hampson, CPCU, President, Insmark Corporation; Francis J. Kelly, Jr., CPCU, ARM, Vice President, Orion Group; Harry E. McCluskey, CPCU, Division Manager, State Farm Insurance Companies; Emmett O'Brien, CPCU, Risk Manager, County of Wake; George M. Periera, Departmental Manager, Royal Insurance; Colin J. Rose, CPCU, Product Consultant, Royal Insurance; and Jerome Trupin, CPCU, CLU, President, Trupin, North, and North, Inc.

We are also grateful to all the American Institute staff members who assisted in the production of this text, especially the Publications and Public Relations Department. Their devotion to quality and attention to detail are reflected literally from cover to cover.

The four authors have now been involved with three editions of this text, for a period spanning more than a decade. Each of us now knows much more than he did ten years ago, and some of our recently acquired knowledge is reflected in this edition. Comments received on the first two editions have greatly aided us. We invite CPCU students and other readers to send us their comments and criticisms in order that we might continue to improve future editions.

We are also deeply interested in the usefulness of this text as a learning device. Accordingly, we welcome constructive comments on how we may improve our presentation. The authors recognize that the text may contain oversimplifications and factual errors—especially if the facts have changed since the text was written, as is almost a certainty in such a dynamic field. Though we have tried to anticipate and minimize such problems, we invite readers to call our attention to any that they may discover. Comments may be addressed to the Curriculum Department of the American Institute.

William H. Rodda
James S. Trieschmann
Eric A. Wiening
Bob A. Hedges

Contributing Authors

The American Institute for Property and Liability Underwriters and the authors of this text acknowledge, with deep appreciation, the work of the following contributing authors:

Donald S. Malecki, CPCU
President
Donald S. Malecki & Associates, Inc.

Samuel L. Rosenthal, CPCU, ARM
Property and Casualty Insurance Consultant
Industrial Insurance Management Corp.

Table of Contents

Special Named Perils Causes of Loss—Extended Form

An Illustration ~ *Analyzing the Exposure; Determining How Much Insurance to Purchase; Payroll or Utility Coverage Options*

**Chapter 6—Miscellaneous "Commercial Property,"
Boiler and Machinery Exposures and
Insurance** **307**

Condominium Property Exposures ~ *Documents Clarifying Status; Barewall Concept Versus Single Entity Concept; Insurance Requirements*

Condominium Property Insurance ~ *Condominium Association Coverage Form; Condominium Unit-Owners Coverage Form*

Builders Risk Property Exposures

Builders Risk Insurance ~ *Builders Risk Coverage Form; Builders Risk Reporting Form; Business Income Coverage for Builders Risks*

Leasehold Interest Exposures and Coverage

Legal Liability Exposures and Coverage ~ *Exposures; Legal Liability Coverage Form; Other Approaches*

Standard Property Policy ~ *Covered Property; Covered Perils; Conditions; Condominium Association Coverage Endorsement*

Glass Exposures ~ *Types of Glass Property; Perils and Loss Consequences; Frequency and Severity of Glass Losses*

The Glass Coverage Form ~ *Eligible Property; Property Covered; Covered Perils; Vacancy Exclusion; Additional Coverages; Coverage Extension—Newly Acquired Glass; Limits of Insurance; Deductible; Valuation and Loss Payment Provisions*

Boilers and Machinery ~ *Loss Exposures—Property and Perils; Controlling Boiler and Machinery Loss Exposures; Other Policies Insuring Boiler and Machinery Losses*

Boiler and Machinery Insurance ~ *ISO Policy Format; Scope of Coverage—Accident to an Object; Covered Property; Coverage Extensions; Exclusions; Limits of Insurance; Conditions; Object Definitions Endorsements; Time*

Element Coverages; Small Business Boiler and Machinery Forms

CHAPTER 1

Commercial Property Exposures

The primary emphasis of this text is on insurance, an important risk management technique. To study insurance properly, it is necessary to study exposures to loss and *all* the techniques that can be used to handle those exposures.

Chapter 1 begins with a brief overview of loss exposures, the goals of risk management, and the risk management process. Identification of commercial property exposures is then developed in detail by analyzing types of property, perils, and loss consequences. Although the discussion may seem rather elementary, it is necessary to lay a base for discussion of the vast variety of property loss exposures to be considered in this course.

Loss exposures cannot be consciously treated until they have been identified. In identifying commercial property loss exposures—the first step in the risk management process—it is desirable to use an organized approach. The latter part of this chapter introduces several structured systems for accomplishing this. The insurance survey method is particularly useful to insurance personnel who are interested in identifying loss exposures primarily so that they can provide insurance that gives appropriate coverage. This method is of less value in identifying exposures that are not generally insured or insurable exposures for which risk management techniques other than insurance should be considered. Other methods or systems of exposure identification—particularly flow chart analysis and financial statement analysis—will also be discussed.

This chapter does not present any magical formula for identifying all insurable and noninsurable property exposures that face producers, underwriters, or risk managers. Even with the aid of computers or the various systems to be explored here, exposure identification requires experience, imagination, insight, and education.

1

LOSS EXPOSURES AND RISK MANAGEMENT

Risk management is the treatment of loss exposures. Insurance is only one technique for treating loss exposures. All risk management techniques other than insurance are referred to in this text as *noninsurance techniques.* Both insurance and noninsurance techniques are used to treat or "manage" loss exposures. It is appropriate to begin this text by answering three basic questions:

1. What is a loss exposure?
2. Why should loss exposures be treated? (What are the objectives?)
3. How can loss exposures be treated? (What are the tools?)

Loss Exposures

A *loss exposure* is a set of circumstances that present a possibility of loss, whether or not a loss actually takes place. *Commercial property loss exposures* are loss exposures that exist because a commercial enterprise or public entity depends on property to help accomplish its objectives.

There are three elements of a property loss exposure:

1. the item subject to loss,
2. the perils, or forces that may cause a loss, and
3. the potential financial impact of the loss.

These three elements will be discussed in detail later in this chapter. For now, a simple example will help clarify the concept. This book, *Commercial Property Risk Management and Insurance, Volume I,* is an item subject to loss. A loss would be caused if the book were stolen. Thus, "theft" is a peril that may cause loss of this book.

Part of the financial impact of the theft would be loss of the immediate value of the book. Suppose the book cost about $25; that purchase price might be one measure of its value. Any inflation in the price since the book was purchased would push the amount upward. At the same time, wear and tear (depreciation) might have made this particular copy less valuable.

Besides loss of the book's immediate value, there would be loss of its availability as an aid to study and preparation for an examination. The value of study time lost while awaiting a replacement text would also be part of the impact of the loss.

By the time you have finished studying this book and have annotated it with various markings and underlinings, it may be worth much more to you than $25, even it you could purchase a fresh, new clean book for $25. This further illustrates the notion that property values are not always easy to measure and may change over time.

The chance of losing $25 or more because this book is stolen is a loss exposure. It is a loss *exposure* even if this book is *not* stolen, because the chance of theft exists. We would like to suppose that demand for this book is so great that there is a high probability of theft. Whether or not that is actually the case, it does illustrate the notion that some exposures are more likely than others to result in loss.

Objectives of Commercial Property Risk Management

Not just risk management, but all management activities are intended to accomplish certain goals. The purpose of management goals is clearly described by Martin J. Gannon:

> Goals serve several useful purposes. Obviously, management must have an overall goal in mind before the organization even comes into existence. This and subsequent, more specific goals help determine the organization's structure. Goals also provide a basis against which management can measure performance. In addition, they serve as a guide when management must make difficult decisions. For example, managers may decide to curtail production of a new product if sales within the first year fall short of expectations. Further, goals can link departments, giving them a target they can seek jointly rather than struggling with one another over scarce resources. Because of the importance of goals, top management typically sets the major objectives to be achieved throughout the organization.

> To be useful, goals should satisfy two objectives: they should be explicit and they should not be in conflict. Top management can insure that goals are explicit by making them as clear and specific as possible. The goal "to improve customer service" does not define customer service; consequently, there is no way to measure whether the organization has achieved it. An explicit version of this goal would be "to provide next-morning delivery on 95 percent of all orders received from the Sales Department by 5:00 p.m."

> If goals are in conflict, they cannot normally be met. Conflict is inherent in the goal, "to provide the highest quality at the lowest cost." Usually there is a trade-off between quality and cost; it is not possible to achieve both objectives simultaneously. A more consistent statement would be, "to produce a product of maximum quality subject to a selling price of $8.50.[1]

Risk management objectives are goals that deal specifically with the management of pure loss exposures. (*Pure loss exposures* present the possibility of "loss" or "no loss." In contrast, *speculative exposures* present the possibility of "loss," "no loss," or "gain.") Risk management objectives have been divided into two categories—pre-loss and post-loss.[2]

Post-loss Objectives   Post-loss objectives relate to the completeness and speed of recovery from losses that have occurred. If a loss actually takes place, a commercial enterprise might wish to accomplish one or more of the following objectives:

- *Survival*—This objective means being able eventually to resume at least some operations, although possibly with substantially fewer assets. Many firms fail to meet this minimal objective and are forced out of business following a major fire or other property loss.
- *Continuity of operations*—A more ambitious objective than mere survival, this objective means continuing operations after a loss with only minimal interruption or impairment. Continuity of operations is particularly important to businesses like banks, newspapers, and dairies where interruption of service could mean permanent loss of customers or suppliers.
- *Earnings stability*—Stabilization of earnings may be important. One way to do this is to obtain income to replace lost earnings. Earnings stability may also be achieved if it is possible to continue operations with no increase in cost. Earnings stability may be an important objective for the owners of a "Ma and Pa" store who depend on the store as a sole source of income. Earnings stability is also an important objective for publicly held corporations, because financial analysts and investors put less value on the stocks of corporations with highly variable rather than relatively stable rates of return. Because insurance helps to stabilize business results against the fluctuations caused by losses, there is a trend toward disclosing information about any significant absence of insurance (especially liability coverages) in a corporation's financial statements. Investors thus can evaluate not only the corporation's recovery from losses that have occurred but also its apparent ability to recover from losses that might occur.
- *Continued growth*—Even more ambitious than surviving, continuing operations, and maintaining earnings stability, may be an objective of continued growth. A business that has experienced steady growth in recent years that may not be willing to forgo its growth pattern following a severe property loss. A business that has extensive plans for future growth, for which it has already made heavy investment, may not be ready to forgo that growth even in the face of some property loss.

- *Social responsibility*—An important post-loss objective often is to protect investors, suppliers, employees, and customers against losses or inconvenience resulting from disruptions of a firm's operations. An organization may also desire to avoid upsetting residents in the area or local, state, or federal government officials.

Pre-loss Objectives Loss exposures, by definition, may or may not result in losses. Risk management—treating loss exposures—involves anticipating losses that *might* happen. Pre-loss objectives should be accomplished whether or not a loss takes place, and usually include the following:

- *Economy*—A firm seeks to accomplish its post-loss risk management objectives in the most economical way possible. In short, the relative cost of various risk management alternatives must be considered.
- *Reduction in anxiety*—Mehr and Hedges call this objective a "quiet night's sleep."[3] Loss exposures involve uncertainty. When loss exposures have been properly treated, there should be less uncertainty concerning loss.
- *Meeting externally imposed obligations*—Some obligations are imposed by outsiders. For example, building codes may require certain safety features that affect the probable frequency or severity of building fires. Smoke detectors are required in certain occupancies so that the occupants can become aware of a small fire that has ignited and can evacuate the building and notify firefighters.
- *Social responsibility*—This is both a pre-loss objective and a post-loss objective. Society is threatened not only by losses that occur but by the threat that losses may occur. Measures taken to prevent losses benefit society.

Conflicts Among Objectives As Martin J. Gannon noted in the excerpt quoted earlier, goals that are in conflict normally cannot all be met. The *economy* objective, for example, is often in conflict with other risk management objectives. The most complete insurance is not the most economical, but it may provide the greatest reduction in anxiety.

For any commercial enterprise, goals need to be stated as explicitly as possible in a manner that acknowledges the trade-offs among conflicting objectives. Rather than expressing its goals as "economy" and "earnings stability," a given firm might more explicitly state as its objective "to minimize expected costs of financing and controlling losses, on the average in the long run, to the extent that this corporation is not exposed to the chance that earnings will be reduced from the current level by more than 5 percent as a consequence of property losses."

Given a series of specific stated objectives, often set forth in a "risk management policy statement," a risk manager can proceed to develop a risk management program that meets the specific objectives of the firm.

This text focuses on risk management tools that enable businesses, nonprofit organizations, public agencies, and other commercial enterprises to meet their objectives that involve managing property loss exposures.

The Risk Management Process

Goals having been set, the risk management process involves:

1. Identifying and analyzing loss exposures
    (a) Identifying things of value exposed to loss
    (b) Measuring potential loss frequency and severity
2. Selecting the technique or techniques to be used to handle each exposure
    (a) Techniques for controlling loss exposures
    (b) Techniques for financing loss exposures
3. Implementing the techniques chosen
4. Monitoring the decisions made and implementing changes when appropriate[4]

The rest of this chapter deals with step (1a) in the risk management process—identifying things of value exposed to loss.

TYPES OF COMMERCIAL PROPERTY EXPOSED TO LOSS

With respect to property loss exposures, identification begins with locating things of value exposed to loss. This section will discuss various types of commercial property. The perils that may cause property losses and the types of loss consequences that may result when property is damaged by a peril will be examined in subsequent sections.

There is no single widely accepted system for classifying commercial property. Property can be divided into the categories of *real property* and *personal property*, but, without further subdivision, these broad categories are not of much use for the present discussion. The approach taken here is to discuss narrower categories of property types, with most of the property in each category having similar loss exposures.

A good classification system is one that meets the needs of its user. The classification system used here merely illustrates one that might be adapted for use by an organization attempting to identify types of property exposed to loss. A brief analysis of each of the property types will make clear the usefulness of this kind of classification. The real property types used for this discussion are land and buildings and structures. Personal property types are money and securities; accounts receivable; inventory; equipment, fixtures, and supplies; machinery; data processing equipment and media; valuable papers, books, and documents; mobile property; and intangible assets. Nonowned property and property off-premises have special characteristics and are presented here as separate property classes.

Real Property

Real property is generally defined as land and whatever is growing on it, erected on it, or affixed to it.

Land Real estate, excluding buildings and other structures, is known as land. Often it is desirable to classify land separately for two reasons: (1) values may be difficult to determine, and (2) perils that can cause loss to land are unique, or at least unusual.

Consider some of the reasons values may be difficult to recognize. Land may contain (1) water (lake, river, creek, springs, or underground water table); (2) mineral resources (coal, iron, oil, copper, bauxite, potash, sand, or stone); (3) natural attractions of commercial value (cave, therapeutic spring or pool, historic site, or artifacts); (4) growing plants (timber, fruit trees, or grazing pasture); or (5) resident wild animals (which, even though not affixed, are legally part of the real property). The principal component of value in much land is location, which is little subject to physical damage.

Improved land may include crops, trees, and extensive and expensive landscaping. Some perils that might affect land are obvious. Growing crops or timber are subject to brush or forest fires and plant diseases. Agricultural crops (such as vegetables and grains) may be damaged by rain, hail, snow, drought, and other weather conditions. The soil itself may be lost by erosion (caused by water or wind), volcanic eruption, mud slide, and landslide. Various activities may also generate wastes or release chemicals that pollute or contaminate the land, reducing its value and utility.

Even unimproved land that is not in use for any purpose has a value. Yet, if it is unattended and unsupervised for long periods, others may obtain rights to the property through easements or "squatter's rights" or the land may be subject to unauthorized dumping of wastes and chemicals.

Most property losses to land are not covered by insurance, although crops are often insured. Yet loss to land may have substantial consequences if the land's resources or use value are reduced or destroyed.

Buildings and Other Structures The loss exposures of buildings and other structures depend primarily on the type of construction, occupancy, and location of the property. Loss potential may be influenced significantly by loss control measures. A sprinklered building, for example, is much less likely to suffer a major fire loss than an identical but unsprinklered building.

The major characteristics of buildings and structures are as follows:

1. They may represent substantial values directly exposed to loss.
2. Income is frequently lost until the damaged property is repaired or replaced—and sometimes longer.
3. These exposures are usually insurable—at least against a large number of perils causing physical property losses.

Buildings and structures under construction are subject to special hazards. Normally, security is poor. Fire detection or prevention devices may not be operational. There are many open spaces through which a fire can spread. Combustible materials are scattered throughout the structure. Construction materials are unprotected from the elements. In addition, there may be several subcontractors working on the same project, with varying degrees of loss control activity. Furthermore, the values of a structure under construction are undergoing constant change as materials and labor are added.

Structures other than buildings are easily overlooked when loss exposures are being identified. Yet, many structures represent substantial values and require special insurance treatment if they are to be covered. Another potential problem is the possibility that ownership of land could be called into question—an exposure that can be addressed with title insurance and other measures described in Chapter 13.

Personal Property

Personal property is everything that is the subject of ownership other than real property.

Money and Securities The term "money and securities" includes many types of monetary assets, such as cash, bank accounts, certificates of deposit, securities, notes, drafts, and evidences of debt.

The magnitude of money and securities loss exposures varies widely by type of operation and is not always related to the size of the organization. Some small firms have relatively sizable monetary assets. A single supermarket, for example, typically has on hand large sums in cash and checks. A large manufacturer, on the other hand, may have a small exposure for cash on hand, yet face the possibility over time of a severe embezzlement loss of cash (or other property). The money and securities exposure fluctuates considerably in some companies. Firms that have seasonal patterns often have wide variations in monetary assets on hand during the year.

Monetary assets are subject to many perils, but one of the most important is theft. Monetary assets may be stolen by employees or outsiders, by simple schemes or by very elaborate, sophisticated plans.

Accounts Receivable The tangible property (paper or other media such as computer disks on which accounts receivable are recorded) is subject to physical damage, destruction, or removal from possession. However, the value of these tangible media usually is insignificant when related to the property right that the media represent. If accounts receivable records are damaged or destroyed, a company may be unable to replace the records or collect on the accounts; or it may be able to reproduce them from underlying data only at a large cost. Either way, the loss can be substantial.

Another outstanding characteristic of this exposure is that loss potential may be substantially reduced by reasonable loss control methods. If complete duplicate records are kept in a remote location, simultaneous loss of both sets of records is practically impossible. Usually, however, the backup records are not entirely up to date.

Inventory For a wholesaler or retailer, inventory represents goods ready for sale and perhaps some goods that are sold but have not yet been delivered to the buyer. For a manufacturer, inventory is usually further divided into raw materials, stock in process, and finished goods.

There are several characteristics of this exposure. One is that inventory is subject to a wide range of perils. Some inventory may be at a fixed location. Other inventory may be subject to the perils of transportation.

Inventory values may fluctuate widely. The value of goods in process is sometimes difficult to determine because value is being added at each stage in the production process. In some cases, raw material is obtained from sources that may be difficult or impossible to replace. In these circumstances, a company can suffer a loss when a supplier has a loss and is unable to deliver its goods.

Furniture, Equipment, and Supplies Examples of personal property in this category include office furniture, file drawers, typewriters, photocopy equipment, showcases, counters, office supplies (such as stationery and printed forms), manufacturing supplies, cleaning supplies, and packaging materials.

This classification includes a miscellaneous category of personal property that would be difficult and impractical to classify otherwise. For many organizations, one outstanding characteristic of this classification has been that usually it consists of many separate pieces of property, most of which have a relatively low value. However, there is a trend towards using expensive, "high-tech" equipment (e.g., computers rather than typewriters) in many operations. Also, replacement equipment and supplies are usually readily available, so an extensive interruption of the business resulting from loss of these items is unlikely. Another characteristic of property in this category is that often it is difficult to establish total values for two reasons: (1) with numerous items of low value, it is impractical to devote much attention to precise valuation of each item; and (2) this type of property frequently shifts from one location to another, making it difficult to keep an accurate inventory.

The above characteristics provide, at best, only a general description of property in this category. Since this is a miscellaneous class of property, there is a real danger that some property will not conform to the general pattern. This exceptional property can cause risk management problems. Suppose, for example, that a risk manager assumes furniture, equipment, and supplies are low-value items that could be replaced easily. A manufacturer, however, may have a significant investment in packaging materials, fuel, chemicals, or cutting oils. And, even if the values are not large and *most* such property is readily replaceable, it is possible that *some* property may not easily be replaced, and that a loss of that property could shut down the firm's operations. It is important, therefore, to analyze the property in this category to determine if it includes any property of special importance. It is easy for special property in this category to escape detection.

Machinery Machinery could logically be included in the previous category—furniture, equipment, and supplies. In fact, machinery might be considered a type of equipment and vice versa. Some items of machinery, however, often have particular characteristics that affect loss exposures.

Machinery may involve large values. Often the values are subject to rapid depreciation—true physical depreciation and obsolescence, as opposed to accounting depreciation.

In many cases, losses caused by breakdown of machinery cause additional loss consequences. Damage to power, heating, cooling, and lighting machinery, for example, may interrupt a company's operations. Since replacement or repair of damaged machinery often requires specialized parts or technical expertise, repair or replacement may require a long time. As a result, the lost income during the business interruption can be substantial.

In addition to the perils affecting property in general, machinery is subject to some unique perils. Mechanical breakdown, for example, may result from improper use or maintenance, electrical malfunctions, inherent defects, metal fatigue, rust, and overheating. Technological advances may cause rapid economic obsolescence. Many of these perils are uninsurable and must be handled by some risk management technique other than insurance.

Data Processing Equipment and Media Many organizations have electronic data processing (EDP) equipment with substantial values. This property classification includes not only computers but also computer programs and data (sometimes called "media") and equipment such as printers, modems, and external disk drives. Word processing equipment, electronic typewriters, and other electronic office or manufacturing equipment may also be included in this classification, as well as large mainframe computer installations.

Some computer facilities require a special environmental control system which represents a significant additional *building* exposure that would not exist were it not for the computer. This may involve separate temperature and humidity controls.

In addition to the usual perils that may cause physical damage to the computer facilities and loss of income if the business is interrupted because the computer is "down," EDP systems make other losses possible. Accidental damage to programs or data can also interrupt operations. Computer fraud by employees and outsiders has increased dramatically in recent years. Usually the criminals intend to steal money, but some ingenious schemes involve the theft of other property. In some cases, an employee or outsider is interested in sabotaging EDP programs or altering data. Sometimes the purpose of the crime is to obtain confidential information that leads to loss of an intangible asset such as a trade secret. Industrial espionage probably has been stimulated by computers because corporate information is now more centralized than it previously was. Even theft of "computer time" can be significant.

Some computers are owned by the user, but others are leased.

Normally, the lessor assumes responsibility for maintenance and accidental losses to the computer and its equipment, but this is not always true. Lease agreements must be reviewed carefully to identify loss exposures.

Valuable Papers, Books, and Documents Even small business firms may generate a huge volume of accounting, financial, and statistical records. Many of these records may be maintained in the form of computer data, but there may also be a substantial exposure to loss of paper records containing unconverted data—data that has not yet been entered into the data processing system. In addition, the operations of many companies depend heavily on valuable books, drawings, films, maps, abstracts, deeds, photographs, and other documents. Physicians maintain medical histories on their patients. Photographers, architects, engineers, journalists, and others maintain files of their previous work in order to become more efficient.

These pieces of property create special loss exposures because they are small, light, and easily destroyed or lost. They can be difficult to evaluate or be quite valuable. If valuable papers can be reproduced promptly, with little cost, the exposure may not be significant. Often, however, reproduction of valuable papers is time consuming or impossible, and a company may lose income or incur additional expenses because of the loss.

Vehicles Autos, aircraft, boats and ships, heavy mobile equipment used by contractors, and other vehicles represent a separate class of property.

Vehicles of many kinds are exposed to special hazards that arise from transportation. Collision is a major cause of loss, but movable property can be damaged or destroyed by a large number of other perils as well.

Often extremely large values are concentrated in single items of mobile property. A single airplane, ship, or piece of earth-moving equipment may be valued in the millions.

Intangible Assets Some assets, although valuable, have no physical substance. These include such items are goodwill, copyrights, patents, trademarks, trade names, leases and leasehold interests, licenses, and trade secrets.

These assets are generally difficult to recognize. If a firm consistently earns a larger profit than seems warranted on the basis of the company's physical assets, the implication is that a portion of the profits may be generated by intangible assets. It is easy to overlook specific intangible assets that are responsible for the level of profits. The larger profits may be a result of a key employee's efforts, trade secrets, or even competitive advantages. Once an intangible asset has been identified, another difficult challenge lies in trying to figure out how that asset may be lost, damaged, or otherwise reduced in value.

Some intangible asset exposures are insurable. For example, a dry cleaner can purchase insurance covering fire loss to customers' property even under circumstances where the cleaner is not responsible for the fire. By compensating customers for the value of their damaged garments—even when not legally obligated to do so—the cleaner preserves customer goodwill. Many intangible asset exposures are not insurable—at least at a reasonable rate. Noninsurance risk management techniques, therefore, are especially important for preserving the value of intangible assets.

Nonowned Property

Losses caused by damage to owned property are fairly obvious. Less obvious are the situations involving nonowned property that can produce losses, such as those involving bailed property, leased property, property on consignment (actually a type of bailment), employees' property, property used as security for a loan or mortgage, or trustee relationships.

In some instances, the legal responsibility for repairing or replacing nonowned property is determined by the type of relationship between the parties involved. In others, an agreement or contract will spell this out. In situations involving the sale of certain types of personal property, provisions of the Uniform Commercial Code will dictate where the exposure to loss falls.

Bailed Property Dry cleaners, laundries, warehouses, repair firms, jewelers, television repair shops, and others have on their premises property of customers (or others) for which they may or may not be legally responsible.

Leased Property Companies often lease from others computers, autos, and other machinery. The terms of the lease agreements usually determine who is responsible for losses.

This also applies to leased real property. Some leases require that the tenant pay for repairs and reconstruction following damage to the premises.

Property on Consignment Distributors and retailers sometimes have property on their premises to be sold, although ownership rests with another entity. Responsibility for losses should be spelled out in a contract between the parties, but this is not always done.

Employees' Property Employees often keep property, such as clothing and tools, on the employer's premises. Some union contracts make the employer directly responsible for loss of employees' tools, imposing a loss exposure where none might otherwise exist. This would be either a bailment or an exposure created by contractual liability.

Property under Lien A lender may suffer a financial loss if a debtor ceases to make payments following damage or destruction to property used to secure a debt. For example, a bank holding the mortgage on a commercial building may suffer loss if the mortgaged building is damaged. Likewise, a merchant who sells a television set on an installment sale may be unable to collect the debt if the TV is destroyed while it is in the purchaser's possession.

Agency Relationships A growing number of condominium associations are given powers of trusteeship with the obligation to insure the real property of the individual unit owners in addition to the common elements. Other agency relationships also exist.

"Contingent" Property Indirect losses may result from direct damage to nonowned property—for example, an interruption of business when a major supplier's plant suffers a loss. The major supplier's property may represent substantial loss exposure for an organization with no ownership interest in that property.

Property Off Premises

To identify property loss exposures, it is necessary to recognize *where* a loss may occur. The situation is not as obvious as it might seem. All types of owned and nonowned property may be exposed to loss that occurs away from the owner's premises. In fact, it is often quite important to consider just what is meant by "premises." For example, do they include an adjacent street, parking lot, or river?

Buildings and Structures Although buildings are essentially immobile, certain building components may be detached and moved to another location. For example, screen and storm windows may be removed for seasonal storage and repair. Other building components may be exposed to off-premises loss before they are delivered to a building site. Equipment intended for installation in buildings under construction is particularly vulnerable to off-premises loss.

Other Property Although some types of tangible property (such as glass showcases) are more or less permanently situated, others (such as autos) are normally used away from the premises. Yet, a showcase may be removed for refinishing, and an owned or nonowned auto may sustain damage while on the premises. Trade fixtures, even though attached to the realty, may be subject to removal and thus, in effect, be in the nature of personal property.

PERILS AFFECTING PROPERTY

A *peril* is a cause of loss, such as fire. The word "perils" used to appear in property insurance policies. However, there has been a trend toward replacing "perils" with the phrase *"causes of loss."* Both terms will be used in this text. "Peril" and "cause of loss" are synonyms. A *hazard* is a condition that creates or increases the probability or likely severity of loss from some peril. A defective chimney is a hazard if it increases the probability that a damaging fire will occur. Hazard identification is important in controlling loss exposures, a topic discussed in detail in Chapter 2. Emphasis here is on identifying exposures so that (1) they can be controlled and (2) the losses that occur due to the exposures can be paid for, or "financed."

A sound property risk management program requires a strong ability to identify potential causes of loss to the various types of property. The frequency and severity of potential losses cannot be analyzed properly unless perils are recognized. More important, an unrecognized peril might produce a loss for which no risk management treatment has been planned. If a large, unanticipated loss occurs, the unintentional retention of the exposure can seriously threaten a firm's survival.

Despite the importance of peril recognition, it is impossible to identify every potential cause of loss. Perils keep changing, and there is no method that guarantees discovery of all perils present now, let alone keeping up with changes.

Some peril classification systems give the illusion that practically all perils have been identified. Indeed, some listings of perils are quite lengthy and detailed, and it is difficult to imagine any perils that have been omitted. However, classification systems always omit some perils, and this inherent limitation must be kept in mind.

Perils may be classified by many different systems. Two systems— the generic classification system and classification by insurance categories—will be discussed here.

Generic Classification System

Under a generic classification system, perils may be divided into three categories: (1) natural perils, (2) human perils, and (3) economic perils. From these broad classes, lists of specific perils can be constructed. Such lists are illustrated in Exhibit 1-1.

As complete as these lists appear to be, they must omit an unknown but huge number of perils. Also some perils do not necessarily fall into only one category. The list can be expanded by

Exhibit 1-1
Generic Peril Classification System

I. Natural Perils		
Sun	Water	Mold
Rain	Flood	Corrosion
Fog	Tides	Rot
Snow	Tidal wave	Fungi
Ice	Perils of the	Vermin
Hail	air (icing,	Weeds
Lightning	clear air	Uncontrollable
Static electricity	turbulence)	vegetation
Wind (tornado,	Perils of the	Landslide/mudslide
hurricane, typhoon,	sea (icebergs,	Erosion
tempest)	waves, sandbars,	Cave-in
Temperature	reefs)	Subsidence
extremes	Fire of natural	(sinkholes)
Humidity extremes	origin	Meteors
Drought	Evaporation	Expansive soil
Volcanic eruption	Rust	
Earthquake		
Mildew		

II. Human Perils		
Fire and smoke	Changes of	Riots, civil
Pollution (smoke,	temperature	commotions
smog, water, noise)	Shrinkage	Sabotage
Excessive odor	Water hammer	War, rebellion,
Toppling of high	Dust	insurrection
piled objects	Discrimination	Theft, forgery, fraud
Building collapse	Sonic boom	Terrorism
Radioactive	Chemical leakage	Kidnapping
contamination	Vibration	Extortion
Discoloration	Strikes	Libel, slander,
Contamination	Loss of trained	malicious
Electrical overload	personnel	prosecution,
Human carelessness,	Arson	infringement of
error, mistake,	Vandalism,	personal or
omission,	malicious	property rights
malpractice,	mischief	
incompetence,	Molten metal	
or incomplete		
knowledge		

III. Economic Perils		
Expropriation, confiscation Inflation Obsolescence	Currency fluctuations Change in consumer tastes	Depreciation Recession Technological advances Stock market declines

imagination and research, but it is sometimes helpful to consider other classification systems.

Classification by Insurance Categories

Perils can also be classified according to an approach somewhat more useful to the student of insurance. Within this system, perils can be divided into (1) commonly insured perils; (2) less commonly insured perils, or perils usually insured only by the government; and (3) generally uninsurable perils.

Insurance does not cover all losses caused by every peril named here. Examining the definitions and limitations of the perils helps identify loss exposures that can be insured, and also those that cannot. Some typical insurance policy definitions and limitations will therefore be examined in the present discussion.

Classification by insurance categories also highlights the fact that certain identified causes of loss are generally uninsurable and require treatment by a noninsurance technique. For example, the inability of retail consumers to pay their debts might generally be considered an uninsurable peril.

Insurance availability is subject to change as loss exposures, underwriting, regulation, and market conditions change. Although such changes affect the categories into which the various perils are placed, they do not affect the value of this approach in classifying loss exposures.

The analysis that follows is presented according to the sequence in which causes of loss are listed in standard insurance policies. The discussion will be kept brief since later chapters are more specific with respect to these perils.

Basic Causes of Loss The following perils are covered under the "causes of loss—basic form" (described in Chapter 4) and may be regarded as a fairly standard set of property perils that are usually insurable under normal circumstances.

Fire. Fire is often defined as rapid oxidation with a flame or glow. For insurance purposes, "fire" is meant to encompass only a hostile fire, or one that goes beyond its intended confines. Thus, with the exception of a very few court decisions, fire is not a fire, for insurance purposes, if it is confined within a fireplace, stove, or furnace. Commonly associated with the fire peril is heat and smoke damage caused by the fire, as well as water damage resulting from extinguishing the fire. In addition, other damage to the property—as for example when firefighters break out windows and knock down doors in order to fight fire—is considered to be the result of the fire peril.

Lightning. Lightning is a discharge of naturally generated electricity. Lightning often provides the source of ignition for a fire, and it is sometimes difficult to establish where lightning damage ceases and fire damage begins.

Explosion. Explosion is a violent expansion or bursting with noise. For insurance purposes, explosion is often subdivided into different types of explosions, insured in different types of policies.

Windstorm and Hail. Windstorm includes damage caused by a wind of unusual strength that has produced general damage in an area at a particular time. Hurricanes, tornadoes, and cyclones are all windstorms. Less violent winds also can cause property damage.

In insurance policies the hail peril invariably accompanies the windstorm peril. Hail is ice particles created by freezing atmospheric conditions. Severe hail can cause substantial damage to autos, buildings, and other property exposed to the elements. Hail is a significant peril for growing crops, which may be insured by "crop hail" insurance, described in Chapter 13.

Smoke. Smoke from many sources may damage property, but not all smoke exposures are insurable. The smoke peril is defined as "sudden and accidental damage from smoke, other than smoke from agricultural smudging or industrial operations." Much, but not all, smoke damage is done by fires, and it could be difficult to determine where fire damage stops and smoke damage begins. The distinction does not matter when both perils are covered in the same policy, as is the usual practice.

Aircraft and Vehicle Damage. Aircraft damage and vehicle damage are usually insured together. These perils involve damage caused by direct physical contact between insured property and the vehicle or aircraft. Also covered is damage caused by objects falling from aircraft or "thrown up" by vehicles (a stone, for example).

Damage done by vehicles owned or operated by the insured or a tenant of the premises is sometimes excluded.

Riot and Civil Commotion. Riot is defined in law. The usual definition is "an assembly of individuals who commit a lawful or unlawful act in a violent or tumultuous manner to the terror or disturbance of others."[5] Civil commotion can be considered as an uprising of citizens. The two perils are quite similar, and it is difficult— and unnecessary—to distinguish between them. As defined, the riot or civil commotion peril typically covers physical damage done by striking employees who are occupying the insured's property during a sit-down strike. The peril also includes loss or damage from looting if such loss occurs during and at the place of the riot or civil commotion.

Vandalism. Vandalism includes damage that might be caused by racketeers, cranks, spiteful employees, and other people who maliciously damage property. Typically, the peril encompasses "willful and malicious" damage to or destruction of the insured property. Glass breakage and damage caused by thieves is often excluded from the vandalism peril, but may be within the scope of other perils covered by the same insurance form or by different forms.

Sprinkler Leakage. The peril of sprinkler leakage includes loss caused by the accidental discharge of an automatic sprinkler system intended to discharge only in the event of a fire. If the system is *accidentally* activated and the discharge damages or destroys insured property, the loss is covered under the sprinkler leakage peril. If a fire starts the discharge and the discharge damages the property, the damage is considered a loss caused by the fire.

Sinkhole Collapse. A peril that has received special attention in some areas is that of *sinkhole collapse*, defined as "sudden sinking or collapse of land into underground empty spaces created by the action of water on limestone or dolomite."

Volcanic Action. The first edition of this text did not even mention "volcanic eruption" in the context of this discussion. In 1978, the likelihood of a volcanic eruption affecting the continental United States seemed remote, and the drafters of many easy-to-read policies had eliminated any specific exclusion for this peril. Since that time, repeated eruptions of Mount St. Helens have underscored both the importance of this peril and the difficulty of properly identifying perils that may cause loss. Many insurance claims were paid because "volcanic eruption" was interpreted as an explosion, because it was somehow considered to be within the scope of another peril, or because eliminating the exclusion was interpreted as an intent to provide coverage. Current policy wording attempts more carefully to address this peril.

Broad Causes of Loss The next group of perils are those covered under the "causes of loss—broad form." These perils may be regarded as less commonly insured than the basic causes of loss.

Breakage of Glass. Technically, one might say that glass breakage is a consequence of loss rather than a peril or cause of loss (except perhaps in situations where the broken glass damages other property). Nevertheless, glass breakage is usually treated as a peril. As such, it encompasses any action that damages covered glass. Glass breakage by vandals would generally be within the scope of the "breakage of glass" cause of loss.

Falling Objects. The falling objects peril includes damage to the exterior of the building caused by any item falling on it. If the exterior is damaged, any resulting interior damage is also covered. For instance, when a tree falls onto a building and damages the structure and its contents, the damage to both the exterior and the contents is covered. If a person drops a load of bricks on a warehouse floor and chips the floor, no coverage exists because no damage occurred to the exterior of the building.

Weight of Snow, Ice, or Sleet. This peril involves situations where the roof or some other part of a building is damaged by the weight of accumulated snow, ice, or sleet. For instance, if a snowstorm deposits two feet of snow on a roof, the roof may collapse, or the rafters may bend or crack.

Water Damage. The water damage peril described in the "causes of loss—broad form" includes only particular types of damage caused by water. This peril includes only damage resulting from the accidental discharge or leakage of water or steam as the direct result of the breaking or cracking of any part of a system or appliance containing water or steam. Damage resulting from sprinkler leakage is specifically excluded because it is usually specifically covered by the sprinkler leakage peril.

Since they are not mentioned in the definition of water damage, destruction resulting from flood, tidal wave, or other natural sources of water damage are not covered. In fact, these perils are also explicitly excluded from most policies.

Boiler Explosion The definition of explosion within the "basic causes of loss" provisions does not generally include damage resulting from an exploding steam boiler unless the explosion is of accumulated gases or unconsumed fuel. Other types of boilers, such as hot water heating and supply boilers fall within the regular explosion peril because they do not normally impose any major threat or explosion. Boiler explosion and related perils are examined in greater detail in Chapter 6.

Crime Perils The crime perils involve the stealing of property. With respect to insurance, there are four major overlapping crime perils: burglary, robbery, theft, and employee dishonesty.

- *Burglary* is the felonious taking of property from a premises where force is used to enter and signs of forceful entry are visible.
- *Robbery* is the use of violence or threat of violence to take property from a person.
- *Theft* is the unlawful taking of another person's property and the most general peril of the four. The theft peril includes burglary and robbery.
- *Employee dishonesty*, or "infidelity" is a category that includes theft by employees or other "insiders."

These and other crime perils are examined in greater detail in Chapters 7 and 8.

Perils of Transportation While personal property is being transported in a car, truck, ship, or aircraft, loss can occur from a variety of causes peculiar to property in transit. Cargo in planes, trains, and cars can be damaged due to collision or upset; cargo in ships can sustain damage due to the "perils of the seas." All those losses result directly from transportation. These and other perils treated by marine insurance will be examined in Chapters 9, 10, 11, and 12.

Other Insurable Causes of Loss The perils named or described in the above insurance categories do not represent a *complete* list of all causes of loss specifically covered in property insurance policies. Many special-purpose property policies cover perils inherent in a particular type of property. It is certainly possible to develop broader "causes of loss" lists, but even a very long list would omit some possible perils.

Because of the difficulty of naming all insurable perils that could be covered, many insurance policies take the opposite approach. Such policies cover "risks of loss" that are not excluded. They then contain detailed lists of excluded perils—perils that are difficult to insure or are better treated in a separate coverage form.

Difficult-to-Insure Perils Two perils traditionally considered difficult to insure are earth movement and flood. These perils are *considered* difficult to insure because they are excluded in most insurance policies covering fixed location property. As noted in later chapters, earthquake and flood coverage are actually available in many cases.

Earth Movement. The term "earth movement" includes earthquake, landslide, mudflow, earth sinking, earth rising or shifting, and, perhaps, volcanic eruption. The earthquake peril is difficult to insure where the threat is great because of its catastrophic nature. If a strong earthquake were to occur in downtown Los Angeles or St. Louis, dollar losses could be in the billions.[6] In earthquake-prone areas of California, premium rates are relatively high and so are deductibles. Some insurers are not anxious to provide insurance. However, in southern Florida, coverage should be readily available, if it is wanted, since that area has an earthquake rating of zero on a scale of zero to three. The rating in California is three. Other areas with "three" ratings include the regions around St. Louis, Missouri, and Charleston, South Carolina.[7]

Flood. The insurance definition of the flood peril includes more than just flooding from streams. It includes overflow of inland or tidal waters, unusual and rapid runoff of surface waters from any source, and mudslides caused or precipitated by accumulations of water on or under the ground. It does not include seepage or backup of sewers or hydrostatic pressure. Flood insurance is discussed in Chapter 14.

Nuclear Reaction. Because of its obvious catastrophe potential, the peril of nuclear reaction is excluded from most property policies. However, coverage is available through a pooling arrangement discussed in Chapter 14.

Generally Noninsurable Perils Perils against which insurance is usually unavailable are numerous. Insurance forms may address these perils by (1) specifically excluding them and/or (2) by not including them as covered causes of loss. Some of these are war; rebellion; insurrection; intentional losses; and losses such as fading, rust, dry rot, pollution, and settling of pavements, foundations, and walls. In addition, most losses resulting from political, production, and marketing activities are not generally considered commercially insurable.[8]

The perils of war, rebellion, and insurrection are typically considered the *war perils* and as a group or singly are usually considered uninsurable. While special forms may be used to insure aircraft and oceangoing vessels against losses caused by war, this coverage is issued primarily by the United States government. The war exposure is usually deemed to be privately uninsurable because of its catastrophic nature. If a hydrogen bomb were exploded over the Chicago Loop, the devastation would be enormous. Losses would be in the billions of dollars. If private insurance companies were providing coverage, they and their reinsurers would be bankrupt. While the losses could be spread throughout the general population, the losses that could happen at one time would be too great for the insurance mechanism to absorb. Perhaps they would even be too great for the government to cover. It should be noted, however, that war perils are regularly insured for ships and cargoes at sea. This is feasible because there is a relatively low catastrophic exposure.

Intentional loss by any means is not insurable for the obvious reason that, if it were, people could readily liquidate assets by deliberately destroying much of their property in order to collect from insurance companies. Any time a business could not sell an old building or its inventory became obsolete, it could burn the property and collect from the insurance company. Beyond the question of insurability, it is against public policy to reimburse a party for its own intentional act—intentional acts of other parties, such as vandals or arsonists other than the insured, are generally insurable.

Fading, rust, dry rot, gradual pollution, and settling of pavements, foundations, and walls can be called the *natural wear and tear perils*. These causes of loss are part of the natural order of things. If iron is exposed to air and moisture, it will rust. If a painting is directly exposed to the rays of the sun, it will eventually fade. A greenish coating (verdigris) forms on copper when it is placed in the open air. After prolonged use, most items simply wear out. These perils do not cause *accidental* losses. The losses are certain to happen, and insuring them would be of no benefit—uncertainty would not be reduced.

Production, marketing, and political activities that cause losses are what might be called *business perils*. While losses may result from them, gains may also be made. These perils are generally considered relevant to *speculative exposures* rather than *pure loss exposures*, and are not generally suitable for insurance coverage. For instance, a firm cannot buy insurance to cover the losses that might be involved if it overproduces or underproduces because of failure to correctly anticipate the market for its product. (However, underproduction caused because the plant was shut down by a fire or other fortuitous occurrences is insurable under business income insurance.)

Likewise, if a company enters a new market, it cannot purchase insurance to cover the losses if it fails. If it could, the company could recklessly enter all types of new markets without fear of financial loss. The chance of production and marketing loss is largely in the hands of the insured. The moral hazard and adverse selection would be just too great to insure.

Classification of perils by degree of insurability is summarized in Exhibit 1-2. Although this list is much shorter than the generic list in Exhibit 1-1, it should be noted that the definitions of these commonly insured perils are rather broad.

Exhibit 1-2
Perils Classification by Insurance Categories

Insurable Perils	Difficult-to-Insure Perils	Generally Noninsurable Perils

Basic Causes of Loss
  fire
  lightning
  explosion
  windstorm and hail
  smoke
  aircraft and vehicle
    damage
  riot and civil commotion
  vandalism
  sprinkler leakage
  volcanic action
  sinkhole collapse
 	
Broad Causes of Loss
  breakage of glass
  falling objects
  weight of snow, ice, or
    sleet
  water damage
 	
Boiler Explosion
 	
Crime
  burglary
  robbery
  theft
  employee dishonesty
 	
Transportation
	Earth Movement
	Flood
	Nucelar Reaction
	Volcanic Eruption
		War Perils
		Intentional Losses
		Wear and Tear Perils
		  fading
		  rust
		  dry rot
		  settling of
		    pavements
		    foundations and
		    walls
		Business Perils
		  production
		  marketing
		  political

PROPERTY LOSS CONSEQUENCES

Discussion to this point has concentrated on types of property that may be lost or damaged, and perils that might cause loss or damage. Exposure identification also requires an ability to recognize the types of consequences that may result when property is damaged by some peril. Property loss consequences include (1) reduction in value, (2) extra cost to replace, (3) cost of debris removal, (4) business interruption, (5) extra expenses to operate, (6) contingent business interruption, (7) contingent extra expenses, (8) loss of rental income, (9) loss of rental value, (10) loss of leasehold interest, (11) cost of refinancing, (12) loss of tuition fees, (13) inability to reconstruct accounts receivable and other records, (14) loss of use value in improvements and betterments, (15) demolition costs and increased cost of construction, (16) changes in condition, and (17) pair or set losses. Many of the loss consequences introduced here are examined more closely in later chapters.

Reduction in Value

When a peril causes actual physical destruction, damage, or disappearance of property, an immediate reduction (sometimes to zero) in the value of the affected property occurs. Such a loss to tangible property is easy to visualize, although the exposure is not always easy to identify. Losses causing reduction of the value of intangible property are also possible. The theft of trade secrets or valuable corporate information, for example, diminishes the value of intangible property.

Extra Cost to Replace

In most cases, the cost of restoring or replacing damaged or destroyed property exceeds the amount by which the property was reduced in value.

For example, suppose the current pre-loss value of a building was $80,000, but, after a loss, it costs $100,000 to erect an equivalent structure to replace the building. In one sense, the extra $20,000 is not a "loss" because it represents a capital expenditure that increases one of the owner's assets. However, there is another aspect to consider: As a consequence of the loss event, the building owner is forced to incur an unexpected $20,000 expense. Before the loss, the owner has a building. After the reconstruction, assuming the owner borrowed the $20,000 necessary to rebuild, the owner has a building and a $20,000 debt.

Cost of Debris Removal

The cost of removing debris is an expense that often accompanies property damage. In some cases, this cost is substantial. Although, to some extent, the presence of debris reduces the remaining value of damaged property, the cost of removing debris may also be considered a separate loss consequence.

Business Interruption

When property used for producing or selling goods or providing services is destroyed or rendered unusable, sales may be impaired and business lost. A business slowdown or shutdown, therefore, may cause business income losses in the form of:

1. loss of net income that would have been earned, and
2. payments for expenses that necessarily continue when the property is damaged or destroyed. (Even if the property is completely destroyed, there may be continuing expenses, such

as taxes on the land, noncancelable contracts for heat, light, and power, interest on debt, and salaries for executives. If no loss occurs, these continuing expenses are offset by continuing income.)

Extra Expenses to Operate

When a business interruption occurs, additional expenses may be required to minimize the loss of income. Some companies can altogether avoid a slowdown or interruption of the business by incurring additional costs. For example, renting a temporary office and couch might enable a psychiatrist to remain in business while a damaged office is being refurbished. Many companies are strongly motivated to continue operations at all costs.

Contingent Business Interruption

Many firms are highly dependent on the activities of other organizations. A contingent business interruption may occur when a company has a single major supplier. For example, if a manufacturer depends on one supplier for a particular unique component, it may be impossible to avert a shutdown if the suppliers property is damaged. In these cases, a direct loss to one company's property causes a loss of income to another company.

The same situation can result when a consumer or wholesaler suffers a loss with the result that the seller or manufacturer no longer has a customer. The consequences to the seller can be substantial if the customer represents all, or a large portion, of the seller's business.

Contingent business interruption can even result when a nearby firm suffers a loss. A number of small stores, for example, may be located near a large store. If the large store is shut down, business at the smaller stores may stop or decrease, even though they are not physically harmed.

Contingent Extra Expenses

Extra expenses may be incurred in order to continue operations following loss of a primary supplier or destruction of a nearby business that attracts customers. These may be termed contingent extra expenses.

Loss of Rental Income

Property that is leased or rented to others produces income. If the property is damaged or destroyed, the lessee or tenant may be excused from rent or lease obligations. The owner of the property, then, would suffer a loss of rental income. In effect, this is a business interruption for those who rent or lease property to others.

Loss of Rental Value

If property is occupied and used by the owner, there is no chance for loss of rental income, but the loss of use represents a loss of rental value (potential rental income). Suppose, for example, that a company owns a five-story building. Four stories are rented to others and one story is used by the owner. If the building is totally destroyed, the company may lose not only rental income, but also the rental or use value of the one story it occupied. The destruction of the building causes the company to lose the *use* of a valuable asset.

Loss of Leasehold Interest

If a company occupies or uses property as a lessee and the lease is subject to cancellation if circumstances render the property untenantable, the company could have a loss of leasehold interest. Consider this example: A company obtains a twenty-year lease on a building in 1988, at a cost of $5,000 per month. In 1998, with ten years remaining on the lease, equivalent property might lease for $12,000 per month. If so, and the company were to lose the lease in 1998, it would lose the present value of $7,000 per month for the remaining ten years of the lease.

Cost of Refinancing

Another loss consequence may be involved when a mortgage or other loan is canceled because property that forms collateral for the loan has been destroyed. If lending rates have changed, the property owner may need to pay a higher rate of interest in order to finance the purchase of replacement property.

Loss of Tuition Fees

Educational institutions have unusual business interruption loss exposures. Tuition fees usually are paid at the beginning of the school year or semester. If major damage to facilities occurs shortly before or after the beginning of school, it is possible for tuition for the entire year to be lost even if the building could be repaired or reconstructed within a short time.

Inability to Reconstruct Accounts Receivable and Other Records

If a business loses its records of accounts receivable (or other transactions), it may not be able to collect the amounts due the company from debtors. Under the worst circumstances, the company would not be able to reconstruct its records, and many customers would not pay their bills. At best, extra costs will be involved in reconstructing the accounts, and collections would be delayed.

Costs involved in the loss of accounts receivable may also include interest charges to borrow money to substitute for delayed collections, extra costs incurred to collect accounts, and expenses to reestablish the records.

Loss of Use Value in Improvements and Betterments

Many tenants install improvements in rented or leased property. If these improvements are permanently attached, they become part of the realty and therefore become the property of the building owner. Nevertheless, they are installed because they have value to the tenant. If destroyed and not replaced by the building owner, the tenant will lose the use of these improvements and betterments for the remaining period of the tenancy. Of course, the tenant might replace the improvements and betterments. The loss then would be the value of the replaced property.

Demolition Costs and Increased Cost of Construction

Building codes may have a significant influence on a loss. Some local codes state that if a building is more than 50 percent destroyed, the entire structure must be demolished and rebuilt according to the prevailing building code. This may involve three major types of loss:

1. the demolition cost,
2. the loss of the *undamaged* property that must be demolished and the cost of removing its debris, and
3. the extra cost of the higher quality construction that the existing building code is likely to require.

In most cases, electrical codes call for more modern wiring, plumbing may be different, and the structure itself might need improvement. For example, a fire-resistive structure might be required in place of a building of frame construction. In addition, the time period needed for restoration may be extended, increasing the related business interruption loss.

Changes in Condition

The term "consequential loss" sometimes is used to describe undesirable changes in condition of property. The identification of such potential losses can be difficult. The variety and variables that can be involved are suggested by a few examples: spoilage of frozen food following failure of a freezer, shutdown or malfunction of a data processing machine following failure of an air conditioning system, or solidification of electrically heated molten metal when electrical power fails.

Pair or Set Losses

Some property items derive a large part of their value from the fact that they are used together. When one part of the set is lost or destroyed, the value of undamaged property may be substantially reduced. For example, consider a clothing manufacturer that produces men's suits. If a fire or other peril destroys a lot of trousers, the matching coats may be worth only a fraction of the value they possessed as part of a suit.

SYSTEMS FOR IDENTIFYING COMMERCIAL PROPERTY LOSS EXPOSURES

Identification of property loss exposures is no simple task. Fortunately, several systematic approaches to exposure identification exist. Unfortunately, no one approach is adequate by itself.

The systems that will be discussed in this chapter include the insurance survey method, flow chart analysis, and financial statement analysis. Other analysis systems are mentioned briefly.

The Insurance Survey Method

One commonly employed system of loss exposure identification is the insurance survey questionnaire. Forms for this purpose are supplied by many insurance companies in conjunction with survey procedures they have developed as an aid to their producers. Insurance survey forms are also available from a few publishing houses that specialize in insurance publications, and some insurance practitioners have developed their own.

All such questionnaires have undergone substantial revision as insurance coverages have been broadened. Some current survey forms include insurance policy applications.

Understandably, insurance survey forms like the one discussed here are totally insurance-oriented. They are designed to reveal the insurable loss exposures of the prospect or client and to provide the information necessary to underwrite and rate each policy that might address these exposures. They do not attempt to develop information on exposures for which insurance is not currently available.

Some insurance companies have several questionnaires, each especially designed to meet the particular requirements of certain classes of business. A retail store questionnaire does not develop the information required to survey a bank. Neither does a manufacturing questionnaire meet the needs of a long-haul truck operation.

Exhibit 1-3 contains those sections of one insurance survey that relate to property loss exposures. By carefully completing each item, the surveyor may develop the information needed to identify most or all of the firm's *insurable* property loss exposures, and also to determine *insurable* values. To a degree, the categories used in the form track with the "types of property" discussion earlier in this chapter. Since the insurance survey is designed as an insurance sales tool, the various headings tend to relate to types of property that fall into different categories for insurance purposes. Some questions develop information necessary to complete an insurance application.

The reader is encouraged to examine Exhibit 1-3 and to ponder the significance of each of the questions asked in the survey. The relevance of some items may not be clear at this point in the text. If so, the exhibit has helped to set the stage for discussion in later chapters.

The insurance survey is one effective way of identifying exposures that can be treated with insurance. When combined with the knowledge, skill, and experience of an insurance professional, the insurance survey can develop the information needed to design a combination of insurance coverages that treats the exposures of the firm surveyed. Because they are insurance-oriented, insurance surveys may lead to the use of insurance when other techniques should be used in addition—or even instead—to meet an organization's risk management objectives. This is a major deficiency of insurance surveys.

Insurance surveys are most useful for a small- to medium-sized organization that uses insurance as its primary loss financing technique. However, the approach can be adapted for use by organizations of almost any size.

To develop the information shown in an insurance survey, typically it is necessary for the surveyor to tour the premises, at least in part, and to interview personnel who are capable of providing the necessary information. Throughout the information-gathering process, the surveyor assimilates the information received and combines it with his or her knowledge of insurance coverages.

Exhibit 1-3
Property Sections of an Insurance Survey

LIFE & CASUALTY

ÆTNA PLAN
QUESTIONNAIRE Date _____ 19 ___

1	Exact operating name of firm.	
2	☐ Corporation ☐ Partnership ☐ Joint Venture ☐ Individual ☐ Other	
3	Post office address and zip code of firm.	
4	a. Is this firm owned or controlled by another? Name of parent company? b. Does this firm own or control other firms? Names? c. Information as to degree of control.	
5	Describe nature of client's business. *Also indicate whether manufacturer, contractor, distributor, wholesaler, retailer or a combination of these.* How many years in this business?	
6	Describe any new or discontinued operations within the last 3 years.	
7	Names and titles of Owners, Executives, Trustees, etc. — a. Co-owners or partners b. Executive officers *(If inactive, so state)* c. Trustees, executors receivers, etc. d. Employed family members.	
8	a. Does the firm have any overseas operations? Give exact name or names under which foreign branches operate. b. Give locations and functions of foreign operations.	
9	Do you bid on federal or state contracts? What types?	

BUILDINGS OR PREMISES

		Location 1	Location 2	Location 3	Location 4
10	Indicate all locations which you own, lease or use. (Be sure to include branches, sales offices, dwellings owned by firm, vacant land, parking lots and locations in foreign countries.) Obtain for each location a copy of any lease agreements. Include zip codes for each location.				
	Exact use of each location.				
11	If property is owned by firm or a related interest, in what name is title held?				

QUESTION NO. 12 APPLIES ONLY TO LOCATIONS OWNED BY CLIENT OR A RELATED INTEREST

			Location 1	Location 2	Location 3	Location 4
	a. Latest Building Appraisal (Obtain copy)	Date				
		Insurable Value				
		Replacement Cost				
	b. What is your estimate of present building value?					
12	c. If property is mortgaged, to whom?					
	d. Are fire or other insurance policies held by mortgagee? Kind — Amount?					
	e. Would any zoning ordinance prevent the repair or replacement of any building damaged by fire or other peril?					

1

continued on next page

BUILDINGS OR PREMISES (Continued)

			Location 1	Location 2	Location 3	Location 4
	QUESTIONS NO. 13 THROUGH 26 APPLY TO ALL LOCATIONS					
13	What part of the premises do you use or occupy? Describe the tenancy of the portion you do not occupy.					
14	If you are owner or general lessee, do you rent 90% or more of the premises (or any entire single building) to tenant who operates elevators, furnishes power, etc.? Describe or diagram.					
15	Area and Frontage	Show(a) Area of buildings and (b) Frontage of property as required for Liability insurance rating purposes.				
16	Construction of Building	Outside walls				
		Floors				
		Roof				
		Number of stories				
17	Hotels, Motels Apartments	Number of rental units?				
		Closed season From—To				
18	Automatic Sprinkler System	Type of system—Wet or Dry?				
		Type of alarm (Describe)				
		Approx. age of system				
		Part of building equipped				
19	Fire Protection	Type of fire alarm?				
		Number of fire extinguishers? Who maintains them?				
		Fire Department service Contract? Cost?				
20	Boilers and Pressure Vessels	Number and description of heating or power boilers				
		Kind of fuel used				
		Description and use of other pressure vessels				
		Which of above items would cause business interruption if damaged?				
		Estimated daily loss if business is interrupted				
21	Power Machinery* (Including refrigeration and air conditioning equipment)	Number of items and description				
		Indicate any item whose breakdown would cause business interruption				
		Estimated daily loss if business is interrupted				
		*Large items of machinery eligible for machinery insurance: motors, engines, turbines, generators, transformers, compressors, pumps, flywheels, switchboards, etc.					
22	Cold Storage or Controlled Atmosphere Rooms	Where located				
		Use				
		Value of perishable contents				
		Auxilliary Generators				
23	Plate or Ornamental Glass	Number of plates, size and description*				
		Value of lettering				
		*Indicate whether Exterior, Interior, Carrara, Bent or other special glass.					
24	Signs	Outside signs (Number, type and value)				
		Inside signs (Number, type and value)				

CONTENTS

			Location 1		Location 2		Location 3		Location 4	
28	Date or dates on which you take stock inventory?									
29	If a manufacturer, what is profit in finished goods on the premises at any one time?									
30	Is there a chattel mortgage on any property? Give details.									
			Month	Amount	Month	Amount	Month	Amount	Month	Amount
31	Stock	Average value*	XXX		XXX		XXX		XXX	
		Peak value								
		Low value								
32	Unattached Furniture and Fixtures	Value of all *unattached* furniture, fixtures, office equipment and supplies?								
33	Permanently attached Furniture, Fixtures, Improvements, Betterments	Value of all *permanently attached* furniture and fixtures?								
		Value and type of improvements and betterments made by client to non-owned premises?								
34	Machinery If appraisal is available, obtain copy	Value of power machinery indicated in question 21?								
		Value of all other machinery?								
35	Electronic Data Processing Media	Value?								
		Owned or leased?								
		If leased, who is responsible for damage?								
		Cost to replace stored data?								
		Time to replace stored data?								
		Any use by others?								
		Who is liable for loss or destruction of data of others?								
36	Dies Patterns Molds, Tools Owned by Client	Value of dies?								
		Value of patterns, molds, forms, lasts and models?								
		Value of tools?								
37	Property of Others In Client's Custody	Description and value of property? i.e.: finished goods—raw material—dies —patterns—property left for repair or processing— employees property— leased equipment								
		How was value determined?								
		Who is responsible for such property and to what extent?								
38	Radioactive Materials	Value and kind of radioactive materials?								
39	Client's Property In Custody of Others	Description, value and location of your property (merchandise, equipment, dies, etc.) in custody of sub-contractors or others for processing, service or repair or leased to others, loaned, rented or on consignment? Who is responsible?								

continued on next page

CONTENTS (Continued)

<table>
<tr><td rowspan="2">40</td><td colspan="5">Indicate the value of any of the following property owned by the client:</td></tr>
</table>

40	Indicate the value of any of the following property owned by the client:				
	Contractors equipment (attach schedule) $_____			Salesmen's samples	$_____
	Scientific instruments $_____			Exhibits	$_____
	Cameras and projection machines and equipment $_____			Radium	$_____
	Were these values included in answers to previous questions? ☐ Yes ☐ No				

41	Valuable Papers	Description, value and exact location where valuable papers are kept? Nature of the valuable papers?				

			Location 1	Location 2	Location 3	Location 4
42	Accounts Receivable	Number of accounts				
		Average, total outstanding, each month? Maximum, total outstanding, each month?				
		Maximum outstanding balance on any single account?				
		Are accounts receivable records kept in fireproof container?				
		Are duplicate records kept? Where? How long? What percent of the records?				
43	Deferred (Time) Payment Sales	Estimated annual amount of deferred payment sales				
		Maximum unpaid balance any one customer				

SHIPMENTS

Method of Transportation	Amount Shipped Annually		Amount Received Annually		Max. amount any one shipment
	Prepaid	F.O.B.	Prepaid	F.O.B.	
Own Trucks					
Public Truckmen					
Rail					
Domestic Air Freight					
Parcel Post					
Registered Mail		XXX		XXX	
Coastwise Steamer					
Intercoastal Steamer					
Overseas - waterborne or air					
First Class or Certified Mail		XXX		XXX	
Armored Car or Messengers		XXX		XXX	
What percent of values are shipped under Released Bill of Lading?					

(Row group number: 44)

NOTES

MONEY, SECURITIES, ETC.

			Location 1	Location 2	Location 3	Location 4
45	Money *(Currency, Coins, Bank Notes, Bullion, Travelers Checks, Registered Checks, Money Orders Held for Sale to the Public)* Show Maximum Amounts	Cash other than payroll on premises				
		Payroll cash on premises				
		Total kept in each safe overnight including undistributed payroll (Identify Each Safe By Number)				
		Cash kept at home of custodian overnight				
		In custody of each bank messenger or paymaster				
		In custody of each truck driver, salesman or collector				
		How often are bank deposits made?				
46	Armored Car Service	Are cash receipts picked up by armored car?				
		Is payroll delivered by armored car?				
47	Other Checks and Stamps *(Including Trading Stamps)* Maximum Amounts for Each	Total on premises at one time				
		Are checks immediately recorded and stamped for deposit only, or photographed?				
		Which locations issue checks? Maximum amount per check?				
		Total kept in each sale overnight (Identify Each Sale By Number)				
		In custody of each bank messenger and paymaster				
		In custody of each truck driver, salesman or collector				
48	All instruments or contracts Representing Either Money or Property including Tokens and Tickets Maximum Amounts	Total kept in each safe (Identify Each Safe by Number)				
		In custody of each bank messenger				
		In safe deposit vault or at other locations (Specify)				
49	Valuable Merchandise or Other Property Maximum Amounts	Total kept in each safe (Identify Each Safe By Number)				
		In custody of each truck driver or salesman				
		In safe deposit vault or at other locations (Specify)				
50	Number of Custodians Away from Premises at Same Time	Bank messengers and paymasters				
		Truck drivers, salesmen and collectors				

SAFES AND VAULTS

	Safe of Vault	Name of Maker	Serial Number	Shape of Door, Thickness of Steel in Door and Walls Excluding Insulation. Special Labels if Applicable.	Location (Use location numbers previously shown and indicate where in building safe is situated.)
51	No. 1				
	No. 2				
	No. 3				
	No. 4				

continued on next page

PROTECTION

52 — Watchmen, Guards Protective Equipment — Main Location Only*

WATCHMEN on duty within premises when closed ________ (Number) ☐ Signal central station hourly ☐ Punch clock hourly

GUARDS on duty within premises when open ________ (Number) with each messenger ________ (Number)

paymaster ________ (Number) Any over 64 years? ☐ Yes ☐ No

LOCKED SATCHEL (approved) used by messenger ☐ Yes ☐ No by paymaster ☐ Yes ☐ No

PRIVATE CONVEYANCE used by messenger ☐ Yes ☐ No by paymaster ☐ Yes ☐ No

BURGLAR ALARM: Make: ________ Protects: ☐ Safe ☐ Vault ☐ Premises

Installation ________ Class ________ Certificate No. ________ Expiration date ________

Describe any other protection (hold-up alarm, tear gas systems, bandit resisting enclosures, etc.)

*Use separate page where necessary to show information relative to watchmen, guards and protective equipment at other locations.

53 — Check any of the following statements which apply to the operation:

a. Audit by independent public accountant - Quarterly ________ Semi-annually ________ Annually ________

b. Audit by employee who is equivalent of public accountant, who has no other duties and makes written and signed periodic reports of such internal audits ________

c. Audit reports rendered directly to individual owner, all partners or Board of Directors ________

d. Require countersignature of checks ________

e. Joint control of securities ________

f. Reconciliation of bank account by someone not authorized to deposit or withdraw ________

g. If there is Fidelity coverage do new employees complete personal application supplied by the Insurer including, at least, a record of previous employment? ________

CLASS 1 AND/OR CLASS 2 EMPLOYEES

	OFFICIALS		ACCOUNTING							
					Asst. Managers	Custodians			Salesmen of Auto Dealers	
	Chairman		Auditors		Branch Managers	Watchmen				
	President		Asst. Auditors		Dept. Managers				Demonstrators	
	Vice President		Cashiers		Superintendents				Canvassers	
	Treasurer		Bookkeepers		Factory Supts.	**SALES**			Collectors	
	Asst. Treasurer		Paymasters		Purchasing Agents	Sales Managers			Drivers	
54	Secretary		Timekeepers		Messengers (Outside)	Asst. Sales Mgrs.			Drivers' Helpers (Other than brewers)	
	Asst. Secretary		Adjusters			Floorwalkers				
	Comptroller				**STOCK**	Buyers			Chauffeurs	
	Asst. Comptroller				Shipping or Receiving Clerks	Asst. Buyers				
			MANAGEMENT			Salesmen (Outside who collect)				
			Managers		Stock Clerks					
									Total Class 1 and/or 2 Employees	
									Total All Employees	

NOTES

BUSINESS INTERRUPTION AND OTHER TIME ELEMENT EXPOSURES

80	Business Interruption	Total annual ordinary payroll (excluding Officers, Executives, Department Managers, employees under contract and other important employees whose pay would continue during period of business interruption).	
		Annual Gross Sales less discounts, returns, bad accounts, prepaid freight.	
		Annual cost of raw materials entering into article produced, or cost of merchandise sold.	
		Annual cost of heat, light and power.	
		Estimated percentage of increase or decrease in profits for coming year.	
		Is continued full-time operation of your plant dependent upon any one supplier or customer?	
		Is your business dependent upon outside heat, light or power? Give details.	
81	Extra Expense	If your premises are damaged, what percentage of your business could be continued at another location?	
		Estimate of "extra expenses" in order to carry on business at another location.	
		If your premises are damaged, what percentage of your business could be continued at your present location?	
		Estimate of "extra expense" in order to continue business at your present location.	
82	Leasehold and Rents Tenant	Is there a written lease?	
		Present monthly rent.	
		Estimated cost of similar facilities elsewhere.	
		Was an advance rental or cash bonus paid?	
		Are premises sublet at a higher rental?	
83	Rental Income or Value Owner	Annual Rental Income from tenants?	
		Annual Rental Value of part of premises occupied?	

NOTES

Flow Chart Analysis

One useful tool in exposure identification is the analysis of a flow chart of a firm's business operations. A flow chart is a diagram of the firm's operations showing, in the case of a manufacturer, the flow from suppliers' raw materials to final customers or users of the finished product.

For many operations, a flow chart will be quite complex. For some organizations, it may be necessary to use several flow charts. There may be a different one for each product line and separate ones for flows of services (such as electric power) and information (such as sales orders and billing data). However, the basic procedures are the same for firms of any size.

It is often desirable to have separate charts for flow of goods within a plant and for movement into and out of the plant. An example of the latter appears in Exhibit 1-4. Such a chart should reveal how a loss at one point could affect operations elsewhere. In Exhibit 1-4, for example, severe damage at the raw materials warehouse might require a slowdown in activity at stages three through six because of lack of raw materials to process. This possibility needs further investigation and evaluation. Note that the key role played by this one building might not be revealed by a questionnaire or insurance survey.

The second chart, or series of charts, depicting the movement of goods within a plant, should reveal critical processes in which a minor direct damage loss could cause substantial business interruption losses, because all goods flow through one machine or one point in the manufacturing process. A chart depicting movement of goods within a plant is illustrated in Exhibit 1-5. In this chart, it will be observed that minor damage to process AB might make it necessary to shut down the entire plant.

Applying the Flow Chart Technique   The number, variety, and format of flow charts that can be drawn depends on the exposures present, the amount of information available, and the creativity of the person making the flow chart(s). For example, in identifying crime exposures, it might be used to trace the flow of cash through an organization that handles large sums of money. Likewise, flow charts might be used to examine the way invoices and vouchers are handled in a firm that desires to identify its employee dishonesty exposures. Flow charts can also be used in restoration of property after a loss. Critical path analysis, described in Chapter 5, is especially useful in this context.

By itself, a flow chart would be inadequate for identification of a firm's loss exposures. As a supplement to other methods, it can identify

Exhibit 1-4
Flow Chart Covering External Flow*

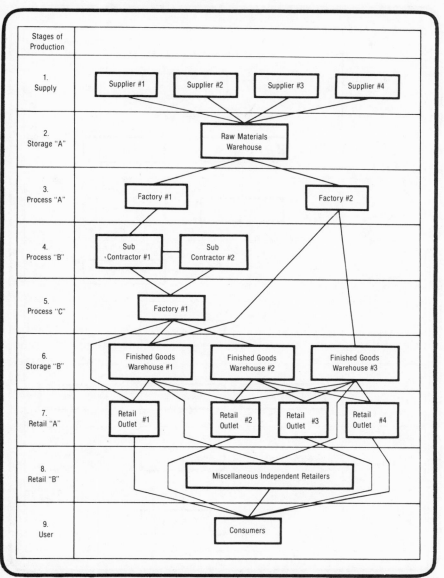

*Reprinted, with permission, from Matthew Lenz, Jr. *Risk Management Manual* (Santa Monica: The Merritt Company, 1976), p. 17.

Exhibit 1-5
Flow Chart Covering Internal Flow*

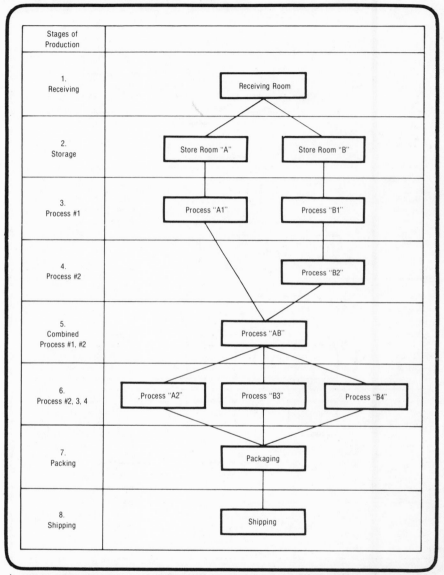

*Reprinted, with permission, from Matthew Lenz, Jr. *Risk Management Manual* (Santa Monica: The Merritt Company, 1976), p. 17.

potential problems that might otherwise be unrecognized. While other attempts at exposure identification may tend to take a static approach, a flow chart shows the dynamics of an organization in action.

There is no one appropriate method, format, or set of symbols that should be used in constructing a flow chart. The flow chart technique can be adapted by the user to meet the needs of many different organizations and exposures.

The Financial Statement Method

Early in the development of risk management, it was recognized that the insurance survey method of identifying loss exposures had a number of inadequacies. Surveys deal primarily with exposures that are commonly insured. Insurance surveys were not designed to encourage objective consideration of alternative methods of treating exposures or to develop information on commercially uninsurable exposures, no matter how serious. Because risk management involves more than insurance, it is necessary that the identification of loss exposures be on a broader basis than the insurance survey.

The initial effort to create a better system for loss exposure identification consisted of expanding the insurance survey into risk management areas. The problem with this effort was that it was still heavily dominated by insurance practices and did not deal adequately with internal procedures that might be changed to control loss exposures.

Since the function of risk management is to protect an organization's capital, assets, and income against loss, or to provide financing in the event that losses do occur, the conclusion was reached by some that risk management is a function of financial management. A method was needed that was sufficiently comprehensive to identify all exposures to accidental loss, whether or not currently insurable. Workable criteria were also required to establish all sources of possible loss causes, analyzing the degree of probability of their occurrence, and evaluating the potential financial consequences. The data source ideally should be one readily available in substantially standardized form for any medium or large organization. The logic of the system should be understandable and acceptable to directors, executives, stockholders, accountants, bankers, and investors. The developed facts should be capable of clear, concise presentation in terms that conform to reports on other corporate matters, as distinct from the jargon of the insurance business. The principles upon which such a system should be based should be logically supportable and universally applicable, so that they can be employed for any type of organization, located anywhere, with assurance that all significant loss possibilities would be disclosed, analyzed, evaluated, and dealt with in a comprehensive manner.

In 1958 it was suggested that such a system could use corporate financial and accounting records as the initial data source. These records are the common denominator of all business organizations, reflecting most of the values owned, all current and past activities involving monetary values and certain types of future activities. For risk management purposes, the surveyor must go beyond the condensed type of annual report usually issued to stockholders. Behind this brief annual report are much more detailed reports for internal use. For example, there are considerable underlying data with respect to asset accounts, income accounts that break down the result of operations by profit centers or by classes of business, administrative or selling expenses, loan agreements, and litigation. From all of these accounts, a substantial index of probable loss exposure can be deduced.

The financial statement method basically involves a careful study of each account title in the various financial statements. A number of questions can be asked about each entry to gain an understanding of the exposures. The major account titles listed in a typical balance sheet are shown in Exhibit 1-6. The following discussion incorporates some of the questions or concerns that might be raised and briefly describes how the specific asset account titles may then aid in identifying loss exposures. The same general approach can be carried into an analysis of other items and other financial statements, but the *specific* questions to be raised will vary with the exposures involved and the answers to questions already asked.

Cash "Cash" is ordinarily the first item in a balance sheet. To identify loss exposures, it is necessary to learn how "cash" comes into the possession of the organization—whether it is in the form of money or checks, what happens to it between the time of its receipt and the time of its disbursement (and even after), the safeguards that are employed, and the amounts that are involved, with particular reference to the maximum amounts that can accumulate at one time in a seasonal business or that can build up over weekends and holidays.

The money loss exposure will vary widely among different classes of business. Retail stores and supermarkets handle a great deal of cash, but the large manufacturer handles only modest amounts.

The next "cash" item to be explored is checks received. A number of questions may be asked. How are they received? Do they go to the office of the organization or is there a post office box number through which they go directly to the bank? What is the deposit practice? What is the ability to reconstruct checks that come to the organization and are then sent out to the bank? What about exposures to money and

Exhibit 1-6
Typical Balance Sheet Items

Assets	Liabilities
Current assets	Current notes payable
Cash	Accounts payable
Accounts Receivable	Interest payable
Inventory	Taxes payable
Marketable Securities	Current capital lease
Noncurrent assets	obligations
Investment in Affiliates	Revenue collected in
Fixed assets	advance
Land	Noncurrent notes payable
Building	Bonds payable
Machinery	Noncurrent capital lease
Equipment	obligations
Vehicles	
Intangible assets	Owners equity
Patents	
Copyrights	

checks that have been banked? Is there a duplicate deposit slip or record from which lost, stolen, or forged checks could be reconstructed? With respect to both cash and checks, it is important to investigate the control procedures involving verification of cash and checks received and credits to customers' accounts.

Accounts Receivable The next asset item is usually "accounts receivable." Very few organizations do business on an entirely cash basis. With respect to those who do a credit business, the amount and terms of credit extension must be determined. One critical characteristic is whether the credit is extended by the organization itself, or by someone else, such as a bank or credit card company. If the organization itself issues credit cards (e.g. gasoline company and department store credit cards), the exposure is very different than for, say, a manufacturer that offers thirty- or sixty-day terms to businesses that buy its products. Losses on receivables can be incurred from inception (e.g. fraudulent inception) up to extinction, so the exposure should be analyzed from the beginning of the process to the end. Accounts receivable entry procedures should be traced from the source document to the ledger posting. The posting of payments and credits to the account should also be checked for procedure and control.

The safeguarding of accounts receivable records should be verified, as should the ability to duplicate them in the event of loss or destruction. The range of protection that will be found will vary from unlabeled filing cabinets to safes bearing two- or four-hour Underwriters Laboratory labels. Another method is to have the accounts receivable ledger cards in rolling trays, which are removed from a protective vault during the day when being used. This temporarily unprotected exposure should not be overlooked.

Accounts receivable records, when not in use, should be kept in a vault or otherwise adequately protected under lock and key, and persons authorized to unlock or remove accounts receivable should be identified. Vandalism by disgruntled employees has caused a number of serious accounts receivable losses. Today, most organizations with extensive accounts receivable have computerized the process, creating a new set of loss exposures.

Inventory The third item appearing on the balance sheet is usually "inventory." Inventories can consist of merchandise purchased ready for sale or of raw material or components that are used to manufacture the final product of the organization. Applying the axiom, "exposure to loss follows title," the task is to ascertain the terms of purchase to determine when title passes to the organization.

If purchases are on a "delivered basis," title passes upon receipt by the buyer at the buyer's premises, and the transit loss exposure falls on the seller. If, on the other hand, the purchase is "F.O.B. Seller's Shipping Dock," title passes when the goods are loaded on board the transporting conveyance and the transit exposure is the buyer's. The transporting conveyance could be a common carrier—railroad, truck, or ship. If so, the goods move under a bill of lading that describes the extent of liability of the common carrier for loss of the goods during transit. This makes it necessary to examine the bills of lading which are representative of the incoming shipments to determine whether or not the carrier's limit of liability is adequate. Some shippers, in order to reduce freight rates, will take what is known as a "released bill of lading," which may limit the liability of the carrier to considerably less than the value of the goods being transported. Under these conditions, the purchaser has a loss exposure equivalent to the excess valuation. A common carrier's liability is not absolute. For example, it has no liability for so-called "acts of God" or "acts of the public enemy." Shipments by rail are delivered to a freight terminal, rather than to the consignee. The railroad will have only a warehouseman's (negligence) liability if the goods are not picked up by the consignee within the stated number of hours.

Another mode of transportation is by contract carriers. Contract carriers are usually used on an annual contract or an individual contract basis. The terms and conditions of the agreement between the purchaser and the contract carrier, with respect to liability, should be carefully examined. Some organizations buying a variety of products might find it advisable to use a so-called freight consolidator. Under this system, goods are accumulated in the terminal of the consolidator until a full load is reached and then shipped. It is important to establish the values that might accumulate at such a location, as well as the values per shipment. Finally, a purchaser might use owned vehicles to pick up purchased materials. If the terms of purchase are "F.O.B. Seller's Shipping Dock," the loss exposure is entirely the purchaser's from the time the goods are loaded. If the organization has a traffic department, this is where this information can be obtained. (Further detail on these issues is provided in Chapters 9 and 10.)

Most organizations use formal prenumbered purchase orders for the majority of their purchases. The terms and conditions, which are usually printed on the back, should be examined with respect to property loss exposures. (Purchase orders also frequently contain contractual provisions that affect products liability exposures.)

Regardless of the mode of transport, the transit loss exposure ends upon arrival at the purchaser's destination. It is important to check the receiving procedures of the purchaser. One question may lead to another. For example, one might ask if the receipt of merchandise is approved only if there is a copy of the purchase order in the hands of the receiving clerk. Does the clerk check for short deliveries and obvious loss of damage? Does the clerk have authority to accept shipments that are short or shipments for which there is no purchase order? How does the clerk report to inventory control? Do the goods move from the seller directly to the purchaser's selling or manufacturing location, or is there an intermediate distribution warehouse? If there is a distribution warehouse, the peak accumulated values are essential, as well as the mode of transport by which the goods get from the warehouse to the point of sale or to the manufacturing location. In the manufacturing process, is a partially completed product sent out to another location for some phase of processing? If so, how does it get there, how does it get back, and what is the peak accumulated value that would be on the premises of the processor? The agreement with the processor is an important document and should be reviewed with respect to who is responsible for the goods during transit, during process, and during return.

In a manufacturing operation, one would be led to inquire what happens to finished products. Are they warehoused at the plant, sent directly to customers, or do they, in turn, go to a distribution warehouse from which they are then delivered to customers? If a distribution warehouse is involved, is it a public warehouse for which there are warehouse receipts, or is it a warehouse owned and operated by the organization? How do finished products get from the distribution warehouse to the customer? Is the sale on a delivered basis or an F.O.B. seller's warehouse? Mode and terms of transport in all instances are important to identification of inventory loss exposures.

The property loss protection in all phases of the inventory movement—from the original seller to the final disposition of it to the final customer—is critical. Are trucks involved equipped with alarm systems? Are warehouses staffed with security people during the day? Are there sprinklers? Are there automatic alarms? Are there guards at night? Are receiving and shipping procedures under adequate control? Are inventory shortages within the "normal range" for the type of business involved. Even though sales may be F.O.B. the seller's plant or warehouse, are there circumstances that still make it necessary for business reasons for the organization to assume responsibility for shipments that are lost in transit to a valued customer?

For insurance or other risk management purposes, it is necessary to obtain values in all stages if the inventory flow from the maximum single shipment in one vehicle or one freight car to the maximum accumulation at manufacturing, warehousing, and processing locations. This can be done with the aid of a flow chart.

Marketable Securities The foregoing items usually constitute what the accountants call "current assets," but some organizations will also own "marketable securities," which are likewise classified as "current assets." These are usually represented by bonds or stock certificates and are most often in a safe deposit box or custodian account at a bank. Sometimes, they may be held by a stockbroker or investment banker. The related loss exposures include:

1. Purchase of stolen, lost, counterfeited, or altered securities. This loss exposure can be eliminated or mitigated by purchasing only from reputable stockbrokers, investment bankers, or banks who are guarantors of good title.
2. Theft, damage, destruction, or disappearance of the securities. These loss exposures can be treated by safekeeping procedures previously referred to, including the requirement of two signatures to enter a safe deposit box or to authorize the purchase or sale of securities. Special care is required with respect to bonds identified as "bearer" or "coupon," which are not registered as to the owner. The risk management treatment is to change them to registered bonds or, where this is impossible, a custodian account. Alternatively, they should be fully insured because of the problem related to replacement.

Investment in Affiliates Corporations that have subsidiaries or affiliated companies may show an entry "Investment in Affiliates." Another way of reflecting subsidiaries is through a consolidated balance sheet in which parents' subsidiaries' assets are all combined and entered directly into an overall balance sheet as cash, accounts receivable, and so forth. The financial statements of any affiliates should be reviewed on exactly the same basis as the parent. However, it is necessary to note any differences in accounting methodology.

Fixed Assets The next set of items in the financial statement will usually be headed "Fixed Assets." Fixed assets consist of land, building, machinery and equipment, and other property items owned by the organization that are not normally sold or used up during a company's normal operating cycle.

As previously pointed out, land may, in special instances, be subject to loss exposures that need investigation. Is land merely a site for a business building, such as a retail store or manufacturing plant, or is it "unimproved" land containing valuable resources that are subject to loss? In either case, one of the loss exposures is impairment of title. Quite frequently, title is secured by title insurance; but in many cases, it is simply verified by a lawyer's search of past transactions related to the property. All facets of a potential title loss exposure should be explored.

The next items are usually buildings and equipment. In the search for building loss exposures, an additional subsystem must be employed to supplement the financial statement method. This subsystem involves physical inspection and an estimation of the replacement value of the property. Physical inspection should cover the basic perils, the hazards of occupancy, the inherent perils of machinery and equipment involved, and loss control systems and procedures. In valuation, obsolescence must be considered if the structure is old and outmoded. Buildings also may be subject to building code restrictions that would require a more expensive type of construction and demolition of the remaining building portion in the event of partial loss. Machinery and equipment may also be obsolete in view of the development of more advanced machines for the process. Another factor is location. In the event of a total or a nearly total destruction, would rebuilding be on the same site? Many businesses have found it advantageous to move from their existing location to other regions of the country. This may be simply a move from a metropolitan district to a nearby suburb or may involve a move from one state to another.

Most organizations own motor vehicles, and some own aircraft, watercraft, or mobile equipment. The fixed asset accounts will contain a schedule of such equipment, original cost, and annual depreciation.

Depreciated values will usually be less than the current actual cash values which, in turn, will usually be less than replacement cost. With respect to automotive equipment, it is not necessary to establish values in order to obtain insurance on an actual cash value basis; but for risk management purposes, individual current values—probably replacement cost values—should be established. It is of critical importance that the concentrated values subject to a single loss be ascertained. Fleet insurance policies sometimes contain a one-location or catastrophe limit. Of course, a company that retains its vehicle loss exposure is vitally concerned about catastrophic losses involving several property items. In one instance, forty loaded trailers were backed up against a terminal building, and an explosion and fire of unknown origin completely destroyed all of them, together with twelve private passenger cars, the terminal, and its contents. When analyzing loss exposures, building and contents would normally be considered subject to a single loss, but the possibility of simultaneous loss to forty loaded trailers would probably be overlooked.

With respect to the vehicle collision peril, the most probable occurrence involves a single vehicle, but collisions between two vehicles of the same owner occur often enough to justify consideration. Most often they occur when two vehicles on the same run are "tailgating" and the lead vehicle has an accident.

Aircraft ownership can vary from a single plane to large fleets. The fixed asset account usually reflects depreciated value—not replacement or current cash value. If several are housed in a single hangar, the concentrated values are important in considering fire or windstorm losses. Midair or taxi collisions of two aircraft of the same owner are much less likely than collisions of two tractor-trailer rigs.

Owned watercraft would also be shown as fixed asset items. Values range from modest to very significant. The most reliable values for insurance purposes are those established by qualified marine surveyors. Cargo values must be included in the loss exposure evaluation if the watercraft carry cargo.

Mobile equipment is necessary for some organizations. Contractors require bulldozers, trenchers, cranes, and road-building and earth-moving machines. Strip miners also require draglines. These items also appear in capital asset accounts on an original cost and depreciated basis. Many have long useful lives beyond the depreciation period, and valuation is an important function of property loss exposure evaluation.

While financial statements are useful in identifying tangible assets subject to loss, they are of only limited use in establishing *values.* The dollar values reflected in assets accounts are subject to various accounting rules. While valuable for accounting purposes, figures based on historical (acquisition) cost, tax-allowable depreciation, and other accounting devices may poorly reflect the potential financial impact if a given asset is damaged or destroyed. Once property exposed to loss has been identified, additional steps must be taken to establish its value.

Intangible Assets Financial statements sometimes contain items relating to intangible assets such as goodwill, patents, and royalties. Such intangible assets may be carried in financial statements at a one dollar nominal value, but in fact, the ownership of the patent, copyright, or process is considerably more valuable. Many organizations have developed formulas or processes that they can license to others on a royalty basis. If the royalty contract with others is such that the organization benefits on the basis of the material produced and sold by the licensee, then a property loss exposure is created with respect to the licensee's business or manufacturing premises.

Contractual Exposures All of the foregoing property loss exposures are derived from the basic principle that the one who owns the property is the first to suffer loss of such property. However, this principle can be abrogated or limited by contract.

By contract—lease or construction contract, for example—the owner organization may effect a noninsurance transfer of all or part of its property loss exposure to the contractor. Conversely, by a premises lease, it may assume the property loss exposure of another owner.

Therefore, a further subsystem of the financial statement method must be introduced (i.e., the analysis of contracts and agreements relating to property loss exposures). Such loss exposure assumption may be considered either a direct property loss exposure or a contractual liability exposure.

Types of contracts that may affect the property loss exposures of an organization include (1) leases of real or personal property, including data processing equipment; (2) construction contracts; (3) mortgages; (4) agreements of sale or purchase of real property; (5) railroad sidetrack agreements; (6) contracts for the transportation of goods; (7) repair and servicing contracts; (8) equipment purchase agreements (special machinery, aircraft, etc.); (9) processing agreements; (10) warehouse receipts; (11) custodial agreements with respect to securities; (12) contracts for services (janitorial, office temporaries, security, "in-plant" maintenance, etc.); and (13) purchase or sales order forms.

Other Financial Statement Items This brief illustration of the financial statement method of identifying loss exposures has been confined to direct property loss exposures that can be identified by an analysis of the assets side of the balance sheet. An analysis of the liabilities shown in the balance sheet may identify further exposures.

Analysis of financial statements other than the balance sheet may further aid in recognizing loss exposures.

Some of the data collected by financial statement analysis also reveals liability exposures. The study of contracts and agreements is as essential to liability loss exposure identification as to property. Additional subsystems have to be employed in the search for liability exposures.

Other Methods and Subsystems

Insurance Coverage Checklists A completely insurance-oriented system makes use of a publication by the Rough Notes Company, titled *Coverages Applicable*. This publication contains sections for each of a number of different business types or categories. For each type of business, there is an outline of the insurance coverages that may be needed. The insurance surveyor is spared the task of examining every form of insurance in order to determine which are applicable to the account under study.

This approach might direct attention to kinds of insurance that would not otherwise have been recognized as applicable. However, it might also overlook important exposures that would be identified by other techniques.

Loss Analysis The loss analysis method used by some consultants may also be called the loss history approach.

A study of losses that have occurred is clearly useful in identifying losses that may occur in the future. Unless a former exposure no longer exists, losses similar to those that have occurred may occur again. The obvious limitation of a loss history is that it will not reflect loss exposures of a catastrophe level with a very low probable frequency of occurrence—the "100-year flood," the longer interval earthquake, the concealed dishonesty loss, the volcanic eruption, the nuclear reaction, and so on. Also, unless the firm is very large, it may go for years without losses that are much more common than the examples cited. Even large firms may not experience common loss types in a few years' time.

Physical Inspection The amount of reliance that can be placed on physical inspection by risk management or insurance personnel depends, of course, on the size, spread, and complexity of the organization. Actual inspection of all the properties in a chain of 250 stores is a different matter from inspection of a single store, plant, or office. Operations spread over a dozen or more states or countries present a different problem from operations confined to one town or country. Eventually, persons from the unit responsible for identification and evaluation of loss exposures need to visit at least each major operating location. But in between visits, other sources of risk management information must be utilized. And while there is seldom anything as good as a personal view, the risk manager and insurance persons dealing with larger organizations have to rely heavily on reports from others persons—safety inspectors, engineers, supervisors, and managers who are on or can visit the scenes of action.

What is different about inspections (whoever makes them) is that they discover what *is*, which is not necessarily the same thing as other sources tell; other sources commonly report what *was*, or what *should be*. Thus, the official sources may say that duplicate records are kept up to within fifteen days of current date; a visit to the actual scene may reveal that a thirty-day gap actually exists. Official records may show a solid fire wall; a look at the site may show a doorway has been cut to speed up flow of materials.

And there are things official records seldom contain at all: cleanliness of housekeeping, actual care in handling materials, where employees take their coffee breaks, eat their lunches, or smoke cigarettes—human activities and practices. These tend, of course, to relate more to the intensity of hazards than to the existence or nonexistence of exposures: more to the *likelihood* of loss of inventory and equipment by fire than to just the *existence* of the exposure ("inventory and equipment may be damaged by fire"). The latter information can be determined from records; the former cannot.

Published Information A wide variety of published information is useful in the exposure identification process. Such published information may deal with (1) the operations of the firm, (2) exposures common to certain industries, or (3) loss exposures arising from certain processes or products.

Information about the firm is more likely to be published if the firm's stocks or bonds are publicly traded. Investment advisory services, such as Moody's or Standard and Poor's, publish extensive data concerning the finances, products, markets, and other pertinent characteristics of such firms. Careful scrutiny of such publications may reveal loss exposures that might otherwise be overlooked.

Published information concerning the loss exposures connected with specific processes or products is especially helpful in the exposure identification process. The potential sources of such information are too numerous to list here in detail. Some particularly helpful sources are the National Safety Council and the National Fire Protection Association. Two agencies of the federal government, the Occupational Safety and Health Administration and the Consumer Product Safety Commission also publish material in this category.

Firms selling protective equipment also publish various types of exposure identification surveys or checklists. These checklists are useful in exposure identification, but risk managers must realize that their objective is usually similar to that of many insurance surveys. Protective equipment manufacturers wish to sell protective equipment, and overreliance on their surveys may lead the manager to use inappropriate control measures for treating loss exposures.

Additional Considerations The exposure identification methods described here are by no means the only ways in which property loss exposures can be recognized by a risk manager, or for that matter, by any other interested party. Through a variety of formal and informal communications within his or her organization, a risk manager can develop an information network that builds a continuing awareness of new and changing exposures. Through interaction with outsiders, and even through regular reading of insurance and risk management periodicals, as well as the trade press of the industry in question, one can learn of property loss problems encountered by similarly situated firms. As noted in CPCU 4, risk managers should analyze contracts entered into by the organization in order to determine what liability exposures may have been assumed or transferred. Where contracts transfer responsibility for property of others, they may also indicate some exposures best handled by applying risk management techniques similar to those applied to owned property.

Comparison and Evaluation of Techniques

Serious mismanagement is much less likely for loss exposures that have been identified or recognized than for exposures that have been overlooked. Therefore, one major objective in identification of exposures is *to assure that nothing important has been overlooked.* However, the amount of time, effort, and expense that can be devoted to exposure identification is invariably limited. Thus, a second major objective must be *to do an adequate job of identification with only the information, time, and personnel that can be obtained for the purpose.*

To meet these two major objectives, the method(s) used to identify loss exposures must be both *effective* (giving a high probability of discovering all that needs to be discovered) and *efficient* (having a high ratio of results to effort).

The use of any identification technique by itself is likely to result in a failure to identify some exposures to loss—that is, using only one technique is usually not effective. This is especially true of the standard questionnaire approach, because the questions must be general enough to apply to many firms. Questionnaires tailored to a specific industry may be less deficient in this respect.

As an example, executives of one large greeting card manufacturer indicated, when interviewed for an insurance survey, that the firm did not have any valuable papers. However, a flow chart analysis of the manufacturing process revealed a storage area containing several thousand items of original artwork that had been used in the company's high-priced lines of greeting cards. Additional questioning revealed that the company earned about a half-million dollars each year by licensing similar firms in foreign countries to use the artwork from the collection. In addition, the firm frequently used the material in its own lower-priced lines. Since the artwork was not shown as an asset on the firm's balance sheet, it is doubtful whether this loss exposure would have been identified by any method other than flow chart analysis or physical inspection.

In general, the questionnaire method and financial statement analysis are likely to be satisfactory in identifying exposures to direct property loss. However, some care must be exercised even in regard to those exposures. Some assets may not appear on financial statements, either because they have been full depreciated or because accountants do not think of them as assets. The greeting card artwork mentioned in the preceding paragraph is an example of the latter.

The questionnaire method also is likely to be satisfactory in identifying details regarding the exposures that are common to a large number of firms, such as employee dishonesty, damage to motor vehicles, boiler explosion, and the more common liability exposures. It is much less satisfactory in identifying unusual exposures to which a particular firm may be subject. The list of such unusual exposures is virtually endless, but examples are (1) the inability to obtain merchandise or raw materials from a key supplier; (2) the increased probability of loss of profits or prolonged loss of profits because of the failure of a key machine or key process; (3) the loss to goods in process and possibly processing machinery if processing is stopped because of power failure or other reasons; and (4) the expense to reproduce research results if records, test animals, or other research materials are destroyed. Such unusual exposures are much more likely to be found through flow chart analysis.

The best approach to loss exposure identification is a combination of several methods. One effective combination relies on flow chart analysis and financial statement analysis for the initial identification effort. A comprehensive questionnaire is then used as a final checklist to be sure that no common exposures have been overlooked in searching for unusual ones. Of course, a physical inspection of the firm's facilities and operations is highly desirable. Other combinations of methods are possible, of course, and each analyst will develop effective and efficient techniques that are compatible with his or her abilities and methods of operation.

It should also be noted that exposure identification is not a one-shot activity. The "final" step in the risk management process—and one that is often underemphasized—is *monitoring*. Effective monitoring requires continuing attention to changing exposures *and* periodic application of a formal process to verify that all current exposures have been identified and addressed.

Chapter Notes

1. Martin J. Gannon, *Management: An Organizational Perspective* (Boston: Little, Brown and Company, 1977), pp. 116–117.
2. Discussion here is based on the CPCU 1 text by C. Arthur Williams, Jr., George L. Head, Ronald C. Horn, and G. William Glendenning, *Principles of Risk Management and Insurance*, 2nd ed. (Malvern: American Institute for Property and Liability Underwriters, 1981), Chapter 1. Williams et al. base their discussion of pre-loss and post-loss objectives on suggestions made by Professors Robert I. Mehr and Bob A. Hedges.
3. Robert I. Mehr and Bob A. Hedges, *Risk Management: Concepts and Applications* (Homewood, IL: Richard D. Irwin, Inc., 1974), p. 3.
4. The risk management process is discussed extensively in the CPCU 1 text, *Principles of Risk Management and Insurance*.
5. FC&S Bulletins, *The National Underwriter*, January 1975, Misc. Fire Sc-5.
6. On October 1, 1987, an earthquake registering 6.1 on the Richter scale jolted Southern California. That quake and its aftershocks caused damage exceeding $137 million. However, the California Department of Insurance estimates that an earthquake of 8.25 magnitude on the Richter scale—the size that occurred in San Francisco in 1906 and in Alaska in 1964—would cause damage of more than $4.9 billion if it occurred in the Los Angeles/Orange County area. Alfred G. Haggerty, "Quake Claims Limited in California" and "Quake Loss Could Have Been Worse," *National Underwriter, Property and Casualty Edition*, October 12, 1987, pp. 1, 3.
7. S. T. Algermissen, "Seismic Risk Studies in the United States," Fourth World Conference on Earthquake Engineering, 1969, p. 26.
8. A. Hawthorne Criddle, CPCU, "How Can the Part Time Insurance Manager Know His Risks?"—address to the Delaware Valley Chapter of RIMS (formerly ASIM), delivered on October 8, 1958.

CHAPTER 2

Measuring and Controlling Commercial Property Exposures

Chapter 1 introduced the risk management process, explained how the risk management process is intended to meet an organization's pre-loss and post-loss objectives and discussed part of the first step in the risk management process—exposure identification. The purpose of exposure identification is to determine what loss exposures exist in a given organization, but not specifically to determine how serious they may be.

Next in the process is measurement of those exposures found to exist. Once a loss exposure has been measured and its dimensions known, one can intelligently select techniques for managing, or treating, the exposure. Measuring loss exposures is the first major subject of Chapter 2.

Before appropriate risk management techniques can be selected, it is necessary to recognize what techniques are available. The techniques for treating loss exposures can be divided into two broad categories—control techniques and financing techniques, as shown in Exhibit 2-1. *Control techniques* alter the exposures themselves. They attempt to lower the frequency, reduce the severity, or improve the accuracy of predicting losses that might occur. In other words, control techniques attempt to change the dimensions of an exposure, so that it will have different measurements. The second major part of Chapter 2 deals with loss control techniques used to alter some of the more important commercial property loss exposures, particularly the fire exposure.

Financing techniques provide funds to finance recovery from losses that actually occur. Subsequent chapters of this text will deal primarily with insurance against fire and related perils. Noninsurance financing techniques (techniques other than insurance) for the same

57

Exhibit 2-1
Techniques for Treating Loss Exposures

CONTROL TECHNIQUES	FINANCING TECHNIQUES
Avoidance	Some Noninsurance Transfers
Loss Control	Insurance Transfers
Loss Prevention	Retention
Loss Reduction	
Separation	
Combination	
Some Noninsurance Transfers	

exposures will be discussed in Chapter 15, which will also provide guidelines for selecting among risk management techniques.

For now, however, it is necessary to note that at least two risk management techniques should generally be considered to treat any specific exposure. Sometimes, an exposure can be avoided, so that it ceases to exist. Otherwise, for exposures that continue to exist, effective risk management suggests the consideration of at least one control and one financing technique. Control techniques other than avoidance attempt to change the dimensions of an exposure, but do not eliminate the exposure altogether; financing techniques must be considered in order to pay for losses that occur despite the controls.

A rather simple example may illustrate the scope of these next few chapters. Assume Patty, the owner of Patty's Burger Shop, has identified the fact that a fire at the shop could cause considerable reduction in value of the restaurant property, as well as a business interruption loss. Measuring these exposures provides Patty with some information regarding the likelihood of a fire, its potential financial impact on Patty, and the reliability of her predictions. By installing an automatic fire extinguishing system over the hamburger grill, Patty controls the loss exposure by reducing the probable severity of damage that could be caused by a grease fire on the grill. Fires may still occur, however, and Patty purchases building, contents, and business interruption insurance to finance losses that may occur. Because the building and contents policy she selects contains a $500 deductible, Patty also uses the retention technique to finance small losses. This rather elementary example illustrates the use of one control technique (the extinguishing system is a loss control measure) and two financing techniques (insurance and retention).

MEASUREMENT OF LOSS EXPOSURES

After loss exposures have been identified, analysis is necessary. The risk manager must formulate a realistic estimate of the economic effect on the organization of losses that may arise from the exposure.

To analyze a given loss exposure, a risk manager needs to study the following:

1. *loss frequency*—the number of events (e.g., fires, thefts, or floods) that are expected to occur within some time interval such as a century, a decade, or a year;
2. *loss severity*—how serious these individual occurrences are expected to be;
3. *total dollar losses*—how serious the total dollar losses are expected to be (the expected number of occurrences times the average expected dollar loss per occurrence, or frequency times severity); and
4. *credibility of loss predictions*—how reliably the risk manager can predict the number of occurrences, the loss per occurrence, and the total dollar losses. In other words, how much confidence can be placed in the predictions?

This information is important to the risk manager for the following reasons:

1. *It reduces uncertainty concerning loss.* A loss exposure that has been measured is better understood than an exposure of unknown dimensions.
2. *It indicates which exposures should receive more immediate or concentrated attention.* When loss exposures have been measured, it becomes easier to identify those exposures that are most serious.
3. *It helps the risk manager determine what risk management techniques would be most appropriate for the particular exposure.* By evaluating how different risk management techniques affect each measurement, the risk manager can test the effects of possible risk management techniques.

In theory, the risk manager should attempt to forecast the impact on an organization of the sum of all losses each year. As a practical matter, the forecast will be limited to those types of losses that lend themselves to forecasting because of the availability of loss data from one source or another, but will also recognize other rarely occurring losses and lump them all together. The risk manager will then attempt to meet the organization's risk management objectives by identifying potential losses that threaten the organization's ability to meet its objectives, and determining how to deal with the exposures.

Potential Loss Frequency

It is sometimes confusing to speak of the "frequency" of something that happens so infrequently as a fire to a given building. Many buildings in the United States have stood for 200 years or more without suffering a fire. To suggest that a certain loss prevention measure would "reduce fire frequency" to a 200-year-old building seems contrary to the normal use of this term. However, there is some "frequency" of the fire losses in buildings of this type, and this is what is referred to. Consider the following case—a pair of dice has been thrown fifty times and no double six has appeared. What is the "frequency" of double six? In the observed case, it *has been* zero out of fifty. (In the one observed 200-year-old building, fire loss frequency *has been* zero out of 200 years.) But, over all throws of two dice, the result is one double six in every thirty-six throws. (Over all buildings similarly situated, the fire frequency is, perhaps, seven per 200 years.)

Thus, frequency can be considered as referring to experience, on the average, over many cases. In this sense, average frequency is another way of stating probability. With a pair of dice, average frequency of one double six in thirty-six throws is a probability of $\frac{1}{36}$ for double six. An average of seven fires per building over 200 years is $\frac{7}{200}$, or 0.035 probability of fire per building per year. Installation of some effective loss prevention technique might reduce the probability to, say, $\frac{1}{1,000}$ or 0.001. Although it is sometimes impractical actually to measure such a low probability (frequency) of loss in real world situations (how many houses, in similar situations, can be observed for two hundred years?), such low probabilities do exist, and each exposure has a specific figure associated with it.

The term "frequency" is used because it can also be applied to cases at the opposite extreme; "probability" cannot be used in such cases. Consider the following example: over the past five years, Corporation H has averaged 2,700 shipping claims per year. The smallest number was 2,350; the largest was 2,910. In the same period, Corporation I has averaged 240 claims per year. Its smallest number was 205; its largest, 265. The realistic probability of having shipping claims next year is 1.0 for both corporations—a sure thing. But the expected frequency for the two is very different—about 2,700 versus about 240. Hence, expected frequency is the more widely useful concept. But, note that it is the *expected* frequency that is comparable to probability. Actually observed, historical frequency is not necessarily the same.

As a general rule, loss frequency is more predictable than loss severity. In fact, loss frequency can be predicted with a fairly high degree of confidence for some exposures for large organizations. For example, an organization with 1,000 motor vehicles probably would be quite confident of its ability to predict accurately the number of accidents involving physical damage during a given time period. A firm that makes dozens of shipments each day can predict within acceptable limitations the number of transit losses it will sustain in a given year. Some firms may even be able to make satisfactory projections of the number of fire losses to be expected each year. An example would be a fast food chain with, say, 2,000 stores throughout the country.

However, significant property losses occur infrequently, and most firms do not have a sufficiently large number of exposure units to permit prediction of loss frequency with enough confidence to include loss expenses in the firm's operating budget. An estimate with a substantial margin for error is better than no estimate at all, as long as the risk manager recognizes its limitations. However, even precise loss estimates are useful only if they affect a risk manager's decision.

Potential Loss Severity

Confident estimation of severity is usually more difficult than confident prediction of loss frequency. The severity of a particular loss, particularly a fire loss, depends on many variables that are highly unpredictable. For example, fires that start at night, when most businesses are closed, commonly cause more damage than fires that start in the daytime when they are likely to be promptly detected and extinguished. The difference between a minor fire and a total loss may hinge on some entirely unpredictable situation, such as an employee erroneously turning off a sprinkler system valve, or a train blocking a grade crossing on a highway used by fire trucks.

It is useful to know the size of loss most likely to occur. However, there is little comfort or value in knowing that the most probable amount of loss was $25,000, if a $1 million loss has actually occurred. In measuring property loss exposures for risk management purposes, it is particularly important to know the size of the largest loss that could occur, or *maximum possible loss*. It is also helpful to determine the largest loss *likely* to occur, or *maximum probable loss*.

Maximum Possible Loss The first important consideration in estimating loss from fire or other perils to buildings and contents is the maximum possible loss, sometimes called the *amount subject*. The *maximum possible loss* is the total value exposed to loss at any one location or from any one event. For direct damage by the peril of fire, this would usually be the total building and contents values exposed to loss within any one building or fire division. It is the maximum *possible* loss that should usually be considered by the risk manager when choosing among loss financing alternatives and in establishing insurance limits if insurance is elected.

The foregoing discussion was couched in terms of fire loss, but fire is not always the most serious peril, in terms of severity, to which buildings and contents are exposed. If a building is fire resistive and well divided by fire walls, fire damage may be relatively minor, even in the worst conceivable situation. However, the fire resistive construction and fire walls may offer little protection against damage by earthquake, windstorm, landslide, subsidence, or explosion.

The maximum possible loss must be considered with regard to other property also, not just for buildings and contents. For example, what is the maximum possible physical damage loss for a fleet of motor vehicles? Is it the value of the most expensive unit? Are several vehicles stored in the same building at night? What are the chances of flood or tornado damage at the company's parking area?

At first glance, the amount to which goods in transit are subject in a single loss would seem to be the value of the largest shipment. However, one must also consider the possibility that several shipments might be in a terminal, warehouse, or staging area at the same time, or that more than one vehicle could be involved in a truck accident or train wreck.

Maximum Probable Loss   The largest loss likely to occur may involve less value than the maximum possible loss. The probable fire loss will be limited by the fire protection available—such as automatic sprinklers, public fire departments, and so forth. This smaller loss estimate might be termed probable maximum loss, or maximum probable loss.

The diagram in Exhibit 2-2 illustrates the concepts described above. The premises consist of two buildings: Building A and Building B. Building A is subdivided into three areas by two fire walls. The values of buildings and contents in Area 1 of Building A are $1 million, $2 million in Area 2, and $3 million in Area 3.

The other building, Building B, is separated from Building A by 300 feet, including a river 200 feet wide, and contains total values of $10 million. In determining the maximum possible loss and maximum probable loss, it might be determined whether the fire walls and the separation distance between buildings will be recognized as effective fire separation. This sometimes calls for a fire protection engineer's evaluation of the premises, considering the combustibility of the materials and the effectiveness of the separations. Assuming the

Exhibit 2-2
Maximum Probable Loss and Maximum Possible Loss Illustration

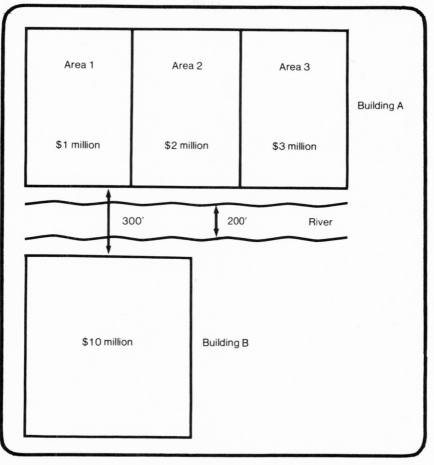

engineer reports that all separations are standard and effective, then the maximum possible fire loss would be $10 million and the maximum probable fire loss would be $10 million (the value of Building B). Building A and Building B would not be deemed subject to a single fire loss. If, however, all buildings are sprinklered with an adequate sprinkler system, the maximum probable loss might be judged some fraction of the values exposed, say 40 percent. The maximum possible loss would stay at $10 million, because automatic sprinklers can be rendered ineffective.

If Building A by itself were considered and the two fire walls met all necessary standards (thus forming separate fire divisions), then both the maximum possible fire loss and maximum probable fire loss might be considered $3 million. However, if the building is of fire resistive construction and combustibility of the contents is low, or if automatic sprinklers have been installed, the maximum probable loss might be considered less than $3 million. A similar analysis might be made of a multi-story building, estimating the probable maximum number of floors to be damaged.

In Exhibit 2-2, it was determined that the maximum possible loss in any one fire was $10 million because it was virtually impossible for a single fire to damage both buildings simultaneously. Such a conclusion must be tempered with the realization that perils other than fire must also be considered. Because Buildings A and B are located alongside a river, it is possible that flooding of the river would result in simultaneous damage to both buildings. The likelihood of a flood at this location must be considered, as well as the degree of damage a flood might inflict. There is also the possibility of windstorm destroying both Building A and Building B. A tornado could simultaneously damage both buildings, although the probability of such an occurrence may be low.

It is important to note that the definitions used and the figures reached represent only one approach used by some underwriters and risk managers—other individuals have different approaches. In any discussion of these terms, it is necessary first to define the terms being used and the conditions under which they are used.

The maximum possible loss concept is of value to risk managers and underwriters who can use the concept to establish the severity of exposures that must be treated. The maximum probable loss concept is of particular use in underwriting, since underwriters are concerned with the averaging effect of a large number of exposure units. However, the concept can also be very useful to risk managers in many situations.

Potential Total Dollar Losses

In determining how serious the total dollar losses are likely to be, it is helpful to recognize two loss categories—(1) normal losses and (2) catastrophic losses. Because dollar losses can involve many different amounts, it is often useful to group losses into various size categories or layers, an approach sometimes termed "stratification."

Working Layer The normal loss rate is that number or amount occurring with enough regularity that plans may be made to establish expense allowances for the exposure in the organization's operating budget. Common examples are the auto collision loss rate in a large

Exhibit 2-3
Losses Over a Ten-Year Period

Size of Loss	Number of Losses	Total Amount of Loss
$0 to $1,000	159	$76,200
$1,000 to $5,000	32	61,412
$5,000 to $10,000	5	41,216
$10,000 to $25,000	2	26,500
Over $25,000	0	0

fleet or the rate of inventory losses caused by dishonest employees. Since these losses occur in a reasonably predictable manner, they sometimes are referred to as the *working layer*.

Catastrophe Layer Rates of loss well above normal (that do not appear with regularity and may not ever occur) may be termed the *catastrophe layer*. While working layer losses can be funded from current revenues as a cost of doing business, catastrophe layer losses normally require advance funding through reserves, insurance, or some other formalized funding or transfer device.

Buffer Layer The *buffer layer* lies between the working layer and the catastrophe layer. If the working layer includes losses that *regularly* happen, and the catastrophe layer includes losses that *rarely* happen, then the buffer layer might be said to include losses that *sometimes* happen. For example, it might be considered that losses of a severity that can be expected at least once every five years, or perhaps once every twenty years, fall in the buffer layer.

Stratification of Loss Levels Loss data may be analyzed most easily if separated into various strata. They may be prepared, for example, as in Exhibit 2-3.

If tables like this one are prepared, covering a large number of exposures during a ten-year period, then a fairly clear picture may be obtained of how many losses of a particular size can be expected. In Exhibit 2-3, no losses over $25,000 occurred in the years represented. It might be reasonable to assume that losses over $25,000 would not normally occur and would therefore be considered in the catastrophe category.

Since a loss in the $10,000 to $25,000 category occurred only twice in ten years, there would be a question whether this was an unusual event or one that might be expected. In this case, the $10,000 to $25,000 layer could be considered a buffer layer. The range above $25,000 would constitute the catastrophe layer.

A table of stratified losses, like Exhibit 2-3, can be very useful in the selection of deductibles or retentions under excess insurance policies. The deductible amount usually should be somewhere within the buffer layer. From Exhibit 2-3, a deductible of $10,000 to $25,000 is indicated. Of course, the firm's ability to absorb the indicated deductible one or more times during the year and the difference in premium levels for insurance with various deductible levels also must be considered. A $5,000 deductible might be reasonable under some circumstances. Or, for an organization with substantial ability to absorb loss, a deductible of $100,000 or more might be indicated.

Simple stratification of loss levels, as described above, is an easy, effective technique for obtaining a picture of the frequency of losses that happen often enough to appear regularly in limited time periods. However, caution is necessary when making risk management decisions based on this type of information. Perhaps no losses over $25,000 *have* occurred during a certain time period, but how likely was it that such losses *could have* occurred? Statistical techniques beyond the scope of this text can be used to provide more precise information leading to sound risk management decisions. For some organizations, the data can be sufficiently well approximated by a probability distribution curve so the curve itself may be used to predict losses at various levels.

Care must also be taken to apply appropriate trend factors to losses of different years, as discussed later in this chapter. One trend that can be fairly well quantified is inflation. Other trends may not be so easy to quantify, such as changes in operating procedures and improvements in protection facilities. Statisticians have several techniques for uncovering trends, and adjusting for them, that can be used. Although forecasting the future always involves an element of uncertainty, better informed forecasts regularly outperform pure guesswork.

Total Loss Concept

The discussion up to this point has dealt with relatively simple events in which a single peril caused only one kind of loss consequence. Unfortunately, actual events are seldom that simple. A risk manager must recognize the "total loss concept." Most losses involve more than one peril, and/or more than one type of loss consequence.

Combination of Property Types. It is possible for loss to involve property in several different classifications. Even a relatively small fire in an office building may cause damage to the building, to money and securities, to accounts receivable records, to data processing equipment and media, and to other equipment and supplies. Damage may involve not only owned but also nonowned property, such as employees' personal property kept in their desks, and leased photocopy equipment.

Combination of Perils When calculating the maximum loss potential, attention must be given to the fact that some major losses can involve several different perils. An earthquake may be followed by a fire. In fact, one research study predicts that more of the losses from a major California earthquake would be from fires following the tremors than from building collapses.[1] Flooding may be accompanied by a fire. Hurricane and flooding may come together, as may hurricane and fire.

The chief reason for considering a combination of perils in assessing an organization's loss potential is to be certain that excessive loss exposures are not retained.

The combination of physical damage perils normally will not exceed the maximum possible loss established for fire loss, but exceptions exist. One possible exception occurs where there is a considerable amount of noncombustible or fire-resistive construction not subject to fire loss and there is an earthquake and ensuing fire. Another appears where two or more buildings or fire divisions are susceptible to a common natural disaster such as flood, tornado, or earthquake.

Multiple Loss Consequences The discussion of maximum possible loss in terms of damage to building and contents was a convenient way to introduce some important concepts. However, it is very important to realize that a loss to building and contents may be, and frequently is, accompanied by other consequences caused by the same peril. It is not sufficient for risk managers to define one maximum possible loss for damage to buildings and contents and a separate maximum possible loss for business interruption. Reduction in building and contents values, business interruption losses, and several other loss consequences (such as liability and workers compensation claims) may be involved in a single incident. When a loss occurs, the entity suffers all of it, and that total effect is what must be managed. *The important figure to consider in measuring loss exposures is the maximum dollar loss that could occur, considering all its aspects.*

Credibility of Loss Predictions

The degree to which losses are predictable plays a large role in

Exhibit 2-4
Loss Prediction

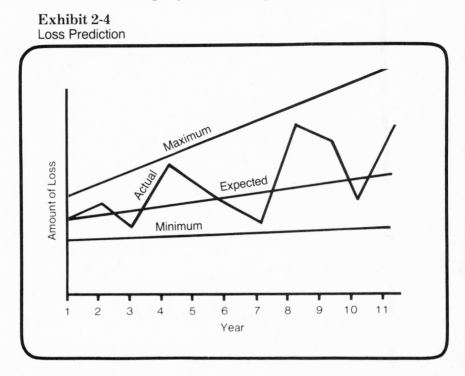

determining what insurance or noninsurance techniques will be used. Suppose, for example, that losses can be predicted within a range as shown in Exhibit 2-4. It might be predicted that average losses would fall along the line labeled "expected," and that the maximum probable loss would lie along the line labeled "maximum." Minimum probable loss levels might also be predicted as shown by the "minimum" line. If such predictions can be made with a high degree of confidence, actual losses will be expected to follow a pattern something like the "actual" line on the graph, deviating from the average from one year to the next but in no case exceeding the maximum or falling below the minimum.

This might be a typical pattern for the transportation claims of a large shipper with ten years in business and a steadily increasing volume. In such a case, there is little uncertainty and the losses can be retained and built into the shipper's operating budget. No insurance or other transfer mechanism is needed to finance these losses, although insurance might be purchased for other reasons.

A more typical situation is illustrated in Exhibit 2-5. This might represent fire losses actually experienced by a large organization with a number of locations. A few losses usually occurred each year. In year 4, however, there were no losses, while in year 8, there was at least one

Exhibit 2-5
Predicted Losses vs. Actual Losses

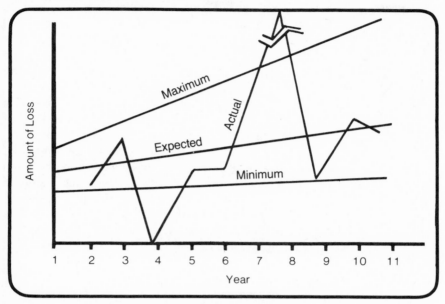

major fire. These losses may have been predictable to a certain extent at lower levels, but possibilities existed for substantial losses above the normal loss levels. To retain these losses and to attempt to finance them out of the organization's operating budget might have been disastrous.

Sources of Data for Measuring Exposures

If projection into the future is to be more than a wild guess, it must have some factual basis. In most cases, the basis for the projection of future loss frequency is past loss frequency—the past loss frequency of the firm under consideration, of a group of firms, or of a geographic area. This information might be obtained from the firm's own records, or it might be based on the experience of other firms, on insurance statistics, or on data from other sources.

Past Experience of the Organization The most useful data for estimating future loss frequency is the past experience of the organization concerned, provided the organization has a sufficient number of exposure units for the figures to have meaning. It is important, however, to evaluate the reliability of experience data before they are used. Some of the factors that may affect the reliability of data are discussed in this section.

Loss Reporting and Recording Procedures. In order to analyze loss data, it is necessary to have a record of all losses kept in some organized system. Property losses present problems in this regard, particularly in a large organization. Many small fire, wind, theft, and other property losses are not reported because they appear trivial, or because the department or branch suffering the losses sees no advantage in having them reported. Thus, true loss frequency data may be unavailable.

A second important problem in reporting property losses is obtaining figures that accurately represent loss severity. The cost of repairing or replacing damaged property is relatively easy to measure, but does not reflect a number of intangibles—such as disruption of work flow, losses or gains in accounting or tax treatments, benefits from replacing old property with new, and many unrecorded expenses such as executive time taken for planning and expediting repairs, long-distance telephone calls, and so on. Such loss costs are sometimes ignored and almost always inaccurately stated.

To the extent that losses have been covered by insurance, a reasonably accurate representative of past insured losses may be made. For uninsured expenses associated with insured losses, an informed estimate is usually the only practical means of producing figures.

Once a loss is reported, it must be recorded. The accuracy and timeliness of records of any kind depend on the diligence and accuracy of the person recording them. Sometimes, insurance loss reports are maintained by an insurance producer or insurance company, in which case the amounts recorded usually include only the incurred or paid insured losses, omitting deductible portions or uninsured losses.

Changes in Organization. All organizations are subject to change, and some are more changeable than others. Any organization may produce different product mixes at different times. It may change officers. There may be a merger. Nearly all such changes affect loss exposures to some extent, so the losses incurred during one year may represent a different environment from that of future years.

Changes in Operations. The Occupational Safety and Health Act, influence of insurance inspectors, and technological changes through the years continually alter property exposures. For the most part, these changes are for the better, but there may be regressions, such as when a hazardous new operation is not accompanied by safety improvements, or when property maintenance is deferred.

Whatever the situation, changes do occur and will affect losses. For example, a firm that makes frequent shipments may have experienced one pilferage claim for each ten shipments over the past three years. If the firm does not contemplate any change in its method of shipping or packaging, it might use this figure to project future pilferage loss frequency. However, if it has recently started shipping all goods in large, sealed containers, it may be desirable to lower the estimate of future loss frequency. On the other hand, if the firm will continue its former methods but will increase its shipments to a terminal where pilferage losses are relatively frequent, the estimate should be adjusted upward to reflect the increased exposure.

Environmental Changes. Changes occur in the economic and social environment in which organizations operate. Inflation is the most apparent change, and past inflation can be measured with at least a moderate degree of accuracy. All dollar figures for losses in different years should be adjusted by an inflation factor if they are to be compared on a common basis. Another environmental change is the increasing restrictiveness of building codes and other laws that may require rebuilding damaged facilities to a higher standard of safety and pollution control.

Environmental and economic factors beyond the direct control of the firm may affect future loss frequency. For example, the shift of many industries from natural gas to coal furnaces and the increasing use of "alternative" energy sources are likely to have some effect on the frequency of fire and explosion losses. The risk manager must reflect such influences in estimates of future loss frequency to the extent possible by modifying the projections used.

Technological Changes. The introduction of new technology is often accompanied by changes in hazards. New chemical or biological processes, for example, may improve certain processes while introducing pollution hazards that have not yet been recognized. One area of special concern involves the emerging field of genetic engineering.

Limited Volume of Data. The extent of past experience is a major determinant of the reliability of data. There must be a sufficient number of exposure units for the data to be statistically credible. The number of exposure units required for statistical credibility varies inversely with the relative frequency of loss. The method of determining the required units is beyond the scope of this discussion. However, it can be noted that the number of exposure units required for confident prediction is larger than is often supposed. In general, the larger the number of units, the more credible the data.

All these limitations do not say that experience is unusable. They simply point out the need for careful analysis and recognition of the need to estimate the degree of credibility for different types of loss reports.

Experience of Similar Organizations In some cases, the experience of organizations in similar fields may be a usable indicator of probable loss frequency. In fact, insurance rates normally are based on the loss experience of many insureds with reasonably homogeneous loss exposures. However, it may be difficult or impossible for some organizations to use the data of others, for several reasons. First, the loss histories of others are pertinent only for organizations with reasonably homogeneous operations, such as gasoline stations having similar construction and protection. Second, organizations large enough to have credible information of their own are not always willing to share it. Even smaller firms may be reluctant to furnish loss information to a competitor. Some trade associations compile data on an aggregate basis in such a way that they can be useful to all members without disclosing the proprietary data of any single member.

A small company, without credible statistical data of its own, might use information regarding similar companies as a basis for its own calculations. A large company, on the other hand, might find that (1) it is not enough like other companies for their data to be useful and, (2) data of its own are statistically credible. Thus, the usefulness of another company's experience diminishes as the size of the company wanting to use the experience increases.

As an example, consider a small retailer owning four stores, each in a different city. The retailer has no basis for confidently estimating probable losses from the experience of the four stores. However, the retailer might be able to determine the experience of a retail chain with 1,000 similar stores scattered throughout the country. These statistics may be useful to the small retailer for such things as estimating the value of electronic labels as a theft reduction device. Nevertheless, it would be impossible to predict with any satisfactory confidence that next year's losses for a four-store chain will be approximately four one-thousandths of those of the large chain.

Insurance Statistics   Loss data collected by insurance organizations represent the most comprehensive accumulation of loss information available. Many insurance companies subscribe to the services of the Insurance Services Office (ISO) or the American Association of Insurance Services (AAIS), rate-making organizations that promulgate insurance premium rates country-wide. As insurers collect data on the losses they pay, information is forwarded to these organizations which then promulgate insurance rates using the loss data. These rates develop a premium which is intended to enable the insurer to pay losses and expenses while making a profit.

For fire insurance, loss statistics are broken down by classes for those types like dwellings that can be class rated. Loss statistics are also considered for adjusting specific rates on larger buildings that are individually rated, giving rating credits for better-than-average features and debits for those below average. Unfortunately, loss statistics are not sufficiently refined to be any more than a rough indicator of future losses for a large *group* of exposure units. It is never possible to predict with much accuracy the losses at a single location. Moreover, insurance statistics are related to premium rates rather than to *values* exposed. Though the aggregate statistics used in rate making may be satisfactory for rating purposes, a fire insurance rate is not a predictor of whether a loss to a given item of property will occur.

Both the Insurance Services Office and the American Association of Insurance Services collect loss statistics for inland marine insurance. However, the data seldom are in sufficient detail to be of much assistance to risk managers. Perhaps the most useful risk management application of such statistics would be the establishment of trends in loss experience. The same limitations apply to crime insurance statistics collected by the Insurance Services Office and fidelity and surety statistics collected by the Surety Association of America.

Other Data Sources Trade organizations represent a good source of data for many industries. The Machinery and Allied Products Institute, for example, collects data on the loss experience of some classes of industrial firms. The National Fire Protection Association is a useful source of information on fire losses. Its publications discuss such subjects as the fire hazards of various industrial processes, the effectiveness of sprinkler systems in extinguishing fires, fire resistance of building materials, and explosion hazards of industrial materials and processes. Underwriters Laboratories and the Factory Mutual Research Corporation also provide information on fire hazards and fire resistance of materials.

The uniform crime reports compiled by the Federal Bureau of Investigation may be of some value in estimating crime losses. They are especially useful in the establishment of loss frequency trends and the comparison of crime trends by geographic area.

The U.S. Army Corps of Engineers is a source of information on flood frequency and magnitude. Though the Corps cannot estimate the dollar loss potential, it can give some indication of the height to which flood waters may rise and the frequency with which floods may affect a given location. For example, it can project that, at one location, flood waters might be expected once every 100 years, on the average.

Earthquake insurance statistics are kept by the Insurance Services Office, but they are of value only in a general way because of the low frequency of damaging earthquakes and the small percentage of earthquake damage covered by insurance. More extensive information on earthquake activity can be obtained from government sources.

Windstorm and hail statistics are well documented by the U.S.

Weather Service and provide a useful background for building design or exposure analysis. Catastrophe data collected by the Insurance Services Office also may be useful in estimating the probability of damage by tornado or hurricane.

Frequency and Severity by Peril

Loss frequency and severity vary rather widely according to the causes of loss involved. This section describes general patterns of frequency and severity associated with some of the more common property perils. Although it is not possible to analyze all perils here, those that are discussed account for a large proportion of property losses.

Fire Among perils with large potential for property damage, fire has the greatest frequency for most operations. The chief difficulty in estimating probable fire loss frequency is obtaining accurate information. Many small fires are extinguished after causing little damage and, therefore, are never reported. Even those that cause moderate damage may not be reported if deductibles are in effect. It is natural for most people to resist filling out a report form unless forced to do so by a management directive with effective penalties for failure to comply. Since few managers consider fire loss reporting to be highly important, the data base may understate past loss frequency.

Fire loss severity potential is best determined by estimates of trained fire protection engineers or underwriters. Severity varies greatly as a result of differences in protection, construction, and occupancy, and care must be used in severity estimates.

Explosion Explosion is quite a different peril from fire and is subdivided for insurance purposes into two types: (1) boiler explosion, and (2) all others. The distinction is made because separate insurance policies are usually employed for boiler insurance and because loss statistics are separately maintained.

Different types of explosions have considerably different characteristics, and their low frequency makes statistical analysis difficult. Certain processes have large numbers of explosion-prone devices. In most cases, however, explosions arise from unpredictable causes, and loss frequency is difficult or impossible to quantify.

Potential severity, on the other hand, is relatively easy to determine, though not with a high degree of accuracy. The severity of a steam explosion is roughly proportional to the total volume of water which may be turned to steam and released by sudden failure of the containing vessel. Higher pressure also means a larger potential explosion. The severity of a liquified gas (e.g., propane) tank explosion is proportional to the quantity of gas contained in the tank. Explosions can be extremely violent, causing damage within a wide radius. Parts of the containing vessel can be hurled hundreds of feet by the force of the explosion. The magnitude of potential explosion damage can be determined by analyzing the value of property surrounding the object, making an informed estimate of the extent of damage possible, and relating that to the value of the property. Exploding pressure vessels, such as air tanks, present much less of a severity problem than either steam or combustion explosions, but they can damage property within a radius proportional to the size and operating pressure of the object.

Explosions not involving pressure vessels are different. Rotating flywheels can explode due to centrifugal force. Combustion explosions can occur almost anywhere. Leaking gas can accumulate in a building and then be ignited, causing widespread explosion damage. A truck containing explosives may explode near a building. Grain or other dusts may explode in storage or processing areas.

In estimating the potential severity of explosion losses, careful consideration must be given to construction characteristics of the building and to explosion control equipment provided. Buildings for which there is a relatively high probability of explosion, such as spice manufacturing or grain grinding operations or others handling combustible dusts, are usually designed with roofs or wall panels that can be blown off easily by explosion without damage to the basic structural components of the building. Explosion suppression equipment (discussed later) is very effective against combustion explosion, though not against explosion of steam vessels or other pressure vessels.

Windstorm Data regarding the frequency and maximum velocity of windstorms in particular areas can be obtained from the U.S. Weather Service, but it is not easy to determine the potential loss severity resulting from such winds. Most buildings and structures are designed to withstand the most serious winds reasonably foreseeable in the area, but experience has proven that weaknesses are often still present, and that damage can be considerable. Roofs, particularly those that are old and in need of repair, are particularly susceptible to loss. Carports and roofs with large overhangs tend to create an airfoil effect and are frequently torn off. Tall structures and movable property items are also especially susceptible. Loss potentials vary with the type of property and can be estimated by (1) outlining the maximum geographical area in which a single windstorm can be expected to be damaging, (2) presuming that mobile equipment and other properties not firmly anchored would be a total loss, and (3) considering that permanent structures anchored to the ground are less likely to be a total loss, depending upon the type of construction and maintenance.

Hurricanes have somewhat different loss-producing characteristics than tornadoes. Hurricanes often have winds of 100 miles per hour or more and may be dozens of miles in extent. Tornadoes are typically more violent in local intensity. As for spread, while a single tornado seldom covers many miles (in terms of its track on the ground), a single weather system can spawn scores of tornadoes over several states. In addition, hurricanes and tropical storms spawn tornadoes as they die out over land, especially when they do so in the Mississippi River Valley. Furthermore, in a single year, there can be more than one catastrophic windstorm in the same place.

In coastal areas, hurricane winds combine with damaging tides and waves. Some hurricanes create tremendous tides. It has been estimated that a hurricane the size of "Camille" would put Miami Beach under twenty feet of water! Wave wash not only produces flooding, but the force of the water can also directly demolish a building or cause its collapse by undermining the foundation. Land values are destroyed by erosion or creation of new dunes.

In inland areas, more hurricane damage is done by floods (both flash floods and "riverine" floods) than by wind.

Hail Hail damage is a peril that is strongly influenced by geography and type of property. Major hailstorms occur only in certain parts of the country, most often in plains areas. In these areas, hailstones the size of golf balls can damage many types of property. Growing crops are particularly susceptible, but wood and aluminum siding and glass also may be severely damaged. Frequency can readily be predicted from weather bureau records. However, severity is not only a function of the property involved, but also of size and type of hailstones and importantly, accompanying wind velocity.

Flood Frequency of floods from heavy rain or similar weather conditions can be estimated from data developed by the U.S. Army Corps of Engineers. In addition, however, there are catastrophic floods from collapses of dams; for these, historical figures of frequency are of no help.

The severity of flood damage is related in part to the height of the floodwaters. For floods caused by nature, probabilities of various heights can be calculated fairly accurately from data given by the Corps of Engineers. Even flood levels resulting from dam breakage can be calculated, and such data are usually available in flood maps obtainable from government sources.

Once the frequency and flood height have been determined, the next step is to question the susceptibility of the concerned property to flood water damage. Masonry buildings can survive a flood with little damage, whereas some paper, electrical equipment, and other property will be seriously damaged by soaking or even by corrosion and mildew from excessive humidity in flooded buildings. A major part of the loss to buildings is the cost of cleanup.

Flood losses are not always confined to riverside areas and flood plains. Sometimes the runoff from unusually heavy rains can wash out hillside areas or create temporary lakes. New structures, construction operations, or temporary barriers of one sort or another can also affect surface water runoff, causing flooding in locations previously immune. Potential frequency and severity of this type of flooding is virtually impossible to determine, but the possibility should be recognized. Some intuitive assessment may be necessary; for example, the possibility of such losses could cause the risk manager to recommend against putting an important computer facility in the basement. Even where the flood frequency is low, the potential severity may be high enough to rule against such a location. (Basement locations are also subject to water damage from accidents to building plumbing, exterior water, or sewage pipes, and from collection of water used to extinguish fires on higher floors.)

Water Damage Water damage from broken pipes or tanks rather than from flood is a peril that has a low frequency and moderate severity. This peril's loss potential can be best judged by consideration of the premises exposed, their layout, and the susceptibility of building and contents to water damage. For example, picture a five-story industrial building with wood floors and an automatic sprinkler system fed by a large wood water tank on the roof. Each of the five floors contains garment manufacturing operations or printing shops, all of which have high susceptibility to water damage. The wood floors would probably not be watertight, so a rupture of this water tank would cause a large loss. The loss probability may not be low, especially if it is an older tank.

In this regard, the risk manager may want to distinguish between a water tank used to supply an automatic sprinkler system, and one that supplies water for domestic or industrial use. Loss from the former can be insured under a policy covering basic causes of loss, while insuring loss from the latter would require a broad causes of loss, or an "all-risks" property policy. Consequently, the frequency estimates may need to be kept separate for analysis of insurance needs.

Earthquake Major earthquake frequency is so slight, even in the most seismically active parts of the world, that statistics are not reliable indicators of future loss probability. Few structures will be subject to more than one damaging earthquake in any century, and no one can say with certainty when, or even within what reasonably precise time span, an earthquake might be expected. In parts of

California, estimates are that major earthquakes occur every sixty to one hundred years, but the accuracy of this prediction is questionable since it is based on only a few hundred years' data.

The matter of severity can more easily be estimated, but precision is not great—at least in the short run. There are many variables: type of ground soil (whether rock or loose-fill), proximity to faults, type of construction, height and configuration, quality of earthquake resistant design, proximity to other buildings, and other factors.

Every structure has the possibility of total loss from earthquake. However, for well-designed buildings, the probability of total loss may be exceedingly small.

Some firms use computer simulation models to assess the potential damage to a particular building by an earthquake of a given intensity. While these models offer considerable promise for the prediction of loss severity, their use is expensive and can be justified only for high-value properties and probably only at the design stage, when corrective measures can be taken. The cost might be justified if the results of the simulation can be used to convince an underwriter to issue insurance coverage on the property.

Tsunamis, giant seismic waves generated by underwater earthquakes, have also been responsible for considerable damage to the islands of Hawaii and the west coast of the continental United States and have actually devastated coastal communities.

Theft   Theft is one of the most important perils affecting personal property. Frequency might be estimated from historical records, knowledge of the environment, type of merchandise, and methods of storage. The Uniform Crime Reports compiled by the Federal Bureau of Investigation also may be useful in determining crime trends in geographical areas. Loss magnitude will depend generally on the quantity of goods concentrated in one area, the marketability of the goods, and the relationships among value, weight, and volume, as discussed further in later chapters.

Some trusted employees, particularly in computer departments or in shipping and receiving areas, can embezzle huge sums of money over a period of time. In 1971, a moderate-sized fruit packing firm in rural California found that a trusted computer programmer had embezzled over $1 million over a six-year period before auditors discovered it. A California bank lost $11 million due to computer crime in 1978. And the Mormon Church has reportedly lost $64 million due to computer fraud. The loss frequency of such crimes is rising and the potential magnitude is indeed high.

Employee dishonesty loss potential is considerably greater than most people realize. This particular exposure will be discussed in greater detail in Chapter 7.

Contamination or Pollution   Increasing attention to health hazards and environmental concerns have highlighted the pollution problem. Contaminated land and buildings may be permanently unusable—or, at least, unusable unless expensive cleanup activities are undertaken.

Organizations that buy property need to exercise safeguards to assure that the property does not contain toxic wastes or other pollutants, because the cost of cleanup can easily exceed the purchase price of the property, turning a would-be asset into a serious liability. For example, a florist shop might purchase a former auto service station building—and then discover that gasoline from leaking underground gasoline tanks has polluted the soil and is entering the water supply, requiring immediate, expensive cleanup.

Miscellaneous Perils   The risk manager is concerned with all perils, whether insurable or uninsurable. It makes no difference to the company financial statement whether a loss occurred from an uninsured insurable peril such as fire, or from a generally uninsurable peril. The dollar result is the same. Identification of the frequency and severity of loss caused by all perils is therefore highly important.

Each firm will have somewhat different exposures to uninsurable perils, and each analysis will depend on the peculiar circumstances of the concern in question. No general procedures have been developed for calculating frequency and severity of loss due to specific miscellaneous perils. The main thing to remember is that these perils exist and that they should be treated, or at least recognized.

Loss Analysis

When the data have been determined, stratified where desirable, and frequency and severity estimated, the most important process can be started: analysis of the data to determine what they may mean. The first step is to evaluate the reliability of data sources, the conditions under which the information was gathered, and the changes that may have occurred from the time data were recorded to the present.

Some conditions will continue into the future, in which case inflation factors need only be applied to the old statistics to bring them up to current values. When conditions have changed, the impact often cannot be expressed accurately in numbers. In such cases, the closest possible approximation should be made in order to convert old figures to current figures. Then, future trends should be estimated.

Exhibit 2-6
Loss History

	Number of Losses	Total Loss	Average Loss
Year 1	9	$ 35,762	$ 3,924
Year 2	7	19,292	2,756
Year 3	72	63,283	879
Year 4	83	129,519	1,560
Year 5	99	108,511	1,096

Exhibit 2-7
Loss History for Years 1 and 2

	Number of Losses	Total Losses	Average Loss
Year 1	9 x 10 = 90	$99,000	$1,100
Year 2	7 x 10 = 70	77,000	1,100

Updating Loss History—An Example The following example illustrates how a loss history can be updated to improve its use as an indicator of future loss trends. The firm in this example has a five-year loss history as shown in Exhibit 2-6.

The risk manager realizes that reporting procedures were lax in Years 1 and 2. A new report form issued to the field after Year 2 brought out more complete and accurate figures. This is indicated by the low number of losses reported in Years 1 and 2 and by the relatively large average loss. Apparently, smaller losses were occurring but were not reported during those two years.

The risk manager estimates (using Years 3 through 5 as a guide) that average losses should have been about $1,100 and number of losses about ten times the number actually reported in Years 1 and 2. Then the loss history for the first two years should have been as shown in Exhibit 2-7.

Inflation has occurred, according to the Consumer Price Index, at the following rates:

Year 1	6 percent
Year 2	5 percent
Year 3	4 percent
Year 4	5 percent
Year 5	6 percent

Exhibit 2-8
Adjustment of Loss Values

Year 1	$ 99,000 x 1.03 x 1.05 x 1.04 x 1.05 x 1.06	=	$ 123,934
Year 2	77,000 x 1.025 x 1.04 x 1.05 x 1.06	=	91,357
Year 3	63,283 x 1.02 x 1.05 x 1.06	=	71,843
Year 4	129,519 x 1.025 x 1.06	=	140,722
Year 5	108,511 x 1.03	=	111,766

While the Consumer Price Index was used for this example, other indexes are more appropriate in most cases. Possible alternative indexes include the wholesale price index, index of industrial commodity prices, construction cost indexes, and others. Modern accounting practices develop data that include adjustment of publicly reported figures for inflation. The adjustments used for those figures can be useful here.

To adjust loss values to equivalent figures at the end of Year 5, they should be factored as shown in Exhibit 2-8. Though 6 percent is the figure for Year 1, the occurrence of losses is assumed to operate uniformly throughout the year. Thus, the average effect on all losses to year end will be one-half of 6 percent, or 3 percent. A similar rationale applies to losses in other years.

At the end of Year 1, management sold one manufacturing facility which was estimated to be responsible for 15 percent of all losses. Thus, the amounts for Year 1 from Exhibits 2-7 and 2-8 were multiplied by a factor of 0.85 (1.00 less the 0.15 decrease for the factory removed) before being used in Exhibit 2-9.

The reconstituted loss history is shown in Exhibit 2-9. This is a very rough estimate, based on the risk manager's knowledge of the reporting system in use in Years 1 and 2, and the average losses in Years 3, 4, and 5. But, rough as it is, it presents better information than the raw data presented in Exhibit 2-6.

Allocating Losses In a large organization, losses—especially liability losses and workers compensation losses—are often considered proportional to an exposure base such as annual sales or payroll. This provides a basis for loss projections, and for charges to be assessed to operating units.

Property losses may be proportional to sales or payroll, but are usually more closely related to property values. They may be further refined into losses per unit value in a certain kind of process. For

Exhibit 2-9
Loss History Reconstituted as of End of Year 5

	Number of Losses	Total Losses	Average Loss
Year 1	77[1]	$105,344[2]	$ 1,368
Year 2	70	91,357	1,305
Year 3	72	71,843	998
Year 4	83	140,722	1,695
Year 5	99	211,766	1,129
Average	80	$104,206	$1,303

[1]90 x .85
[2]123,934 x .85

Exhibit 2-10
Property Losses Related to Property Values

	Sales Division		Manufacturing Division	
	Values	Losses	Values	Losses
Year 1	$1,500,000	$212	$ 385,000,000	$ 38,512
Year 2	1,600,000	42	398,000,000	87,608
Year 3	1,600,000	0	430,000,000	25,012
Year 4	1,700,000	36	512,000,000	118,606
Year 5	1,900,000	0	590,000,000	59,718
Totals	$8,300,000	$290	$2,315,000,000	$329,456
Average	$1,700,000	$ 58	$ 463,000,000	$ 65,891
Losses per $1 million of values		$ 34		$ 142

example, a conglomerate would maintain data on losses in office buildings separately from the data on losses in factory buildings. An example is shown in Exhibit 2-10.

Results show that the Sales Division might anticipate future losses of $34 per million dollars of property values next year while the Manufacturing Division can project $142 per million.

Larger organizations also may make use of statistical analysis where the loss data are fitted to curves representing different loss distributions. If losses fit a particular distribution curve, it is possible to show the probability of losses of a certain size occurring. This can be done even for sizes of loss for which there has been no actual experience. Such estimation can be very helpful in identifying which exposures demand the greatest attention and selecting among risk management alternatives. For example, a loss that has a probability of one in 10,000 may call for special protection devices before a loss which has a probability of one in a million. In some cases, statistical analysis may be useful in determining whether or not insurance should be purchased.

All loss projections should be tempered by the knowledge that, even if the probability of a specific loss is remote, if a loss *can* happen, it *may happen today.* The fact that the probability was low will be little consolation if no positive action has been taken to treat the loss exposure.

RISK MANAGEMENT TECHNIQUES FOR TREATING LOSS EXPOSURES

After loss exposures have been identified and measured, a risk manager is in a position to select among the various alternatives available in the formulation of a risk management program. The discussion in this section is general, and serves only as an introduction to the various risk management techniques. Most of this text will deal with the specific treatment of commercial property loss exposures, including both insurance and noninsurance techniques.

The techniques available can be divided into two classes, as was illustrated in Exhibit 2-1.

Control techniques attempt to change the exposure itself by reducing loss frequency and/or loss severity, or by improving the organization's ability to predict losses with greater confidence. These techniques include:

- avoidance,
- loss control,
- combination, and
- some noninsurance transfers.

Financing techniques are designed to provide funds to handle the losses that do occur. Financing techniques include:

- some noninsurance transfers,
- insurance, and
- retention.

Each of these techniques will be examined briefly in turn.

Avoidance

One method for dealing with any loss exposure is never to have it, although in most cases this is not practical.

Loss Control

The second *control* technique is called *loss control*. In general, loss control measures are designed to change the loss exposure by either reducing the frequency of loss occurrence (loss prevention) or minimizing the adverse financial impact or severity of such occurrences (loss reduction), or both. Although exposures are changed, some chance of loss remains.

Because of the savings in human and material resources that may result, loss control efforts always deserve serious consideration. They may not, however, always pay off in success or in benefits that justify the costs. For example, in designing a new building, the question often arises as to whether or not it should be provided with automatic sprinklers for fire protection. Sometimes a key question is, "Is the cost of insurance for a sprinklered building plus the cost of sprinklers less than the cost of insurance without sprinklers?" Sometimes the answer to this question is obvious. Borderline decisions are determined by a careful analysis of all pertinent facts including insurance costs, expected cost of retained losses, initial cost of sprinkler installation, maintenance costs, and taxes. Similar decisions are often necessary for property with a high theft potential to determine whether or not elaborate security measures are cost-effective.

Notwithstanding the cost-effectiveness of loss control activities, it is often necessary to consider factors less tangible than cost, such as worker safety or the loss of market that could follow a fire loss. Loss control measures are of value, even when not indicated by readily measurable costs, if control reduces other costs and losses not readily reducible to specific figures.

One special form of loss control is *separation*. Separation means spreading the loss exposure over a larger number of completely segregated locations. For example, instead of building one large warehouse exposed to fire, explosion, vandalism, and other perils, a business might build many widely scattered smaller warehouses. In addition to reducing loss severity, separation makes future loss experience more predictable because it increases the number of exposure units.

Combination

Combination means the acquisition of more exposure units in order to improve the predictability of future losses by increasing the number of exposure units. As a practical matter, the combination approach is not used by organizations other than insurance companies just to help make future loss experience more predictable. However, when organizations acquire many units for operational purposes, combination does occur, and predictability often improves.

Noninsurance Transfers

Transfers may be used as control techniques or financing techniques. *Control-type transfers* alter the organization's exposures in an attempt to reduce the loss frequency or the loss severity experienced by the organization or to improve the organization's ability to predict losses with confidence.

Financing-type transfers transfer only the financial consequences of certain loss exposures to another organization. The organization gets someone else to pay for losses the organization suffers. Financing-type noninsurance transfers differ from insurance in that the exposures are transferred to some entity that is not an insurance company. Financing-type noninsurance transfers appear in many kinds of contracts. For example, a building owner may lease a building to a tenant and in the lease agreement require the tenant to be responsible for all loss. (This is frequency done in what is termed a "net lease.") On the other hand, the owner may agree to retain the exposure of loss to the property.

As another example, when a contractor works at a large construction site, the construction contract may state that the owner will be responsible for all losses of property, which could include the property being installed by the contractor. On the other hand, the contract may make the contractor responsible for such damage.

Insurance

Insurance is a transfer technique. Insurance contracts transfer the financial consequences of potential accidental losses from an insured organization to an insurance company. Proper use of the insurance technique is a key risk management responsibility.

Mandatory Insurance The options available to a risk manager may be limited because insurance is required by law or by contract. Under such circumstances, the principal duty of the risk manager will be the selection of the most suitable coverage and the insurer best able to provide the needed coverage and service at the most attractive price. The risk manager should also help the organization avoid contracts that require it to purchase insurance against losses that could be more efficiently financed some other way.

Required by Law. Property insurance is sometimes required by law. For example, federal law requires flood insurance for any real property located in a flood zone and financed by a lender who is federally insured or financed. Federal regulations also require some interstate common carriers to carry cargo insurance.

Required by Contract. It is quite common for mortgages and other contracts to require that certain property be insured. Leases sometimes require the tenant to carry fire insurance or other coverages on the leased property. Leases on personal property may contain similar provisions. A risk manager should review all leases, of either real or personal property, to determine whether such requirements exist. In some cases—particularly when it would not be cost-effective to purchase insurance—the lessor will agree to modify the contract so that the lessee is responsible for losses but is not required to purchase insurance.

Likewise, there is a trend in condominium bylaws requiring the condominium association, as a trustee, to insure the real property of individual units.

Bond indentures and other loan agreements sometimes include requirements that certain of the firm's assets be insured. For example, bond indentures on the convention center and on Angels' Stadium in Anaheim, California, require millions of dollars of earthquake insurance. Such contractual obligations often are overlooked.

If a firm wants to retain losses despite contractual obligations to insure them, it may be able to satisfy its insurance requirements by arranging for an insurer to "front" for the firm and to file a certificate of insurance with the other party. The insurer would require an indemnity agreement in which the firm would agree to reimburse the insurer for any losses paid under the certificate. Some consideration for the certificate would be required, since the insurer is exposed to the possibility that the firm might be unable to fulfill the indemnity agreement. The consideration might be a specific charge for the certificate, the placement of other coverages with the insurer, or both.

Voluntary Insurance Insurance is usually the most practical technique for transferring large loss exposures. In addition, insurance organizations through the years have developed appraisal, loss control, claims administration, boiler inspection, and other services that are important adjuncts of the insurance contract. These may influence the decision to purchase insurance.

Retention

Retention is, simply, keeping or retaining all or some of the elements of a loss exposure. To the extent that an organization retains a loss exposure, it bears the financial consequences of any losses. Whenever a business does not transfer the potential financial consequences to someone else, that consequence has been retained.

Retention may be voluntary or involuntary. Since insurance and other transfers never cover all of an organization's exposures, there must always be some retention. The only decision here is whether to accept the risk or avoid it.

The act of retention may be consciously or unconsciously selected. Failure to identify certain loss exposures sometimes means that the organization unknowingly retains these loss exposures. Only by chance might this be the best thing to do. On the other hand, the organization may explore the alternatives and consciously decide that the best course of action is retention. Or, the unrecognized exposure might nevertheless be transferred along with recognized exposures, perhaps via "all-risks" insurance.

PROPERTY LOSS CONTROL

Loss exposures are often susceptible to some type of loss control. Loss control measures should always be considered even when losses are financed by insurance or by a funded retention program. Effective *loss prevention* measures will lower the expected loss frequency. Effective *loss reduction* measures will reduce loss severity. Thus, effective loss control measures serve to lower both expected dollar losses and the cost of financing retained losses. In addition to their dollar benefits, loss control measures can serve to reduce uncertainty and provide "a good night's sleep" and to meet the specific risk management objectives of any organization. Moreover, since there are always some loss costs that are not covered by insurance (such as the value of employee time devoted to handling the paperwork), loss control reduces loss financing costs even with full insurance. Even if they do not directly affect insurance premium rates, loss control measures are likely to make it easier to obtain and keep insurance coverage.

Many insurance policy provisions relate to loss control measures in one way or another. For example, some provisions relate to the maintenance of fire alarms and other protective devices. Some loss control measures even introduce a need for insurance coverage. For example, automatic sprinkler systems suggest a need for coverage against the peril of sprinkler leakage.

Loss Control in General

Losses result from chains of events. The 1967 McCormick Place fire in Chicago is a good illustration of a sequence of events that led up to a major loss. The loss and its severity resulted from a connected series of things that went wrong. In the McCormick Place exhibition hall, the exhibitors' need for electrical outlets had not been anticipated. Available circuits were overloaded with extension cords. One exhibitor used a defective cord that ran among other exhibits made of light, combustible materials such as cardboard, light pressed panels, and paper. Since combustibility of contents had not been specifically considered during the design phase (despite the building's intended use) and the ceiling was extremely high, the exhibition area was not sprinklered. A fire began while the guard was in another part of the building, and the blaze had grown substantially before he saw it. It took three or four minutes for him to reach an alarm station. When fire-fighters arrived, they found that valves on the lines to the fire hydrants had been left partially closed, seriously reducing dynamic water pressure. The firefighters did not know where the valves were. This series of events resulted to a $52.5 million fire and one death.[2] Many unsafe acts and physical hazards combined to produce this result, and not all of them have been mentioned. (For example, the valve problem with the hydrants was itself caused by a chain of events.)

Loss control measures are designed to break vital links in the chain of events that leads to a serious loss. Naturally, the use of specific measures depends on the nature of the particular perils and exposure conditions being attacked.

In general, loss control measures take one or both of two approaches. The *engineering approach* involves attack by design and location of properties and equipment to reduce the number of physical hazards. The *human behavior approach* attacks the problem by modifying the behavior of people to reduce the frequency of unsafe acts. Although losses are usually caused by unsafe acts (note the several "people" failures in the exhibition hall loss chain), engineering often can be used to limit the losses resulting from unsafe acts (e.g., automatic sprinklers can successfully interrupt fire loss chains that people have started).

Fire Loss Control Principles

To break a chain of loss-causing events, it is necessary to know how the events proceed—how one thing leads to another. In elementary terms, fire losses proceed by chemical processes—heat causes rapid oxidation of fuel. Thus, three things are required to have a fire: (1) an initial source of heat; (2) oxygen; and (3) fuel—material that will burn, given the amount of heat and oxygen available. And, once started, the chain reaction must be uninterrupted.[3] As more fuel burns, the amount of heat present usually increases. Strong fires create their own air drafts, thus bringing more oxygen to the fuel. So fires grow, engulfing more and more fuel as the burning process literally feeds upon itself.

It follows that most fire prevention centers on removal of one or more of the three common essentials (heat, oxygen, and fuel) from the scene.

Heat Sources Four types of energy can create heat sufficient to cause a fire—electrical energy, chemical energy, mechanical (frictional) energy, and nuclear energy.

- *Electrical heat energy* may come from natural sources (such as lightning) or artificial ones (such as power generating plants). It may be dynamic (for example, power flowing through power lines and operating motors) or static (such as the temporarily quiescent static electricity in the air or the charge in a storage battery).
- *Chemical heat energy* is released as part of a chemical reaction. Examples include the ignition of a match, the burning of a welding torch, and spontaneous combustion of oily rags left in a closet.
- *Mechanical or frictional heat energy* is developed when objects rub together. The brakes on a car create heat, as does the friction of a grinding wheel on a piece of metal, a belt running through a pulley, or a defective bearing.
- *Nuclear heat energy* is released by nuclear fission or fusion. Controlled nuclear reaction creates a source of heat that is converted to electricity in nuclear power plants. Uncontrolled release in a nuclear accident, or the controlled or uncontrolled release of a nuclear weapon, can cause widespread damage.

It is important to identify all the important heat sources from which fire damage might arise in order to give each of them proper loss control treatment. The specifics of treatment differ according to whether the source is planned or unplanned, fixed or mobile.

Planned Versus Unplanned Heat Sources. Planned sources are of two main types: those in which the heat energy is desired, and those in which it is not. Standard examples of the former include a wide variety of heat-creating equipment, ranging from cigarette lighters to blast furnaces. Heating furnaces, boilers, and many types of electrical apparatus are planned heat sources.

Other planned sources of heat are those in which heat is an unwanted by-product. Certain equipment or other items that are wanted produce heat—but the heat itself is not wanted. The most common unplanned heat source is electrical wiring. Heat may also be generated by machinery or from grinding operations. Many natural fibers generate heat while in storage, and many chemical processes necessarily produce unwanted heat.

Unplanned heat sources consist primarily of those which management has not been able, or has not tried, to control. Examples include smoking by employees and visitors, the use of personal coffee pots in a work area, and off-premises elements such as lightning that no amount of planning can eliminate.

Fixed Versus Mobile Heat Sources. Some planned sources of heat are fixed, while others move around. Furnaces and boilers for heating buildings are fixed. Welding and cutting torches are common mobile sources of heat, as are forklift trucks and other vehicles.

Fuels For a fire to start, continue, or spread, it must have fuel. Fuels vary greatly in the ease with which they can be ignited. Gasoline vapor is thus generally more hazardous than paper, paper more hazardous than lumber, lumber more hazardous than steel, and so on. The relative combustibility or flammability of a fuel depends on the amount of heat required to cause it to produce burnable vapors. In a practical situation, two characteristics of a fuel are important: the temperature at which it vaporizes (a function of its chemical composition) and the extent to which it holds heat rather than spreading it (a matter strongly affected by the size and shape of the item, as well as by its chemistry).

Temperature at Which Substances Vaporize. An important characteristic of solid substances is the *ignition temperature*. The ignition temperature of a substance may be defined as the "minimum temperature to which it must be heated for it to ignite."[4] A substance that has reached the ignition temperature will continue to release vapors that burn and will continue to burn until they are consumed or the fire is extinguished.

An important characteristic of liquids is the *flash point*. The flash point is "the minimum temperature at which a liquid gives off vapors that can be ignited by a spark or flame." Gasoline, for example, has a flash point of −45°F, compared to kerosene's flash point of 100°F.[5] At room temperature, gasoline releases vapors that can be readily ignited. Kerosene must be heated above room temperature before it releases ignitable vapors.

Form of the Material. Wood in a toothpick and the same kind of wood in a dry log both have the same ignition temperature. But, when the surface of a toothpick is heated, there is little place else for the heat to go and so the toothpick quickly ignites. In a log, however, some of the heat at the surface is dissipated into the interior. Hence, it takes a hotter or longer sustained supply of heat to get the log to burst into flame. And when external heat is removed, the cool interior of the log may absorb enough heat to bring the temperature below the ignition temperature.

Steel in most forms cannot burn because of its density and the fact that steel is a good conductor of heat. A flame applied to a steel beam is rapidly conducted away from the point of contact, which remains below the ignition temperature. Steel wool, on the other hand, can be ignited by a match because its low density reduces its ability to dissipate heat.[6]

Continuing fire represents an ongoing reaction. Thus, when one starts a wood fire in a fireplace, initial heat may be created by friction (striking a match). It is then continued by burning of the chemicals in the match head. When the fire so generated has burned long enough, the wood of the match flames. The temperature thus created is not extremely high, but the shape and material of the match cause it to be a self-sustaining chain reaction. In the fireplace, fire is ignited in paper and light wood materials with ignition temperatures below that produced by the match. As more fuel catches fire, a higher temperature is generated. If this temperature is sustained long enough, logs can be induced to flame because heat (from already burning materials) is being applied more rapidly than it can be dissipated into the air and into the logs' interior. Eventually, if enough heat is produced rapidly enough, logs can continue to burn on their own, without any continuing outside source of heat.

The process is the same with most hostile fires. In severe cases, the buildup of heat from the fuels that have, one by one, been heated to flaming point, increases with each additional bit of fuel consumption until the fire reaches such a point that it cannot be stopped until it has completely consumed all available fuel.

Building Contents as Fuel. The variety of building contents that may be exposed to fire is, of course, tremendous. Depending on type of operations and particular location, inventory may be paper or pig iron, alcohol or asbestos, sulfur or silicon. Equipment and furnishings may be combustible or noncombustible, oily or clean, light or heavy. Not only the inherent combustibility of each type, but also its spacing and arrangement determine its actual significance as fuel for fire. Each occupancy, and in some cases each part of a single occupancy, presents different exposures. Each must be evaluated on its own merits, or at least according to its own particular class. Overall, the possibilities range from a well-arranged office with metal furniture and a minimum of paper, to a stockpile of sulfur.

The expected amount of combustibles available as fuel for a hostile fire in a given area is called the *fire load*, commonly expressed in terms of weight of combustibles per square foot. Heat to be expected in a fire is estimated on the basis of known calorific content of those combustibles present in a building's contents and structural components. (The "calorific content" of any thing is the amount of heat—number of calories—produced when it burns.) Since physical arrangement of the material greatly affects the amount of heat produced in any given amount of time, estimation of fire load in specific cases requires expert judgment.

Most high fire loads do not result from materials recognized as especially hazardous; where possible, care is taken to limit the amount of such exposure in a building. Rather, the usual high load cases come from bulk storage or relatively low hazard materials packed together in great quantity in a minimum of space. Modern lifting equipment allows stacking to considerable height, which can create extreme fire loads. The very heaviest fire loads, however, occur in situations with large quantities of extraordinarily hazardous materials: highly flammable liquids such as light petroleum products, lacquers, or alcohols; materials that burn explosively, or nearly so, such as sulfur and some sulfides, many nitrates, some peroxides, many types of metallic or organic dusts; and so on.

Buildings as Fuel Fire load includes the combustible parts of a building. Wooden buildings, of course, contribute more ready fuel for fire than do buildings of masonry, non-combustible, or fire-resistive materials. When building materials are combustible, the common result is more damage to the building itself and faster spread of the fire to other fuel inside or outside the building.

The following discussion of construction types is based on the construction definitions used by the Insurance Services Office (ISO) in determining property insurance rates:[7]

1. **Frame:** Buildings with exterior walls, floors and roof of combustible construction, or buildings with exterior walls of non-combustible or slow burning construction, with combustible floors and roof.

2. **Joisted Masonry:** Building with exterior walls of fire resistive construction (not less than one hour), or of masonry, and with combustible floors and roof.

3. **Non-Combustible:** Buildings with exterior walls, floors and roof of non-combustible or slow burning materials supported by non-combustible or slow burning supports (including non-combustible or slow burning roof decks on non-combustible or slow burning supports, regardless of the type of insulation on the roof surface.)

4. **Masonry Non-Combustible:** Buildings with exterior walls of fire resistive construction (not less than one hour), or of masonry, and with non-combustible or slow burning floors and roof (including non-combustible or slow burning roof decks on non-combustible or slow burning supports, regardless of the type of insulation on the roof surface.)

5. **Modified Fire Resistive:** Buildings with exterior walls, floors and roof constructed of masonry materials described in 6. below, but deficient in thickness; or fire resistive materials described in 6. below, but with a fire resistance rating of less than two hours, but not less than one hour.

6. **Fire Resistive:** Buildings constructed of any combination of the following materials:

   Exterior Walls or Exterior Structural Frame:
   Solid masonry, including reinforced concrete,
   Hollow masonry not less than 12 inches in thickness,
   Hollow masonry less than 12 inches, but not less than 8 inches in thickness, with a listed fire resistance rating of not less than two hours,
   Assemblies with a fire resistance rating of not less than two hours.
   Note: Panel or curtain sections of masonry may be of any thickness.

   Floors and Roof:
   Monolithic floors and roof of reinforced concrete with slabs not less than 4 inches in thickness,
   Construction known as "Joist Systems" with slabs supported by concrete joists spaced not more than 36 inches on centers with a slab thickness of not less than 2 3/4 inches,
   Floor and roof assemblies with a fire resistance rating of not less than two hours.

   Structural Metal Supports:
   Horizontal and vertical load-bearing protected metal supports (including horizontal prestressed concrete units) with a fire resistance rating of not less than two hours.
   Note: Wherever in this Schedule reference is made to "prestressed," this term shall also include "post-tensioned."

Frame Construction. Wood frame construction is illustrated in Exhibit 2-11. This classification includes buildings with non-combustible or slow-burning exterior walls with combustible floors or roof. For example, a building with a single thickness of brick (brick veneer) on

Exhibit 2-11
Wood Frame Construction*

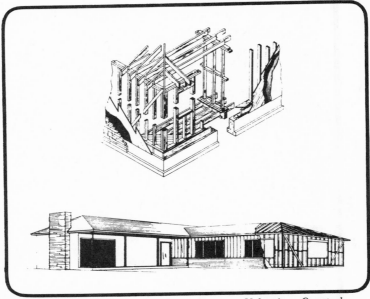

*Reprinted with permission from *Stevens Valuation Quarterly* (Los Angeles: Marshall and Swift Publication Company, July 1973), p. A-12.

the walls, with the combustible floors and roof supported by wood framing, is considered a frame building.

Many dwellings and small mercantile buildings are of frame construction, but the popularity of this type varies considerably by geographic region. The combustibility of wood makes frame buildings susceptible to fire damage. Everything is held up by wood in a frame structure. When the wood burns, the structure, or the involved part of it, is destroyed.

Jointed Masonry Construction. In this type of construction, also called "ordinary," "ordinary masonry," "brick," "brick joisted," or "wood joisted," the walls are self-supporting masonry—they stand without wood supports. Other supporting elements, however, are wood. Joists and beams supporting floors and roof are wood; so, usually, are the roof and floors themselves. Joisted masonry construction is illustrated in Exhibit 2-12.

In a fire of considerable intensity, only a shell will be left—the bare walls. In such a fire, some significant portion of the walls may even fall, be knocked down by fall of the roof, or be pulled or pushed down by

Exhibit 2-12
Joisted Masonry*

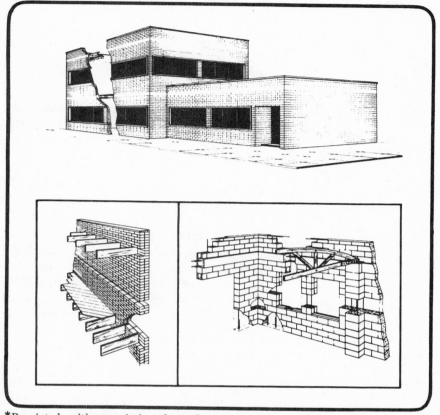

*Reprinted with permission from *Stevens Valuation Quarterly* (Los Angeles: Marshall and Swift Publication Company, July 1973), p. A-11.

collapsing wooden support beams. Even the bricks themselves can be damaged beyond use by heat when of sufficient intensity and duration.

In the much more frequent, less intense fires, the exterior bearing walls usually remain in usable, or nearly usable, condition; they continue to support the roof, and walls and roof provide some degree of protection for the interior. Obviously, joisted construction is usually preferable to frame construction when fire occurs.

Non-combustible Construction. "Non-combustible construction" is a specialized term in fire protection and fire insurance. Non-combustible construction is illustrated in Exhibit 2-13. The term is *not* applied to all buildings of non-combustible materials—many such buildings fall into the fire resistive category. A building is in the non-combustible

Exhibit 2-13
Non-combustible Construction*

* Reprinted with permission from *Stevens Valuation Quarterly* (Los Angeles: Marshall and Swift Publication Company, July 1973), pp. A-11 and A-12.

class when its walls, partitions, and structural members are of materials which will contribute little if any fuel to a fire.

One common type of non-combustible construction, illustrated in Exhibit 2-13, is all-metal construction—light metal walls and roof, with light metal supports. Many light non-combustible buildings do not add fuel to fires but are readily susceptible to heat damage. Their structural members expand, twist, crack, and otherwise deteriorate in fires. Therefore, such structures often collapse in fires. This produces loss of the building, increased damage to contents, and increased threat to life safety. Although they do not contribute fuel to a fire, non-combustible buildings are not necessarily "safer" than buildings of frame or joisted masonry construction.

Masonry Non-combustible. Like non-combustible construction, masonry non-combustible construction includes floor and roofs of metal or some other non-combustible material. The walls are usually of masonry material but may be of fire resistive construction. Masonry non-combustible construction is illustrated in Exhibit 2-14.

Fire Resistive Construction. Fire resistive construction provides more fire protection than all other types of construction, but no construction is "fire-proof." Building materials used in fire resistive construction resist heat longer than materials required for protected ordinary or noncombustible construction, but they do not resist it forever, and they do not keep fires—including large and dangerous fires—from happening. Even fire resistive buildings can be totally destroyed by fire.

There is also construction known as "modified fire resistive." True fire resistive construction requires certain thicknesses of masonry materials, and the fire resistance rating of structural assemblies must be at least two hours. Modified fire resistive construction may include masonry materials slightly deficient in thickness or structural assem-

Exhibit 2-14
Masonry Non-combustible Construction*

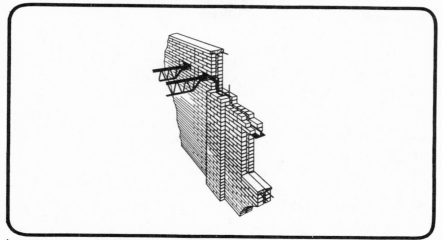

*Reprinted with permission from *Stevens Valuation Quarterly* (Los Angeles: Marshall and Swift Publication Company, July 1973), pp. A-11 and A-12.

blies with a fire resistive rating of at least one hour but less than two hours.

Fire resistance ratings of materials are determined by standard tests in laboratories. Fire resistance of building materials as typically assembled is commonly rated by testing in furnaces specially designed for exposing the assemblies to a standard fire. An assembly rated one-hour fire resistance would meet a furnace test under load without failure for approximately one hour. Two very important practical points about the resultant ratings are the following:

1. Standard fire tests take into consideration the capacity of materials and, in some cases, assemblies, to perform intended functions during fire exposure, and their subsequent load capacity. There is no reference to their suitability for further use (e.g., in a repaired or reconstructed building).
2. There are many reasons why performance in a standard test and performance in an actual building fire may differ.[8]

Materials commonly used to meet fire resistive requirements are reinforced concrete and protected structural steel for framing, reinforced concrete or masonry for bearing walls, and lighter noncombustible materials in other parts, such as curtain walls (walls that are enclosing but not load bearing).

There is a type of joisted masonry construction called *heavy timber* or *mill* that is considered more fire resistant than typical joisted masonry. Heavy timber construction, illustrated in Exhibit 2-15, is a special variety of heavy timber supports and masonry wall construction used primarily in industrial buildings. The wood timbers must be of certain minimum dimensions. For example, beams and girders must not be less than ten inches deep and six inches thick; columns must be not less than eight inches in any dimension. Loads are carried on beams resting on but not attached to the outside walls and on heavy wood (sometimes steel) columns. Floors are planks providing an assembly four inches thick.[9]

Large, solid pieces of wood are extremely difficult to burn. Thus, a bare wooden beam eight inches by ten inches in diameter ordinarily resists fire damage better than a bare steel beam with the same loadbearing capacity. Although the steel beam will not burn, it will warp and twist in a large fire and lose its strength. (That is why fire resistive construction requires that structural steel be protected by a layer or layers of fire resistive insulating materials.)

Other Definitions of Construction Types. It should be noted that The National Fire Protection Association, various building codes, appraisal guides, or insurance publications use definitions somewhat different from those used by the ISO. In each case, construction types are categorized according to the needs of those using the classifications.

Oxygen, Air Flow, and Related Factors Heat, fuel, and oxygen are prerequisites to a fire. Having discussed heat sources and fuels (in particular, buildings and contents as fuels for fire) the discussion proceeds to the third element of fire—oxygen.

Fires consist of fast oxidation of materials. Oxidation is a process in which some of the chemical elements of the items burned are released from their original molecules and recombined into compounds containing oxygen. The normal temperature, humidity, pressure, and oxygen of the atmosphere cause some oxidation (e.g., rusting of iron, yellowing of paper). Some substances can burst into flame under ordinary atmospheric conditions, but these, of course, are very special cases.

Obviously, oxidation requires oxygen. The vast majority of fires obtain their necessary supply from ordinary air (about 20 percent of which is oxygen). When they cannot get enough oxygen, they die (are "smothered"). Heat hastens the oxidation process; so, often, does an increase in the oxygen supply. A hot fire tends to develop its own air supply by creating a draft—air heated by the fire rises, leaving a low pressure area below into which fresh air flows.

The more favorable the arrangements for oxygen supply, the faster and better the fire burns, and when there is an abundance of

Exhibit 2-15
Heavy Timber Construction*

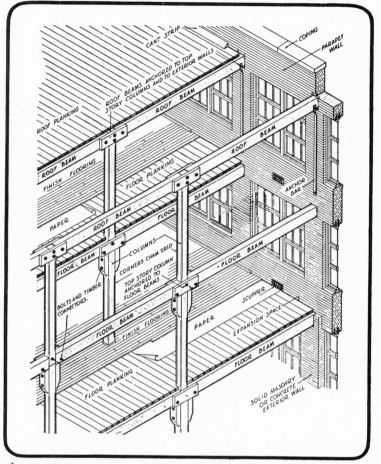

*Reprinted with permission from *Fire Protection Handbook*, 15th ed. (Boston: National Fire Protection Association, 1981), p. 5-26.

oxygen, fuels flame at lower temperatures. Consequently, oxygen-rich atmospheres (used in oxygen tents in hospitals, for example, and in some industrial processes) increase the probability of a fire.

However, while an ample supply of oxygen-containing air favors flaming, too fast a flow of air can have the reverse effect, as seen in the blowing out of a match or candle. In such a case, it is partly the cooling effect of the air flow that reduces the temperature below that required for a self-sustaining fire.

Flammable (Explosive) Range. Fire requires a ratio of fuel vapor to air that is neither too low ("lean") nor too high ("rich"). In an auto engine, an excess of gasoline in proportion to the amount of air can "flood" the engine—a condition brought about by too rich a mixture. On the other hand, if the choke does not operate properly, the gasoline-air mixture may be too lean for the engine to fire.

The *lower flammable limit* is the percentage of vapor below which a fire cannot occur because the mixture is too lean. The *upper flammable limit* is the range above which there is not sufficient air for a fire. The range between the lower flammable limit and the upper flammable limit is the *flammable range* or *explosive range.* For example, low octane gasoline, at room temperature in a normal atmosphere, has a flammable range from 1.4 percent to 7.6 percent.[10] Fires can be prevented if vapor concentrations can be kept below or above the flammable range, or when vapors within this range are kept free from an ignition source. Thus, it is important for firms handling flammable and combustible liquids or gases to be aware of the properties of these materials.

A few substances can burn without an outside oxygen supply. All of these are self-oxidants (e.g., nitrous oxide, nitro cellulose); their physical structure includes enough combined oxygen to support flame for a while. And a few special chemical combinations can produce fire without any free oxygen.

Effect of Construction Characteristics on Oxygen Supply. The way a building is arranged is important in fire protection. Layout and construction have an effect on creating, stopping, or controlling air flows. In tightly enclosed spaces (e.g., a vault), a fire may be smothered for lack of oxygen, but this is not a practical solution to most building fires. Most important is the control of the hot gases rising from the fire. These hot gases heat materials with which they come into contact, and the heated materials give off vapors that mix with air drawn in with the fire gases. When the mixture is hot enough and sufficient air is present, flames are created, more heat and gases are generated, and the process compounds itself.

Given sufficient air supply, important factors affecting the speed of fire spread are (1) the presence of fuels above the fire, where the first and most intense heating occurs; and (2) the size of the enclosed space above the fire (in larger spaces heat is dissipated faster; in smaller spaces, heat is more concentrated and temperatures rise more rapidly). Thus, vertical shafts (elevators, stairs, atriums) promote spread of flame, particularly when the shafts contain combustible materials.

Loss Control Measures. There are standard fire control measures that utilize the concentration of heat rising from a fire. By means of baffles or curtain boards, in conjunction with roof vents, the hot gases may be prevented from spreading throughout the building and instead be conducted to a roof vent which will remove heat from the building, thus inhibiting fire spread.

When an automatic sprinkler system is in operation, it is usually desirable to get sprinklers immediately above the fire to open quickly (by concentration of heat), and to avoid opening many sprinkler heads at once. Should a considerable number of sprinkler heads open due to the spread of rising heat, many would not be over the fire, and water pressure and flow may be reduced in heads over the fire. Such dilution of water concentration can inhibit extinguishing action, allowing the fire to spread. Baffles and vents can be arranged to reduce spread of heat over many sprinkler heads.

Counteracting Fire

Once fuel, heat, and oxygen have interacted to start a hostile fire, fire-fighting activities can be initiated to hold down loss severity. Usually these operate by removing one or more of the three described fire elements. In addition, it is possible to stop fires by interfering with the chain reaction mechanism in a way proven effective although not yet fully understood.

Removing the Fuel The idea of removing fuel after a fire has started is elementary and generally requires no special explanation. But its usefulness is restricted to those situations in which the fuel feeding the fire is fairly specific and subject to full control. The simplest example is turning off the supply of gas or oil in a line that has ruptured and caught on fire. Fire detection devices frequently used in restaurants shut off the supply of gas to a gas-fired stove or deep-fat fryer when a fire flares up.

A more difficult technique is the creation of a backfire to remove fuel from the path of an oncoming forest or brush fire. This technique has been successfully employed in many forest fires and in some large fires in congested cities.

Reducing the relative amount of vaporized fuel in a mix by increasing the amount of other gases (blowing out the candle) can be considered a special case of controlling fire by removing fuel. It has occasional practical application: compressed air blasts can be effective on some fires, and explosives are sometimes used to blow out oil well fires. However, removal of fuel has limited possibilities as a means of fighting most fires.

Removing the Heat Most fires are extinguished by cooling. The principal value of water in fighting fire is its strong cooling effect.

Water. When enough water can be applied to hot and burning surfaces, they are cooled below the temperature necessary to maintain combustion. Water absorbs a great deal of heat as it is converted to steam and in addition is able to cling to many substances, thus prolonging the cooling effect. A further advantage is its ability to enter cracks and crevices and to seep through many surfaces; this characteristic increases its ability to reach some spots needing to be cooled. Water is usually easy to obtain and store in large quantities at minimal cost.

However, water has some limitations as a cooling agent. It conducts electricity, so it may be dangerous where there is electrical exposure. Some chemicals react violently with water, burning more actively or even exploding. Water neither wets nor mixes with some types of fuel. For example, many flammable liquids float on water, so application of water merely makes it easier for such fluids to spread flames over a large area. Burning gases cannot be wet by water. In addition, water does not cling well to some surfaces, and it has limited ability to reach deep inside closely packed materials, such as rolls of paper or bales of cotton.

Sometimes, fire fighting with water is hampered by low temperatures, and problems are presented in those special cases where operations or materials are kept at temperatures below freezing. The storage of water for fire fighting purposes, both in piping for automatic sprinklers and in tanks and standpipes, is restricted to situations in which the water will not freeze while waiting to be used. However, dry-pipe automatic sprinkler systems, or systems containing antifreeze solutions, can be used in freezing temperatures. In a dry-pipe system, the sprinkler piping contains only compressed air or gas until a sprinkler head is opened, allowing the air to escape and water to enter the system. Other measures can also prevent freezing, such as heating the storage tanks or using a pump to keep water in circulation.

Other Cooling Agents. There are other cooling agents. Sand, for example, when spread thoroughly over a burning surface, can act to cool or smother the fire. Clearly, it is more difficult to get solid materials, such as sand, to reach and stay in contact with many burning surfaces than it is to get water (or other liquids) to do so. Nevertheless, there is one class of fires in which the cooling effect of solid particles is preferable to the use of water. Some combustible metals react violently with water; some are partially or completely self-oxidizing, so smothering does not work; some have both characteristics. For fires in many of these difficult cases, special extinguishing powders are available— different powders for different metals. Some of their effect is by cooling; some is by smothering; and some by breaking the chain reaction, depending on the powder and the type of burning metal.

Inert gases can get into small spaces better than solids or even water and can have some cooling effect. However, most of their efficacy depends on smothering (discussed below). As previously noted, ventilation is also commonly used to remove heated gases from a burning building.

Removing the Oxygen Smothering fires—interfering with their supply of oxygen—is a standard fire-fighting method, especially in fires where water has an adverse reaction. Covering the fire in a pan of grease and snuffing a candle are examples of extinguishment by removal of oxygen. The use of smothering foam on major oil fires applies the same principle.

Removal of oxygen is also the principle by which carbon dioxide (CO_2) fire extinguishers work. The CO_2 or other inert gas dilutes the oxygen available to support a fire. To be completely effective, separation of fuel and oxygen must be accompanied by enough cooling of the fuel to avoid re-ignition when the oxygen block ceases. This point limits the usefulness of CO_2 for ordinary fires; after the flames have been extinguished, ordinary materials often retain heat longer than a blanket of CO_2 lasts. When oxygen again reaches such materials, they can re-ignite.

The smothering effect of foams, however, lasts longer and, since foams include water, they also cool hot surfaces. Also, foam is less dense than any of the flammable liquids. Unlike water, foam can float on top of (and smother and cool) fires in liquids. Because they contain some water, however, foams are not suitable for electrical fires or for fires in materials that react violently with water.

Breaking the Chain Reaction Experimentation has uncovered the possibility of extinguishing fire with certain chemicals, such as some halogenated hydrocarbons (halogens or "Halon") and inert salts (dry chemicals). Apparently these work by interfering with the chemistry of chain reaction in a fire rather than by either cooling or smothering. Since some of these chemicals are toxic or corrosive in varying ways, care is necessary in their selection and use.

Many of the halogenated extinguishing agents, because they are either gases or liquids that rapidly vaporize in fire, leave little corrosive or abrasive residue after use. Another advantage is that they have a less toxic effect than many other extinguishing agents. (Carbon dioxide, for example, smothers people when applied in sufficient concentration to smother fires.) Because halogenated agents inflict little, if any, damage to property when released, and because of their low toxicity, these agents are frequently used to protect such things as computer equipment or computer rooms where evacuation of employees would be difficult. A disadvantage, however, is that Halon extinguishing agents are quite expensive.

Dry chemicals are very effective in extinguishing flames that can be reached with these chemicals. Many can be used on electrical fires and flammable liquids. This effectiveness and versatility, plus ease of application, have made them popular for general use. The principal disadvantages of dry chemicals are limited penetrating power, low cooling effect, and production of a sticky residue that may damage some equipment. In order to obtain cooling, water or foam may be used. However, many foams and dry chemicals are incompatible, and combinations of these must be chosen carefully.

Applying Fire Control Principles

Fires that have begun to burn can be counteracted by removal of heat, fuel, or oxygen, or by breaking the chemical chain reaction. While reducing fire severity is important, fire prevention is no less important. This section on applying fire control principles will discuss some of the means available to prevent the occurrence of fires or to lower their severity.

The lines of attack to apply fire loss control principles are fairly obvious. Fires can be prevented by controlling heat sources and by maintaining a distance between fuel and heat. Fire severity can be reduced by reducing the damageability of property exposed to the fire peril and by taking other loss reduction measures. Furthermore, it is necessary to recognize that not all fires are accidental in origin. Steps must also be taken to control arson losses.

Controlling Heat Sources Much fire loss may be prevented by having no buildup of heat energy in heat sources not necessary to operations. For example, appropriate rules and procedures should be enforced in connection with smoking, personal cooking and heating equipment, and burning trash.

Planned Heat Sources. The necessity of planned heat sources should be questioned. Are all the sources planned for energy actually required? With sources in which heat is an unwanted by-product, can storage of the heated material or use of the heat-producing process be avoided by practical alternative arrangements?

The second question is equally important: Where there must be energy, has care been taken not to have more than is necessary? Are electrical devices overheated? Are more furnaces, forges, kilns, or other heating devices in use than necessary? Are fires larger or hotter than necessary? Are there flames where something else (e.g., hot water) will do? The answers to these questions may identify planned heat sources that can be reduced or eliminated.

Heat as a By-Product. When heat is an unwanted by-product, a variety of options is often available. In lighting, fluorescent tubes are cooler than incandescent bulbs. Machines differ in the amount of friction heat they generate. Clearly, with self-heating materials and supplies, quantities stored should be controlled, and separation of such materials into smaller amounts at segregated locations is desirable.

The release of heat energy can be controlled by dissipating heat slowly through some kind of cooling. That the atmosphere around hot processes should be kept cool seems obvious, but only methodical, step-by-step analysis gives good assurance that such a move will not be overlooked.

Electrical Heat Energy. The rate and path of release of electrical energy can be controlled with proper fuses or automatic circuit breakers, and with adequate grounding. Grounding can be used both to protect power circuits and to control static electricity created by moving machinery, liquids, and dust. It also applies to the mightiest "unplanned" electrical source—lightning—which can be grounded by lightning rods.

Separation—Friendly Fires or Heat Sources The measures that may be used to prevent friendly fires or heat sources from becoming a source of hostile fire vary, depending on whether the heat sources are planned or unplanned, fixed or mobile.

Fixed Location Planned Heat Sources. When fixed location planned heat sources have been identified, flammable or combustible materials must be kept away from them. The National Fire Protection Association, Factory Mutuals, Industrial Risk Insurers, and others have developed standards that serve as a guide. Some involve only common sense. For example, the furnace room is not the place to keep trash, paper stocks, or janitors' materials. Other standards require more specific information. Building timbers and wood partitions should not be too close to furnaces and flues, but how close is too close? Here, recommendations are available from the above sources and should be followed.

With cooking stoves, the major fuel hazard comes from cooking oils, greases, and fats in foods. Besides the immediate exposure, there is a buildup of greasy deposits in hoods and flues—a frequent factor in restaurant fires. Regular removal of the deposits is indicated as a standard fire protection measure.

With electrical equipment, the first and most important separation device is insulation of wiring, of motor compartments, of switches, and so on. Where there is or may be arcing—as there is in most electrical switches, motors, and generators, common sense again dictates separation from flammable materials. When they are in the presence of a heat source, finely divided particles of any kind, including lints, metal dusts and shavings, may provide fuel for a fire. Lubricating greases and oils are other obvious fuels. (It follows that finely divided particles that are oily compound the exposure.)

Mobile Planned Heat Sources. Mobile planned heat sources are a significant problem in fire loss control. Welding and cutting torches are a frequent cause of fires, and portable heaters of various kinds are also significant. Even an ordinary flashlight can ignite a fire in an explosive atmosphere. "Explosion-proof" flashlights are designed for such applications.

With fixed planned sources, buildings, equipment, and operations can be designed to keep fuels away. Since the exposure does not change rapidly, the plans are relatively easy to manage effectively. With mobile equipment, the specific exposures keep changing. The equipment has to be taken where it is needed, and is not necessarily restricted to use in areas free of fuels. Furthermore, a major psychological difficulty exists because people are less impressed with the need to take elaborate precautions for an exposure that is going to last only a few minutes or even a few hours. If it takes, say, fifteen to thirty minutes to make an area thoroughly safe for a repair job that will last an hour and involve only several minutes of torch work, with another fifteen to thirty minutes to restore the area to operational condition, it can be difficult to get operators, and even supervisors, to take full care. Furthermore, under a variety of possible circumstances, it may be difficult to phrase rules and procedures that always define adequately what "full care" means.

Unplanned Heat Sources. With unplanned sources of heat, the obvious approaches are prohibition and restriction, as in having "no smoking" areas and possibly areas specifically reserved for "smoking breaks." Employees' hot plates or coffee makers may be prohibited or restricted in number or size, and there may be a supporting practice of providing convenient alternatives in planned lunchrooms or coffee nooks. There should be a set of procedures for anticipating and handling unusual situations such as the disposal of trash during a collectors' strike or the provision of temporary heat or power to a critical operation when its regular supply has been cut off.

Separation—Hostile Fires If friendly fires or heat sources are not adequately separated from fuel, the result may be a hostile fire. The severity of hostile fires may be reduced by effective building design.

Separation of fuel heat may be by clear space, by barriers, or both. Within a building, how much clear space may be interposed between heat sources and possible fuels depends on the building's area relative to the space needed for storage and equipment. Inadequate space often means that materials will be crowded together and too close to heat sources. Increasing building size beyond minimum operational requirements ordinarily does not do much to separate heat from fuel effectively. When a fire does get started in some materials, its chance to reach more can be increased when there is a lot more material in the same building. Large unbroken areas within buildings can spawn large fires. Indeed, avoiding large, open areas is one of the most basic propositions in fire loss control.

Limiting Vertical Fire Spread. Fire spread can be encouraged by vertical openings that allow heat to rise past combustible property. The most frequent examples of such vertical openings are stairwells and elevator shafts, ducts and flues, and openings used to allow pipes and wiring to get from floor to floor. Windows can also contribute to the spread of fire from one floor to another as the fire shoots out of one window and into the next one above. This action is called "looping."

Another major exposure involves high stacking in storage. In hundreds of warehouses (and in many stores), goods in cardboard containers are stacked up, row above row, for dozens of feet. Fires that start in lower rows are thus well supplied with fuel on which to grow. Whiskey warehouses, containing alcohol in well-seasoned wood containers, present the same type of exposure but with even greater intensity, as do some drying sheds and lumber yards.

Limiting vertical rise of fire is of prime importance in designed buildings for fire loss control. Of course, it is also important to maintain the integrity of fire barriers originally designed into a building. Although this principle should seem obvious, it is frequently violated in practice. Conveyor belts may be installed to deliver goods from one floor to another, piercing what was a fire-resistive floor. Electrical, plumbing, or heating equipment may be installed leaving a large rough-cut opening through which fire can spread. Fire doors originally installed in order to separate passageways between stories may be damaged or may suffer from improper maintenance.

Openings through which building service lines (pipes, wires, ducts) pass should be filled with adequate noncombustible material. Of course, air ducts are designed for movement of air through the building, and when a hostile fire occurs, its hot gases can move the same way. Therefore, insertion of movable stops (fire dampers) in all but the smallest ducts is recommended. These may be actuated by various fire-sensing devices.

Interior spaces in hollow walls and below floors (above ceilings) are other weak points. Finished walls in any type of construction may have open spaces. Open spaces between the floor of one story and the ceiling of the story below are standard features of frame and ordinary construction and are common in finished areas of other types. There are three reasons why such spaces contribute significantly to spread of fire:

1. Being concealed, fire in these spaces can burn for a considerable time before it is noticed.
2. These spaces commonly contain some quantities of combustible debris, including dust.
3. With only a limited volume of air to heat, a fire in a small, contained space produces higher temperatures than it would in the open (like a fire in a stove, for example). For these reasons, *fire-stops* should be inserted. These are solid pieces running from support to support of the wall or floor. In frame buildings, fire-stops inside walls often are wooden two-by-fours, running horizontally from stud to stud. Although such stops are combustible, they do not burst into flame easily and they accomplish the purpose of delaying the flow of heat.

Attics are also hazardous for the same reasons. In addition, they are in the path of rising heat. In row buildings, for example, fires starting in one structure have bypassed brick walls by spreading through the common attic. Here again, while good fire-resistive materials are best in the dividers, lighter materials can delay spread until firefighters control the original fire.

Spread of heat through an attic or along the underside of any roof or ceiling can sometimes be reduced by venting, which protects by cooling (controlling the rate of release of fire energy) and by directing the flow of heat into the open, away from combustibles in the building (a form of separation of heat from fuel). Built-in venting can also prevent the problem of sudden flaming when firefighters vent the building after a fire in it has already heated the interior.

Looping of fire from one story to the next through exterior windows is less common but can be serious. The generally recommended controls are metal framing with wired glass or other installations that will not readily burn out, soften, or fall out in high heat. Staggering the lines of windows may help. Another device is installation of parapets that extend out between in-line windows.

Limiting Horizontal Fire Spread. A fire may spread horizontally almost as easily as it spreads upward. In the presence of readily flammable materials, there is no significant difference. (In bowling alleys, for example, the alley surfaces have sometimes supported flash spread, so that within a few minutes the whole playing area has been involved.) Nearly all materials used to make walls, partitions, or doors in buildings have some value in slowing fire spread. (Unwired glass panels are a major exception.) Even a wooden stud partition with a half-inch of bare fir plywood on each side has a standard test rating of twenty minutes. Many plaster or wallboard partitions with wooden studs test at one hour. Even twenty minutes can make a large difference in the effectiveness of prompt fire fighting; in most fires, an hour's resistance means a contained fire. The problem, however, is that fires are not always noticed right away, and then the difference between combustible and fire resistive barriers becomes important.

As with vertical separation, adequate horizontal separation calls for barriers with no holes for heat to get through. The ideal is an unbroken wall that extends from the floor at the lowest level through and beyond the roof, with no windows near it in the exterior walls. Next in desirability is a wall with openings properly protected with fire doors. When the doors are not as fire resistant as the wall, then the strength of the whole is limited by the strength of the doors. The doors should shut automatically whenever not actually in use (*self-closing doors*) or be arranged to close themselves in the presence of fire heat (*automatic fire doors*). Automatic fire doors are illustrated in Exhibit 2-16. Automatically closing equipment must not be blocked or rendered inoperable. Unfortunately, such blockage or interference is fairly common practice. A fire wall with an open door or other sizable opening is hardly more of a fire-stop than a wall of combustible materials, occasionally even less (depending on how long it takes the fire to find the opening—a process which may be increased when the opening provides an exhaust channel for fire gases).

When equipment (such as a conveyor line) makes solid closure impossible, special water spray protection can be used. Special sprinklers are also needed where shafts cannot be fully enclosed (as with escalators, for example). Outside sprinkler heads may be used to help protect window openings in the event of a fire from outside the building.

Full Separation. When one space is sufficiently separated from another, the two are called separate "fire divisions." A self-supporting solid wall the full width and height (including lowest basement) of the building plus adequate extensions (*parapets*) beyond any combustible roofs or walls, with appropriate fire resistance rating, is a *fire wall* that separates a building into *fire divisions*. Under most circumstances, a fire, even a very severe one, will not pass through or around a fire wall. (There is another type of divider, less strong, and usually not extending from basement to roof, called a *fire partition*. Although it can reduce the spread of fire, a fire partition does not create fire divisions.)

The other way to create a fire division or its equivalent is by

Exhibit 2-16
Automatic Door Equipment*

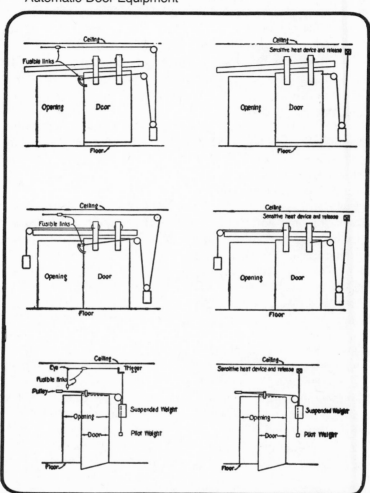

*Reprinted with permission from *NFPA*, 4th ed. (Boston: National Fire Protection Association, 1976), p. 260.

outdoor open space separating two buildings. The amount of space necessary for reliable separation depends on the possible intensity of the exposing fire, the combustibility of the surfaces (walls and roofs), and the size and nature of windows and other openings in both buildings. The relative heights of two exposing buildings is also a factor. Common standards for adequacy of clear spaces regularly assume that firefighters will arrive and be able to hep protect the

2 • Measuring and Controlling Property Exposures—111

exposed building. When this is not the case, the amount of clear space required is much greater. (More open space may be required than is often considered necessary. A fire in Massachusetts once spread 100 feet across a river and upwind to ignite another building.)[11]

In addition, the clear space needs to be *clear*. Too frequently, the value of open spaces has been compromised to the point where their effectiveness is all but destroyed by their being cluttered with combustible yard storage, small structures, etc., or by allowing grass and brush to grow between the structures.

Protected openings in a fire wall substantially reduce the reliability of the wall as a fire barrier, since there is no assurance that the protection will be properly in place when needed. Therefore, the possible spread of a fire from one side of the wall to the other (i.e., no actual fire division) must be taken into account.

The protection of external openings and exposed surfaces against communication of fire or heat across a clear space increases the effectiveness of the clear area. Among the recommended devices are water spray, steel shutters, and wired glass in metal frames.

Naturally, full separation is desirable between hazardous fire sources and less hazardous operations, such as between manufacturing and office occupancies, and between operations involving materials with low ignition temperatures and other materials.

A special type of full separation is provided by a fire resistive vault. Valuable records, money, securities, jewelry, furs, or fine arts enclosed in a fire resistive vault can often survive destruction of the rest of the building. Such fire protection also provides some protection against other perils. For full protection, the vault must not only resist entry of flame; it must also insulate the contents against increase of temperature within the vault to the point where contents can ignite or be damaged. It also must withstand rupture from collapse of the containing building. (Lesser degrees of protection, as in a fire resistive file with, say, one-hour fire resistance are, of course, an improvement over ordinary cabinets or open filing with respect to fire damage.) Safes and vaults will be discussed in greater detail in Chapter 7.

Physical separation between records and duplicates of them, at totally different locations, is often the most practical method of controlling fire loss from damage to an organization's valuable papers and records.

Reducing Damageability A major method of fire control is substitution of noncombustible or combustible materials. With respect to the major components of building—as in the differences among wood frame, ordinary masonry, noncombustible, and fire resistive construction—this is obvious. It is also generally recognized in connection with special hazards, such as flammable and combustible liquids and gases. Combustibility is less frequently considered with ordinary property, such as desks and chairs. The use of steel instead of wood, or of heavy materials rather than light, can reduce damageability. Hotels and hospitals can use noncombustible bedding, rugs, drapery, and furnishings. Of course, the gain in resistance to fire (and other) damage, compared to the increase in cost of the safer equipment, is commonly much smaller in low hazard occupancies (such as offices) than in more hazardous ones. Combustibility of buildings and contents has actually increased in recent years with the growing use of plastic furnishings and structural components.

Other Loss Reduction Measures   Once a hostile fire has begun, effective counteraction requires that it be detected and extinguished. Detection can be accomplished by visual observation and a voice alarm (someone sees the fire and yells "fire") or through simple or sophisticated automatic smoke or fire detection systems.

The two chief ways in which hostile fires are extinguished are through the use of automatic extinguishing systems and through the use of trained fire-fighting personnel. Either way, rapid response is essential.

The major virtue of automatic extinguishing systems is that, when properly designed, installed, and maintained, they provide effective response with more reliability than any other device or procedure. The major drawback of trained fire fighting is the frequent delay in getting proper personnel, equipment, and supplies to the scene. The most frequent cause of this delay is in getting notification to the fire fighters that they are needed.

First Aid.   Fire-fighting efforts are generally divided into two classes: immediate, simple, limited efforts, sometimes called first aid fire fighting; and fully equipped efforts. The former can be accomplished by regular personnel of the organization. Portable fire extinguishers or standpipes and hoses may effectively combat a small fire. Turning off fuel supplies and electrical power and closing fire-stops are some other possible first aid measures.

Reliance on first aid fire fighting has some serious dangers. Delay is a big problem. There is a common tendency to delay action other than first aid on the assumption that simple, limited measures will quickly extinguish the fire. As a result, there can be failure to get people out of endangered premises and delay in notification of fully trained and equipped fire fighters. Thus, when "first aid" measures are inadequate, both personal injury and property damage losses can be greatly magnified.

Users of fire extinguishers often have no training in such use. This can cause further delay while they find the equipment and learn how to use it. Untrained personnel may also use the wrong type of fire extinguisher on a fire. A fire extinguisher may be relied on to extinguish only the type(s) of fire for which it is labeled. The various types of fire extinguisher ratings are illustrated in Exhibit 2-17. Fire extinguishers should be periodically inspected and maintained to assure their operation when needed. Even trained "first aiders" are sometimes subject to another problem, having been shown only the effectiveness of the equipment, not its ineffectiveness.

All employees should be regularly trained in the most essential elements of fire response. Most important is that immediate notice of any fire be given to supervisors responsible for personnel safety and to the fire brigade or fire department, regardless of first aid efforts. Training should include drills on transmitting such notice. Supervisors must be *skilled* in (not just "know") evacuation rules and procedures. Nonsupervisory employees generally should also be given practice and/or training in using fire extinguishers and in proper exit procedures.

Trained Fire Fighters. The "fully trained and equipped fire-fighting personnel" may be a private fire brigade or public fire department. It is not enough for fire fighters to be fully trained—they must also be fully equipped. Inadequate water pressure and/or volume are all too frequently a problem. Also, fire fighters may encounter blank walls that impede entrance, and bad weather (high winds or extremely cold or hot, dry atmospheres).

A handicap that sometimes arises with large and special exposures is failure to acquaint public fire department personnel with plant layout, hazards, and fire-fighting resources ahead of time. This lack of preplanning delays effective counteraction (and sometimes even leads to ineffective or dangerous courses of action) when fire does occur. For example, fire fighters may apply water to a substance that reacts violently with water. Or, they may fail to hook their pumper to a hidden siamese sprinkler connection to boost water pressure at the sprinkler heads. Fire fighters can also get lost or trapped in an unfamiliar building.

Personnel responsible for fire safety can develop *pre-planning programs* in cooperation with their local fire department. Fire departments are usually happy to assist in such an endeavor. Among the items that should be considered in preplanning are informing the fire department of building floor plans, locations of exits, what hazardous materials are present and where they are located and which valuable files should be removed from the burning building if at all possible.

Delays in getting adequate equipment and personnel to a fire

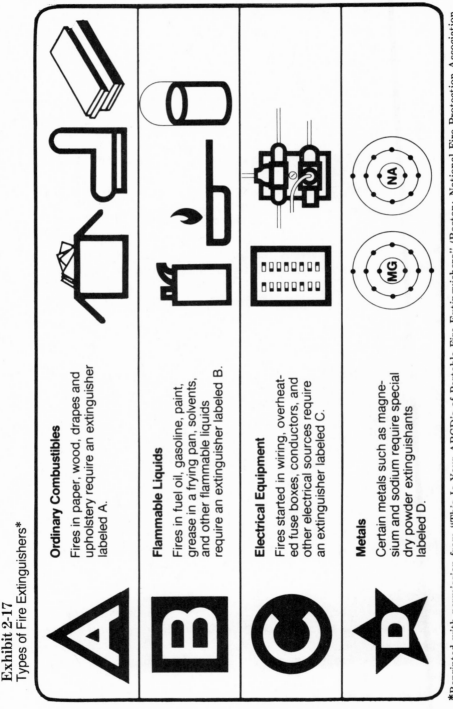

Exhibit 2-17
Types of Fire Extinguishers*

Ordinary Combustibles

Fires in paper, wood, drapes and upholstery require an extinguisher labeled A.

Flammable Liquids

Fires in fuel oil, gasoline, paint, grease in a frying pan, solvents, and other flammable liquids require an extinguisher labeled B.

Electrical Equipment

Fires started in wiring, overheated fuse boxes, conductors, and other electrical sources require an extinguisher labeled C.

Metals

Certain metals such as magnesium and sodium require special dry powder extinguishants labeled D.

*Reprinted with permission from "This Is Your ABCD's of Portable Fire Extinguishers" (Boston: National Fire Protection Association, 1976).

sometimes occur because of traffic or because resources are already tied up elsewhere. However, most delays are caused by delays in alarm. Therefore, automatic alarms are desirable for all situations in which there is special flammability or damageability of property or danger to life.

Alarms and Detection Devices. Fire detection or alarm services include (1) the manual fire alarm found in the halls of many buildings, (2) automatic smoke detection devices, (3) automatic heat detection devices, and (4) water-flow alarms that are activated when water begins to flow through a sprinkler system because a sprinkler head has opened.

Once an automatic or manual alarm has been actuated, it signals one or more of the following types of alarm systems:

1. A *local system* sounds an alarm inside and/or outside the protected property, thus alerting the occupants and/or nearby people to a fire. However, one cannot be certain that an occupant will always hear the alarm unless the premises are occupied twenty-four hours a day, 365 days a year. Occupants who hear a local alarm do not necessarily realize that they must call the fire department. Passersby are even more unlikely to do so.

2. A *remote station system* conducts the alarm to equipment in a remote station such as a fire or police station where someone is always on duty.

3. *Central station systems* are owned, operated, and maintained by a private concern which, on observing the alarm, will notify the fire department and may also send its own investigator to the scene of the alarm. Central station alarm companies generally provide high quality service and see to it that the transmission lines between the protected premises and the alarm company are in operation at all times.

4. *Proprietary systems* are similar to central station systems but differ in that the alarm is received at a central office on the protected property.

5. *Auxiliary systems* conduct the signal from a detection or alarm device to actuate a fire alarm box on a circuit of a municipal fire alarm system.[12]

Of these types of alarm systems many feel the central station service is best (when available) because the system is continuously monitored by the alarm company. However, the mere presence of a central station type alarm does not assure its effectiveness—a lesson many have learned the hard way. Underwriters Laboratories Inc. (U.L.)

has a program for certifying central station and alarm installations that comply with the requirements of both U.L. and the National Fire Protection Association (NFPA). A sample certificate is shown in Exhibit 2-18. Notice the periodic tests and prompt repairs specified in the certificate. Note also that a U.L. certificate applies only to the specific services described in the certificate.

Many factors are relevant in determining the type of alarm system most useful in a given situation. For firms with low-hazard levels for both people and property, probabilities as to fire frequency and speed of spread are often considered too low to warrant the expense of automatic alarm systems. But where danger is greater—e.g., to people in schools, hospitals, hotels, theaters, night clubs, department and other large stores; or to property wherever there are readily flammable materials, concentrated property values, or large undivided areas—automatic detection and/or extinguishing systems are of prime importance in loss control. In fact, such detection and extinguishing systems are required by many building codes.

Automatic Sprinkler Systems. Automatic sprinkler systems are among the most effective fire-fighting tools ever developed. One example of a sprinkler system is shown in Exhibit 2-19.

An automatic sprinkler system usually consists of pipes placed along the ceilings of a building. These pipes are equipped at intervals (commonly ten- or fifteen-foot intervals) with sprinkler heads containing valves which generally are held in position by fusible links. Depending on the type, when the air around a sprinkler head reaches a given temperature, the fusible link melts ("fuses"), the valve in a sprinkler head opens, and water is sprinkled on the area below, thus extinguishing any fire. The heat that activates the system can originate from any source, since the fusible link in a sprinkler head cannot distinguish between fire heat and heat from other sources.

Sprinkler systems may be "wet pipe" or "dry pipe." A *wet pipe system* contains water (or sometimes an antifreeze solution) in the pipes, and these pipes are connected to a water supply so that an immediate and constant supply of water is released upon the fire. In a *dry pipe system*, shown in the refrigerated area in Exhibit 2-19, there is air instead of water in the pipes down the line (behind the valve) under pressure. Quickly (although not instantly) after the opening of a sprinkler head, the air escapes through the sprinkler head and water rushes to it. Wet systems have a faster response time than dry pipe systems. However, dry systems are necessary where temperatures are such that the water might freeze (e.g., in refrigerated areas, unheated warehouses, or loading docks).

Some automatic extinguishing systems use extinguishing agents

Exhibit 2-18
Underwriters Laboratories Alarm Certificate*

UL UNDERWRITERS LABORATORIES INC.
111 PFINGSTEN ROAD NORTHBROOK, ILLINOIS 60062

an independent, not-for-profit organization testing for public safety

CENTRAL STATION SIGNALING SYSTEM CERTIFICATE

This certifies that the Central Station Alarm Company whose name appears on the reverse side of this form is included by Underwriters Laboratories Inc., in its Directory as being capable of furnishing the signaling system described hereon and is authorized to issue this Certificate to the equipment described hereon as its representation that such equipment and all connected wiring and devices which form a system together with installation and maintenance service are in compliance with the requirements established by Underwriters Laboratories Inc. This Certificate does not apply in any way to the installation of any additional alerting systems such as medical emergency, burglary, holdup, industrial process monitoring, or otherwise that may be connected to or installed along with the system described hereon.

★ ★

The Central Station Alarm Company issuing this Certificate bears the responsibility for inspecting, testing, maintaining and providing any necessary repairs for the system described in the Certificate. All required service is to be provided for in an appropriate contract.

Bimonthly tests are required for transmitters, waterflow actuated devices, automatic fire detection systems and valve supervisory devices.

Semiannual tests are required for manual fire alarm boxes, combination night guard and fire alarm boxes, tank water level devices, building and tank water temperature supervisory devices and other sprinkler system supervisory devices.

Alarm signals require the dispatch of a runner or technician (arrival time not to exceed one hour) to the protected premises when equipment must be manually reset. Supervisory signals also require the dispatch of a runner or maintenance person (arrival time not to exceed one hour) unless the abnormal condition can be restored to normal through the subscriber's efforts. Trouble signals or other signals pertaining solely to equipment maintenance require the dispatch of a runner or maintenance person (arrival time not to exceed four hours) to initiate the necessary maintenance.

Repairs are required to be commenced within four hours after notification of a need for service and are to continue until completion.

★ ★

LIMITATION OF LIABILITY
Underwriters Laboratories Inc. makes no representations or warranties, express or implied, that the alarm system will in any way prevent any loss as might be caused by fire, smoke, water damage, or otherwise, or that the system will in all cases provide the protection for which it is installed or intended. This Certificate only evidences that UL conducts countercheck field inspections of representative installations of the installing company. UL does not assume or undertake to discharge any liability of the installer or any other party. UL is not an insurer and assumes no liability for any loss which may result from failure of the equipment, incorrect certification, non-conformity with requirements, cancellation of the Certification or withdrawal of the installing company from inclusion in UL's Directory prior to the expiration date appearing on this Certificate. If an installation is found not in conformity with UL's requirements, it is the responsibility of the installing company to bring the system into conformity or the Certificate is subject to cancellation.

© 1983 U.L.

FC 0003753

Alarm Company: _____

Central Station

   Location : _____

Subscriber : _____

Address   : _____

         : _____

Responding Fire Department: _____

Authority Having Jurisdiction: _____

UL File No. **S**_____

Service

Center No. _____

Issued _____

Expires _____

(Not to be issued for a term of more than 5 years)

ALARM TRANSMISSION TO CENTRAL STATION

☐ Multiplex

☐ McCulloh

☐ Digital Communicator

ALARM RETRANSMISSION TO FIRE DEPARTMENT

Primary   Secondary

☐ . . . Code Transmitter

☐ . . . Direct Telephone . . . . ☐

☐ . . . To Unlisted Telephone . . . . . ☐

☐ . . . To Public Telephone . . . . . . ☐

911 . . . . ☐

AUXILIARY EQUIPMENT

Local Annunciator . . . . ☐

Local Sounding Device . . . . . ☐   No. of devices _____

Manual Fire Box . . . . ☐   No. of boxes _____

SAMPLE

SPRINKLER SYSTEM WATERFLOW ALARM AND SUPERVISORY

No. of waterflow risers

Waterflow Indicators:

   No. of coded waterflow transmitters _____

   No. of noncoded waterflow switches _____

   Activating _____ waterflow transmitters

Sprinkler Shutoff Valve Supervision: ☐ Yes ☐ No

   No. of shutoff valves _____

   No. of shutoff valves supervised _____

Number of shutoff valve and other supervisory transmitters _____

Other Supervisory Equipment: _____

Other Supervisory Services Provided:

Pressure	☐	Water	No. of devices _____
	☐	Air	No. of devices _____
Temperature	☐	Water	No. of devices _____
	☐	Room	No. of devices _____
Water Level	☐		No. of devices _____
Fire Pump	☐	Running	No. of devices _____
	☐	Power	No. of devices _____

AUTOMATIC FIRE DETECTION AND ALARM SERVICE

Coverage: ☐ Full   ☐ Partial (If partial, indicate locations)

_____

Spot type detectors -	Number	Line type detectors -	Number
Heat, fixed temperature (FT)	_____	Heat (No. of circuits)	_____
Heat, rate of rise (ROR)	_____	Smoke	_____
Heat, combination FT & ROR	_____	Duct smoke detectors -	_____
Smoke	_____	Number of coded fire signals	_____
Smoke and heat combination	_____	Number of coded trouble signals	_____
Other (specify) _____	_____		

MANUAL FIRE ALARM SERVICE

No. of coded stations _____

No. of noncoded stations _____

    activating _____ fire alarm transmitters

No. of combination manual fire alarm and guard tour coded stations _____

GUARD'S TOUR SUPERVISORY SERVICE

No. of coded stations _____

No. of noncoded stations _____

    activating _____ transmitters

Compulsory guard tour system comprised of _____ transmitter stations and _____ intermediate stations

_____   _____   _____

    (Signed)   (Title)   (Date)

© 1983 U.L.

* Reprinted with permission from Underwriters Laboratories, Inc.

Exhibit 2-19
Automatic Sprinkler System*

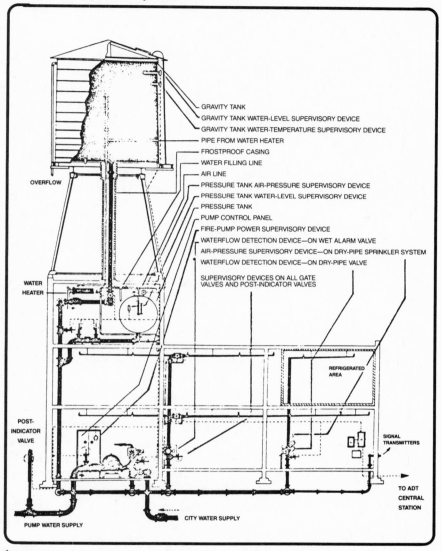

GRAVITY TANK
GRAVITY TANK WATER-LEVEL SUPERVISORY DEVICE
GRAVITY TANK WATER-TEMPERATURE SUPERVISORY DEVICE
PIPE FROM WATER HEATER
FROSTPROOF CASING
WATER FILLING LINE
AIR LINE
PRESSURE TANK AIR-PRESSURE SUPERVISORY DEVICE
PRESSURE TANK WATER-LEVEL SUPERVISORY DEVICE
PRESSURE TANK
PUMP CONTROL PANEL
FIRE-PUMP POWER SUPERVISORY DEVICE
WATERFLOW DETECTION DEVICE—ON WET ALARM VALVE
AIR-PRESSURE SUPERVISORY DEVICE—ON DRY-PIPE SPRINKLER SYSTEM
WATERFLOW DETECTION DEVICE—ON DRY-PIPE VALVE
SUPERVISORY DEVICES ON ALL GATE
VALVES AND POST-INDICATOR VALVES

OVERFLOW

WATER
HEATER

REFRIGERATED
AREA

POST-
INDICATOR
VALVE

SIGNAL
TRANSMITTERS

TO ADT
CENTRAL
STATION

PUMP WATER SUPPLY

CITY WATER SUPPLY

*Reprinted with permission of ADT Security Systems.

other than water, such as carbon dioxide, Halon, or a dry chemical extinguishing agent.

Although sprinkler systems are very beneficial in extinguishing fires, they introduce a new exposure—accidental discharge from the system can damage property. The sprinkler system will activate at a given degree of temperature or rate of change in temperature, regardless of the heat source. Discharge can be caused by a welder's torch, overheating of unit heaters, or sunlight through a skylight in an attic room. A combination of high heat and a low temperature fuse can cause accidental discharge. Other events that can cause leakage include freezing of pipes in unheated areas, mechanical injury to sprinklers or pipes (e.g., from the operation of lift trucks), settlement of water storage tanks, and disintegration of fusing material on old sprinklers. A large water storage tank is frequently installed to assure adequate water—quantity and pressure—to a system. Collapse of such a tank can cause much damage.

Automatic sprinkler systems solve more problems than they create, however, and have greatly reduced loss severity for firms so equipped. The possibility of an undetected discharge from a sprinkler system can be reduced by a simple local gong, driven by water pressure, that sounds when water flows through a system. More sophisticated systems, like that pictured in Exhibit 2-19, sound an alarm at a central station of an alarm company, such as Wells Fargo or ADT (American District Telegraph Company), whenever water flows. The primary purpose of these alarms is to alert plant personnel and fire departments to a fire, but they may well cause a false alarm.

Automatic sprinkler systems have an impressive record in limiting fire loss severity. (Of course, they have little effect on loss frequency since sprinklers are usually activated only after a fire has begun.) In cases where sprinklers have not been effective, the deficiency is almost always due to causes that could have been corrected.

A primary cause of automatic sprinkler ineffectiveness is failure to keep the sprinklers turned on. Some fire protection engineers suggest that sprinkler valves be chained and locked in an open position. It is further possible to attach to the sprinkler valve a sensing device that sounds an alarm when a sprinkler valve is tampered with. (This can be of particular value when an arsonist attempts to defeat a sprinkler system by closing the sprinkler valve before setting a fire.)

Another common deficiency is partial sprinkler protection. If a fire starts in or spreads to an unprotected area, a blaze may develop of such intensity that the sprinkler heads in the protected area cannot effectively extinguish the resulting blaze. However, proper design and maintenance can overcome or greatly mitigate these problems. And, as mentioned in an earlier section, sprinklers can be specially designed to reduce transmission of fire through unenclosed openings and from one building to another.

Controlling Loss from Arson For loss control, arson cases must be divided into crimes *against* the property owner and crimes *by* the property owner. While insurers need to consider the possibility of both types, only crimes against the owner will be considered in this discussion of risk management devices other than insurance. (Arson by the owner would not be a fortuitous loss cause.)

Arson loss severity can be limited—with the same types of loss control devices used to limit severity of other hostile fires—sprinklers, alarms, fire walls, and so forth. In addition to normal loss control measures, other measures are particularly useful in combating the arson hazard.

The chance of an effective arson attempt is reduced when an arsonist's opportunity to enter the premises is made difficult and when the presence of an intruder will be quickly detected. Locks, guards, alarms, and other systems effective in protecting against forcible entry of a burglar can also serve to prevent entry by an arsonist. Of course, it is necessary that areas vulnerable to an arsonist be protected, as well as those areas attractive to a thief. Loss control measures for crime losses will be discussed in greater detail in Chapter 7.

Sprinkler valves, fire alarm control devices, and similar protective devices can be protected so that any tampering by an arsonist will sound an alarm. Although such alarms may not eliminate the arsonist's opportunity to set a fire, they can reduce the amount of time during which the arsonist can work undisturbed and may send fire fighters to the scene even before the fire has been started. Any device that restricts entry or reduces the amount of time during which a would-be arsonist can work uninterrupted can reduce the chance of arson loss.

Controlling Water Damage Most fire fighting is done with water, and occasionally the water causes more property damage than the fire. (Of course, if there were no water, the fire would do more damage—an elementary point that is sometimes overlooked.) Also, automatic sprinklers sometimes release water when there is no fire, with some resultant damage. (Plumbing systems sometimes break or overflow, spreading water which results in the same type of damage but from a different insurable peril.) Control of water damage is therefore of interest in property loss control.

Control starts with sources. With sprinkler systems, an obvious point is proper design, installation, and maintenance. There are various ways to design automatic sprinkler systems so they are less likely to respond to stimuli from sources other than hostile fires. For example, there are differing temperatures at which different sprinkler heads will open. Sprinkler heads should be chosen that will not respond to ambient temperatures produced by normal operations, and vulnerable sprinkler heads can have guards which reduce the probability of accidental damage.

Also important in reducing water damage loss severity is to provide means for water to move out of the building with minimum damage. Impermeable floors, and drains and scuppers to channel the water outside, are common means of control. Also, inexpensive skids or pallets that keep stock off the floor help to reduce water damage losses.

Most sprinkler systems have water-flow alarms that sound when water begins to flow through the system. Their primary purpose is to serve as a fire alarm. However, such alarms are also useful in providing prompt notification of an accidental discharge from a sprinkler system. In addition, sprinklers can be designed to withhold or interrupt water flow unless combinations of stimuli are received that confirm the presence of a hostile fire rather than something else. For example, there is a sprinkler head that automatically resets itself (shuts itself off) when the temperature cools. This type of head could thus automatically extinguish a small fire and then cease spraying. Due to their expense, such heads are not frequently installed.

When there is a fire and valuable property is exposed to water damage from fire hoses, crews trained and equipped to put waterproof covers in place can greatly reduce loss severity. Of course, it is ordinary wisdom to minimize water damageable property in basements or in lower floors below upper stories where there is serious fire exposure or other source of potential water damage.

Finally, where the possible loss from water damage is large, automatic extinguishing systems containing CO_2, dry chemicals, Halon, foam, or systems that emit water in a very fine spray (fogging systems) may be used. (Even though foam and fogging systems contain water, it is so finely divided that it has little or no effect on many materials that are damaged by water in its usual form.)

Experience has shown that the danger of water damage from sprinklers has often been overestimated. Electronic data processing equipment, for example, is often assumed to be highly damageable by water from sprinklers. Experience with modern EDP equipment has shown otherwise.

Personnel Safety in Fires Most of the discussion of fire loss control in this text deals with property damage. But no discussion of the factors in origin, spread, and control of fires is adequate without special attention to personnel protection.

The key to personnel safety in hostile fires, beyond not having such fires in the first place (fire prevention), is keeping the people away from fires that do occur. This in turn involves containing fires in areas away from the people and moving the people away from areas where a fire is in progress (evacuation). The first of these approaches is adequate only where fire containment is absolutely assured, a condition nearly impossible to guarantee in advance. Because of this and because a fire is always possible where people are, evacuation must always be contemplated and prearranged.

A majority of fire deaths are caused, not by burns, but by asphyxiation and smoke inhalation. Thus, it is important to protect personnel not only from the heat of a fire, but also from the toxic gases generated by a fire. Evacuation is often the best way to accomplish this.

Safety of evacuation depends on how much faster the people can be moved out than the fire can spread. The speed of evacuation depends on (1) speed of notice that evacuation is to commence, (2) the ability of the exit routes to speed movement, (3) the path of the exit routes in relationship to the fire, and (4) the behavior of the people in the evacuation process.

Speed of notice to the fire department has already been touched on in discussion of fire fighting responses to fire. Even more important is the necessity for prompt notice to the occupants of a burning building.

Ability of exit routes to speed movement is a function of distance to be traversed and number of people that can be handled at once. Obviously, long or narrow exit routes cause delays. Dark or unusual routes, or routes with mechanical difficulties (e.g., steep stairs, vertical ladders, slippery surfaces) also slow exit.

Human behavior is well known to be a critical factor in safe evacuation. In several notorious cases, panic has caused scores of injuries and deaths. A fire at the Beverly Hills Supper Club in Southgate, Kentucky illustrated the problems that can be caused by panic. Shortly after 9:00 P.M. a busboy interrupted a comedy act to announce that there was a small fire in the kitchen and to ask everyone to leave the building. Many ignored the warning until smoke, billowing from behind closed doors, prompted a stampede toward the exits. The scene became pandemonium, and when it was over the huge nightclub was gutted and 165 were dead, victims of burns, trampling, and smoke inhalation.[13] In a fire in a modern skyscraper office building in Brazil, many persons were trapped in stories above the blaze. Many of the 189 deaths were caused by leaps from windows, some of them after the fire had been brought under control.

Fire protection specialists have noted that people commonly try to leave a public place by the door, elevator, or staircase through which they entered, even when that route is dangerous and others are safe. Fire gases and smoke can impair both thinking and motor control. All these factors affect efficiency of evacuation. The longer a fire and its dangerous products—heat, smoke, gases—can be kept from the people and their exit routes, the more likely a safe evacuation. Not the least of the reasons for this is reduced likelihood of panic.

Personnel safety is also, of course, a function of fire control. A fire put out in minutes by an automatic sprinkler, for example, is unlikely to cause personal injury. But an uncontrolled fire that persists and grows presents a threat, both directly (by actually causing injury) and indirectly (by inducing panic). Worst, of course, are fires that attack exit routes. This is why protection of stair openings (a natural channel of fire spread) is crucial, and fire-resistive protection of stairways is among the requirements for many types of property.

Rapid spread of flame by decorative surfaces, trim, and furnishings is a serious hazard for safe exit. Many such items, particularly upholstery and plastics, produce toxic fumes, compounding the difficulty.

High-rise office buildings and apartments are nearly impossible to evacuate totally, especially if people are at levels above the fire. The solution has to be provision of safety zones away from the fire, getting the people into them, and convincing them of their safety while there. This can be difficult. Besides building construction adequate to contain the fire against vertical spreading, it is necessary to inform the occupants as to where they should go and how to get there. The number of separate organizations in a high-rise office building, their turnover in personnel, the presence of visitors, and the lack of direct communication between the building operator and individual occupants all make advance instruction extremely difficult. (Hotels and restaurants obviously present very special problems.) Communication to and management of persons must be a major part of well laid plans for disaster management. Finally, personnel safety in high-rise buildings requires that fire fighters be able to control fires before they threaten safety zones or cause the people there to panic. Since fires many stories above the ground cannot be fought from the outside, building design must include proper equipment, such as standpipes and sprinklers.

Hospitals and some other institutions have a problem when it is necessary to avoid moving some patients or inmates. For these, a safely separated area is needed. But there still must be a safe way to move out of the building should that need arise. Preferably, any required movement should only be lateral, avoiding the problems of stairs.

After the Fire Is Out   Loss control continues to be possible after a fire is out. Property losses can be minimized by good salvage techniques, and business interruption losses can be minimized by the use of alternate resources or by expediting repairs.

Fire salvage is a specialized skill. For anyone who rarely deals with fire losses, the services of an experienced salvor are needed. The salvor may be supplied by an insurer or hired directly.

Alternate resources may be arranged in advance by having standby or underutilized equipment and facilities at another location.

For some organizations, competitors' facilities may be available; occasionally there is even pre-loss understanding of mutual aid in this respect. More often vacant facilities will have to be found, refurbished, and adapted to the organization's needs. Of course, temporary operation requires financing in addition to outlay for repair and reconstruction. Whether operations can be continued may depend on whether arrangements for loss financing have been adequate to cover all these expenditures.

Explosion Control

Many explosions have the chemistry of extremely rapid combustion. These explosions are, in essence, nearly instantaneous fire over the whole of a large quantity of material. Examples include explosions of flammable liquid vapors and gases, dust explosions (for example, grain elevator explosions), and the action of commercial explosives. The principles of explosion control are very similar to those for the slower combustion of fires. A major difference, of course, is the much shorter time available for explosion counteraction. There are, however, explosion suppressors that can act effectively the instant an explosion is initiated in order to suppress what would otherwise be a major explosion. Such suppression equipment detects a sudden abnormal increase in pressure and automatically floods the incipient explosion with a suppressing agent. This equipment resembles an automatic fire extinguishing system but differs in the type of detection and the extreme rapidity of response.

To prevent initial combustion that could lead to explosion, explosive materials should be properly handled. Sometimes, in addition, the material may be kept in a low-oxygen or oxygen-free atmosphere. (This is done by replacing much or all of the air in a chamber with inert gas, such as carbon dioxide or nitrogen.) Similar treatment may be provided for electrical equipment, or electrical equipment may be of explosion-proof design appropriate for the explosive environment.

For explosions that are not prevented or suppressed, venting is the standard method of control—directing the force toward open air and/or a solid barrier such as an earthen bank. Thus, for example, dynamite is stored in "igloos" with light roofs (so the explosive force is directed upwards); the "igloos" are surrounded by earth or concrete banks.

Explosion of pressure and vacuum vessels is the other major type of explosion. (Technically, vacuum vessels, which rupture inward rather than outward, suffer "implosion" rather than "explosion," but the difference is not important here.) Explosions occur in such equipment when the pressure exerted exceeds the capacity of the vessel to contain pressure. Such excess can occur from either an increase in the amount of pressure or a decrease in the strength of the vessel. Changes in strength or pressure must therefore be prevented or controlled. This exposure will be dealt with in greater detail in Chapter 6.

Control of Windstorm Damage

Although the energy source in windstorms cannot be controlled, it is possible to locate away from areas with frequent severe storms, such as hurricanes and tornadoes. However, it is usually impractical to avoid the windstorm exposure with a choice of location. Yet, there are certain factors, such as type of building construction, that affect the probability of windstorm damage to property. Some buildings resist wind damage better than others. There is considerable correlation between ability to resist fire damage and ability to resist wind damage because stronger structures resist both types of damage.

Plate glass, attached exterior trim, and roofing are particularly susceptible to windstorm damage. Ordinarily glass is readily damaged by windblown objects. When hurricane Alicia swept the Texas coast, extensive glass damage was done to buildings in downtown Houston. Many panes were damaged by pebbles blown from pebble-and-tar roofs on nearby buildings. When the glass area is large, glass can be broken by the high wind itself; light trim can be torn off by winds; and high velocity wind passing over a building creates forces that tend to lift the roof. Inadequate anchorage of the roof assembly will result in loss of the roof, followed by more loss to exposed contents. When the roof itself holds, its surface can suffer considerable stress and there may be much damage to shingles, tiles, or other attached coverings. This possibility must be considered in selection and attachment of roof surfaces. Proper maintenance is necessary, as strength of materials and their fastenings can deteriorate over time.

Flood and High Water Losses

Water damage may be caused when the hazard of low ground is combined with the peril of high water. In major hurricanes there is more damage from flooding than from force of wind. Natural flooding, whether from hurricanes or other storms, may be classified as three types: flooding from high tides; riverine floods—from rising water in rivers, streams, and lakes; and floods from inadequate runoff of rain water (flash floods). The best method of treating this exposure is to avoid areas known to have had flood experience. Since construction and rearrangement of the surface of the ground change runoff and flood patterns, consideration has to be given as to how these patterns may change. The consideration should, of course, be given before construction commences.

Where property is exposed to high water, design of grounds and buildings should take this into account, as should location of particular property in the building.

Many loss control measures are possible:

1. Placement of dams and other impoundments of water can cause, modify, or reduce energy buildup.
2. The rate and direction of release of water energy can be controlled by creating channels and impoundments to control direction and rate of runoff and by creation of open areas over which flooded waters can be spread out, reducing their depth and speed of flow.
3. Dikes and other barriers may be used to separate flood waters from property (and people) to be protected. Channels also effect such separation. Placing property at a high level (on high ground or in upper stories of a building) is another example of separation.
4. Property may be designed for strength against the pressure of flood waters and the effects of dampness. This can be done by making structures more solid and by giving them shapes that offer less direct impedence to water flow around and past them. Provision for runoff or pumping out water when the flood has subsided may also be necessary. (Dikes and levees sometimes increase loss by keeping water impounded longer.)
5. Buildings in flood prone areas can be constructed so that the bottom floor is above the 100-year flood level. On beach front properties, construction on pilings serves not only to elevate the structure but also to withstand the pressure of waves.
6. Counteraction includes such activities as emergency sandbagging, moving property to higher levels, speeding draining by pumping, and promptly drying and cleaning damaged property to minimize adverse effects.

Losses Caused by Earth Movement

As a practical matter, little attention is paid to earthquake loss control except in geographic areas that have had a history of damaging earthquakes. Where a serious earthquake exposure exists, the effects of an earthquake can be reduced by careful attention to building design and construction, taking into consideration the conditions of the soil upon which the building will rest. Earthquake-resistant buildings are designed so that the structure as a whole will resist the forces of earth movement. Mortar between bricks is not strong enough to hold walls together during an earthquake without some type of reinforcing. In fact, ordinary masonry buildings have done poorly in resisting earthquakes. The most common method of designing an earthquake-resistant building is to build a rigid structure with walls, columns, and pillars tied securely to floors and roofs by horizontal, vertical, and cross members carried through to the foundations.

Landslide, mud slides, subsidence (sinking), volcanic eruption, and expansive soil are other types of earth movement that may result in severe property damage. Of these, the one that does the most annual damage is expansive soil: $1.9 billion (10 year average). *Expansive soil* contains clay that, when wet, expands to fifteen times its volume when dry.[14] The major device for controlling losses from these various earth movements is care in siting buildings.

Chapter Notes

1. All-Industry Research Advisory Council, "Fire Following Earthquake," as reported by Karen Huelsman, "Fires Will Cause Most Losses After California Quake: Study," *Business Insurance,* 1 June 1987, p. 18.
2. *Fire Protection Handbook,* 13th ed. (Boston, MA: National Fire Protection Association, 1969), pp. 1-69.
3. An "uninhibited chain reaction" is sometimes considered the fourth element necessary to have a fire. This element is of little importance in fire *prevention.* However, some chemicals used in fire extinguishers or extinguishing systems control or extinguish fires by breaking the chemical chain reaction.
4. *Fire Protection Handbook,* 16th ed. (Boston, MA: National Fire Protection Association, 1986), pp. 4-4 to 4-5.
5. NFPA *Inspection Manual,* 4th ed. (Boston, MA: National Fire Protection Association, 1976), pp. 146-148.
6. Any attempt to verify this statement should be made with caution because the hot particles shot away from burning steel wool can cause eye injuries if protective equipment is not worn.
7. Revision No. 4, 4-78 CFRS, Copyright 1976, Insurance Services Office.
8. *Fire Protection Handbook,* 16th ed., pp. 7-83 to 7-84.
9. NFPA *Inspection Manual,* p. 232.
10. NFPA *Inspection Manual,* pp. 147-148.
11. *Fire Protection Handbook,* 14th ed., pp. 6-14.
12. NFPA *Inspection Manual,* pp. 290-293.
13. Richard L. Best, "Analysis of the Fire," Section III, *Reconstruction of a Tragedy: The Beverly Hills Supper Club Fire,* National Fire Protection Association, Boston, 1978.
14. *Building Losses from Natural Hazards: Yesterday, Today and Tomorrow,* report on study for National Science Foundation, by J. H. Wiggins Company, Redondo Beach, California, ca. 1978.

CHAPTER 3

Building and Personal Property Coverage

Insurance is widely used for transferring the financial consequences of loss to property. This chapter explores insurance coverages available for commercial buildings and business personal property. The chapter begins with a brief discussion of the scope of modern "commercial property" insurance, followed by a description of the historical development of fire insurance. A great deal of current insurance practice evolved from this heritage.

The next segment of the chapter describes the structure of modern property insurance policies—in particular, the structure of the simplified ISO commercial policies introduced during 1985, 1986, and 1987. Many elements of the program are common to all commercial insurance policies. Since these common elements form a basis of most commercial insurance policies, they are examined in some detail.

The remainder of the chapter is devoted to an analysis of the *building and personal property coverage form* (BPP). This form, accompanied by other essential documents, is designed to handle the basic building and/or contents coverage needs of most commercial insurance buyers. It serves a key role in most property insurance programs and therefore receives more emphasis than any other coverage form examined in this text. Many other coverages are best analyzed by comparison with the building and personal property coverage form.

Chapter 3 concentrates on the types of property and the types of loss consequences covered by the unmodified building and personal property coverage form. Alternatives to this basic approach, as well as the various causes of loss that may be insured, are then examined in Chapter 4.

NATURE OF "COMMERCIAL PROPERTY" INSURANCE

"Commercial property" insurance is one of several categories of property insurance. In a broad sense, commercial property insurance is all insurance that covers real and/or personal property exposures of business firms, as well as governmental bodies and private nonprofit organizations. The title of this text reflects that broad usage. However, as explained below, the so-called "commercial property" forms address only one segment of the commercial property insurance field.

Historically, commercial property insurance that relates to buildings and their contents has been referred to as "commercial fire and allied lines insurance." The relevant section of the current Insurance Services Office (ISO) *Commercial Lines Manual* (CLM) is titled "Commercial Lines Manual Division Five—Fire and Allied Lines." However, the manual begins by stating that "Division Five contains the rules, rates and rating procedures and state exceptions for the Commercial Property Coverage Part." Thus, both labels—"commercial fire and allied lines" and "commercial property coverage" refer to the same segment of the commercial property insurance field. In this text, we refer to this particular segment as "commercial property" in quotation marks and omit the quotation marks when referring to the entire spectrum of insurance coverage on commercial property.

"Commercial property" (fire and allied lines) insurance can be characterized according to:

- property and locations covered,
- perils (causes of loss) insured against, and
- covered loss consequences.

Property and Locations

Buildings and Contents "Commercial property" coverages usually have the location of each covered structure specified in the policy. Personal property may be covered while it is contained in the specified structure or within a given distance of it. Personal property is often loosely referred to as "contents," but it is not necessarily required that personal property be *contained* within the described building for coverage to apply. It is common to include coverage for personal property within 100 feet of the described premises.

Incidental Off-Premises Property As explained later, "commercial property" policies may also provide incidental coverage for property in transit or otherwise temporarily away from the premises.

However, "commercial property" coverage is not designed to insure items with extensive transit exposures. Businesses that ship, deliver, or receive materials or goods generally use a marine insurance form to protect that property.

Property Not Generally Covered "Commercial property" forms generally do not cover property that is better handled by another type of coverage. Such items as watercraft, bridges, tunnels, autos used on public highways, and aircraft are generally excluded. They can be covered under specially designed policies such as ocean marine or inland marine insurance policies, auto policies, or aviation policies. Likewise, money, securities, valuable papers, and records are generally not covered by "commercial property" policies (or are covered on a very limited basis). Property of this type is more specifically covered under crime or inland marine forms, discussed later in this text.

Perils

Because fire and allied lines insurance has centered on buildings, the perils covered traditionally have been those that damage buildings—perils such as fire, lightning, windstorm, hail, explosion, and riot. Conspicuous by their absence from this list are such perils as burglary, robbery, collision, and jettison—these perils primarily affect personal property.

Traditionally, fire and allied lines insurance has been written on a named perils basis. Many policies are issued for only the basic causes of loss. However, there has been a trend toward making available a broad list of named perils or even "all-risks" type protection on buildings and contents. (Rather than listing the perils that are covered, "all-risks" type coverage, in the so-called "special" forms, simply protects against direct losses from "risks" that are not excluded.)

Loss Consequences

The *Commercial Lines Manual* (CLM), which contains rules and rates for ISO commercial insurance policies and forms, effectively divides fire and allied lines insurance into four categories. All forms in these categories are "commercial property" forms, and their form numbers begin with "CP."

1. *Building and personal property coverage.* The forms treated in this section of the manual are generally those covering the reduction in value of existing buildings and their contents. These forms will be examined in detail in Chapters 3 and 4.

2. *Builders risk coverage.* Coverage for buildings under construction is discussed in Chapter 6.
3. *Time element coverage.* This section of the manual includes policies that cover business interruption, extra expense, and related exposures. These coverages are examined in Chapter 5. The term *time element* relates to the fact that the extent of loss is directly related to the passage of time during which the use of property is interrupted or limited.
4. *Other coverages.* This miscellaneous section of the manual includes the following coverages:

- glass, examined in Chapter 6;
- leasehold interest, examined in Chapter 6;
- legal liability for fire damage, in Chapter 6;
- mortgage holder's errors and omissions, in Chapter 13; and
- tobacco in sales warehouses—a special-purpose form not discussed further in this text.

To summarize discussion to this point:

- Commercial fire and allied lines insurance, also called "commercial property" insurance, *generally* applies to buildings at a fixed location and property inside those buildings.
- This insurance has traditionally been written on a named-perils basis, but broader coverage—including "all-risks" type coverage—is now widely available.
- Some "commercial property" insurance covers the reduction in value of buildings and contents, and other forms cover business interruption, extra expense, and related "time element" exposures.

EVOLUTION OF THE MODERN "COMMERCIAL PROPERTY" POLICY

The 1943 standard fire policy (SFP) was a major component of most commercial property insurance contracts for over thirty years. However, the SFP and the forms that accompanied it have gradually been displaced by more simplified forms. A brief look at the historical development of fire insurance coverage forms provides a background that helps one understand the present situation.

Early History

As fire insurance developed in the 1800s and early 1900s, a great deal of product differentiation came about. The absence of standardized forms and wide variations in the wording among fire insurance contracts gave rise to numerous problems, both for insureds and insurers. Consumers thought they knew what the policy was supposed to do; however, most insureds had not studied their contracts in detail and were not aware of many implications of the policy provisions. Fire insurance contracts were too often carelessly drafted and ambiguous since insurers were independently developing their own contracts without common wording. As a result, problems came about in interpretation of coverage, litigation of claims, and settlement of loss where dual coverage existed. The need for a simple, standard fire policy became increasingly apparent.

Fire Policy Standardization

Massachusetts was the first state to adopt a standard form for fire insurance. The Massachusetts standard policy was made mandatory for all insurance companies writing business in the state after 1880. The New York legislature adopted a standard policy in 1887. While formally designated the "General Standard Fire Policy," it was popularly known as the "1886 form" (even though it was adopted in 1887).

In 1916, the National Convention of Insurance Commissioners (now the National Association of Insurance Commissioners), following several years of deliberation, recommended a new standard form. This new form significantly decreased the number of clauses that dealt with moral hazard.

Furthermore, "while" clauses were substituted for the old "if" clauses. The old clauses *voided* the entire policy "if" and when the specified hazard appeared. The newer clauses provided that the coverage was only *suspended* "while" the hazard was present. Other changes were recommended and, in 1918, New York adopted the resulting "200 line form" which became known as the "Commissioners' form."

In 1936, a committee of the National Association of Insurance Commissioners recommended revision of the 1918 form. Recommended changes in the policy included (1) the addition of (a) lightning and (b) fire caused by riot as perils covered; (2) the modification of the policy to an "interest" contract which did not require that the insured be the sole and unconditional owner of the property in order to have coverage; (3) allowing assignment of the policy with the insurer's consent; (4) providing for the liberalization of vacancy and unoccupancy clauses to allow such conditions if for less than sixty days; and (5) adding a stipulation that in the event of loss (and multiple coverage) the loss would be prorated among insurers according to the face amounts of the coverage, whether collectible or not. On July 1, 1943, New York adopted this "165 line form." It became known as the New York standard fire policy, the standard policy, or the "165 lines." This standard fire policy is shown in Exhibits 3-1 and 3-2.

The 1943 New York Standard Fire Policy

The 1943 New York standard fire policy was eventually used in nearly all states. In most of these states, it was made "standard" or "approved" by the insurance code of the state or by insurance department regulation. Variations existed in some of these states.

Physically, the standard fire policy may be set up in one of two ways. The first is to insert a declarations page into a "jacket" which contains the insuring agreement on one page and the 165 lines on another. The second way is to print the insuring agreement on the declarations page as illustrated in Exhibit 3-1 and place the 165 lines on a succeeding page as shown in Exhibit 3-2. In either case, about two-thirds of a page is devoted to information identifying (1) the insured, insurer, and the policy number; (2) the inception and duration of the insurance; and (3) the subject(s) of the insurance coverage, the perils insured against, the rates charged for each unit of coverage, the total premium charged for the coverage, and the specific items of property insured. This page is commonly referred to as the "declarations" because most of the information comes from statements made by the insured or selections of coverage and peril options made by the insured.

The insuring agreement of the standard fire policy, which may be found on the declarations page, is a general statement of what the insurer agrees to do under the contract.

The second page of the standard fire policy consists of the numbered 165 lines. These provisions, stipulations, and conditions are standardized by statute, insurance code, or insurance commissioner regulation, and they set forth definitions, limitations, exclusions, and procedures for loss adjustment.

The standard fire policy declarations contain the words: "Subject to form No(s). Attached Hereto." When the policy is issued, the person or computer preparing the policy enters in the space following these words the numbers and edition dates of each form attached to the standard fire policy.

In order to be complete this policy must be combined with at least one additional "form" that defines and explains important aspects of coverage. Over the years, as the attached forms were refined, they modified or superseded more and more of the provisions of the standard fire policy. It became increasingly difficult to read and interpret the combined documents—many of the provisions printed in the 165 lines

Exhibit 3-1
Standard Fire Policy Declarations and Insuring Agreement

STANDARD FIRE INSURANCE POLICY for Alabama, Alaska, Arizona, Arkansas, Colorado, Connecticut, Delaware, District of Columbia, Florida, Georgia, Hawaii, Idaho, Illinois, Indiana, Iowa, Kansas, Kentucky, Louisiana, Maine, Maryland, Michigan, Mississippi, Missouri, Montana, Nebraska, Nevada, New Hampshire, New Jersey, New Mexico, New York, North Carolina, North Dakota, Ohio, Oklahoma, Oregon, Pennsylvania, Rhode Island, South Carolina, South Dakota, Tennessee, Utah, Vermont, Virginia, Washington, West Virginia, Wisconsin and Wyoming.

No.

NONASSESSABLE

STANDARD FIRE POLICY

Insured's Name and Mailing Address

Policy Term: INCEPTION (Mo. Day Year)   EXPIRATION (Mo. Day Year)   YEARS

$
Div. on Exp. Pol.   Renewal of

It is important that the written portions of all policies covering the same property read exactly alike. If they do not, they should be made uniform at once.

INSURANCE IS PROVIDED AGAINST ONLY THOSE PERILS AND FOR ONLY THOSE COVERAGES INDICATED BELOW BY A PREMIUM CHARGE AND AGAINST OTHER PERILS AND FOR OTHER COVERAGES ONLY WHEN ENDORSED HEREON OR ADDED HERETO

Item No.	DESCRIPTION AND LOCATION OF PROPERTY COVERED — Show address (No., Street, City, County, State, Zip Code), construction, type of roof and occupancy of building(s) covered or containing property covered. If occupied as a dwelling state if building is a seasonal or farm dwelling. If commercial state exact nature of product (and whether manufacturer, wholesaler or retailer) or the service or activity involved.	Pro-tection Class	Dwelling Business Only			
			No. of Families	Feet From Hydrant	Miles From Fire Dept.	Zone
1.						

Item No.	PERIL(S) INSURED AGAINST AND COVERAGE(S) PROVIDED (INSERT NAME OF EACH)	Per Cent of Co-Insurance Applicable	Deductible Amount	Amount of Insurance	Rate	Prepaid or Installment Premium Due At Inception	Installment Premium Due At Each Anniversary
1.	FIRE AND LIGHTNING			$		$	$
	EXTENDED COVERAGE			x x x x x x x			

Special provision applicable only in State of Mississippi—**Total Insurance**—See form attached—
Item 1, $; Item 2, $; Item 3, $ TOTAL(S) $ $

Special provision applicable only in State of So. Carolina—**Valuation Clause**—See form attached—
Item , $; Item , $; Item , $ TOTAL PREMIUM FOR POLICY TERM PAID IN INSTALLMENTS $

Subject to Form No(s).   attached hereto.

INSERT FORM NUMBER(S) AND EDITION DATE(S)

Mortgage Clause: Subject to the provisions of the mortgage clause attached hereto, loss, if any, on building items, shall be payable to:

INSERT NAME(S) OR MORTGAGEE(S) AND MAILING ADDRESS(ES)

		AGENT
COUNTERSIGNATURE DATE	AGENCY AT	

IN CONSIDERATION OF THE PROVISIONS AND STIPULATIONS HEREIN OR ADDED HERETO AND OF the premium above specified, this Company, for the term of years specified above from inception date shown above At Noon (Standard Time) to expiration date shown above At Noon (Standard Time) at location of property involved, to an amount not exceeding the amount(s) above specified, does insure the insured named above and legal representatives, to the extent of the actual cash value of the property at the time of loss, but not exceeding the amount which it would cost to repair or replace the property with material of like kind and quality within a reasonable time after such loss, without allowance for any increased cost of repair or reconstruction by reason of any ordinance or law regulating construction or repair, and without compensation for loss resulting from interruption of business or manufacture, nor in any event for more than the interest of the insured, against all **DIRECT LOSS BY FIRE, LIGHTNING AND BY REMOVAL FROM PREMISES ENDANGERED BY THE PERILS INSURED AGAINST IN THIS POLICY, EXCEPT AS HEREINAFTER PROVIDED,** to the property described herein while located or contained as described in this policy, or pro rata for five days at each proper place to which any of the property shall necessarily be removed for preservation from the perils insured against in this policy, but not elsewhere.

Assignment of this policy shall not be valid except with the written consent of this Company.

This policy is made and accepted subject to the foregoing provisions and stipulations and those hereinafter stated, which are hereby made a part of this policy, together with such other provisions, stipulations and agreements as may be added hereto, as provided in this policy.

TA8-3

Exhibit 3-2
Standard Fire Policy "165 Lines"

1 **Concealment,** This entire policy shall be void if, whether
2 **fraud.** before or after a loss, the insured has wil-
3 fully concealed or misrepresented any ma-
4 terial fact or circumstance concerning this insurance or the
5 subject thereof, or the interest of the insured therein, or in case
6 of any fraud or false swearing by the insured relating thereto.
7 **Uninsurable** This policy shall not cover accounts, bills,
8 **and** currency, deeds, evidences of debt, money or
9 **excepted property.** securities; nor, unless specifically named
10 hereon in writing, bullion or manuscripts.
11 **Perils not** This Company shall not be liable for loss by
12 **included.** fire or other perils insured against in this
13 policy caused, directly or indirectly, by: (a)
14 enemy attack by armed forces, including action taken by mili-
15 tary, naval or air forces in resisting an actual or an immediately
16 impending enemy attack; (b) invasion; (c) insurrection; (d)
17 rebellion; (e) revolution; (f) civil war; (g) usurped power; (h)
18 order of any civil authority except acts of destruction at the time
19 of and for the purpose of preventing the spread of fire, provided
20 that such fire did not originate from any of the perils excluded
21 by this policy; (i) neglect of the insured to use all reasonable
22 means to save and preserve the property at and after a loss, or
23 when the property is endangered by fire in neighboring prem-
24 ises; (j) nor shall this Company be liable for loss by theft.
25 **Other Insurance.** Other insurance may be prohibited or the
26 amount of insurance may be limited by en-
27 dorsement attached hereto.
28 **Conditions suspending or restricting insurance. Unless other-**
29 **wise provided in writing added hereto this Company shall not**
30 **be liable for loss occurring**
31 (a) while the hazard is increased by any means within the con-
32 trol or knowledge of the insured; or
33 (b) while a described building, whether intended for occupancy
34 by owner or tenant, is vacant or unoccupied beyond a period of
35 sixty consecutive days; or
36 (c) as a result of explosion or riot, unless fire ensue, and in
37 that event for loss by fire only.
38 **Other perils** Any other peril to be insured against or sub-
39 **or subjects.** ject of insurance to be covered in this policy
40 shall be by endorsement in writing hereon or
41 added hereto.
42 **Added provisions.** The extent of the application of insurance
43 under this policy and of the contribution to
44 be made by this Company in case of loss, and any other pro-
45 vision or agreement not inconsistent with the provisions of this
46 policy, may be provided for in writing added hereto, but no pro-
47 vision may be waived except such as by the terms of this policy
48 is subject to change.
49 **Waiver** No permission affecting this insurance shall
50 **provisions.** exist, or waiver of any provision be valid,
51 unless granted herein or expressed in writing
52 added hereto. No provision, stipulation or forfeiture shall be
53 held to be waived by any requirement or proceeding on the part
54 of this Company relating to appraisal or to any examination
55 provided for herein.
56 **Cancellation** This policy shall be cancelled at any time
57 **of policy.** at the request of the insured, in which case
58 this Company shall, upon demand and sur-
59 render of this policy, refund the excess of paid premium above
60 the customary short rates for the expired time. This pol-
61 icy may be cancelled at any time by this Company by giving
62 to the insured a five days' written notice of cancellation with
63 or without tender of the excess of paid premium above the pro
64 rata premium for the expired time, which excess, if not ten-
65 dered, shall be refunded on demand. Notice of cancellation shall
66 state that said excess premium (if not tendered) will be re-
67 funded on demand.
68 **Mortgagee** If loss hereunder is made payable, in whole
69 **interests and** or in part, to a designated mortgagee not
70 **obligations.** named herein as the insured, such interest in
71 this policy may be cancelled by giving to such
72 mortgagee a ten days' written notice of can-
73 cellation.
74 If the insured fails to render proof of loss such mortgagee, upon
75 notice, shall render proof of loss in the form herein specified
76 within sixty (60) days thereafter and shall be subject to the pro-
77 visions hereof relating to appraisal and time of payment and of
78 bringing suit. If this Company shall claim that no liability ex-
79 isted as to the mortgagor or owner, it shall, to the extent of pay-
80 ment of loss to the mortgagee, be subrogated to all the mort-
81 gagee's rights of recovery, but without impairing mortgagee's
82 right to sue; or it may pay off the mortgage debt and require
83 an assignment thereof and of the mortgage. Other provisions

84 relating to the interests and obligations of such mortgagee may
85 be added hereto by agreement in writing.
86 **Pro rata liability.** This Company shall not be liable for a greater
87 proportion of any loss than the amount
88 hereby insured shall bear to the whole insurance covering the
89 property against the peril involved, whether collectible or not.
90 **Requirements in** The insured shall give immediate written
91 **case loss occurs.** notice to this Company of any loss, protect
92 the property from further damage, forthwith
93 separate the damaged and undamaged personal property, put
94 it in the best possible order, furnish a complete inventory of
95 the destroyed, damaged and undamaged property, showing in
96 detail quantities, costs, actual cash value and amount of loss
97 claimed; **and within sixty days after the loss, unless such time**
98 **is extended in writing by this Company, the insured shall render**
99 **to this Company a proof of loss,** signed and sworn to by the
100 insured, stating the knowledge and belief of the insured as to
101 the following: the time and origin of the loss, the interest of the
102 insured and of all others in the property, the actual cash value of
103 each item thereof and the amount of loss thereto, all encum-
104 brances thereon, all other contracts of insurance, whether valid
105 or not, covering any of said property, any changes in the title,
106 use, occupation, location, possession or exposures of said prop-
107 erty since the issuing of this policy, by whom and for what
108 purpose any building herein described and the several parts
109 thereof were occupied at the time of loss and whether or not it
110 then stood on leased ground, and shall furnish a copy of all the
111 descriptions and schedules in all policies and, if required, verified
112 plans and specifications of any building, fixtures or machinery
113 destroyed or damaged. The insured, as often as may be reason-
114 ably required, shall exhibit to any person designated by this
115 Company all that remains of any property herein described, and
116 submit to examinations under oath by any person named by this
117 Company, and subscribe the same; and, as often as may be
118 reasonably required, shall produce for examination all books of
119 account, bills, invoices and other vouchers, or certified copies
120 thereof if originals be lost, at such reasonable time and place as
121 may be designated by this Company or its representative, and
122 shall permit extracts and copies thereof to be made.
123 **Appraisal.** In case the insured and this Company shall
124 fail to agree as to the actual cash value or
125 the amount of loss, then, on the written demand of either, each
126 shall select a competent and disinterested appraiser and notify
127 the other of the appraiser selected within twenty days of such
128 demand. The appraisers shall first select a competent and dis-
129 interested umpire; and failing for fifteen days to agree upon
130 such umpire, then, on request of the insured or this Company,
131 such umpire shall be selected by a judge of a court of record in
132 the state in which the property covered is located. The ap-
133 praisers shall then appraise the loss, stating separately actual
134 cash value and loss to each item; and, failing to agree, shall
135 submit their differences, only, to the umpire. An award in writ-
136 ing, so itemized, of any two when filed with this Company shall
137 determine the amount of actual cash value and loss. Each
138 appraiser shall be paid by the party selecting him and the ex-
139 penses of appraisal and umpire shall be paid by the parties
140 equally.
141 **Company's** It shall be optional with this Company to
142 **options.** take all, or any part, of the property at the
143 agreed or appraised value, and also to re-
144 pair, rebuild or replace the property destroyed or damaged with
145 other of like kind and quality within a reasonable time, on giv-
146 ing notice of its intention so to do within thirty days after the
147 receipt of the proof of loss herein required.
148 **Abandonment.** There can be no abandonment to this Com-
149 pany of any property.
150 **When loss** The amount of loss for which this Company
151 **payable.** may be liable shall be payable sixty days
152 after proof of loss, as herein provided, is
153 received by this Company and ascertainment of the loss is made
154 either by agreement between the insured and this Company ex-
155 pressed in writing or by the filing with this Company of an
156 award as herein provided.
157 **Suit.** No suit or action on this policy for the recov-
158 ery of any claim shall be sustainable in any
159 court of law or equity unless all the requirements of this policy
160 shall have been complied with, and unless commenced within
161 twelve months next after inception of the loss.
162 **Subrogation.** This Company may require from the insured
163 an assignment of all right of recovery against
164 any party for loss to the extent that payment therefor is made
165 by this Company.

IN WITNESS WHEREOF, this Company has executed and attested these presents; but this policy shall not be valid unless countersigned by the duly authorized Agent of this Company at the agency hereinbefore mentioned.

did not apply, and some of the provisions in the attached form(s) were incomplete without the 165 lines. Despite these problems, for many years states continued to require that the standard fire policy be a part of all policies providing fire and allied lines coverage. Gradually, however, forms were introduced that combined all the necessary provisions into a single policy and eliminated those provisions that did not apply.

A further blow to the standard fire policy developed in the late 1970s and early 1980s, with the push for policy simplification and readability. Not only was the standard-fire-policy-plus-form approach unnecessarily complex, but also the language failed to meet readability tests. For example, the insuring agreement was one 229-word sentence, and another sentence was thirteen lines long (lines 90 to 113). The trend in the 1980s has been to use the standard fire policy only where it is required by law. This is usually done by an endorsement that says, in effect, "The law requires that your policy include these words." In Michigan, for example, the policy begins:

> The provisions of the Standard Fire Policy are stated below. State law still requires that they be attached to all policies. If any conditions of this form are construed to be more liberal than any other policy conditions relating to the perils of fire, lightning or removal, the conditions of this form will apply.[1]

Standard "Commercial Fire" Policies

Today, the most widely used standard insurance policies are those developed by Insurance Services Office, Inc. (ISO). ISO is a national nonprofit corporation of property-liability insurance companies that exists to serve the needs of those member companies. ISO was formed in 1971 through the consolidation of six separate national service bureaus. Nine local or regional property bureaus were also brought into ISO.

Before the formation of ISO, each rating bureau had its own forms and rates. After ISO, standardization did not immediately take place. In its earlier years, ISO maintained varying coverage forms for different sections of the country. Though ISO was a national organization, it still had regional forms. Thus, the ISO form that was used to provide building and contents coverage in California was different from that used in the Northeast, while the southeastern states used yet another set of forms. In the late 1970s, however, ISO introduced national "commercial fire" forms, with form numbers bearing the "CF" prefix.

Package Policies and the SMP

While "commercial fire" policies were evolving, other sets of policy forms were also being developed independently by insurance companies and rating bureaus. Commercial package policies began to appear during the 1950s. A variety of forms, developed by a variety of rating bureaus, eventually took on some uniformity in the early 1960s with the introduction of standard package policies for certain commercial classes of business such as motels, apartment houses, hotels, and offices.

These separate programs were unified in 1966 under a Special Multi-Peril (SMP) Program. The SMP program underwent major revisions in 1973 and again in 1977, before being replaced by the Commercial Package Policy Program in 1986-87.

While the original SMP included the standard fire policy, the 1977 edition was designed to be complete without the 165 lines. Instead, the "general conditions form" included all applicable provisions of the standard fire policy, modified in some cases to provide broader coverage.

The SMP was a package policy providing both property and liability coverages through an appropriate combination of forms. A package discount reflected the reduced cost of handling a variety of coverages and also the fact that SMP policies were intended primarily for preferred-risk accounts (at least, this was the intent at the inception of the program).

Policy Simplification

As of the early 1980s, there were two ways of providing similar commercial property coverage:

- a *monoline* policy comprising a standard fire policy and a "commercial fire" form, or
- a *package* special multi-peril (SMP) policy, including more modern conditions in place of the 165 lines (and the 165 lines if required by state law) and also including liability coverage—and possibly also inland marine, crime, and boiler and machinery coverages.

Each successive change increased the similarity between monoline and package property policies; yet, the commercial fire and the special multi-peril forms differed in many details. The previous edition of this text devoted a number of pages to pointing out these distinguishing details. Current readers may be grateful that these distinctions no longer exist in the simplified forms.

During the early 1980s it became obvious that ISO needed to update most commercial forms, especially the comprehensive general liability form that had been in use since 1973. Since this change would require substantial revision of a major portion of its commercial policies, the decision was made to make a simultaneous across-the-board revision of most commercial policies, so that all would follow the same "simplified" policywriting style. At the same time, rating programs were simplified, modernized, and revised. The initial simplified forms bore 1985 dates and were phased into use during 1986 and 1987.

There is no real name for the forms in ISO's current policy series. Where a label is needed, they are usually referred to as "simplified" policies or forms; earlier versions are then called "pre-simplified" or "nonsimplified." The current forms are, indeed, much simpler than their predecessors. The writing style is more readable, the format is more easily followed, and the coverages have been made more straightforward.

A major result of the "commercial lines simplification project" is that differences between monoline and package policies have been eliminated. The standard fire policy is no longer used (except in states that require the 165 lines to appear somewhere in the document). The difference between a monoline policy and a commercial package policy is that a commercial package policy must include two or more of the following coverage parts:

1. Boiler and Machinery
2. Commercial Auto
3. Commercial Property
4. Commercial Crime
5. Commercial General Liability
6. Commercial Inland Marine
7. Farm
8. Liquor Liability
9. Owners and Contractors Protective Liability
10. Pollution Liability
11. Products/Completed Operations Liability

A commercial package policy is eligible for a premium discount, called a *package modification factor*, if the policy includes:

1. a "commercial property" coverage form that provides building and/or personal property coverage with an 80 percent or higher coinsurance clause[2] and
2. any coverage part that includes premises and operations liability coverage for bodily injury and property damage.

Exhibit 3-3
Contents of the ISO Commercial Package Policy (CPP)

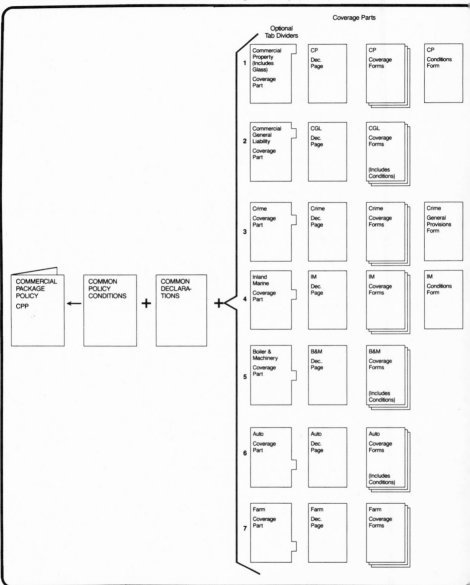

A commercial general liability form is usually used to meet the second requirement, but a farm or garage liability form would also be acceptable.

SIMPLIFIED COMMERCIAL POLICIES

Simplified commercial package policies can be used to provide many different coverages to businesses and other organizations. A simplified commercial policy requires several different forms, as illustrated in Exhibit 3-3.

Commercial Policy Structure

Most simplified policies are modular in nature. All such commercial policies contain two modules:

- *common declarations*—containing such things as the name and address of the insured, and
- *common policy conditions*—containing some basic provisions that apply to all policies, regardless of which coverages are included.

Beyond that, the selection of forms for any given insured depends on what coverages are needed. If property insurance is desired to cover a store's direct loss exposures arising out of its building and contents, the following forms would be added:

- *commercial property declarations form*—containing such things as a description of the covered building,
- *commercial property conditions form*—a module containing a variety of basic provisions that apply to policies that include property insurance,
- *building and personal property coverage form (BPP)*—stating precisely what types of property the insurer intends to cover and including other relevant provisions, and one or more
- *causes-of-loss forms.*

Endorsements might be added, as appropriate.

Three different "causes-of-loss" forms are available, and the choice depends on what perils are to be insured. The *causes of loss—basic form* lists eleven covered perils. The *causes of loss—broad form* lists fifteen. The *causes of loss—special form* is an "all-risks" type form that does not list covered perils, but instead covers perils that are not excluded. The same "causes-of-loss form" may apply to both building and contents—and also to business income coverage: or different causes-of-loss forms may be selected for the different coverages. By combining the right set of forms and making appropriate entries in the declarations, it is possible, for example, to construct the policy so that the building is covered for "all-risks," while the contents are covered for broad named perils, with business income coverage for basic causes of loss.

If the intention is to provide general liability insurance coverage for the same storeowner, a commercial general liability coverage form can be added and the combination is known as a "commercial package policy." Boiler and machinery, crime, and inland marine coverages are among others that may be added.

Terminology

Before progressing further, it is necessary to clearly distinguish among coverage parts, monoline policies, commercial package policies, and commercial package policies qualifying for a discount (package modification factor).

Coverage Part A *coverage part* consists of:

- one or more *line of business declarations,*
- one or more *coverage forms,* and
- applicable endorsements.

Monoline Policy A coverage part becomes a *monoline policy* with the attachment of:

- *common policy declarations* (which may be combined with the line of business declarations in a single form), and
- *common policy conditions.*

Commercial Package Policy Alternatively, a coverage part may become part of a *commercial package policy* (CPP) in combination with:

- at least one more *coverage part,*
- a *common policy declarations,* and
- a *common policy conditions.*

A package policy is eligible for a premium discount, known as a *package modification factor,* if it includes (1) "commercial property" building and/or contents coverage and (2) premises and operations bodily injury and property damage liability coverage, as noted earlier. Because an insurer uses the same set of policy forms to create either a monoline or package policy, there is no difference in coverage between monoline policy forms and policy forms used in a commercial package, but the package may involve a lower premium.

Most ISO commercial lines forms fit into the modular format described here. There are exceptions, however—notably the monoline standard property policy (a "bare bones" property policy described in Chapter 6) and the businessowners policy (a more-or-less indivisible package policy described in Chapter 13).

COMMON POLICY CONDITIONS

For policies using the simplified, modular format, a single set of conditions applies to all coverages in the policy. These conditions apply to both property and liability insurance contracts.

The term *first named insured* has special significance for some provisions in the common policy conditions. The policy assigns to this one insured individual who is named first (who may indeed be a corporation or a partnership, if so shown in the declarations) the duty and rights of representation of all named insureds in some cases—for example, payment of premium. The reason for this is that many commercial policies are written on exposures in which a variety of parties have an interest, as subsidiaries or parents, as lenders, as joint venturers, and so on. In order to avoid the confusion that such a plethora of interests would create in administrating an insurance policy, the contract reduces the number of parties with whom the insurer must deal to one, for management's sake.

All parties to the transaction must give special attention to who is shown as the *first* named insured in the policy, since this will be the party with whom the insurer will deal.

Cancellation

The cancellation clause states how the insurer and the insured can go about canceling the policy. The *first named insured* may cancel the policy by mailing or delivering to the insurer advance written notice of the cancellation, stating the future date on which coverage is to cease.

The *insurer* may cancel by giving written notice to the first named insured. Ten days' notice is required when the insurer cancels for nonpayment of premium; otherwise thirty days' notice is required. Many state laws require longer advance notice and restrict the reasons for which an insurer may cancel a policy. These state requirements may or may not be reflected in an endorsement to the policy. To effect cancellation, the insurance company must mail or deliver notice to the last known mailing address of the first named insured shown in the policy. This notice must state the effective date of the cancellation.

When the *insurer* cancels, a pro rata refund of unearned premium must be sent to the first named insured. The pro rata refund is equal to the number of days left on the policy divided by the number of days in the policy term and multiplied by the total policy premium. When the *insured* cancels, the refund may be less than pro rata. The "short rate" is often 90 percent of the pro rata refund. An exception to the short rate rule applies when the insured cancels because the insured no longer has an insurable interest in the covered property. In such cases, manual rules state that the insurer should make a pro rata refund, but there is no provision in the policy itself addressing such situations.

Changes

Modifications in the policy may be made by the first named insured if the insurance company consents. To effect the change, the insurer issues a written endorsement which is made a part of the policy.

Perhaps the most significant part of the changes provision is not that it permits changes, but that it *limits* policy changes. The provision states that the written policy contains all agreements between insurer and insured and that these agreements can be amended or waived *only* when the insurer issues a written endorsement and makes it a part of the policy. (Note, however, that court decisions have frequently held that such "entire contract" provisions may themselves be waived orally or in writing by the insurer.)

Examination of Books and Records

The insurer has the contractual right to examine the books and records of the insured that relate to the insurance policy during the policy period and up to three years after the policy has expired. This condition is included so that the insurer can verify that statements made by the insured are accurate and, in the case of auditable policies, to determine the correct premium.

Insurance premiums for commercial insurance policies are often based on such things as annual payroll, annual sales, dollar value of goods in stock, or similar things that are recorded in the insured's financial records. *Premium auditors* employed by insurance companies need to examine these financial records in order to determine the proper premium to charge. The examination of books and records provision makes it clear that the insured must permit the premium auditor to examine the books and records as necessary.

Inspections and Surveys

Many insurance companies employ *loss control representatives* to inspect the premises and operations of businesses that apply for insurance. While the policy is in force, loss control representatives may also make inspections and surveys, give reports to the insured, and recommend changes that the insurer would like to see made. A typical recommendation might be that fire extinguishers be of a proper type and capacity to handle a given situation.

The inspections and surveys provision makes it clear that the insurance company has the right to make such inspections and surveys.

The condition also states that these are not safety inspections, that the insurance company does not take on the responsibility of protecting workers or the public from injury, and that the insurance company does not warrant that the business it inspected is safe or healthful or complies with applicable laws. This disclaimer is included because certain courts have held insurers liable for losses supposedly related to the inadequacy of such inspections.

This clause gives not only the insurer, but also various rating and advisory organizations, the inspection right. An ISO subsidiary, Commercial Risk Services, Inc. (CRS) conducts property rating surveys on commercial and personal properties to help companies set accurate premiums for those buildings. This policy provision includes the CRS field rating representative under the protection of the disclaimer.

CRS and other organizations also provide loss control service to insurers for a fee. These organizations must also be permitted to make inspections and surveys, according to policy terms.

Transfer of Rights and Duties Under the Policy

This so-called *assignment provision* deals with two situations in which it may be desirable to assign the policy to another party. One type of situation arises when the named insured sells an insured property or business operation and desires to transfer the insurance to the new owner along with other assets. The provision states that the named insured's rights and duties cannot be transferred without the insurer's written consent. Insurance is a personal contract, and the insurance company needs to be able to decide whether it wants to protect each individual insured; such underwriting approval would not be possible if coverage could be transferred at will from one person to another.

The second situation occurs when a named insured dies. The property usually continues to exist—and to be exposed to loss. In such a case, the insured's rights and duties in connection with covered property are automatically transferred to anyone having proper temporary custody of property. Coverage also applies to the named insured's legal representative, once he or she is appointed. The legal representative is not protected for other ventures, and is covered only while performing duties as a legal representative.

As a practical matter, insurers are seldom requested to assign insurance coverage. When a property or business is sold, the named insured's interest ceases and the named insured is entitled to receive a pro rata refund of the unearned premium. The new owner then purchases his or her own insurance. But when a named insured dies, this provision facilitates an orderly transfer of continuous coverage to the named insured's heirs.

"COMMERCIAL PROPERTY" CONDITIONS

The commercial property form contains nine conditions. These conditions apply to all "commercial property" insurance contracts, whether monoline policies or part of a commercial package.

Concealment, Misrepresentation, or Fraud

This provision states that the coverage part is void in case of fraud related to the insurance. In addition, intentional concealment or misrepresentation of a material fact with respect to the coverage part, covered property, or the insured's interest in the property voids the policy. Statutory or case law in a given state will void any contract affected by fraud, whether or not the contract addresses the situation. But there is no doubt as to the effect of a concealment or misrepresentation when the insurance contract is explicit.

Control of Property

If the insured does not have control of the property (for example, when an entire building is rented to another firm), any act of neglect by others will not affect coverage. The insured is not held responsible for the actions of others who are not under his or her direction.

On the other hand, certain types of neglect and intentional acts of the named insured will affect coverage. In situations where more than one location is insured, a violation of policy conditions with respect to one location will relieve the insurer of its duties to cover loss *at that location*. Coverage at other insured locations is unaffected.

Insurance Under Two or More Coverages

Some items of property might conceivably be covered by both building and personal property coverage. Similarly, theft of a building's contents might be covered by a crime coverage form, as well as a personal property coverage form in the same commercial package policy. In situations where more than one of the policy's first-party coverages may apply to damaged property, the insurer will not pay more than the actual amount of the loss. If duplicate coverage exists in the same policy, the insured receives full payment for the loss but is not allowed to collect twice.

Legal Action Against Us

Before an insured can sue or otherwise bring legal action against the insurer under the terms of the insurance contract, he or she must comply with all the terms in the coverage part and must initiate any such action against the insurer within two years of the date of the loss.

Liberalization

Protection is automatically broadened if the insurer broadens (or "liberalizes") the coverage part (that is, any "commercial property" form that is part of the policy) (1) within 45 days before or (2) at any time during the policy period. This condition applies only if the broadened coverage does not increase the premium of the policy.

This condition benefits both the insured and the insurer. The insured receives the broadened coverage, and the insurer does not have to issue a new policy or a set of endorsements to every current insured every time a liberalization is made.

The liberalization clause may operate to broaden coverage, but it will never restrict coverage. If the insurer adopts a revision that narrows coverage, the new restriction does *not* apply to policies already issued.

No Benefit to Bailee

Sometimes property is damaged while it is in the custody of a bailee—such as a trucking company, airline, railroad, or repair service. In such circumstances, the commercial property form will pay the insured(s) for any covered loss, but will not treat the bailee as an insured. In fact, the insurer may subrogate against the bailee. The bailee is supposed to be accountable for his or her own actions, and it is not the insurer's intention to protect the bailee.

An important exception lies in the words "other than you [the named insured]." The *no benefit to bailee provision* does not void coverage of the named insured if the named insured is a bailee of property that sustains damage.

Other Insurance

The "other insurance" clause addresses two situations and offers two different solutions. In one, the insurer pays on a pro rata basis; in the other, on an excess basis.

- When another policy is subject to the same terms, conditions, and provisions as the coverage part, the insurer agrees to pay its share on a pro rata basis (policy limit of the coverage part divided by the total of all applicable policy limits, times the loss).
- If the other insurance does not have the same terms, conditions, and provisions, the insurer agrees to pay on an excess basis (the other insurer exhausts its limits, and then the insurer that issued this policy pays).

Because other insurance can take many forms, this brief "other insurance" clause clearly does not take into account every conceivable situation. Most insurers abide by a set of principles designed to allocate liability among insurers whose policies differ and to preserve protection for insureds. These principles are expressed in a document known as the *Guiding Principles—Casualty, Fidelity, Inland Marine—First-Party Property Losses and Claims*,[3] usually referred to as simply the *Guiding Principles*.

Policy Period and Coverage Territory

The policy period is determined by the date(s) or time period shown on the policy declarations page. It usually starts at 12:01 A.M. standard time of the address shown on that page. The coverage territory is the United States of America, Puerto Rico, and Canada. Property located in Mexico, South America, and other parts of the world is not insured under the "commercial property" coverage part.

Transfer of Rights of Recovery Against Others to Us

This subrogation condition describes the insurance company's right to recover from third parties who may be responsible for damage to the covered property. After the insurer has paid an insured for the damage to the covered property, the insurance company has the right to seek recovery from any third party to the extent the insurer made payment to the insured. If the insurer paid the insured $50,000, then it may seek to recover up to $50,000 from the third party through a process called *subrogation*. The insured is not supposed to take any action after the loss that will hinder the insurer's ability to subrogate.

The named insured may waive his or her right of recovery if done in writing before the loss occurs. After the loss occurs, the insured can waive its recovery rights against:

- someone else covered by the "commercial property" form (e.g. where property not owned by the named insured is covered by the policy),
- a business firm that is owned by the named insured or one that owns the named insured's firm (e.g., if ABC owns XYZ, ABC's insurer may not subrogate against XYZ and XYZ's insurer may not subrogate against ABC), and
- a tenant of the named insured.

CANCELLATION CHANGES ENDORSEMENT

The anti-arson *cancellation changes endorsement* provides that the insurer may cancel the commercial property coverage with only five days' notice in the following five situations.

Vacancy or Unoccupancy

The cancellation changes endorsement may be invoked when the building has been *vacant* or *unoccupied* for sixty consecutive days or more. In insurance terminology, *unoccupied* means operations or other activities in the building are suspended, but contents remain in the building. *Vacant* means the building does not contain any contents pertaining to the operations or activities customary to the occupancy of the building.

Either vacancy or unoccupancy presents problems for an insurer. For example, an unoccupied building attracts vandals and burglars. Problems such as a defective heating system may not be discovered before serious damage results. A vacant building, with no contents to protect, may have little security. Both extended vacancy and unoccupancy suggest that a building is providing no economic value to its owner.

"Commercial property" forms suspend coverage after sixty days of vacancy for loss by vandalism, sprinkler leakage, building glass breakage, water damage, and theft or attempted theft. For all other perils, loss recovery is reduced by 15 percent after sixty days of vacancy. Full coverage for a vacant building may be "bought back" for an additional premium by adding a *vacancy permit* endorsement. Of course, underwriters will examine the circumstances behind the vacancy before granting a vacancy permit.

The cancellation changes endorsement explicitly does *not* permit the insurer to cancel with five days' notice in three situations:

1. *Seasonal unoccupancy*—some schools, canneries, and recreational facilities, for example, are seasonal in nature. Off-season unoccupancy does not reflect an unusual condition.
2. *Buildings in the course of construction, renovation, or addition*—Such buildings clearly do not suggest a lack of economic value, since the owner is actively increasing their economic value.
3. *Buildings to which the vacancy permit endorsement applies.*

Unrepaired Damage

Coverage may be canceled with five days' notice if, after damage by a covered cause of loss, permanent repairs have not started and have not been contracted for within thirty days of the initial payment of loss. Insureds are expected to repair a damaged building after the loss occurs and they have received payment from the insurer. Damaged structures are more likely to suffer losses by vandalism or damage by natural elements than buildings that are in good repair.

Condemned Buildings

The insurer may cancel coverage with five days' notice on a building that has an outstanding order to be vacated or demolished or has been declared unsafe by governmental authority. Buildings that are subject to any of these proceedings are likely candidates for arson, as they are probably insured for more than they are now worth. Since the moral and morale hazards are high, the insurer needs to be able to cancel quickly.

Buildings Being Stripped

Another danger signal, and a situation where cancellation is often necessary, applies to buildings whose fixed and salvageable fixtures have been removed and are not being replaced. Removal of such items for renovation and remodeling is permitted.

Failure to Maintain Property or Pay Taxes

Failure of the insured to provide necessary heat, water, sewer service, or electricity for thirty consecutive days (except for seasonal unoccupancy situations), or failure to pay property taxes for one year (unless there is a bona fide dispute with the taxing authority) also provides grounds for the insurer to cancel with five days' notice.

The Arson Problem

The issues surrounding the anti-arson *cancellation changes endorsement* are sensitive. Arson presents very serious problems for insurers and for society. In one recent year, the U.S. Fire Administration listed arson as the cause of almost one in every four fires in nonresidential structures, including schools, restaurants, garages, and manufacturing plants. The National Fire Protection Association estimated 110,500 fires that year of incendiary or suspicious origin, with $1.41 billion in direct property damage and 530 civilian deaths.[4] Measures are in order to reduce the economic incentives for arson, and this endorsement is one such step.

This is not to say that every arson is committed so that the insured can "sell" distressed property to the insurance company—a situation known as "arson for profit." Fires are intentionally set for many other reasons as well, including personal grudges, attempts to cover up criminal activity, and pyromania. Nor would it be fair to say that every building that is empty, unrepaired, and so forth is a sure-fire candidate for arson. Insurers need to exercise their cancellation rights with extreme care. Counterbalancing the arson problem are the often legitimate needs of insureds to maintain continuous coverage. Insurers are likely to receive very little praise, but a great deal of unjustified blame, when they invoke the cancellation changes endorsement to cancel coverage—even though, in some cases, cancellation literally prevents arson.

In many states, the cancellation changes endorsement is not available since it would contradict the terms of state cancellation and nonrenewal laws and regulations. Even so, such symptoms of potential arson are seriously considered by insurers when coverage is to be granted or continued.

THE BUILDING AND PERSONAL PROPERTY COVERAGE FORM (BPP)

The ISO building and personal property form (BPP) is the form most widely used to insure commercial buildings and their contents. Most other building and contents forms, described in later chapters, will be analyzed by noting how they compare with the BPP. Discussion in this text is based on the November 1985 edition of the BPP and a few subsequent endorsements, mentioned later. This form began to be used during 1986 and 1987. The material in this section of the chapter will be most easily understood if the reader has a copy of the form at hand.

The discussion will first deal with the categories of property covered by the form—real property, owned personal property, and nonowned personal property. Following this, the discussion deals with:

- locations at which property is covered,
- rights of insureds,
- additional coverages,
- clauses defining the amount of covered loss, and
- provisions dealing with loss adjustment.

Covered causes of loss (perils) will be discussed in detail in Chapter 4. Likewise, analysis of the BPP in this chapter does not deal extensively with valuation of insured property, which is also discussed in Chapter 4.

Categories of Covered Property

Descriptions of the exposures covered by the BPP appear under three different headings:

1. Covered Property,
2. Additional Coverages, and
3. Coverage Extensions (which apply only when a coinsurance percentage of 80 or higher is shown in the Declarations).

Also highly relevant in determining the extent of coverage is the portion of the BPP titled "Property Not Covered."

Three broad categories of covered property are described in the building and personal property coverage form (BPP):

1. building(s),
2. personal property of the insured, and
3. personal property of others.

The commercial property coverage part declarations page notes that:

Insurance at the described premises applies only for coverages for which a limit of insurance is shown.

Therefore, coverage in any of these categories applies only when an amount of insurance for that category is indicated in the declarations. For example, if the declarations show no limit for building coverage, the policy provides no building coverage—even though the BPP contains a section describing building coverage.

Many insureds do not require coverage in every category.

- The owner of a building rented to others might purchase coverage only for the building.

- A tenant might cover only personal property of the insured, or might also purchase coverage on the personal property of others.
- An owner-occupant with a bailee exposure might purchase coverage in all three categories.

Real Property The description in the declarations includes the building's location, construction, and the nature of its occupancy. If these descriptions are materially wrong, the coverage *may* be voidable, since coverage applies only to items specifically described. Usually, covered real property is owned by the insured. However, it would not be inappropriate for a lessee to insure a leased building if required to do so by the terms of the lease.

The building and personal property coverage form (BPP) describes what property is covered under the "building" coverage as follows:

> **Building,** meaning the building or structure described in the Declarations, including:
> (1) Completed additions;
> (2) Permanently installed fixtures, machinery and equipment;
> (3) Outdoor fixtures;
> (4) Personal property owned by you that is used to maintain or service the building or structure or its premises, including;
>   (a) Fire extinguishing equipment;
>   (b) Outdoor furniture;
>   (c) Floor coverings; and
>   (d) Appliances used for refrigerating, ventilating, cooking, dishwashing or laundering;
> (5) If not covered by other insurance:
>   (a) Additions under construction, alterations and repairs to the building or structure;
>   (b) Materials, equipment, supplies and temporary structures, on or within 100 feet of the described premises, used for making additions, alterations or repairs to the building or structure.

Earlier policies used a long paragraph to describe these items. By numbering the various categories of property, the simplified policy makes it easier to modify or delete coverage by endorsement for a certain type of property.

Besides the building and additions, the building coverage provisions include some additional property. Inclusion of permanently installed fixtures, machinery, and equipment means that building coverage would apply to refrigeration equipment in cold storage houses, fixed seats in theaters, and permanently installed pipe organs in churches. Also noteworthy is the inclusion of some furnishings under the building coverage. Covered furnishings include carpets and refrigerating, ventilating, cooking, dishwashing, and laundering equipment owned by the landlord.

The building coverage section also provides protection for personal property used to maintain or service the building or its premises. Window washing and floor cleaning equipment and materials are examples of such personal property. Coverage for this property applies while the property is located on the described premises. Outdoor fixtures and furniture (flagpoles and patio furniture, for example), are also protected by the building coverage. The reason for this is to provide coverage for a limited amount of personal property that is owned by a landlord and to avoid the need to purchase small amounts of coverage on personal property. However, in owner-occupied buildings, this overlaps with the personal property coverage.

Some property is specifically not covered. Although the BPP does not separate property not covered into a "building" category, many excluded items might properly be classified as building items—or, at least, as real property.

Not covered are:

- land;
- water;[5]
- bridges;
- roadways, walks, patios, or other paved surfaces;
- retaining walls that are not a part of the described building;
- piers, wharves, or docks;
- the cost of excavations, grading, backfillings, or filling;
- pilings;
- foundations below the lowest basement floor or, if there is no basement, the surface of the ground; and
- underground pipes, flues, or drains.

With respect to the last two items, note that foundations *are* covered, *except* for those that are below the basement or, if there is no basement, below the surface of the ground. Likewise, pipes, flues, and drains *are* covered property, except when they are underground.

Excavations are not covered property. When a building is a total loss, the excavation (the hole for the basement and foundations), underground pipes, and so forth are seldom damaged.

If these items were covered, the insured would have to include their value in determining the amount of insurance to be carried to meet coinsurance requirements (explained later). Thus, the insured would be required to purchase insurance against exposures with a very low probability of loss. To prevent this, such property is excluded from coverage and is thus not included in determining values to meet coinsurance requirements. It should be noted, however, that while the probability of loss to this property is extremely low, such property is not *totally* immune from damage, as from an explosion. Coverage can generally be added by endorsement, where it is desired.

To determine just how significant the removal of this property from coverage is, one can investigate building cost data. Foundations for most building types account for between 2.5 percent and 5 percent of total building value. Excavation costs may contribute from 0.22 percent to 5.5 percent of the total cost of constructing a building.[6] These figures can represent a substantial amount of money, and insureds need to realize that excavations and some foundations are not covered. If a building is totally destroyed and new excavation work and new foundations have to be completed, the insured will have to provide the extra funds. Since this provision may be removed by endorsement, it can be important to determine whether the exposure is serious. When the exclusion is removed, the amount of insurance should reflect the increased coverage.

A second category of excluded property could be loosely classified as plants and other outdoor property—specifically:

- growing crops and lawns;
- outdoor grain, hay, straw, or other harvested crops;
- outdoor trees, shrubs, and plants;
- outdoor fences, radio and television antennas or towers, and signs not attached to buildings.

These items would generally not be considered part of a building, but might qualify as real property. It would not make sense to include their values as part of the building item, and they are not necessarily exposed to the same losses as buildings. Exceptions exist, of course. For example, lawns can be badly damaged by firefighting equipment.

On the other hand, others of these excluded items are so susceptible to some causes of loss that they are uninsurable for those perils. For example, outdoor trees are rather routinely damaged by wind, as are fences and outdoor signs.

Although outdoor trees, shrubs, plants, fences, and signs attached to a building are specifically excluded from the broad coverage of the BPP, limited coverage is provided as a coverage extension. Regardless of whether basic, broad, or special causes of loss to the building are covered, these outdoor items are covered only for the perils of fire, lightning, riot or civil commotion, and aircraft.

The effect of this treatment is that these outdoor items are not covered for the perils for which loss can routinely be expected—windstorm or hail, vehicle damage, smoke, or vandalism. Such coverage would usually result in high frequency, low severity losses best handled by noninsurance techniques. Where loss occurs due to a covered peril, coverage under this extension is limited to a nominal amount.

Another condition applies: For the coverage extension to be activated, there must be an 80 percent or higher coinsurance clause. This extension of coverage adds $1,000 of additional coverage to the policy, but only $250 or less may be used to replace any one tree, plant, or shrub.

Insureds needing more extensive coverage on landscaping can purchase a separate amount of insurance applying specifically to such property.

Owned Personal Property   Coverage for owned personal property can be handled in a variety of ways. In older policies, a building's contents were separated into two categories—(1) stock, and (2) contents other than stock. Later practice was to combine both categories as "contents" or "personal property of the insured." The BPP has gone back in the other direction and describes six categories of *personal property of the insured*, each of which can be written under a separate limit or included in a blanket "personal property" limit without differentiation. Four of the categories are:

1. furniture and fixtures,
2. machinery and equipment,
3. "stock," and
4. all other personal property owned by you and used in your business.

The other categories are discussed later.

Such a broad definition is best examined in the light of what it does *not* cover, as provided elsewhere in the policy. Also, coverage is either restricted or eliminated for some types of personal property.

Money, notes, and securities are excluded, as are accounts, bills, currency, deeds, and evidences of debt. Essentially the same list of excluded property appeared in the 1943 standard fire policy.

Motor vehicles, aircraft, and watercraft are subject to exclusions in most fire and allied lines insurance forms. Where significant exposures exist, coverage usually must be purchased separately in auto, aircraft, or marine insurance policies. The BPP exclusions, however, are not so broad as to exclude all coverage for these classes of personal property.

Rowboats and canoes out of the water are covered because of an exception to the exclusion.

Coverage generally applies to aircraft, watercraft, and other vehicles that:

1. are *not* licensed for use on public roads,

2. are operated primarily on the described premises, and
3. are manufactured, processed, or held for sale.

For example, self-propelled lawn mowers held for sale by a garden shop would be covered, but mowers used in its landscaping operations would not.

A separate exclusion eliminates coverage for autos held for sale (for example, used cars in a dealer's garage). Coverage may, however, be added by describing such vehicles in the policy declarations or by endorsing coverage to the policy. This might be done when vehicles in a fleet for which physical damage losses are otherwise retained are garaged in the same building overnight. On the road, the maximum probable loss is small and within the organization's ability to absorb loss. At night, the concentration of vehicles may raise the maximum probable loss beyond the level the firm wishes to retain, so it may choose to insure only this "overnight" exposure.

Animals owned by the insured are specifically excluded in the BPP. However, the exclusion applies only to animals not held for sale or boarded. A kennel exposure, for example, would be covered.

Valuable papers and records coverage was quite limited under earlier forms. Books of account, abstracts, drawings, card index systems, and other records (except electronic data processing records) were insured—but only for the cost of blank materials and the cost incurred to transcribe such records. Electronic data processing records were covered only for the cost of blank cards, tapes, and disks. In effect, only the intrinsic value of the materials containing the records was covered. The cost of redeveloping the information and any loss suffered because the information could not be redeveloped were not.

At first glance, the BPP seems to provide similar treatment. However, a coverage extension adds a small amount of true valuable papers insurance—$1,000 may be used to cover the cost of research and other expenses to replace or restore damaged records, including those existing in computerized form. This protection applies only when the policy is subject to an 80 percent or higher coinsurance clause.

The $1,000 of coverage provided here will meet only incidental needs. It is not intended to cover valuable papers and records losses of any real significance. Moreover, even when the special causes-of-loss form applies, coverage is limited to certain specified perils—those covered by the causes of loss—broad form. If a serious loss exposure exists, regular "all-risks" type valuable papers coverage or a form specifically designed for electronic data processing exposures should be purchased. Such forms are discussed in later chapters of this text.

Nonowned Property Two, types of nonowned property are addressed in the BPP: (1) tenant's improvements and betterments (which are real property) and (2) personal property of others.

Tenant's Use Interest in Improvements and Betterments. The sixth category of property listed in the personal property coverage provision protects a tenant's use interest in improvements that have been added by the tenant to the landlord's building. This is not quite the same thing as saying the improvements and betterments are covered property.

Since improvements and betterments are actually real property, rather than personal property, one might wonder why coverage falls under the "contents" portion of the policy. The reason is that the *need* for coverage accompanies the personal property exposures of a tenant, rather than the building exposures of a landlord. A party with building coverage would have no need to separately specify improvements and betterments coverage. If the building owner has building coverage, this automatically would include his or her interest in the improvements and betterments.

In the BPP, a tenant's use interest in improvements and betterments is automatically included whenever coverage on personal property of the insured is provided. The specific description of the covered exposure reads as follows:

> Your use interest as tenant in improvements and betterments. Improvements and betterments are fixtures, alterations, installations, or additions:
> (a) Made a part of the building or structure you occupy but do not own; and
> (b) You acquired or made at your expense but cannot legally remove.

The above definition of *improvements and betterments* does not include repairs or maintenance, such as painting the inside or the outside of the building. An improvement or betterment generally changes the building and enhances its value—that is, it "improves" or "betters" the real property. Examples of improvements and betterments include a new store front, partitions, accoustical insulation, elevators, floor coverings, and central air conditioning systems.

The question often arises whether an item is a trade fixture or an improvement. Ideally, such questions should be settled in the lease agreement, but often they are not. *Trade fixtures,* characterized by the right (or obligation) of the tenant to remove them when the premises are vacated, may include counters, machinery, and appliances. Whether an item is a trade fixture cannot always be established by looking at it—not even by examining the apparent firmness of its attachment to the structure. Many cases are determined by trade customs. Thus, walk-in freezers and refrigerators in a restaurant, and the stage machinery in a theater, although completely built-in and necessarily firmly attached to the structure are, by custom, trade fixtures and not building improvements. When a tenant buys improvements and betterments coverage, what is covered depends on general legal interpretation as to which installations constitute improvements to the landlord's building and which remain the tenant's trade fixtures.

As noted, a landlord's interest in any improvements is included under the landlord's building coverage. The amount of building insurance carried by the landlord, therefore, should reflect any values that tenants have added to the structure. Since landlord and tenant have simultaneous but separate insurable interests in the same property, each may buy insurance. In fact, in order to avoid a coinsurance penalty, the landlord should include the value of improvements and betterments when selecting a building insurance limit. Such coexistent insurance on separate interests is enforceable: The landlord can collect for the *loss* of owned property, and the tenant can collect on the basis of *loss of use* of the property. Paying for such separate insurance on the same property can be inefficient, and other solutions are available.

One alternative is for the owner and tenant to be named as insureds in a single policy. This arrangement negates the possibility of subrogation against either of the parties when that party's negligence causes the loss. Otherwise, the landlord's insurer, for example, may collect from the tenant when the tenant is legally responsible for the landlord's insured loss.

Owners and tenants do not always favor the idea of sharing a policy. When owner and tenant are jointly insured, acts of one may conceivably affect the coverage of the other. For example, contracts are voidable in the event of fraud by an insured. Another problem is that since the first named insured would have the right to cancel the policy, one named insured may have more control over the coverage than the other. These problems do not develop when each party has its own insurance.

A second alternative is for the lease to oblige one party to make repairs in the event of damage. Then the other party is protected to the extent the obligor can fulfill its obligation. A common arrangement is to assure financing by requiring the obligor to carry adequate insurance on the property. One premium, in effect, pays for protection for both parties. Yet, there is the possibility that the coverage may be abrogated by acts or omissions of the insured party.

The most common arrangement is for the landlord to carry insurance on the building, including the landlord's interest in the improvements, while the tenant insures its interest in the improvements. This is why many standard forms, including the BPP, provide automatic coverage on a tenant's interest in improvements when the tenant buys contents coverage.

Since the tenant's interest in the improvements lies in its right to use them, measurement of the tenant's loss requires special attention. The BPP specifies three different approaches that may be used in determining the tenant's recovery:

1. When the owner replaces the improvements without charge to the tenant, the tenant's insurance pays nothing.
2. When the tenant makes prompt repairs, the improvements and betterments coverage pays based on the actual cash value of the improvements just as though the tenant owned the improvements. In this case, the improvements and betterments are treated as any other covered property.
3. When the improvements are not replaced, payment is based on unamortized cost.

This third approach might best be explained with an example. Suppose improvements costing $50,000 were installed on June 1, 1988. On June 1, 1993, the improvements are destroyed and not replaced. At the time of the loss, the tenant has a lease running to June 1, 2003. The tenant invested $50,000, expecting to use the improvements for a period of fifteen years (1988 to 2003). However, only five of those fifteen years— or one-third of the expected life—had been used up at the time of the loss. The insurer will pay two-thirds of the original $50,000, or $33,333, to cover the tenant's loss.

Note the following points about this third method:

1. The dollar figure used as the basis is the *original* cost, including necessary cost to prepare the premises before the improvements could be installed. Neither actual cash value nor replacement cost is relevant.
2. The lease whose expiration date is considered is the one in effect *at the time of loss.* If the lease contains a renewal option, then the expiration of the renewal option period is used instead.
3. There is no requirement that the lease be in writing. But, if it is oral, the insured may well have trouble proving the expiration date.

Personal Property in the Insured's Custody. Three different policy provisions apply to personal property in the insured's custody.

First, an insured who has expended resources in repairing, storing, or servicing the property of others has an interest in the value of those resources, if not in the property itself. Usually, the insured also expects to collect a fee for its services. The contents coverage or—to be more precise, the coverage for "your business personal property"—includes protection on:

Labor, materials or services furnished or arranged by you on personal property of others.

Note that this covers only the insured's expenses, not its prospective profit from services rendered.

A second provision is found among the "coverage extensions." At the option of the named insured, coverage may be extended to cover personal property of others in the insured's care, custody, or control. The insurance provided here is limited to $2,500. Note that the named insured *"may* apply" the coverage. The insurer is obligated to pay only when the named insured so chooses. There is no coverage at all unless the relevant coverage on owned property is subject to 80 percent or higher coinsurance. However, the covered property of others is not included in computing coinsurance requirements, and the amount provided for property of others is in addition to the amount of coverage purchased on owned property.

Third, insureds who need more than $2,500 coverage on property of others may purchase *personal property of others* coverage in an appropriate amount. The coverage will then be indicated in the declarations, with an amount of insurance and premium shown. Many organizations should seriously consider this coverage, especially service organizations who perform work on others' personal property or organizations selling goods on consignment. However, the BPP does not always provide the best approach to filling this coverage need. For many bailees, some form of inland marine insurance is more appropriate, as discussed in Chapter 10.

Locations at Which Property Is Covered

As noted earlier, fire and allied lines insurance applies almost exclusively to property at fixed or specified locations, and this is certainly true of the building and personal property coverage form (BPP). However, the BPP does extend some coverage—for both building and personal property items—to other locations.

Building There are a few exceptions in the BPP to the requirement that the only building property insured is at the location specified in the policy declarations. These exceptions involve newly acquired buildings at other locations, newly constructed buildings at the insured location, and off-premises building items. These exceptions are handled by coverage extensions that apply when the policy contains at least an 80 percent coinsurance clause.

Newly Acquired or Constructed Buildings. Newly acquired buildings at different locations are handled under a coverage extension. For coverage to apply, the new building must be used either for purposes similar to those of the building described in the declarations or as a warehouse.

Buildings being constructed at the insured location are also covered. There is no condition relating to the purpose of the new building, but this is a moot point since future occupancy has little bearing on the exposures of a building under construction.

In either case, coverage is limited to 25 percent of the indicated building coverage, with a maximum of $250,000 per building.

The purpose of the coverage extension is to handle the named insured's coverage needs on a temporary basis until the insured has time to arrange formal coverage. The automatic coverage is available ("you *may* extend the insurance") as soon as the new building is acquired or construction begins. Coverage ends:

- when the policy expires,
- when the insured reports the values of the new building, or
- when thirty days of automatic coverage have elapsed.

A premium for the new exposure is payable from the date the exposure begins. This is an automatic coverage extension—not free coverage.

Property at Other Locations. In the BPP, building attachments (such as awnings and storm windows) that are covered when on the building are also covered when removed. Like building service materials and equipment, they are covered while stored in any building on the designated premises, and are also covered temporarily at other locations the named insured does not own, lease, or operate, but they are not covered while in or on a vehicle. Awnings, for example, would not be covered property while they were being transported to a storage location, but would be covered once they arrive.

Coverage applies only when the building insurance is subject to an 80 percent or higher coinsurance clause. Coverage is limited to $5,000.

Personal Property The contents coverage of the BPP covers "stock" and other personal property while in a described building and while in the open (or in a vehicle) within 100 feet of the described premises. Elsewhere, personal property—other than stock—is covered by the same extensions of coverage that apply to building items. "Stock" is defined in the policy to mean merchandise, as well as raw materials, goods in process, and finished goods. Packing and shipping supplies are also considered "stock."

Personal Property at Newly Acquired Locations. The BPP's coverage for personal property of the named insured at newly acquired locations is similar to the coverage for newly acquired buildings. For policies with at least an 80 percent coinsurance clause, automatic coverage is provided for up to thirty days for property within the territorial limits of the policy.

Excluded is property located at fairs and exhibitions. Off-premises coverage under this extension is limited to 10 percent of the personal property limit, with a maximum coverage of $100,000.

Property at Other Locations. Property temporarily away from the named insured's premises is automatically covered, subject to a $5,000 limit. As usual, this coverage extension applies only when the policy contains at least an 80 percent coinsurance clause. Excluded are:

- stock;
- property at any fair or exhibition;
- property in the care, custody, or control of salespersons; and
- property in or on a vehicle.

When the causes of loss—special form is used, an additional coverage extension applies to property in transit, as detailed in Chapter 4. Excluded property can often be covered by one of the inland marine forms described in Chapter 10.

Personal Property of Others Property belonging to persons other than the insured is covered only while on premises described in the policy or within 100 feet of those premises.

Multiple Locations To this point, discussion has centered on organizations having one building or one set of premises. Some have a need for building and personal property coverage at several locations.

The basic way of insuring several locations in a single policy is to list each in the policy declarations, with a specific amount of insurance applying to each covered type of property at each location. The effect is the same as though a separate policy had been issued for each item. For an insured with a large number of locations, this method is somewhat cumbersome and lacking in flexibility. "Blanket" insurance, discussed in the next chapter, sometimes provides a better approach.

Rights of Insureds

"Commercial property" insurance deals with two basic classes of insureds. One class consists of those who may file claims on their own initiative and in their own names. The other basic class consists of those whose interests are protected only if the named insured chooses to apply the protection.

Insureds Who Can File Claims Two types of insureds may directly enforce claims for coverage:

- named insureds—including their legal representatives, and
- named mortgage holders (for real property).

Named Insureds. Named insureds and their legal representatives may enforce the contract—subject, of course, to their having fulfilled all policy conditions. An important point to be noted here is that when a policy condition has been violated by *any one* of the named insureds in a particular policy, that violation may, in some cases, give the insurer a defense against claims by *any* named insured in the same policy.

First Named Insureds. As noted in the common policy conditions, the *first named insured* is the insured that may cancel the policy, is required to make the premium payment, and will receive any premium refund that should become due. Although the first named insured has somewhat greater control over the policy bcause of these provisions, the first named insured has no rights superior to other insureds when it comes to making—or collecting for—a claim.

Named Mortgage Holders. A named mortgage holder (mortgagee) is entitled to be paid, as its interest may appear, for covered loss or damage to a building.

Coverage of named mortgagees is generally not voided by acts of named insureds. However, the mortgage holder is obligated to notify the insurance company of any change in ownership, occupancy, or substantial "change in risk" of which the mortgage holder is aware. (Former policies used the phrase "increase in hazard," which would probably be a more precise phrase in this context.) Failure to do so could void the mortgage holder's right to collect under the policy.

In circumstances where the mortgagee has protection under the policy but the named insured does not, the insurer is subrogated to the mortgagee's rights under the mortgage to the extent of the amount paid by the insurer. If, for example, the named insured is convicted of setting fire to the building to collect the insurance, the insurer will pay the mortgage holder, but has a right of recovery against the named insured.

The insurer also has the option of paying to the mortgage holder the balance due on the mortgage, then taking over the entire mortgage. In such a case, the named insured then owes the entire balance due on the load to the insurance company. The mortgage holder cannot require the insurance company to take this step—it is done strictly at the option of the insurance company.

Those Protected at the Option of the Insured Within the group of persons whose interests are protected only if the named insured chooses to enforce the protection are two subclasses—owners of "property not owned by the insured" and loss payees.

Owners of "Property of Others." Most of the BPP provisions relating to insurance on the property of persons other than the named insured have already been mentioned. The named insured's goodwill interest is protected by applying some insurance to the ownership interest of others *when the named insured wants this done.*

In addition to provisions previously detailed, the BPP has an extension that allows a small amount of coverage to be applied to the *personal effects* of owners and employees of the insured organization. (Coverage is subject to the $2,500 limit that also applies to property of others.)

Since this coverage extension, like others, states that the named insured "may extend" coverage, it is up to the named insured whether to submit a claim for such personal effects. The owners of the personal effects have no choice in the matter, nor does the insurance company have any obligation toward those owners if the named insured does not choose to extend the insurance to provide coverage.

Named Loss Payees. Also protected are those *named as loss payees* in a *loss payable provisions endorsement.* Loss payable clauses fall into three categories:

1. *Loss payable*—used when the loss payee has some interest in the property,
2. *Lender's loss payable*—used when the loss payee's interest is that of a lender, and
3. *Contract of sale*—to protect the seller of real estate where the seller retains legal title to real property being transferred under an installment land contract.

For covered property in which both the named insured and a named loss payee have an insurable interest, the insurer agrees:

● to adjust losses with the named insured, and
● to pay any claim jointly to the named insured and the named loss payee(s) "as interests may appear."

If the insured enforces a claim against the insurer, a loss payee is entitled to be named on the claim check for covered damage to property in which the loss payee has an interest. But if the insured chooses not to pursue the claim, the loss payee has no independent right to do so. The loss payee cannot collect if the named insured cannot—for example, if the named insured has violated policy conditions—unless the *lender's loss payable clause* (number (2) above) is in effect. In other cases, a mortgage holder has rights superior to those of a loss payee.

A loss payable clause usually is attached to the policy at the request of a creditor who has a claim against specific personal property covered by the insurance. Chattel mortgages, conditional sales, and installment sales are common examples of such claims.

Additional Coverages

Several so-called *coverage extensions* of the BPP have been previously discussed. Coverage extensions automatically provide additional amounts of insurance—over and above policy limits—when the policy contains at least an 80 percent coinsurance clause. The values covered by these coverage extensions are not taken into account in determining compliance with a coinsurance provision.

The *additional coverages* discussed here are distinguished from those coverage extensions in two ways. First, most of the "additional coverages" do not exactly povide additional amounts of insurance over and above policy limits. Rather than adding to coverage, they tend to clarify what costs, relating somewhat indirectly to the direct loss, are also covered by the policy. Another distinguishing feature is that the "additional coverages" apply even when the policy contains no coinsurance clause.

The building and personal property coverage form has been modified in most states by a *changes—pollutants endorsement*, which revises the "debris removal" additional coverage in the basic BPP and adds another additional coverage for "pollutant clean up and removal." As modified, the policy contains four "additional coverages":

1. debris removal,
2. pollutant clean up and removal,
3. fire department service charge, and
4. preservation of property.

Each will be examined in turn.

Debris Removal   It can be argued that the presence of debris increases the "actual cash value" of a building loss. The extent of this effect is readily measured by the cost of removing the debris. According to this argument, no separate debris removal coverage would be required. However, this argument does not apply particularly well to coverage on contents for a tenant who also may have to pay for the removal of debris.

Furthermore, adding the cost of debris removal to the value of the direct damage loss may develop a sum greater than the actual cash value of the property before the damage—a situation that could easily result in underinsurance.

The unendorsed BPP sidestepped this debate by specifically including the cost of removing debris of covered property as a subject of coverage. (Note that only debris of covered property is addressed. Removal of downed trees, retaining walls, and so forth does not involve covered debris removal expense.) The BPP provided for payment of debris removal expenses, as well as the value of the direct loss, up to the policy limit. To forestall the possibility of an underinsurance problem, the BPP included a provision that it would pay up to $5,000 beyond the policy limit when debris removal expenses made it necessary.

This approach essentially continued the practice under former policies and even added another $5,000 of coverage. However, the *changes—pollutants endorsement* adds some restrictions to debris removal coverage. Interestingly enough, the restictions were considered necessary because of changes—not in the property insurance field, but in the area of liability insurance. During the early 1980s, the courts became increasingly generous toward insureds in their interpretation of the pollution exclusion in general liability policies—so much so that insurers reacted by refusing to provide any pollution liability coverage at all. With coverage for pollution claims excluded from liability policies, insureds began looking for other sources of recovery in pollution cases. The result was that claims began to be made on the basis that pollution cleanups should be covered under the debris removal coverage of property insurance policies. The predictable response was that property insurance policies were endorsed to limit pollution coverage.

The *changes—pollutants endorsement* replaces the debris removal clause of the BPP with another clause that covers only those debris removal expenses reported to the insurer within 180 days of the date of the direct loss. Additional wording makes it clear that the direct loss must occur within the policy period if debris removal coverage is to apply. Debris removal coverage is limited to $5,000 plus 25 percent of the value of the direct loss. (The $5,000 limit may be increased by endorsement, for additional premium.) Deductibles are ignored in determining the value of the direct loss. For example, following a $10,000 direct loss covered under a policy with a $500 deductible, the insurer would pay no more than $7,500 (that is, [25% × $10,000] + $5,000) to cover the cost of debris removal. And, furthermore, debris removal coverage does not apply to land or water pollution cases, as described in the endorsement, which are the subject of another additional coverage.

Pollutant Clean Up and Removal As stated in the *changes—pollutants* endorsement, the BPP will pay up to $10,000 of the expense to extract "pollutants" from water or land at the described premises, provided that the original release, discharge, or dispersal of the "pollutants" was caused by a covered cause of loss that occurred during the policy period. "Pollutant" is broadly defined, using exactly the same wording as the pollution exclusion of the commercial general liability coverage form (CGL). Clean up and removal expenses will be paid only if they are reported within 180 days of the end of the policy period.

An aggregate limit applies to this coverage. The insurer will not pay more than $10,000 for each location insured for pollution clean up and removal expenses from covered causes of loss during each twelve-month policy period. (This amount may be increased for an additional premium.)

There are some subtleties in this coverage that should not pass unmentioned. The problem with liability coverage for pollution losses was that the courts did not agree with insurers' interpretations of policy language intended to provide coverage for "sudden and accidental" pollution losses. Liability insurers responded by excluding virtually all pollution coverage. Property insurers took a different approach by explicitly providing coverage and then making it subject to relatively low limits of $10,000 (over and above policy limits). Furthermore, the 180-day reporting period should eliminate the problem of "long-tail" claims being reported long after the polluting incident.

Fire Department Service Charge   The insurer will pay up to $1,000 if a fire department imposes a service charge that is either required by local ordinance or agreed to before the loss. However, the fire department must have been called to save or protect covered property from damage by a covered cause of loss.

This additional amount of coverage is not subject to any deductible—a feature of questionable value, since the deductible would normally be applied to direct damage involved in the same incident. Still, there are situations where the feature could be of value—for example, if firefighters are called to keep a building from being damaged by a fire in a neighboring field. The service fee could be incurred even though no building damage results, but an insurance company would have little reason to complain about paying a service fee to a fire department that prevents a major insured building fire. Note, also, that there is no exclusion under this coverage for false alarms.

Preservation of Property   As is typical of property insurance policies, the BPP requires the insured, in the event of a loss, to "take all reasonable steps to protect the covered property from further damage." The *preservation of property* additional coverage protects the insured who faithfully exercises this duty, since moving property to a temporary location is likely to expose it to some hazards. For one thing, it may be subject to the perils of transportation while it is being moved, and it may be susceptible to theft during and after the move.

If it is necessary to move covered property from the described premises to preserve it from loss or damage by a covered peril, the insurer agrees to pay for *any* direct loss or damage to that property while it is being moved or temporarily stored. This broad protection—which is, in effect, "all-risks" coverage—lasts for ten days after the time the property is first moved. During that ten-day period, the insured may arrange for specific coverage on the property. Otherwise, the usual off-premises coverage—which is somewhat more limited—may apply.

The preservation of property additional coverage contains no dollar limit of its own. Coverage is subject to policy limits. This may seem like a particularly generous coverage, but, remember, it applies to property that might otherwise have been totally destroyed, and the insurer is fortunate that the property has been given a second chance.

In early policies, including the 1943 standard fire policy, this coverage was treated as though it applied to a peril—termed the "removal" peril. The treatment in modern policies makes more sense, since the removal is actually a hazard that increases the likelihood of loss from other causes—it is not the removal itself that is the cause of loss.

PROVISIONS DEALING WITH AMOUNTS OF RECOVERY

Coinsurance Clause and Deductible Provision

The coinsurance clause is fundamental to many of the coverages discussed earlier. While examining the coinsurance clause, it is also desirable to examine the deductible provision and the relationship between coinsurance and deductibles in calculating the amount to be recovered following a loss.

Coinsurance Clause   The building and personal property coverage form (BPP), like most property forms, has a coinsurance clause. The coinsurance clause reads:

> If a Coinsurance percentage is shown in the Declarations, the following condition applies.
> a. We will not pay the full amount of any loss if the value of Covered Property at the time of loss times the Coinsurance percentage

shown for it in the Declarations is greater than the Limit of Insurance for the property.

Instead, we will determine the most we will pay using the following steps:

(1) Multiply the value of Covered Property at the time of loss by the Coinsurance percentage;

(2) Divide the Limit of Insurance of the property by the figure determined in step (1);

(3) Multiply the total amount of the covered loss, before the application of any deductible, by the figure determined in step (2); and

(4) Subtract the deductible from the figure determined in step (3).

The amount determined in step (4) is the most we will pay. For the remainder, you will either have to rely on other insurance or absorb the loss yourself.

The coinsurance percentages most commonly used are 80, 90, or 100 percent. In exchange for a reduced premium rate, the insured agrees, so to speak, to carry insurance at least equal to the specified percentage of the actual cash value of the building. If the specified amount of insurance is not carried, the loss is adjusted according to the formula:

$$\left(\frac{\text{Limit of insurance}}{\text{Value of covered property} \times \text{coinsurance percentage}} \times \begin{array}{c}\text{Total amount of}\\ \text{covered loss}\end{array} \right) - \text{Deductible} = \begin{array}{c}\text{Most that will}\\ \text{be paid by}\\ \text{insurance}\end{array}$$

Insurance students often condense this formula to "Did over should times loss minus deductible," or, in formula form:

$$\left(\frac{\text{Did}}{\text{Should}} \times \text{Loss} \right) - \text{Deductible}$$

"Did" is the amount of insurance carried. "Should" is the minimum amount that should have been carried to meet the coinsurance requirement.

The effect of this clause is to penalize an insured who does not insure to at least the specified percentage of value, the penalty being proportional to the amount of underinsurance. Even when insurance meets the requirements of an 80 or 90 percent coinsurance clause, the amount paid following a loss will never exceed policy limits. It might be misleading to say that a firm with enough insurance to satisfy the coinsurance clause is insured in full. Unless the amount of insurance is as great as the full value of the property plus costs of debris removal (when they exceed $5,000, as discussed earlier), the insurance is not sufficient to pay for a *total* loss, even without considering any business interruption loss.

We stated earlier that the premium rate is "reduced" when a

coinsurance clause is used. It really is not quite that simple. Usually, the 80 percent coinsurance rate is used as a starting point, and that rate is increased if the coinsurance clause is not used. When coinsurance is mandatory, rates for coverage without coinsurance do not exist, and there really is no "reduction" in rate for coinsurance.

When higher coinsurance percentages are used, the rate is reduced. Using the 80 percent rate as a basis: In exchange for a 90 percent coinsurance clause on building or contents insurance, the rate is reduced 5 percent. Thus, the rate per hundred dollars of insurance is lower for the organization that agrees, so to speak, to purchase a higher ratio of insurance to insurable value. The organization that "promises" to insure for 100 percent of insurable value pays a premium rate that is 10 percent lower than the organization that "promises" to insure for 80 percent or suffer a post-loss penalty if underinsured. The organization with a higher coinsurance percentage must also purchase more insurance to escape coinsurance penalties.

Failure to comply with a coinsurance requirement is usually the result of a mistake in valuation, a failure to keep up with inflation, or a misunderstanding of insurance requirements. However, insureds sometimes intentionally become coinsurers because they intend to retain part of any loss to covered property. The disadvantages of this form of partial retention will be discussed in Chapter 15.

Deductible Provision The BPP contains a "per occurrence" deductible, with the amount of the deductible shown in the commercial property coverage part declarations page. The basic deductible is $250, but the amount of the deductible is often increased, in exchange for a premium credit. A $100 deductible may also be available at extra cost.

Note that the deductible applies to each occurrence, rather than to each item of covered property. A loss to both building and contents, for example, would be subject to only one deductible, as would a loss to two or more buildings arising out of a single occurrence (such as a windstorm).

The insurer pays nothing for losses that do not exceed the deductible. For larger losses, the insurer pays the amount of loss or damage in excess of the deductible, up to the applicable limit of insurance.

Coinsurance and the Deductible Before the 1985 revision of "commercial property" forms, some practitioners disagreed whether the deductible should be applied before or after the adjustment for any coinsurance penalty. The BPP leaves no doubt that the deductible is subtracted *after* the adjustment, if any, for coinsurance. If an insured has a $1,000 deductible, a $14,000 loss, did carry $100,000 of insurance, and should have carried $140,000, the insurer pays $9,000:

$$\left(\frac{\$100,000}{\$140,000} \times \$14,000\right) - \$1,000 = \$9,000$$

(If the deductible were subtracted before the coinsurance adjustment, the insurer would pay an additional $286:

$$\frac{\$100,000}{\$140,000} \times (\$14,000 - \$1,000) = \$9,286$$

This formula is wrong; the simplified form clearly does *not* operate this way.)

To try to make certain that the coinsurance clause cannot be misunderstood, the BPP contains three examples—one illustrating underinsurance, one adequate insurance, and one blanket insurance. (Blanket insurance is described in Chapter 4.)

Valuation Provisions

It is not possible for the insurer to pay for a loss to covered property without placing a value on the property (or, at least, on the cost to restore the property). Logically, it is necessary to use the same approach to valuation in deciding how much insurance to purchase in the first place.

As with most other property insurance policies, the basic approach in the BPP is to pay losses based on actual cash value. *Actual cash value (ACV)* is generally defined as "replacement cost minus depreciation," with replacement cost measured at the time of the loss at the location where the property is damaged. For insurance purposes, depreciation is subtracted from the replacement cost—not from the original acquisition cost. This basic actual cash value approach and some alternative approaches are examined in Chapter 4. However, the BPP itself also contains some exceptions that must be noted here.

Small Building Losses When the amount of *building* insurance carried satisfies coinsurance requirements ("did" at least equals "should"), then *building* losses of $2,500 or less are covered on a replacement cost basis. That is, there is no deduction for depreciation. This special provision does not apply to:

- awnings;
- floor coverings;
- appliances for refrigerating, ventilating, cooking, dishwashing, or laundering; or
- outdoor furniture and equipment.

As mentioned earlier, such items fall within the building coverage. However, they are more like personal property in that they are subject to relatively rapid wear and tear and depreciation, as compared with the building as a whole which may actually gain in value over time.

Safety Glass Many communities have building codes that require the use of safety glazing materials, rather than ordinary plate glass, when replacing glass in doors, shower stalls, and similar places where humans are exposed to injury by broken glass. When required by law, replacement of ordinary glass with safety glazing material is covered in full by the BPP.

Stock "Stock" that has been sold, but has not yet been delivered, is valued at its selling price minus any discounts that might have been applicable and expenses that the insured might otherwise have had—such as the expense of renting a truck to deliver an unusually large item. This *selling price clause* has the effect of protecting the insured's net profit in goods "sold but not delivered."

PROVISIONS DEALING WITH LOSS ADJUSTMENT

In a sense, all insurance policy provisions deal with loss adjustment. However, some of the insured's duties are not relevant unless and until a loss occurs. The insured who desires to have the loss paid must follow a certain procedure and abide by certain conditions, as specified in the policy.

If a law has been broken, the police must be notified. Thus, in situations where robbery is a covered cause of loss, the insured must notify the police if he or she expects to collect from the insurer. This provision helps to reduce fraud, since people are somewhat more reluctant to involve the police than an insurance representative. It also helps to assure that questionable circumstances are promptly recorded and, where applicable, investigated. Recovery is sometimes possible if the criminal is apprehended.

The insured is also required to give prompt notice of the loss to the insurer and to describe the type of property that was damaged. In addition, the insured should give details of how, when, and where the loss occurred. This information is necessary to make an accurate determination as to whether the loss involved a covered location and a covered peril occurring during the policy period.

The insurer may require the insured to give a complete inventory of damaged and undamaged goods—including quantities, costs, values, and amount of loss claimed. The insured must allow the insurer to inspect the property and to examine the records proving the loss. The inventory and record inspection requirements are useful to the insurer in determining the amount of property at hand at the time of the loss—information necessary for purposes of applying the coinsurance clause.

The inspection helps to reduce the number of fraudulent claims and to allow the insurer to make an accurate determination of the loss.

The insured is required to cooperate in the investigation or settlement of the claim and to submit to questioning under oath concerning the claim. The insured's answers are to be in writing and signed by the insured. These provisions are designed to aid in settling the claim, reducing intentional losses, and developing information for possible defense of a claim filed by an insured who does not tell the truth.

In general, the "duties in the event of loss" provisions inform insureds that, if they are to collect under the policy, they must be honest and helpful.

One of the last requirements made of the insured is the "signed, sworn statement of loss," often called a *proof of loss*. Before settling the loss, the insurer may require insureds to sign a sworn statement of loss containing information requested by the insurer. The insured is given sixty days to return the signed statement to the insurer, after the insurer provides the necessary forms. (Earlier policies contained a lengthy description of the information to be provided by the insured. The "simplified" policies simply note that the insurer will provide the necessary forms. The insured does not need to know all the questions that will be asked until there is a claim, and the nature of a particular claim may determine the information the insurer considers relevant to analysis of that claim.)

If the insurer and the insured disagree about the value of the claim, the *appraisal clause* may be activated by either the insured or the insurer. The appraisal process, described below, may expedite the handling of a claim. The appraisal clause states:

> If we and you disagree on the value of the property or the amount of loss, either may make written demand for an appraisal of the loss. In this event, each party will select a competent and impartial appraiser. The two appraisers will select an umpire. If they cannot agree, either may request that selection be made by a judge of a court having jurisdiction. The appraisers will state separately the value of the property and amount of loss. If they fail to agree, they will submit their differences to the umpire. A decision agreed to by any two will be binding. Each party will:
>
> a. Pay its chosen appraiser; and
> b. Bear the other expenses of the appraisal and umpire equally.
>
> If we submit to an appraisal, we will still retain our right to deny the claim.

The appraisal process may be used to resolve disputes over either the value of the property or the amount of the loss. However, it does not apply to disputes as to whether or not the policy provides coverage for a given loss.

Chapter Notes

1. Form SFP-1, Ed 10-86, Ed 10-86, Michigan. Copyright ISO.
2. An inland marine physicians and surgeons equipment coverage form may be substituted.
3. *Guiding Principles—Casualty, Fidelity, Inland Marine—First-Party Property Losses and Claims* (New York: Association of Casualty & Surety Companies, et al., 1963).
4. *Insurance Facts* 1986-87 pp. 64-5.
5. The water exclusion is not in the November 1985 edition of the BPP, but is added by the *changes—pollutants* endorsement of April 1986.
6. Marshall and Swift Publication Company, Marshall Valuation Service, Section 96, pp. 1-2, August 1980, Los Angeles, CA.

CHAPTER 4

Valuation, Covered Causes of Loss

In conjunction with declarations, common conditions, and a causes-of-loss form the unmodified building and personal property coverage form (BPP) described in Chapter 3 might be considered a "basic approach" to providing direct loss insurance coverage on real and personal property at fixed locations. A wide array of alternative approaches is also possible.

Chapter 3 provided a detailed analysis of the BPP, with emphasis on the types of property covered and excluded. The important matter of property valuation was not emphasized there, but was reserved for the opening segment of this chapter. This material describes the basic approach to amounts of insurance, as well as alternatives.

Chapter 4 also describes the standard causes-of-loss forms in considerable detail, with emphasis on the perils covered and excluded. Optional alternatives to broadening and restricting coverage are also discussed.

AMOUNTS OF INSURANCE—THE BASIC APPROACH

The basic approach of the BPP was designed for organizations with unchanging property values at one or a few locations. The standard deductibles and the built-in additional coverages and coverage extensions presume a typical small-to-medium-sized business operation. The basic approach to amounts of insurance involves the following:

- actual cash value,
- coinsurance,
- fixed dollar amounts of insurance with a premium based on policy limits,

- specific coverage, and
- a deductible of $250 per occurrence.

When a firm's insurance needs are met by this basic coverage arrangement, there is no need to use a more complicated method. In fact, the most basic approach may be not only adequate but also advantageous. More sophisticated approaches can cause confusion and may lead to a partial recovery in cases where a more straightforward approach would have provided for complete recovery.

On the other hand, many organizations' insurance needs are better handled by alternative approaches. After more closely examining the basic BPP approach to determining the value of insured property and the amount of loss payment, alternatives to the basic approach will be examined.

Actual Cash Value

The basic approach in the BPP is to pay losses based on the actual cash value of the covered property. As noted in Chapter 3, *actual cash value (ACV)* is generally defined as "replacement cost minus depreciation." While this generalization provides a workable textbook definition, it would be misleading to suggest that it clearly describes a precise approach to measuring insurable property values. In the book *Adjustment of Property Losses*, Paul I. Thomas and Prentiss B. Reed, Sr. put it this way, after noting that the terms *actual value* and *actual cash value* are interchangeable:

> The courts, understandably, have not been consistent or in full agreement on what constitutes the cash value of a building. The cash value has variously been held to be replacement cost less physical depreciation, or market value; the difference between its cash value immediately before and immediately after the loss, where the building had been condemned prior thereto; its intrinsic value; and a reasonable value.

> Insurers, brokers, and agents, in a sincere effort to find a rational formula for determining the proper amount of insurance to be carried on a building, generally use *replacement cost less depreciation.* Recognizing that *depreciation* means a decline in value, no one offers violent objection to this formula. The difficulty arises in distinguishing between physical depreciation (wear and tear) and economic depreciation (obsolescence), and particularly in finding some measure or yardstick for determining obsolescence.[1]

Although depreciation is difficult to measure, it seems clear that any applicable depreciation will be deducted in adjusting losses and should also be deducted when establishing values in order to select appropriate limits of insurance.

The BPP contains several automatic extensions of coverage that affect valuation in some instances. These extensions, which were discussed in Chapter 3, include the following:

- replacement cost coverage on losses less than $2,500,
- selling price recovery (less discounts and remaining expenses) on stock that has been sold but not delivered, and
- safety glass to replace nonsafety glass where required by law.

Coinsurance

The basic approach contemplates that a coinsurance provision of 80, 90, or 100 percent will apply. Failure to insure to the amount required by the applicable coinsurance provision may result in a penalty for underinsurance at the time of a loss adjustment.

The applicable coinsurance percentage is shown in the commercial property declarations. Several coverage extensions apply only when a coinsurance percentage of at least 80 is shown in the declarations.

Fixed Amounts of Insurance;
Premium Based on Policy Limit

The *limit of insurance* for each type of covered property is shown in the commercial property coverage declarations. It is generally expected that the limit reflects the actual cash value of covered property in an amount sufficient to comply with coinsurance requirements. Since the limit then reflects the values exposed to insured loss, the premium is based on the limit.

The basic approach contemplates that the stated limit of coverage will apply for the duration of the policy. However, an endorsement may be used to increase or decrease the amount of insurance, with an appropriate adjustment to the premium.

Although this method ignores changing values attributable to inflation, it works for those who have fairly stable amounts of insured property. Examples of such situations include a building to which no major alterations or additions are likely to be made and the contents of an office, which are likely to be fairly constant. Situations not compatible with this approach include a building under construction and the inventory of a seasonal business like a garden shop.

Specific Coverage

Coverage is specific to a particular category of property at one stated location and therefore does not apply to other types of property or to property at other locations.

For example, if the declarations indicate that a $20,000 limit applies to personal property located at 1988 Washington Avenue, then no coverage is provided for property at 1992 Washington Avenue; and when the damaged property is a building but coverage applies only to personal property, no coverage applies even if the loss occurs at 1988 Washington Avenue.

An organization with several locations may shift valuable property items from one location to another. Under the basic approach, the organization would repeatedly have to change policy limits for the affected locations to maintain proper coverage. Substantial paperwork might be involved. Since premium adjustments would also be made, both the insurer and the insured would incur additional accounting expenses. In short, while flexibility is not impossible with this basic approach, it can be had only at some inconvenience and expense.

Deductibles

Although a wide variety of deductibles *may* be used with "commercial property" forms, a standard $250 deductible is contemplated by the basic rates. The applicable deductible is shown in the declarations.

The deductible applies only once per occurrence. Thus, when both building and contents are insured and damaged in the same fire, only one deductible applies. Similarly, if insured property at more than one location is damaged by the same windstorm, the deductible applies only once to the whole loss.

AMOUNTS OF INSURANCE—ALTERNATIVE APPROACHES

Alternatives to Actual Cash Value

According to traditional insurance principles, an insured who sustained a property loss would be reimbursed for the actual cash value of the damaged property. Traditionally, it was held that any payment over and above the actual cash value of the loss would violate the principle of indemnity because it would leave the insured in a better position after a loss than before. For example, if the insurer paid for a new building, the insured's value in the new building was supposedly greater than the value in the new building that had been destroyed;

thus the insured would profit from a loss. Thus, actual cash value insurance was necessary to prevent overindemnification.

On the other hand, the insured who has suffered a property loss is not truly whole after receiving a sum of money that approximates the depreciated value of the damaged property. The insured is not really whole until the property is again whole and properly functioning.

The total cost of recovering from direct property damage is the actual expense required to repair or replace the damaged property. Actual cash value insurance may pay only a portion of those expenses, and insureds with actual cash value face the chance of having to pay the difference between their insurance recovery and the total cost of repair or replacement. With actual cash value insurance, the amount of this difference (depreciation) presents a potential loss that should be identified and treated. Replacement cost insurance, a popular approach which provides for the full cost of replacing property, is one means of treating the exposure.

However, replacement cost insurance is not suitable for every situation. Underwriters generally do not write replacement cost coverage when the difference between the present value and the cost of new replacement is extremely large. In such situations, other alternatives to actual cash value coverage may be used.

Replacement Cost The replacement cost (RC) alternative is so popular that it is preprinted in the BPP as an optional coverage—there is no need to attach an endorsement. Coverage is activated by entry in the commercial property declarations.

Insurers were historically reluctant to write replacement cost coverage because potential for betterment, following a loss, increases the moral hazard. Contemporary thinking, arising in part from rapid increases in construction costs and real estate values, presumes that the potential cost to repair or replace damaged property is a loss exposure that can validly be treated with insurance. Thus, replacement cost coverage has come into rather common usage.

With replacement cost coverage, an insured recovers on the basis of replacement cost at the time and place of the loss. There is no deduction for loss of value through physical depreciation.

Replacement cost coverage is usually added at no specific additional charge. However, the coinsurance clause is then applied to the *replacement cost*, rather than the actual cash value, of property covered for replacement cost. *Therefore, with replacement cost coverage, the insured must usually carry higher limits of insurance to avoid a coinsurance penalty, and the premium increases in proportion to the increased coverage.*

Even when the replacement cost option is in effect, the insured has the opportunity to elect adjustment on the basis of actual cash value. When this is done, the coinsurance clause is applied to the ACV of the covered property—not the RC—in order to determine whether a coinsurance penalty should apply.

Eligible Property. According to the ISO *Commercial Lines Manual,* only some categories of property are eligible for replacement cost coverage:

1. buildings and permanent machinery, fixtures, and equipment that is covered with the insured building;
2. tenants' improvements and betterments;
3. machinery, furniture, fixtures, and equipment; and
4. merchandise and stock—covered only when the "including 'stock'" option is indicated in the commercial property declarations.

The language of the BPP itself is much less restrictive than the above eligibility rules would seem to indicate. The commercial property declarations simply indicate whether the replacement cost coverage applies to buildings or personal property and, if to personal property, whether "stock" is included. The only property items actually excluded from replacement cost coverage in the BPP are as noted in the next paragraph.

Property Not Covered at Replacement Cost. Even when the replacement cost option is chosen, certain types of property are valued on the basis of their actual cash value:

- property of others;
- contents of a residence;
- manuscripts; and
- works of arts, antiques, or rare artifacts—including etchings, pictures, statuary, marbles, bronzes, porcelains, and bric-a-brac.

Stock is also valued at actual cash value unless the "including 'stock'" option is indicated in the declarations.

Actual cash value, rather than replacement cost, is also used in determining compliance with coinsurance requirements on these types of property. Thus, when determining an appropriate amount of insurance and when determining compliance with coinsurance provisions, some property is valued at actual cash value, other property at replacement cost.

Loss Settlement. To recover replacement cost, the insured must actually repair or replace the damaged property as soon as reasonably possible. The insurer is not obligated to pay the replacement cost claim until the replacement has been completed. An insured who wishes to collect something more quickly can make a claim on the basis of actual cash value. If the insured then notifies the insurer within 180 days of the loss of an intention to collect on a replacement cost basis, the appropriate additional amount will be paid when replacement has taken place.

If the insured does not replace or rebuild the property, the claim will be settled on an actual cash value basis.

Supposing the insured does replace or rebuild, the limit on claim payment is the smallest of:

1. the limit of insurance applicable to the lost or damaged property;
2. the cost to replace the property on the same premises with other property of comparable material and quality, used for the same purpose; or
3. the amount *actually* spent that is *necessary* to repair or replace the property.

The first condition restricts coverage to the applicable policy limits. If the policy is for $100,000 and the loss is valued at $105,000, the insurer will not pay more than $100,000. Of course, any failure to meet coinsurance requirements may reduce the recovery to less than the $100,000 limit of insurance.

The second condition limits recovery to the cost of repairing or replacing at the same location for the same occupancy, using materials of comparable quality. This clause does not *require* the insured to rebuild according to the specified conditions—same premises, same occupancy, same use. It merely says that the insured will not be paid more than what it would cost to reconstruct under those conditions. It seems to follow that if the insured replaces with a more expensive building, whether at the same location or a different location, the insurer will pay no more than the amount it *would have* cost to replace the original building at the original location.

The third condition states that the *actual expenditure* limits recovery. The policy limit may be $200,000, and the cost to replace for the original occupancy and use at the original location may be $190,000, but if the insured builds at a different location for $150,000 or decides on a smaller building at the same location for $150,000, the insurer will pay only $150,000—the smallest amount of the three limits. (If the actual cash value of the damaged property was, say, $160,000, this could be a situation in which the insured would be better off in opting for an actual cash value settlement.)

This third condition says nothing about either the same premises or the same occupancy and use. The question arises: Does the replacement cost coverage apply to replacement with a significantly different structure? Suppose, for example, that an auto service station is insured for $200,000 on a replacement cost basis and that the cost to repair or replace it with a comparable service station building would be $200,000. Would the insurer pay $200,000 if the insured were to replace a destroyed service station with a $200,000 restaurant? The answer seems to hinge on the extent to which a different structure can be considered a replacement for the old one—especially when the different structure is erected on different premises. Specific cases may involve questions of fact best decided by the courts.

Time of Replacement. Replacement cost coverage requires that the replacement be accomplished "as soon as reasonably possible after the loss or damage." As noted, the insured may choose to disregard the replacement cost coverage and make a claim on the basis of actual cash value. This option might be exercised, for example, if the insured chooses not to repair or replace the damaged property. Even after electing an actual cash value recovery, the insured can claim the additional replacement cost by notifying the insurer of this intention during the first 180 days following the loss.

Functional Replacement Cost In some situations it would not be practical to replace damaged or destroyed property with new property of comparable material and quality. The *functional replacement cost endorsement* provides an alternative for such situations where neither actual cash value nor replacement cost coverage provides a match with insurance needs.

In the endorsement, property that is to be valued at its functional replacement cost is described in a schedule. For each described item, the schedule lists both the functional replacement cost of that item and a limit of insurance that applies.

Functional replacement cost is defined as "the cost to replace the property with similar property intended to perform the same function when replacement with identical property is impossible or unnecessary." The wording of the endorsement closely resembles that of the replacement cost optional coverage, except that it does not make reference to material "of comparable material and quality."

Functional replacement cost coverage does not apply to certain types of property that have a tendency for rapid depreciation:

- awnings or floor coverings;
- appliances for refrigerating, ventilating, cooking, dishwashing, or laundering; and
- outdoor equipment or furniture.

The coinsurance condition does not apply to property valued on a functional replacement cost basis. Instead, the following approach is used: if the limit of insurance is less than the functional replacement cost, the insured's maximum recovery is prorated according to the following formula:

$$\left(\frac{\text{Limit of Insurance}}{\text{Functional Replacement Cost}} \times \text{Loss}\right) - \text{Deductible} = \frac{\text{Maximum}}{\text{Recovery}}$$

In most cases, the limit of insurance equals the scheduled functional replacement cost, in which case no proration will be necessary.

Market Value Yet another approach may be used to insure property whose market value is substantially less than its actual cash value. An example might be a sound commercial building that would be difficult to sell because it is in a blighted area that is currently considered an undesirable business location.

According to the *market value—property other than stock endorsement*, property is covered on a functional replacement cost basis if the insured contracts for repair or replacement within 180 days of the loss. Unless the insured makes a claim on that basis, the insurer will not pay more than the "market value at the time of loss of the damaged or destroyed property, exclusive of land value." *Market value* is not defined in the form, but is generally considered to be the price the property would command in the market.

Manufacturer's Selling Price As noted earlier, the BPP contains *a selling price clause* (sometimes referred to as the *mercantile selling price clause)* which values stock that is sold, but not yet delivered, at its selling price (less discounts and expenses). A *manufacturer's selling price endorsement* applies the same approach to the value of finished "stock" manufactured by the insured—whether or not it has been sold.

Alternatives to Coinsurance

The basic coinsurance clause encourages the purchase of insurance to value by imposing an underinsurance penalty, at the time of the loss, for those who do not insure to value. However, there are two problems:

1. In some cases the coinsurance clause tends to force the purchase of an excessive amount of insurance.
2. In many cases, there is a threat of less-than-complete loss recovery. This is because of the difficulty in determining, at the beginning of a policy period, what the value of the property will be throughout that period.

Both of these problems can be avoided through the purchase of a policy with less than 80 percent coinsurance, "flat insurance," or the use of an agreed value approach.

Less than 80 Percent Coinsurance or Flat Insurance Coverage is sometimes written with a coinsurance percentage of less than 80, or with no coinsurance at all. The rate per hundred dollars of insurance generally increases by at least 50 percent when this is done.

The term *flat insurance* is sometimes used to refer to property coverage with no coinsurance requirement. No endorsement or special policy provision is required to effect flat insurance or a lower coinsurance percentage. The appropriate percentage is merely entered in the commercial property declarations, or the coinsurance block is left blank. Remember, however, that the coverage extensions of the BPP do not apply unless at least 80 percent coinsurance is in effect.

Agreed Value It is often difficult to predict property values accurately enough to avoid any possibility of a coinsurance penalty. Concern over a possible coinsurance penalty is avoided when the agreed value approach is used instead. Like the replacement cost optional coverage, the agreed value option is preprinted in the form and is activated by an entry in the commercial property declarations. This option provides an alternative to coinsurance.

When the agreed value option is selected, the insured completes a *statement of values*, listing the actual cash value or the replacement cost value of the various covered property items. Assuming the insurer accepts the insured's statement, these dollar amounts are then listed in the "agreed amount" space of the commercial property declarations.

Usually, the *limit of insurance* for property subject to the agreed value option equals the agreed value. When this is the case, any covered loss is paid in full, subject to deductibles—with no consideration of coinsurance or coinsurance penalty—up to the applicable limit of insurance. If, for any reason, the limit of insurance is less than the agreed amount, the insured will recover the proportion of the loss that the limit of insurance bears to the agreed value. In other words, the loss will be adjusted according to the following formula:

$$\left(\frac{\text{Limit of Insurance}}{\text{Agreed Value}} \times \text{Loss}\right) - \text{Deductible} = \text{Insured's Recovery}$$

It is difficult to imagine a situation involving unintentional underinsurance with an agreed value provision, but underinsurance may sometimes be intentional. In some cases, the value of a building exceeds the amount of coverage an underwriter is able to provide, and the insured then expects to participate in every loss in proportion to the extent of the underinsurance. In other cases, two or more insurers participate in insuring the same property; while each policy underinsures, the total amount of insurance in all policies equals the agreed value.

The agreed value approach is available only with some extra effort. The insured must complete a moderately detailed statement of values, and the insurer must agree with the insured's valuation. A statement of values is normally valid only for one year, and a new statement must be completed for each succeeding year for which agreed value coverage is desired. If a new statement is not filed, the coinsurance clause is restored, based on the coinsurance percentage shown in the commercial property declarations.

The rules of the ISO *Commercial Lines Manual* suggest that it is possible to select an amount of insurance equal to 80, 90, or 100 percent of the agreed value. However, the language of the 1985 BPP form does not provide for 80 percent or 90 percent insurance-to-value, but prorates coverage unless the amount of insurance equals the full agreed value. This apparent discrepancy may be resolved in a future revision.

Since the agreed value option displaces the coinsurance approach, it might seem unnecessary to enter a coinsurance percentage in the commercial property declarations. Note, however, that a coinsurance percentage should appear in the commercial property declarations even when coverage is written on an agreed value basis, for two reasons:

1. The percentage shown in the declarations will apply at any point when the statement of values expires.
2. The *coverage extensions* of the BPP apply only when a coinsurance percentage of 80 or more appears in the declarations.

Alternatives to Fixed Limits and Premiums Based on Limits

The alternatives to the basic approach that fit in this category include the inflation guard option, the peak season endorsement, and the value reporting form.

Inflation Guard   Because of inflation, the dollar value of property changes even when everything else remains unchanged. Another popular preprinted option is the so-called *inflation guard*—a catchy term borrowed from homeowners insurance policies. Earlier commercial property policies used the stodgier title "automatic increase in insurance"—but practitioners still called it "inflation guard."

With the inflation guard option, the insured selects a figure that reflects the expected rate of inflationary increases in property values during the coming policy term. Coverage automatically increases throughout the policy term, with the increase in coverage prorated on a daily basis.

For example, suppose the insured purchases building coverage of $100,000 and selects the inflation guard option with an annual percentage of 10 percent. Suppose the insured sustains a building loss after a one-year policy has been in force for seventy-three days. The inflation guard would increase the available amount of insurance by 2 percent, and the amount of insurance available to cover the building loss would be $102,000—determined as follows.

$$\frac{73 \text{ days}}{365 \text{ days}} \times 10\% = 2\%$$

$$2\% \times \$100,000 = \$2,000$$

$$\$100,000 + \$2,000 = \$102,000$$

The inflation guard coverage may be used for buildings and personal property. The additional premium for this coverage is based directly on the additional limits of coverage it provides.

Except by chance, fixed percentage increases do not exactly match inflationary increases in property values. Nor do they help much when applied to insurance that is inadequate in the first place. But they do address a problem imposed during periods of high rates of economic inflation. An alternative approach, used by some insurers, is to increase policy limits in accordance with some type of cost index, such as a construction cost index or a consumer price index.

Although the inflation guard option is designed to address increases in value caused by inflation, there seems to be no reason why it could not also be used to reflect an expected steady increase in the amount of property owned by a particular business. Where the pattern of property value changes is predictable but does not reflect a steady increase throughout the policy term, the peak season endorsement may be more appropriate.

Peak Season Endorsement   Some firms have inventories that fluctuate according to predictable cycles. A toy store, for example, may predictably double its inventory during the months preceding Christmas, with inventory values declining rapidly just before Christmas and stabilizing for the next nine months.

The peak season endorsement simply provides differing amounts of insurance for differing time periods during the policy term, as indicated by specific dates shown in the endorsement. For example, a toy store may have a BPP providing $100,000 coverage on personal property with a peak season endorsement increasing coverage to $200,000 during the period from October 1 to December 31. This would have exactly the same effect as using the "basic approach" endorsing the policy on October 1 to increase the coverage, and endorsing it again on December 31 to reduce the coverage—however, the bother of these extra transactions is eliminated.

Usually, the peak season endorsement is attached when the policy is issued—although it may be added mid-term—and a pro-rata increased premium is charged for the period during which the limit is increased.

Value Reporting Form Fluctuating personal property values are a problem for many businesses—especially those with widely varying inventory levels. Whatever the cause of the instability, an insured usually wants insurance to adjust to the circumstances and give efficient, economical protection year-round.

The basic approach of a single, fixed amount of insurance, with premiums based on that policy limit, is unsatisfactory for such situations. To fully cover temporarily large accumulations, the insured would have to purchase and pay for high limits of insurance. At times when inventory values are reduced, the organization would pay for unneeded insurance. Conversely, the insured could choose a limit of insurance that is less than adequate to cover peak values. This keeps premiums lower but provides a coverage limit that is inadequate at times when inventory levels are high.

The value reporting form modifies the BPP's coverage on personal property to prevent this dilemma. Briefly, it works like this: A limit of insurance is set high enough to cover the insured's maximum expected values at any time during the policy period. Premiums are based not on the *policy limit* but on the *values exposed to loss*. Values are reported to the insurer by the insured at periodic intervals specified in the form. At the end of the policy period, the insurer computes the average values that were exposed to loss and uses that average to determine the premium.

The major distinguishing features of the value reporting form are:

- the reporting requirement,
- the penalties,
- the provisional premium,
- the use of the limit of insurance, and
- the treatment of specific (nonreporting) insurance.

Reporting Requirement. The insured must submit to the insurance company a periodic report of dollar values covered by the policy. The period of time for which new reports of value are due is referred to as a *reporting period.* Each reporting period has a specified interval at which reports are required. Five options are available:

DR—daily values reported monthly,

WR—weekly values reported monthly,

MR—monthly values reported monthly,

QR—quarterly values reported quarterly, and

PR—(policy year) monthly values reported at the end of the policy year.

The code letters DR, WR, and so forth appear in the commercial property declarations in place of the coinsurance percentage. (Since the declarations do not then show a coinsurance percentage of 80 or higher, unless other provisions are made it would seem that the BPP coverage extensions do not apply when the value reporting form is used.) When covered values are to be reported "monthly," the reporting period ends on the last day of each month. For quarterly reports, the reporting period ends on the last day of March, June, September, and December. For policy year reports, the reporting period ends on the policy anniversary date.

The insured must file the required report within thirty days of the end of each reporting period and at the expiration of the policy. The reports must separately list the total value of covered property at each location as of the *report dates* required by the *reporting period,* in order to avoid a penalty.

Penalties. In order for the value reporting approach to work properly—and for the insurer to collect appropriate premiums—the insurer must have timely information that accurately reflects the values exposed to loss. To enforce this need, the form contains penalties for failure to submit any reports, for late reports, and/or for inaccurate reports.

- *Failure to report.* If the *first* required report of values was due, but had not been received, as of the time of the loss (for example, the first monthly report has not been received by the end of the second month, and a loss subsequently occurs), then the insurer will not pay more than 75 percent of the amount that would otherwise have been paid. Thus, the insured who fails to submit the initial report will be forced to retain *at least* 25 percent of any loss.
- *Late report.* As noted earlier, reports are due within thirty days of the report date. If a report—other than the first required

report—is overdue at the time of the loss, the insurer will pay no more than the values last reported for the location that suffered the loss. This could be a serious penalty for an organization whose values are rising, but would have no effect on an organization whose values are lower than they were at the last report date.

● *Inaccurate reports.* The value reporting form replaces the coinsurance provision of the BPP with a *full reporting clause*, which is essentially the same thing as a 100 percent coinsurance clause. (This clause is sometimes referred to as an *honesty clause.*) The clause simply stipulates that, if the last report showed less than the full value of covered property at the affected location on the report date, then the insurer will pay claims according to the following formula:

$$\left(\frac{\text{Values reported}}{\text{Actual values}} \times \text{Loss}\right) - \text{Deductible}$$

Provisional Premium. As with other types of insurance, the insurer will never pay more than the applicable policy limit at the time of the loss. But, unlike other property coverages previously discussed, the limit of insurance for property subject to the value reporting form is not intended to reflect directly the value of covered property; rather, the limit is usually set comfortably higher than the maximum expected values that will be encountered at any one time during the policy term.

Because the limit does not directly reflect the exposures, it would not be appropriate to charge an initial premium based on the full limit of insurance. Instead, the insured must pay, at the beginning of the policy period, a *provisional premium*—typically 75 percent of the annual premium that would be required to purchase nonreporting coverage with the same limit.

The earned premium during the entire policy period depends on the average values reported during the policy term. At the end of the policy period, an additional premium may be due or a refund may be owed to the insured. Refunds and additional premiums are calculated on a pro-rata basis.

As long as the insured complies with the policy conditions, the earned premium, in effect, increases or decreases automatically. Moreover, unless values exceed the limit of insurance, the applicable amount of coverage is adequate to cover any loss—even when the values on hand at the time of the loss are greater than the values reflected in the last report.

Use of the Limit of Insurance. A specific limit of insurance applies to property at each location, and the insurer's obligation is limited by this maximum.

The insured is required to report all property on hand as of each report date. If $250,000 worth of property is on hand and the limit of insurance is $150,000, then the insured must still report $250,000. Since the premium is based on the *reported values*, the insured must also pay a premium based on $250,000. However, coverage is still capped by the $150,000 limit of insurance. If such a situation occurs, the insured should increase the limits or purchase specific insurance to cover the additional $100,000 of value. (Insurance companies and agencies may also set up systems to trigger a review in any case where values approach or exceed limits, but the ultimate burden of monitoring lies on the insured.)

Specific Insurance. Reporting insurance may be combined with other, nonreporting insurance covering the same property. This other insurance is then referred to as specific insurance. (Terminology could get confusing here since "specific" is also used as the opposite of "blanket," as explained later.)

The value reporting form defines specific insurance as:

...other insurance that:
    a. Covers the same Covered Property to which this endorsement applies; and
    b. Is not subject to the same plan, terms, conditions and provisions as this insurance, including this endorsement.

Coverage on property subject to the value reporting form is excess over the amount *due from* specific insurance plus the deductible applying to specific insurance. In effect, the reporting form acts as though the specific insurance had no deductible.

If the specific insurance has a coinsurance clause, the reporting form coverage is not counted when determining whether the specific insurance's coinsurance requirement has been met. For example, suppose insured goods are valued at $250,000. An 80 percent coinsurance clause under the specific insurance contract would require $200,000 of coverage in order to avoid a coinsurance penalty. If the actual amount of specific insurance is $100,000, (and ignoring deductibles for the moment) then the specific insurance coverage would pay only half of any loss up to $200,000, determined as follows:

$$\frac{\$100,000}{80\% \times \$250,000} = 1/2$$

The reporting coverage would pay the amount of loss in excess of the specific insurance payment—subject, in all cases, to policy limits. Suppose the specific insurance has a $5,000 deductible and the reporting insurance has a $1,000 deductible. On a $150,000 loss:

- The specific insurance would pay $70,000. ($\frac{1}{2} \times$ $150,000 = $75,000.) $75,000 − $5,000 = $70,000.
- The reporting insurance would pay $74,000 (assuming its limit is adequate and the last report of values was accurate and timely).
- The insured would retain $6,000—the $5,000 deductible plus the $1,000 deductible.

When the specific insurance has no coinsurance clause (i.e., is "flat" insurance), the specific coverage pays the loss to its policy limit and the reporting insurance pays the balance, (assuming adequate limits and timely reports).

When specific coverage is combined with reporting coverage, the insured always receives recovery in full (subject to deductibles)—as long as the combined limits (specific plus reporting) are adequate and the reporting requirements are complied with.

When the value reporting insurance is excess over specific insurance, the premium for the reporting form is based only on the excess of covered value over the amount of specific insurance at each location. Thus, with specific insurance of $100,000 at a location and value of $250,000 in covered property, the reporting form premium rate is applied against the $150,000 difference. The insured and the insurer must be alert to any change in specific coverage. In particular, when any specific coverage expires, the change must be noted in the next report.

Advantages and Disadvantages   For some insureds, the value reporting form is an ideal way of dealing with values that fluctuate substantially. As long as values do not exceed the limit of insurance, coverage is adequate to cover any loss in full, with no penalty for underinsurance. Yet, the insured does not need to pay for more insurance than is needed, since the premium directly reflects the values exposed to loss. Moreover, the premium rates used are 100 percent coinsurance rates, which are generally 10 percent lower than the more common 80 percent rates. In short, the insured can get the effect of full coverage at a lower rate without paying for more insurance than is necessary.

On the other hand, the value reporting form must be used with extreme care, or the cure might be worse than the disease. The penalties for nonexistent, late, or inaccurate reports can be severe. Late reports are an all-too-common problem with reporting forms. The penalties present a compelling reason why a reporting form should not be used unless there is reason to believe that reports will be produced promptly and accurately.

Inaccurate reports are sometimes made because the insured realizes that lower reported values will develop lower premiums. More frequently, inaccuracy reflects an inadequate system for developing the needed information. Sometimes inaccuracy stems from a misunderstanding as to the values that should be included in the report. For example, the insured might report only inventory values, when furniture, fixtures, and equipment are also among the items covered by the policy.

Even honest and timely reporting sometimes creates a problem: As noted earlier, when the value on hand exceeds the policy limit, the insured is still required to report the value and pay a premium for it, even though it is not fully covered. Obviously, such a situation is undesirable and constitutes a problem.

In short, the value reporting form presents a sound solution to the problem of fluctuating values—but only when the insured submits timely, accurate reports that fully reflect all reportable values *and* care is taken to be sure that the exposure does not exceed the policy limits.

Alternatives to Specific Insurance—Blanket Coverage

(Here is that other meaning of "specific" coverage.) According to the *Commercial Lines Manual*:

> Insurance is specific when the entire amount of insurance under a particular item applies at one location to one type of property such as a single building, personal property of the insured or personal property of others situated in a single building. . . .

Blanket insurance is defined as insurance that:

> covers under one amount: a. One type of property in more than one separately rated building; or b. Two or more types of property in one or more separately rated buildings.

Four "types of property" that might be insured within one blanket limit are:

- building(s);
- personal property of the named insured;

- personal property of others in the care, custody, or control of the named insured; and
- tenants' improvements and betterments.

No endorsement or other policy modification is used to effect blanket insurance. All that is necessary is to indicate in the policy declarations that several types of property are covered as a single item, subject to a single limit of insurance. The word "blanket" would probably be included in the wording used to describe covered property.

The blanket approach can be a particularly effective method for insuring contents that may be moved from one building to another, if the total contents value of all insured locations does not fluctuate widely. Examples of firms that could benefit from blanket coverage include the following:

- An organization having a warehouse that supplies several retail outlets. The contents of the warehouse and the outlets may be blanketed.
- A firm whose stock is located in several different buildings, with an inventory control system that gives total values but does not break out values in each building.
- A manufacturing operation that moves property from one building to another in the normal course of manufacture so that total values are relatively constant, but the value in any given building may vary substantially from week to week.

In general, the greater the number of locations and the smaller the proportion of total value at any one location, the greater the virtue of blanket insurance. From the insured's point of view, there may be little benefit in knowing exactly how much value is at any particular place at any given time, and it may be onerous to report insurable values by location. (Note that blanket insurance is not a good substitute for sloppy record keeping. In the event of a substantial loss at any one location, the insured needs to be able to establish the values that were lost!)

From the insurer's viewpoint, the greater number of locations and the dispersion of values make it less important to know exactly the amount of exposure at each location, because of the greater credibility or predictability of the insured's overall average experience.

Coinsurance Requirement While the blanket approach makes it unnecessary for the insured to know precisely where property values are located at all times, this advantage is available only at an additional cost. Except when personal property of others or tenants improvements and betterments are insured, the minimum coinsurance clause is 90 percent—but the premium rates are the same as for 80 percent coinsurance on a policy providing specific coverage.

The premium for blanket insurance is about 5 percent higher than the premium for the same amount of specific insurance with the same coinsurance percentage. With *specific* insurance, a 90 percent coinsurance clause earns a 5 percent reduction from the 80 percent coinsurance rate. A 100 percent coinsurance clause earns a further 10 percent reduction. For *blanket* insurance, however, a 90 percent coinsurance clause uses the same rate as an 80 percent clause would use with specific insurance, and a 100 percent clause earns only a 5 percent reduction. These higher rates are justified because an insured with blanket coverage does not have to buy insurance equal to 100 percent of total values to have 100 percent coverage at each separate location—unless, of course, the policy is subject to a 100 percent coinsurance clause. This is so because the entire blanket limit of liability applies to loss at any particular location even though most insured losses would involve only one location.

The following example illustrates why this is the case. A tenant owns property in two buildings on opposite ends of a large town, with property at each location valued at $50,000. Both are covered by the same blanket insurance policy with a 90 percent coinsurance clause. The policy limit is $90,000. If the contents of one building are totally destroyed, the amount of insurance required to meet the coinsurance requirement is $90,000, calculated as follows:

$$\text{Value of covered property: } \$50,000 + \$50,000 = \$100,000$$

$$90\% \times \$100,000 = \$90,000$$

Since the coinsurance requirement is met with $90,000 of blanket coverage, the amount recovered in a $50,000 loss would be $50,000 (less any applicable deductible). Of course, there is $100,000 of property exposed to loss and a loss payment could never exceed the $90,000 limit, but this is a moot point unless both locations are involved in a single loss. In short, all possible losses would be covered in full. With specific insurance, the tenant would have had to purchase two separate $50,000 policies ($100,000 total insurance) to obtain the same loss adjustment.

Rating As noted above, the premium rate for blanket insurance is about 5 percent higher than the rate for the same dollar amount of specific insurance. Another potential disadvantage of blanket coverage arises when more than one rate applies to property covered by the form. The rating bureau may require that the highest rate on the various types of property be used on all contents at all locations. However, this obstacle is usually eliminated by the use of a blanket average rate. The average rate is a weighted average based on values at each location and the premium rate at each location. The insured must submit a *statement of values* to be used in developing the blanket average rate.

Alternative Deductibles

Although the basic per-occurrence deductible is $250, per-occurrence deductibles can be increased to as much as $75,000 or more. Higher deductibles are subject to negotiation between insurer and insured.

The use of a large per-occurrence deductible presents the possibility of substantial retained losses in the event a number of separate occurrences take place. That possibility can be controlled with the use of an aggregate deductible.

Aggregate Deductibles With a true aggregate deductible, the insured's *total* loss retention for the policy year is limited to a specified amount (aggregate), regardless of the number of occurrences. The simplified ISO forms do not have a true aggregate, but accomplish the same general effect with what is called a *deductible insurance plan with annual accumulation*. The policy is modified by a *deductible limitation endorsement* which explains how the *annual accumulation* is handled.

When this approach is used, the annual accumulation (similar to an annual deductible as explained below) must be at least $5,000 and at least twice the per-occurrence deductible, according to ISO rules.

Although the aggregate deductible concept is very simple, some complexity is introduced because it becomes necessary to state exactly what losses will be counted towards the aggregate. While it might at first seem logical simply to count every loss, remember that a major reason for deductibles is to eliminate the expense and paperwork involved with handling every small loss as an insurance claim. That purpose would be defeated if every claim had to be recorded in order to keep tabs on progress towards the annual accumulation. Furthermore, disputes might develop in deciding which cases to count—which could lead to coverage disputes in cases that would never result in insurance payment anyway.

The *deductible limitation endorsement* handles this problem by ignoring losses that are less than 10 percent of the per-occurrence deductible, until the annual accumulation amount is reached. For

Exhibit 4-1
How Deductible Limitation Operates*

Loss Date	Loss Amount	Loss Above per Occurrence Deductible	Losses Retained	Annual Accumulation	Annual Accumulation to Date	Losses Paid by Insurer
Jan 14	$ 800[1]	$ 0	$ 800	$ 0	$ 0	$ 0
Feb 12	10,000	0	10,000	10,000	10,000	0
Mar 5	500[1]	0	500	0	10,000	0
Mar 15	1,000	0	1,000	1,000	11,000	0
May 1	25,000	15,000	10,000	25,000	36,000	15,000
Jun 30	5,000	4,750	250[2]	n/a	n/a	4,750
Jul 29	15,000	5,000	250[2]	n/a	n/a	14,750
Sep 5	4,000	n/a	250[2]	n/a	n/a	3,750
Oct 26	15,000	5,000	250[2]	n/a	n/a	14,750
Dec 20	700	n/a	250[2]	n/a	n/a	450
	$ 77,000	$ 29,750	$ 23,550			$ 53,450

* Per occurrence deductible, $10,000; annual accumulation amount, $30,000.

[1] Loss less than 10 percent of per occurrence deductible.

[2] The $250 per occurrence deductible is reinstated after the annual accumulation amount is reached.

example, with a $100,000 per-occurrence deductible, only losses of $1,000 or more would be reported to the insurer, and a running tally of all such losses would be kept. Once the tally reaches the annual accumulation amount, the insured is required to report any loss greater than $250. The insurer will then apply a $250 deductible to each loss for the remainder of the policy year.

Exhibit 4-1 contains an example of what might happen in one policy year in a policy with a $10,000 per-occurrence deductible and a $30,000 annual accumulation amount. After the May 1 loss, the insured would absorb only a $250 deductible in future losses. No more than $250 per loss is deducted, even for losses below the $10,000 per-occurrence deductible. For the one-year policy period, rather than retaining $29,750, as would have been the case with a $10,000 per-occurrence deductible with no aggregate, the insured retains $23,550.

The deductible limitation has obvious risk management advantages when used to supplement a per-event deductible. It allows the risk manager to be more confident when anticipating such important items as cash flow and profits. However, from the insurer's point of view, the use of the aggregate deductible can lead to a larger payout to the insured. Also, the insurer must incur some expenses in verifying and tallying losses that lead to the annual accumulation. Given these possibilities, it should be no surprise that the use of the deductible limitation reduces the rate credit that would otherwise apply for the per-occurrence deductible with no aggregate.

Use of Deductibles   When evaluating deductibles, the percentage reduction in the premium is not all that matters. The actual number of dollars saved is highly important.

For example, suppose a $10,000 per-occurrence deductible could save 25 percent on the normal premium. If the normal premium is $2,000, the resulting $500 saving might not be significant—especially when compared with the potential cost of one or more sizable losses during the policy year. One loss of $10,000 would use up twenty years of premium savings. On the other hand, if the normal premium is $8,000, a 25 percent reduction would save $2,000 and the insured could, in effect, pay for a $10,000 loss with only five years' premium savings. Of course, a larger premium usually reflects more value insured, a higher insurance rate reflecting greater hazards, or both. These factors should obviously have a bearing on the risk manager's decision.

The basic concept involved here has been concisely stated as: "Don't risk a lot to save a little." More sophisticated analysis would take into consideration not only the payback period (twenty years or five years, in the example), but also the time value of money and the tax implications of insurance expenses and of uninsured losses.

CAUSES OF LOSS FORMS—OVERVIEW

The first insurance policies on property at fixed locations covered only fire losses. Subsequently, because it was sometimes difficult to separate lightning losses from fire losses, fire insurance policies were extended to include coverage against the peril of lightning.

Insurance for additional perils became available over time, and coverage for the most popular perils was eventually combined in a package of perils known as *extended coverage,* or *EC* for short. The *extended coverage perils* consisted of the following:

- windstorm and hail,
- smoke,
- explosion,
- civil commotion, riot, and riot attending a strike, and
- aircraft and vehicle damage.

A later development was the addition of *vandalism or malicious mischief—VMM* for short—as an insurable peril. Perhaps the most popular set of coverages for a commercial building involved "Fire, EC, and VMM"—a phrase that tripped readily from the tongues of many insurance people. A "sprinkler leakage" endorsement was often added when insuring a sprinklered location.

A broader grouping of named perils was offered with package policies, such as the special multi-peril policy (SMP). Later, an optional perils endorsement was introduced for commercial monoline policies as well. These broad form perils options presented a second tier of coverage. A third tier of coverage involved the "all-risks" approach, described under the next heading.

One of the simplifications of the Commercial Lines Simplification Program was a further expansion of perils packages, still maintaining the idea of three tiers of coverage.

The basic approach, reflected in the *causes of loss—basic form,* covers against the perils of:

- fire,
- lightning,
- the old extended coverage perils,
- vandalism,
- sprinkler leakage,
- sinkhole collapse, and
- volcanic action.

Windstorm or hail, vandalism, or sprinkler leakage coverage may be deleted by endorsement. The addition of the "volcanic action" peril can be attributed directly to the eruption of Mount St. Helens. Eleven distinct perils are listed, as detailed later.

The *causes of loss—broad form* goes beyond the basic approach, adding the four *perils* of

- breakage of glass;
- falling objects;
- weight of snow, ice, or sleet; and
- water damage.

The broad form also adds one *additional coverage*—collapse.

Still broader coverage is available with the *causes of loss—special form,* an "all-risks" type form that covers direct physical loss except for items excluded or limited. The special form also adds an additional coverage extension for property in transit.

"All-Risks" Type Coverage

In rather general terms, the idea of "all-risks" insurance policies is to cover loss by any cause except for certain excluded perils that are considered uninsurable or difficult to insure. The typical "all-risks" policy covered "all risks of direct physical loss" subject to exclusions and other policy conditions. A typical "all-risks" policy contained exclusions for war, nuclear reaction, flood, earthquake, and a variety of maintenance-type items such as wear-and-tear.

For many years this approach worked satisfactorily. In the early 1980s, however, the *doctrine of concurrent causation* raised some serious issues that resulted in widespread changes to what had been known as "all-risks" insurance.

Concurrent Causation

The eruption of the doctrine of concurrent causation had an effect on property insurance even more significant than the eruption of Mt. Saint Helens. The effect has been to threaten the very concept of "all-risks" coverage.

The doctrine of concurrent causation evolved, in part, from a case in which record rains broke through flood-control facilities and inundated parts of the city of Palm Desert, California. As far as insurers were concerned, this "flood" loss was clearly excluded. However, the holders of "all-risks" homeowners policies alleged that the proximate cause of the loss was "negligence of the water district"—a cause of loss that was not excluded. The court supported the policyholders' position, on the basis that (1) the flood and (2) the negligent act of constructing flood control structures were independent, concurrent causes that interacted with each other to produce the loss. Similar decisions were reached in other California cases. In a case involving earth movement—actually, a landslide—the policyholder successfully argued that a "faulty installation of a drain by a third party" was the cause of the landslide, and such negligent actions by third parties were not excluded.

The effect of the concurrent causation doctrine is that the insurer with a so-called "all-risks" policy must pay if *any one* of the causes of loss is not specifically excluded. Stated differently, if a loss to property can be attributed to two causes—one excluded by the policy and one covered—the policy covers the loss. In short, the doctrine seemed to say that none of the perils exclusions of an "all-risks" policy had any effect if it was possible to identify another, nonexcluded peril, that was somehow involved in the loss event![2]

In response to these decisions, "all-risks" policies began to be revised late in 1983. The revised policies deleted the "all" from "all-risks"—a change intended to de-emphasize the breadth of coverage or its presumably comprehensive nature. In addition, the exclusions were restructured to clarify the insurers' intent. For example, some of the policy language makes it clear that certain losses are "...excluded regardless of any other causes or event contributing concurrently or in any sequence to the loss."

The exclusions of the current "all-risks" type form will be discussed in greater detail later in the chapter. The concurrent causation doctrine has been mentioned here in order to clarify the reasoning behind some of the policy wording, which is reflected not only in the special ("all-risks" type) form, but in the other causes-of-loss forms as well.

A further response to the concurrent causation doctrine has been the preparation of a so-called "special named perils" causes-of-loss form. This form is intended to replace the "all-risks" type of form if future court decisions fail to uphold the exclusions of those revised forms. From the perspective of insurers, the only remaining solution might be to return to named-perils type coverage with the broadest practical list of named perils. At the time of this writing, a set of special named perils forms has been drafted, but there is no plan to implement them. However, they could rapidly be put into use, if needed. The special named perils forms will be discussed briefly later in the chapter.

Content of the Simplified "Commercial Property" Forms

Property insurance coverage can be characterized according to (1) covered property, (2) covered perils, and (3) covered causes of loss. The simplified "commercial property" forms follow this approach, to some extent.

The basic idea of the simplified "commercial property" forms is to describe covered property in one form and covered causes of loss in another. However, the forms are not as "pure" as this explanation would suggest. Scattered throughout the BPP and other covered property forms are provisions relating to causes of loss, and scattered throughout the causes-of-loss forms are references to certain types of property that are covered or excluded.

The basic insuring agreement is found in the "covered property" forms. However, both "covered property" and "covered causes of loss" forms contain exceptions to exclusions, some of which expand the scope of coverage and thus serve, in effect, as additional coverages. Both types of forms also contain provisions distinctly labeled as additional coverages.

As to covered consequences, the costs covered and excluded by "commercial property" forms vary to a much greater extent than first meets the eye. The *reduction in value* of covered property is invariably covered by the BPP, so long as the damage is done by a covered peril as provided in a causes-of-loss form. Certain other costs are covered, too—but only in connection with certain perils.

An example of additional coverage granted by exception to an exclusion appears under the "sprinkler leakage" peril:

> ...we will also pay the cost to...tear out and replace any part of the building...to repair damage....

An example of property excluded within a perils provision is the following, which appears under the "sinkhole collapse" peril:

> "This cause of loss does not include the cost of filling sinkholes."

This chapter integrates these various dispersed items, whether relating to types of property, perils, or consequences, by making reference not only to the causes-of-loss forms, but also to the BPP.

CAUSES OF LOSS—BASIC FORM

The *causes of loss—basic form* represents what might be considered the basic approach to covered perils. The form provides coverage for eleven named perils in a single package. The old "Fire, EC, and VMM" grouping has been combined with sprinkler leakage and expanded with some additional perils. However, it is possible to write a policy without windstorm or hail, vandalism, or sprinkler leakage coverage, since these perils can be excluded by endorsement.

Discussion in this section examines closely all eleven perils insured against in the causes of loss—basic form. These perils were examined in Chapters 1 and 2 from the standpoint of exposure identification and analysis. Discussion in this chapter concentrates on the ways these various perils are described in the various causes-of-loss forms. Some perils are merely listed in the form without further elaboration. However, as the chapter progresses, it will be shown that many of the perils descriptions tend to limit the scope of coverage to something more restrictive than would seem to be indicated if only the names of the covered perils were listed. Other descriptions define the perils in a broad way that might broaden the scope of coverage beyond a mere listing.

Fire

The "fire" peril is merely listed, without further description or definition. However, the range of losses that may be considered "fire" losses has been interpreted in a wide variety of court decisions over many years during which insurers have offered policies covering the peril of fire.

Flame and Oxidation To fall within the fire peril, there should normally be (1) a flame or glow and (2) rapid oxidation. The flame or glow requirement causes some problems when a substance begins to smoke because of a buildup of heat. In one situation, cotton seed stored in a warehouse began to smoke (with no flame or glow) and, when firefighters removed the top portion, the seed broke into flames. This loss was considered a fire loss by the court. It should be mentioned, however, that this is considered a liberal interpretation of the flame or glow requirement, and other courts might reach a different conclusion.

Friendly Versus Hostile Fire For insurance purposes, the fire peril refers to a hostile fire.

- A *hostile fire* is generally considered one that is outside its intended receptacle and does damage.
- In contrast, a *friendly fire* is one that is intentionally ignited and remains inside its intended receptacle.

For instance, a fire in a fireplace or at a gas burner on a kitchen range is a friendly fire. If an ember jumps out of the fireplace onto a carpet, which catches fire, then the fire is considered hostile and any resulting loss could be covered by fire insurance. In an industrial setting, a similar relationship would hold between a fire in a melting furnace and a fire ignited when the heated contents escape from the furnace and ignite combustible materials.

Excessive Heat The modern trend seems to categorize a fire as hostile if it burns abnormally (hotter, longer, and so on), even if the flames remain confined to the intended place. Usually such excessive heat losses involve furnaces with defective controls. The control does not work properly and the furnace overheats—and may even self-destruct.

In an agricultural case, a defective thermostat failed to curtail the heating in a hog barn, the temperature rose to 120 degrees, and fifteen sows died. The Minnesota Supreme Court ruled that the loss was a fire loss under the excessive heat principle. In this case, the court actually extended the principle to include the concept of excessive time. The furnace did not actually overheat—it just operated for an excessive time and allowed the barn to become too hot for the hogs.[3]

Lightning

Like "fire," "lightning" is listed without further description in the basic causes-of-loss form.

Lightning is considered to be an electrical charge generated by nature, as opposed to man-made or "artificially generated" electrical currents. This point is reinforced by an exclusion that specifically precludes coverage for loss or damage caused by artificially generated electrical current.

As an example of the relevance of this difference, suppose a malfunction in a 235-volt line destroys a fuse and terminal. This event causes refrigeration units to stop and some meat to spoil. The policyholder would have coverage if the loss were caused by lightning, but not if the loss were due to another electrical disturbance. In this particular set of circumstances, the loss would not be covered.[4]

If lightning strikes and a surge of electricity goes through a firm's electrical lines, causing damage to building or equipment, the loss is covered under the lightning peril. Other property losses that naturally flow from such damage are considered proximately caused by lightning. Hence, food spoilage due to lightning damage to refrigeration equipment or, in one case, suffocation of hogs due to lightning damage to ventilating equipment, has been held to be covered.

Usually a lightning strike will not start a fire, but will cause property damage. It is said that there are at least two types of lightning bolts—hot and cold. A hot bolt is orange in color, has high amperage, and will start a fire. A cold bolt has an explosive nature, but is not likely to start a fire. It literally can bounce around a room knocking holes in the wall, without starting a fire.[5]

Windstorm and Hail

Except in policies covering growing crops, the perils of windstorm and hail go together. The terms "windstorm" and "hail" are not defined, but coverage is partially delineated by describing what is *not* included within those perils.

The "windstorm or hail" peril of the causes-of-loss form provides no coverage for losses occurring from (1) frost or cold weather, or (2) ice (other than hail), snow, or sleet—whether driven by wind or not.

If the force of wind, or a substance driven by the wind, first causes external damage to an insured structure (e.g., by breaking a window), then subsequent damage to the interior of the building or to its contents *caused by rain, snow, sand, or dust* is covered. For example, damage caused by rain blown through an open window or under roof openings or through cracks is not covered. But if wind breaks the window and wind-blown rain enters the structure through the broken window, coverage exists.

Windstorm damage to the interior of the building or to contents is covered even when there is no damage to the exterior. For example, damage to expensive draperies that are shredded during a windstorm because a window or door was left open would be covered.

Damage due to flood, surface water, waves, tidal water or tidal wave, overflow of streams or other bodies of water, or spray from any of the foregoing—whether driven by the wind or not—is not within the scope of the windstorm or hail peril. This point is reinforced by the *water exclusion* of the form. So even though windstorm damage caused by a hurricane is covered by the windstorm peril, much of the water damage that occurs during a hurricane is not.

Riot or Civil Commotion

The basic causes-of-loss form treats these perils together, but does not define them. Riot has statutory definitions, but the definitions are not the same in all states. A common definition is:

> Whenever three or more persons, having assembled for any purpose, disturb the public peace by using force of violence to any other person or to property or threaten or attempt to commit such disturbance or to do an unlawful act by the use of force or violence, accompanied with the power of immediate execution of such threat or attempt, they are guilty of riot.[6]

Some states say two people can commit an act of riot while other states require up to five people.

Civil commotion has been described as an uprising of citizens.[7] "Civil commotion" and "riot" are quite similar, and the two terms should include most uprisings.

The peril specifically includes acts of striking employees while occupying the described premises. An example that illustrates the potential severity of this peril occurred in 1975 when strikers at the *Washington Post* became violent and damaged many of the newspaper's presses.

Looting frequently accompanies riots, but theft is not one of the basic causes of loss. However, looting occurring at the time and place of a riot (or civil commotion) is specifically within the scope of the riot or civil commotion peril.

Smoke

The basic causes-of-loss form limits coverage to smoke causing sudden and accidental loss or damage, other than smoke from agricultural smudging or industrial operations.

The smoke may originate on or off premises. The smoke may be from a fireplace, stove, or furnace. All these represent friendly fires, and smoke from them would not be covered within the fire peril.

One source of debate is the question of what constitutes an industrial operation. A Georgia Court of Appeals ruled that smoke that damaged a dress shop's contents as a result of fire in a small neighborhood bakery did not involve an industrial operation, and the court held that the dress shop's insurer should pay.[8]

Agricultural smudging refers to the use of smudge pots to protect oranges and other crops against frost damage.

Aircraft or Vehicles

These two perils are treated together in most property forms. In general terms, these perils are intended to cover losses occurring when a car, truck, or airplane crashes into insured property.

Vehicles are not defined in the policy, but have been described elsewhere as "vehicles running on land or tracks but not aircraft." The peril requires physical contact between the aircraft." The peril requires physical contact between the vehicle, or an object "thrown up" by a vehicle, with the damaged property or the building containing the property. This does not necessarily encompass all cases in which a vehicular accident is the proximate loss of a property loss. Examples of losses in which the physical contact requirement is not literally met include the following:

- A vehicle collides with a pole owned by a telephone company and the pole hits the insured property.
- A chain is attached to a loading dock and to the vehicle, and the vehicle drives away, causing damage to the dock.

It is difficult to predict how the courts might interpret coverage in situations such as these.

Damage caused by vehicles owned or operated by the named insured is not covered.

Aircraft are not defined either, but the form tends to clarify the intention of this peril by stating that the aircraft itself, a spacecraft, a self-propelled missile, or an object falling from the aircraft must contact the property or a building or structure containing it. There is no exclusion for aircraft owned or operated by the named insured.

The physical contact requirement eliminates coverage *under the aircraft peril* for sonic boom claims. However, this is not an important consideration, since sonic boom losses are no longer excluded under the explosion peril.

Explosion

The basic causes-of-loss form does not actually define "explosion," but does describe the extent of coverage under this peril. The accepted meaning of the word includes such things as sudden combustion of gunpowder, dynamite, gasoline, and natural gas. Damage caused by a contractor's blasting would be covered within the explosion peril, as would loss due to the explosion of a container of compressed air.

Sonic Boom   A sonic boom is the explosion-like sound produced when a shock wave formed at the nose of an aircraft traveling at supersonic speed reaches the ground. A sonic boom is not an explosion in the usual sense, but it is the result of air compressed by a supersonic aircraft. Presimplified commercial property forms specifically excluded sonic boom losses under the explosion peril. Since the sonic boom exclusion has been removed, it would seem that a sonic boom loss would now be covered.

Water Damage   The basic causes-of-loss form clearly states that explosion coverage does not apply to loss or damage by:

> Rupture or bursting due to expansion or swelling of the contents of any building or structure, caused by or resulting from water.

For example, when moisture in a grain storage silo or elevator causes a sudden expansion and collapse of the structure, that is not considered an explosion.

Pressure Relief Devices   Another provision of the explosion peril makes it clear that "rupture, bursting or operation of pressure relief devices" is not an explosion. This provision refers to the potential damage that might ensue from the operation of safety valves on steam boilers, hot water tanks, air tanks, and so forth, which intentionally release excess pressure to avoid damage to the unit to which the safety valve is attached.

Furnace Firebox Explosions Covered   Most furnaces are operated by the combustion of solid or gaseous fuel which passes through certain passageways while heating water, steam, or air and then escapes through a flue or chimney. Explosion of such fuel or gases is included within the explosion peril. Explosion of the container holding water or steam might also be considered explosion; coverage for boiler explosions is precluded by a separate exclusion in the basic causes-of-loss form.

Boiler Explosion Excluded   The basic causes-of-loss form specifically excludes some explosions that are best covered by boiler and machinery insurance. In general terms, the form excludes coverage for explosion of steam boilers, steam pipes, steam engines, or steam turbines, unless a fire or combustion explosion results.

The relationship between the explosion peril of "commercial

property" forms and the causes of loss covered by boiler and machinery forms will be examined in more detail in Chapter 6.

Volcanic Explosion In the wake of the Mt. St. Helens volcano, some people considered volcanic eruptions to be explosions according to their interpretation of the language of some policies that did not specifically exclude coverage for volcanic eruptions. The basic causes-of-loss form is silent on the question as to whether a volcanic eruption is an explosion—a moot point, since volcanic action is specifically included as a covered peril.

Vandalism

As noted earlier, a riot usually involves three or more people behaving in an unlawful manner and disturbing the peace. Situations involving only one or two people, or people who act quietly, are not included within the riot peril but can be considered acts of vandalism.

Definition of Vandalism Earlier forms included the peril of "vandalism or malicious mischief," often abbreviated as VMM. The simplified forms do not treat "malicious mischief" as a separate peril. However, the same effect is accomplished because the term "vandalism" is defined as "willful and malicious damage to, or destruction of, the described property." Note that both intent ("willful") and motive ("malicious") must be established for a loss to be considered vandalism.

Vacancy Provision If a building is vacant beyond sixty consecutive days, vandalism coverage is suspended. This provision is not found in the causes-of-loss form, but in the BPP—an example of the fact that some perils provisions are found in the property forms.

Buildings Under Construction or Reconstruction. As far as the vacancy provision is concerned, a building under construction is not considered vacant. While vacancy does not exactly cause vandalism, it should be obvious that the probability of vandalism is greatly increased when a building is vacant or unoccupied.

While this may seem clear and logical, the question arises about the status of a building that is vacant while it is being repaired following damage by an insured peril. By its terms, the vacancy provision of the BPP is triggered by vacancy that has been continuous for more than sixty days prior to loss. It is not triggered by vacancy that begins following a loss. The "under construction" exception is intended to provide coverage if a loss occurs when the building is in the process of original construction for more than sixty days.

Reduction or Cancellation of Coverage on Vacant Buildings. Loss of vandalism coverage is not the only problem associated with vacant buildings. When a building is vacant beyond sixty days, coverage is also lost for the perils of sprinkler leakage (if the system was not protected against freezing), building glass breakage, water damage, theft, and attempted theft. For other perils the amount of any claims payment is reduced by 15 percent. Also, as mentioned in Chapter 3, the *cancellation changes endorsement* gives the insurer the right (but not the obligation) to cancel coverage with only five days' notice on a building that has been vacant more than sixty days—unless the vacancy permit endorsement is purchased.

Vacancy Permit. The *vacancy permit endorsement* may be used to extend coverage during an extended period of vacancy, subject to an additional premium and the approval of the insurer.

Exclusions. The vandalism peril is further limited by exclusions pertaining to glass and theft.

Glass. The glass exclusion states that loss or damage "to glass (other than glass building blocks) that is part of a building, structure, or an outside sign" is not covered. However, damage to *other property* caused by breakage of glass by vandals is covered. For example, if vandals were to throw a brick through a plate glass display window of a furniture store, the window would not be covered, but the displayed furniture that is damaged by the brick and the flying glass would be.

Theft. Loss caused by or resulting from theft is not covered by the vandalism peril; however, damage caused by the forcible entry or exit of burglars is.

The general idea is that crime losses should be covered by crime insurance, while vandalism losses should be covered by "commercial property" insurance. Unfortunately, burglars and other criminals may willfully and maliciously damage property, and vandals may steal property—and it is difficult to draw a line that clearly separates vandalism by thieves from theft by vandals. This point will be examined more closely in Chapter 8, where it can be analyzed in the context of both "commercial property" insurance and crime insurance.

Sprinkler Leakage

The basic causes-of-loss form defines "sprinkler leakage" to mean:

leakage or discharge of any substance from an Automatic Sprinkler System, including collapse of a tank that is part of the system.

The term *discharge of any substance* indicates that the peril includes not only the discharge of water, but also accidental discharges from a system containing extinguishing agents such as CO_2 gas, Halon gas, a dry chemical powder, or an antifreeze solution. The protective systems often found above restaurant cooking equipment would clearly be included here.

Automatic sprinkler system is broadly defined in the form to include items such as sprinkler heads, piping, tanks, pumps, and standpipes.

The second part of the definition of sprinkler leakage involves the collapse of automatic sprinkler system tanks. Such tanks are sometimes located in separate water towers, but they often stand on the roof of a building. One such tank was illustrated in Exhibit 2-19. When such a tank collapses, the weight of the collapsing tank itself can cause extensive damage. In addition, a tremendous amount of water may be released. For example, a 9,000 gallon elevated tank filled with water weighs about 75,000 pounds. The collapse of such a tank can cause considerable damage.

Further elaboration in the form deals more with covered property—or, more specifically, covered property damage—than with covered causes of loss. It is intended to make it clear that coverage applies to some building damage caused by sprinkler leakage when the building is covered property:

> If the building or structure containing the Automatic Sprinkler System is Covered Property, we will also pay the cost to:
> a. Repair or replace damaged parts of the Automatic Sprinkler System if the damage:
>   (1) Results in sprinkler leakage; or
>   (2) Is directly caused by freezing.
> b. Tear out and replace any part of the building or structure to repair damage to the Automatic Sprinkler system that has resulted in sprinkler leakage.

Protective Safeguards Endorsement A major factor affecting the severity of damage done by accidental discharge from a sprinkler system (excluding fall of a tank) is the amount of time elapsing before a leaking sprinkler head is plugged or the master valve on the system is turned off. Therefore, rate discounts are given when a sprinkler alarm system or watchman service will note the running of water in the system and sound an alarm.

Given such a discount, the insured must use due diligence to maintain the service. The insurer may attach to the policy a *protective safeguards endorsement* which states that coverage is automatically suspended on the property if the sprinkler system is not operational. In cases where the system is shut off due to breakage, leakage, freezing conditions, or the opening of sprinkler heads, the insured has forty-eight hours to notify the insurer before coverage is suspended.

Vacancy Clause As with vandalism, the vacancy clause of the BPP suspends sprinkler leakage coverage when a building is vacant for more than sixty days, unless the system is protected against freezing or a vacancy permit is obtained.

Sinkhole Collapse

Sinkhole collapse was not included among the extended coverage perils and has not traditionally been among the causes of loss covered within a basic property insurance program. Sinkhole collapse coverage, however, was available by endorsement in those areas of the country susceptible to sinkholes—and was even a required coverage in Florida.

Sinkhole collapse coverage is not included in the basic causes-of-loss form. *Sinkhole collapse* is defined in the form as:

> loss or damage caused by the sudden sinking or collapse of land into underground empty spaces created by the action of water on limestone or similar rock formations.

Dolomite and limestone are the principal rock types involved in sinkhole losses.

Although sinkhole collapse is a covered peril, the intention is to pay for building and contents damage caused by sinkhole collapse—not to pay for damage to the land on which the building was situated. As noted in Chapter 3, land is not covered property. This intention is strengthened by a statement that appears as part of the sinkhole collapse peril, which specifically precludes coverage for the cost of filling sinkholes.

One wonders whether the exclusion for the "cost of filling sinkholes" will be upheld by the courts if the only way of providing a meaningful or lasting repair of the insured structure is to stabilize the ground first. Alternatively, replacement cost coverage does not require that the insured replace the structure on the same site in order for the replacement cost coverage to apply. But what if the premises are unstable—will the insurer be liable for the cost of a new lot as a replacement site, or will the exclusion of "land" from insured property and "the cost of filling sinkholes" from the "sinkhole collapse" peril force the insured to sustain the cost of a new site in order to obtain replacement cost coverage for the damaged structure?

Because the sinkhole collapse peril refers to "empty spaces created by the action of water on limestone or similar rock," it would not seem to cover *mine subsidence*—collapse of land into an underground mine.

Mine Subsidence Coverage Endorsement A mine subsidence coverage endorsement is required to be offered by insurers on certain structures in several states.

Volcanic Action

Another peril now included in the basic set of covered perils is the peril of volcanic action, defined as:

> direct loss or damage resulting from the eruption of a volcano when the loss or damage is caused by:
> a. Airborne volcanic blast or airborne shock waves;
> b. Ash, dust or particulate matter; or
> c. Lava flow.

Simply put, volcanic action encompasses the above-ground effects of a volcano.

The peril of *volcanic action* should not be confused with the peril of *volcanic eruption*. The *earth movement exclusion* of the basic causes-of-loss form specifically excludes coverage for "volcanic eruption, explosion or effusion" while noting that resulting damage by volcanic action or fire is covered. Coverage for earthquake and volcanic eruption is available in an endorsement described later.

As the quotation from the form shows, the perils actually covered under the term "volcanic eruption" are carefully specified: blast and shock waves, particulate matter, and lava flow. Fire, another important peril, is covered by regular fire insurance. But flood is *not* among the perils covered, and this is an important omission: Following the eruption of Mt. St. Helens in Washington in 1980, much of the damage resulted from floods caused by melting of the mountain's blanket of snow, plus part of a mountain lake sloshed out by mudflows and heavy rains created by condensation of steam from the eruption.

Other sources of damage include still other flows. The following is a description of events of Mt. St. Helens:

> The ash eruption was accompanied by pyroclastic flows, or *nanuées ardentes*, which consist of a mixture of gases, hot ash, and hot but solid fragments. Too dense to rise into an ash cloud, the mixture pours down the slope of a volcano from an erupting vent at speeds of up to 60 miles an hour. Sometimes pyroclastic flows are mistakenly called lava flow, but true lavas—surface flows of viscous molten rock—move much more slowly.
>
> An additional calamity that occurred [when Mt. St. Helens erupted] was a series of mudflows, which are slurries of volcanic ash and water that may be cold or warm but involve mainly liquid water rather than steam.[9]

The limits and deductibles of the BPP apply on a "per-occurrence" basis. There might be some question as to whether successive eruptions of a volcano are one occurrence or multiple occurrences—subject to one set of limits and deductibles or several. This problem is avoided by the clarifying statement under the volcanic action peril that all volcanic eruptions that occur within a specified time period will constitute a single occurrence.

Another statement attempts to make it clear that insurers intend to cover actual damage, rather than merely paying to remove volcanic debris. The cost to remove ash, dust, or particulate matter that does not cause direct physical loss or damage is specifically excluded.

CAUSES OF LOSS—BROAD FORM

The *causes of loss—broad form* provides broader coverage. That is, it provides coverage against a longer list of perils than the causes of loss—basic form. The broad form covers all the perils of the basic form and adds four more covered causes of loss. Also added with the broad form is an *additional coverage: collapse.*

Breakage of Glass

The broad causes-of-loss form covers only glass that is part of a building or structure. Furthermore, coverage is limited by both a $100 "per item" type limit and a $500 "per-occurrence" limit. To be more specific, the $100 limit applies to "each pane, multiple plate insulating unit, radiant or solar heating panel, jalousie, louver, or shutter."

Coverage would apply to the pane of glass itself, and also to property cut or otherwise damaged by breaking glass—even if the glass simply breaks for no obvious reason. Thus, coverage is actually for all causes of loss (perils) not specifically removed by the form's exclusions. However, the main effect of this peril is to cover nominal amounts of glass breakage by vandalism. (Remember, glass is not covered property so far as the vandalism peril is concerned.) The $100/$500 limits would have no effect when glass is broken by perils such as fire or windstorm, since there is no restriction on glass coverage under those perils.

Many signs include glass, sometimes in the form of neon tubing, but coverage for sign glass is limited. Since the only signs that are covered property under the BPP are signs attached to buildings, breakage of glass on a detached sign would not be covered. Furthermore, neon tubing on signs attached to a building or structure are not covered property so far as the glass breakage peril is concerned. The bottom line is that only glass (other than neon tubing) on signs attached to buildings is covered—and then only for the limits mentioned above.

It should also be noted that there is no glass breakage coverage after the building has been vacant for more than sixty consecutive days.

The *glass coverage form*, described in Chapter 6, can be used to provide full glass coverage.

Falling Objects

The causes of loss—broad form does not define what a falling object is. Thus, it could be anything—such as a tree branch falling from a tree or an entire tree that tips over onto a building. A falling object could be a rock, a meteorite, drops of rain, spilled paint, a clumsy squirrel, or anything else.

To avoid carrying coverage to a ridiculous extreme, this peril is limited—not by defining the peril, but by excluding certain types of property from coverage:

- Personal property in the open is not covered.
- The interior of a building, and contents of the building, are not covered unless the roof or an outside wall is first damaged by a falling object.

Weight of Snow, Ice, or Sleet

The approach taken here is similar to that of the falling objects peril. Snow, ice, or sleet are not defined, but certain types of property are excluded from coverage:

- Gutters and downspouts are not covered.
- Personal property outside of buildings or structures is not covered.

Although different phrases are used, there would seem to be no significant difference between the falling objects coverage for property "in the open" and the snow-ice-sleet coverage for property "outside of buildings or structures."

Water Damage

In broad terms, if somewhat oversimplified, this peril covers damage caused by leaky plumbing and appliances. Since sprinkler leakage has its own peril, it is excluded from coverage under the water damage peril. More specifically, the water damage peril is defined in the form as:

accidental discharge or leakage of water or steam as the direct result of the breaking or cracking of any part of a system or appliance containing water or steam, other than an Automatic Sprinkler System.

As detailed below, two exclusions within the water damage peril—for seepage and freezing—narrow the scope of water damage losses covered. Other provisions restrict the types of property covered. Water damage coverage is also affected by the *power failure exclusion* in the broad causes-of-loss form, described later. Also, as stated in the *vacancy provision*, water damage is not covered in a building that has been vacant for sixty days or more.

Seepage Exclusion Any loss due to continuous or repeated seepage or leakage of water or steam from an insured system is excluded if it occurs over a period of more than fourteen days. This provision eliminates coverage for losses (such as rotting of flooring or structural members) that result from a gradual seepage of water down a wall or through a floor.

Property policies generally exclude losses that are gradual in nature—especially if they could be detected and prevented with some diligence. However, words and phrases such as "sudden and accidental" and "gradual" are subject to varying court interpretations. The reference to fourteen days presumably defines in precise, quantifiable terms the insurer's intent of covering relatively sudden, but not gradual, losses.

Freezing Exclusion Freezing can generally be anticipated and prevented. Two approaches are obvious:

- Provide enough heat to prevent freezing temperatures, or
- Drain the water from pipes and appliances that will be exposed to freezing temperatures.

The intention is to cover only losses that occur despite reasonable preventive measures. Therefore, water damage caused by freezing is not covered unless:

- the insured does its "best" to maintain heat in the building or structure, or, if heat is not maintained,
- the equipment is drained and the water supply is shut off.

What constitutes a "best" effort involves a question of fact that may have to be decided by the courts.

Types of Property Covered and Excluded One subtle characteristic of water damage losses is that the cost of getting to the leak often costs more than fixing it. Plumbers often need to punch holes in walls, floors, and ceilings in order to get to a leaky pipe. The intentional damage required to make repairs is logically a part of the loss that insurers intend to cover.

Provisions in the water damage peril make it clear that the cost to tear out and replace any part of the building or structure, in order to repair damage to the leaky system or appliance that caused the water damage, is covered. However, the cost of repairing or replacing the system or appliance itself is not. Paying for the maintenance-like costs of replacing worn-out pipes, water heaters, and appliances is not a purpose of insurance.

Impact of Power Failure Exclusion Loss caused by "the failure of power or other utility service to the described premises, however caused," is excluded if the failure occurs away from the described premises. At first glance, this exclusion would seem to preclude water damage coverage for losses caused by failure of natural gas, electrical service, or water utilities originating off-premises. (Loss of gas or electricity might cause a failure of heating systems. Loss of water might result in a valve being accidentally left open, causing a problem when water service is restored.)

However, this exclusion adds the statement that resulting loss or damage by a covered cause of loss is covered. Since water damage is a "covered cause of loss," these provisions combine to affirm the existence of coverage for water damage losses caused by power failure or other off-premises utility problems.

Additional Coverage: Collapse

Earlier policies treated "collapse" as an insured peril, without extensive elaboration. Some writers have felt that this approach was somewhat flawed:

> Like "glass breakage," another so-called peril, collapse is not actually a *cause* of loss by itself; rather it is the *effect* of some property damaging peril. A stone thrown by vandals or a passing truck may cause glass to break; termite damage may cause a building to collapse. Sometimes the cause of glass breakage or collapse may not be verifiable, but the fact remains: Some peril inevitably causes the breakage or collapse.[10]

Moreover, insurers feared that if the concurrent causation doctrine were broadly applied, the collapse *peril*, if covered, could be the basis of a claim for almost any serious loss, so long as the claimant could find a contributing peril that was not specifically excluded. On the other hand, if it were not specifically treated, collapse could be considered a nonexcluded peril.

Since 1983, when property insurance policies were revised in reaction to the concurrent causation doctrine, collapse has been treated as an "additional coverage " rather than as a peril. This is accomplished by stating that coverage applies to loss "involving" collapse of a building or any part of a building caused by certain named perils. The named perils include all the perils of the causes of loss—broad form, plus the following additional perils:

- hidden decay;
- hidden insect or vermin damage;
- weight of people or personal property;
- weight of rain that collects on a roof;
- use of defective materials or methods in construction, remodeling, or renovation *if the collapse occurs during the course of construction, remodeling, or renovation.*

Certain types of property that may be excluded under other perils are covered for losses involving collapse and caused by hidden decay and the other perils listed above—but only if the loss is a direct result of a building collapse:

> outdoor radio or television antennas, including their lead-in wiring, masts or towers; awnings; gutters and downspouts; yard fixtures; outdoor swimming pools; fences; piers, wharves and docks; beach or diving platforms or appurtenances; retaining walls; walks, roadways and other paved surfaces.

Collapse to a completed building caused by defective materials or construction methods is not covered.

Collapse is not defined, but is limited by a statement that it does not include settling, cracking, shrinkage, bulging, or expansion.

Unlike the "additional coverages" of the BPP form, the additional collapse coverage of the causes-of-loss forms does not increase the limit of insurance. As far as limits are concerned, "collapse" is handled the same way as are covered perils.

CAUSES OF LOSS—SPECIAL FORM

The broadest option in the "commercial property" program, in terms of perils insured against, is the special form. The "all-risks" type form covers (all) direct physical losses unless they are excluded or limited. Although the word "all" no longer appears in the insuring agreement, the phrase "all-risks" is deeply seated in the jargon of insurance and will continue to be used in this text to describe coverages of this type. (Recently, a few writers have introduced the phrase "open perils" as a synonym that eliminates that troublesome phrase "all-risks.")

Whereas the basic and broad forms cover perils traditionally associated with what has been termed "fire and allied lines" insurance, the "all-risks" type forms include what were traditionally considered "inland marine" and "crime" coverages (as well as "elevator collision" which was, in the past, handled as a general liability coverage). For many insureds, the crime coverage is the most significant expansion of the "special" forms.

"All-Risks" Versus Named Perils

"All-risks" insurance begins with an insuring agreement that simply provides coverage for direct physical loss to covered property. With this statement, the *burden of proof* as to coverage falls on the insurer—not the insured. Unless the *insurer* can prove that an exclusion applies, the loss is covered. (In contrast, named perils policies such as the basic and broad causes-of-loss forms place the burden on the insured. Unless the *insured* can prove that one of the named perils caused the loss, there is no coverage.) The burden of proof can make a major difference in a case where the cause of a given loss is not entirely clear.

As noted earlier, one of the main advantages of "all-risks" coverage is that theft coverage is provided. Beyond that, since the named perils of the broad causes-of-loss form seem to encompass most imaginable circumstances, students of insurance sometimes ask for examples of "all-risks" type losses that would not also be covered under a broad form. Common examples include:

- Spillage—situations where a substance (other than a pollutant) is spilled or overturned. For instance: Paint is spilled onto a floor, acid is spilled onto machinery, or a fuel tank is suddenly punctured, causing loss of oil and damage to the tank.
- Falling objects—named perils forms generally require exterior damage to the building before interior damage is covered, but "all-risks" forms do not.
- Vehicle damage—coverage exists in "all-risks" forms whether or not the damage-causing vehicle is owned or operated by the insured, and whether or not there is direct physical contact.

These few examples help to illustrate the breadth of "all-risks" coverage. The key point is this: If a cause of loss is not excluded, the peril is covered.

Additional Perils Excluded and Limited under the Causes of Loss—Special Form

The special form contains a number of provisions intended primarily to assure that coverage is at least equal to that of the broad form. Many of the broad form's provisions are expressed under the heading of the specific peril to which they relate. Obviously, this approach cannot be taken in an "all-risks" form that does not specifically name covered perils. The first group of exclusions and limitations under this heading fall into that category and will be given only a quick overview.

In specified causes-of-loss forms, there is no reason to exclude a peril that is not covered in the first place (although exclusions are sometimes used anyway to make the insurer's intention absolutely clear). In an "all-risks" form, an exclusion is the only way to exclude a peril that the insurer does not wish to cover. Therefore, the special form contains a number of exclusions not found in the specified causes-of-loss forms and directed at perils that might otherwise be covered.

The special form also contains limitations defining the extent to which certain types of property are covered for certain perils. Those with greater exposures should consider a different type of coverage directed specifically at that type of exposure.

Another group of exclusions addresses the issues raised by the concurrent causation doctrine.

Provisions to Match the Broad Form Coverage The special form contains several exclusions and limitations primarily intended to match the coverage provided by the broad form:

- *Artificially generated electrical current.* "Artificial electricity" coverage is excluded, but ensuing fire damage is covered.
- *Weather.* Rain, snow, sleet, ice, sand, or dust damage to the interior of a building is not covered unless the building itself is first damaged. However, an exception in the special form provides coverage for loss or damage resulting from the thawing of snow, sleet, or ice on the building or structure. Thus, loss caused by water backing behind an ice dam on the roof would be covered by the special form.
- *Smoke from agricultural smudging operations* is excluded.
- *Boiler and machinery explosion.* Firebox explosions are covered.
- *Glass breakage.* Coverage is limited to $100 per item or $500 per occurrence.
- *Weight of ice, snow, or sleet.* Damage to gutters and down-spouts is not covered.
- *Water damage.* Seepage or leakage beyond fourteen days is excluded, as is freezing that occurs because the insured failed to take appropriate safeguards.

Maintenance-Type Exclusions A number of exclusions eliminate coverage for losses that are in the nature of ordinary property maintenance, with one exception that provides the equivalent of broad form coverage. The actual exclusions state:

> We will not pay for loss or damage caused by or resulting from...
> d. (1) Wear and tear;
>   (2) Rust, corrosion, fungus, decay, deterioration, hidden or latent defect or any quality in property that causes it to damage or destroy itself;
>   (3) Smog;
>   (4) Release, discharge or dispersal of contaminants or pollutants;
>   (5) Settling, cracking, shrinking or expansion;
>   (6) Insects, birds, rodents or other animals;
>   (7) Mechanical breakdown, including rupture or bursting caused by centrifugal force; or
>   (8) The following causes of loss of personal property:
>   (a) Dampness or dryness of atmosphere;
>   (b) Changes in or extremes of temperature; or
>   (c) Marring or scratching.

To this exclusion is added the following exception:

> But if loss or damage by the "specified causes of loss" or building glass breakage results, we will pay for that resulting loss or damage.

The *"specified causes of loss"* to which this provision refers are listed in the definitions section of the form. The "specified causes of loss" are the perils listed under the broad form, but without the detailed elaboration of that form. In some cases, the lack of elaboration has the effect of providing broader coverage. For example, since there is no exclusion for vehicle damage when the property owner is driving the vehicle that damages covered property, marring or scratching caused by an owner-driven vehicle would be covered.

As another example, loss due to change in temperature is excluded. However, suppose a marble statue becomes very hot in a fire and then breaks when water from a fire hose touches it. Although this is a change in temperature (excluded), the loss would fall under the fire peril (covered).

Property Covered Only for Specified Perils Although the "all-risks" approach applies to most property subject to coverage by the causes of loss—special form, some types of property are covered only for the " 'specified causes of loss' or building glass breakage." These include:

- *Valuable papers and records.* "All-risks" coverage is available on an inland marine form discussed in Chapter 10.
- *Animals.* Animals that are covered property are covered only when they are killed or their destruction is made necessary because of direct loss by a specified peril.

- *Fragile articles.* "Glassware, marbles, chinaware and porcelains" are given as examples of property subject to this restriction. Building glass, photographic or scientific instrument lenses, and containers of property held for sale are exempt from this restriction. This exemption could be of considerable value to an organization that manufactures or sells a product contained in glass bottles.
- *Builders' machinery, tools, and equipment owned by or entrusted to the named insured.*

Theft Coverage Exclusions Unlike the basic and broad forms, the special form does cover theft losses. However, there is no coverage for loss by *employee dishonesty* or *voluntary parting* with property. Employee dishonesty coverage is available in crime insurance policies, and coverage for some instances of voluntary parting may also be available.

Closely related to the theft coverage exclusions are limitations for (1) theft of building materials and supplies not attached as part of the building or structure, and (2) what was, in earlier policies, called *mysterious disappearance.* The simplified policy does not use the term "mysterious disappearance," but generically refers to property that is missing without physical evidence to show why it is missing—such as is the case with an inventory shortage.

Some types of property are covered, but the coverage is subject to dollar limitations when the property is lost by theft:

- $2,500 for furs, fur garments, and garments trimmed with fur.
- $2,500 on patterns, dies, molds, and forms.
- $2,500 on jewelry, watches, precious stones, and metals (gold, silver, platinum). Jewelry and watches with a value of less than $100 are not included in this $2,500 limit.
- $250 for stamps, tickets, and letters of credit.

Crime and inland marine policies are available to provide higher limits and broader coverage on property of these types—which are highly susceptible to theft.

Indirect Loss Exclusion An exclusion unique to the special form reinforces the intention to provide coverage only against direct physical loss. The exclusion precludes coverage for loss caused by or resulting from "delay, loss of use, or loss of market."

Concurrent Causation Exclusion Another exclusion in "all-risks" type forms is intended to exclude coverage for losses that would not be covered in the absence of the doctrine of concurrent causation. The exclusion contains a reference to "paragraph 1," which we will clarify after quoting the exclusion itself:

We will not pay for loss or damage caused by or resulting from any of the following. But if loss or damage by a Covered Cause of Loss results, we will pay for that resulting loss or damage.

   a. Weather conditions. But this exclusion only applies if weather conditions contribute in any way with a cause or event excluded in paragraph 1. above to produce the loss or damage.

   b. Acts or decisions, including the failure to act or decide, of any person, group, organization or governmental body.

   c. Faulty, inadequate or defective:

      (1) Planning, zoning, development, surveying, siting;

      (2) Design, specifications, workmanship, repair, construction, renovation, remodeling, grading, compaction;

      (3) Materials used in repair, construction, renovation or remodeling; or

      (4) Maintenance; of part of all of any property on or off the described premises.

The reference to "paragraph 1 above" refers to that part of the policy where the earthquake, flood, war, nuclear, governmental action, power failure, and building ordinance exclusions appear. Other weather-related losses—such as windstorms—would be covered.

Paragraphs b. and c. address the "concurrent causes" of third-party negligence with respect to planning, maintenance, quality of construction materials, or poor decisions of governmental planning bodies. If a building code permits the construction of buildings that cannot withstand an earthquake—and an earthquake damages such a building, the special form will not pay the loss because a poorly planned building code was a concurrent cause of the loss. Likewise, coverage does not apply to flood losses, whether or not faulty design of a flood dike is a concurrent cause.

Additional Coverages

Although the causes of loss—special form has three "additional coverages," only one expands the coverage beyond that of the broad form. The *collapse* coverage is the same as that in the broad form, as previously described. And the *water damage* coverage is the same as the coverage within the water damage peril of the broad form. However, the *property in transit* provision does provide a noteworthy addition.

Property in Transit This extension modifies the policy to provide a modest additional amount of coverage on an additional category of property—property in transit. Specifically, this extension provides $1,000 of additional insurance for damage to the insured's personal property in or on a motor vehicle that is more than 100 feet from the premises. (Recall that the named insured's business personal property within 100 feet of the premises is already covered, subject to the limit of insurance, without the extension.)

Some additional conditions or limitations apply. To be covered, the property must be in or on a motor vehicle owned, leased, or operated by the insured while between points in the coverage territory (United States, Canada, and Puerto Rico). Since the intention here is to provide coverage for incidental exposures, property in the care, custody, or control of salespersons is excluded. (An appropriate inland marine coverage would be in order for this exposure of salespersons' samples.)

Although the special form is an "all-risks" type policy, property in transit is covered only for certain named perils:

- The "basic perils" of fire, lightning, explosion, windstorm or hail, riot or civil commotion, or vandalism.
- The "crime peril" of theft—subject to some substantial limitations. Theft is covered only when an *entire* bale, case, or package is stolen from a *securely locked* body or compartment of the vehicle by a thief who leaves *visible marks* of the forced entry.
- The "inland marine peril" of collision and upset.

EXCLUDED PERILS AND HAZARDS

One group of perils and hazards is specifically excluded in all three causes-of-loss forms—basic, broad, and special:

- building ordinance,
- earth movement,
- governmental action,
- nuclear hazard,
- power failure,
- war and military action, and
- water.

Some of these perils and hazards are considered uninsurable. Others can be insured with the use of other coverages or endorsements. Discussion here will deal not only with the exclusions, but also with means of obtaining insurance for the excluded exposures, where applicable.

Building Ordinance

Many jurisdictions have building codes or other laws regulating building construction. Buildings already standing when such regulations are adopted are usually allowed to continue in use—that is, they are "grandfathered." However, when a nonconforming building is severely damaged, the regulation may provide that it may not be rebuilt unless it conforms to current requirements.

Suppose a building subject to such a law suffers damage equal to, say, 75 percent of its value. Repair would not be permitted by the ordinance. Instead, the remainder of the old structure must be demolished. If a replacement building is erected, it must conform with the code.

Where they exist, such laws create a hazard—they increase potential loss severity. Because of the operation of this law, the insured actually loses the value of the undamaged 25 percent of the building and also incurs the expense of demolishing the undamaged 25 percent and removing its debris. If it is more expensive to erect a conforming building as a replacement than it would be to erect an identical building, the insured may also incur an increased cost.

Although many insureds face this hazard, most do not. The basic approach in "commercial property" forms is to exclude coverage for the added loss costs incurred because of this hazard. The building ordinance exclusion states that the insurer will not pay for loss caused by:

The enforcement of any ordinance or law:
(1) Regulating the construction, use or repair of any property; or
(2) Requiring the tearing down of any property, including the cost of removing its debris.

Even without this exclusion, neither actual cash value nor replacement cost coverage would pay for additional features that were not in the old building but are now necessitated by construction regulations. Such features might include additional fire exits; installation of a roof more resistant to fire; or wiring, heating, or plumbing systems that comply with the current code.

This exclusion has not been uniformly applied by the courts.

Most of the reported decisions interpreting the ordinance or law exclusion involve [situations where] the enforcement of a building ordinance or law results in an increased cost of reconstruction or repair following an admittedly covered loss by an insured peril. . . .In cases where a building was physically if not legally repairable after a loss, some decisions, applying the exclusion, have denied recovery to the insured for the difference between the hypothetical cost of repair of the damage and the total value of the condemned building. Other decisions, however, even in non-valued law states, have refused to apply the exclusion and have allowed the insured to recover as for a total loss to the insured building where a combination of an insured peril and the operation of a building ordinance prevented repair. In valued policy law states, the courts have uniformly rejected the application of the exclusion where due to a combination of damage by fire and operation of building laws, the insured sustained a constructive total loss. However, where building laws increase the cost of repair, but do not create a constructive total loss or prohibit repair, the exclusion has been held to apply to the increased cost of repair, even in a valued policy law state. Thus the exclusion stands the best chance of being successfully asserted in situations where the building ordinance or law merely increases the cost of repair, rather than where the law creates a constructive total loss.[11]

Protection against the exposures created by this hazard is available by endorsement.

Building Ordinance Coverage Endorsement This endorsement provides coverage for losses occasioned by building ordinances. Specifically, the insurer agrees to pay for:

- the increased cost of repairing or replacing the damaged property with one that is in conformity—and is intended for similar occupancy, unless otherwise required by zoning or land use law.
- the cost to demolish the undamaged structure, and
- the cost of removing debris of the undamaged structure that has been demolished.

In addition, the insurer agrees to pay for increased construction costs, provided the property is actually repaired or replaced as soon as possible after the loss. The insurer is not obligated to pay increased construction costs unless the reconstruction is made within two years, although the period may be extended. The replacement building may be on the same premises or elsewhere.

With the building ordinance coverage endorsement, the insured is also indemnified for property that is not directly damaged by an insured peril but must be destroyed anyway because of the operation of building laws.

Merely adding the endorsement to the policy does not address all the problems. Two more steps must be taken.

- The endorsement does nothing to change the basic actual cash value approach of the basic form. This important need must be met by activating the replacement cost optional coverage.
- Although it covers some significant added costs, there is no limit of insurance in the endorsement itself, and the endorsement does not provide an additional *amount* of insurance. This problem must be addressed by increasing policy limits to an amount adequate to cover claims resulting from the increased coverage.

When building ordinance coverage is in effect, careful attention must be paid to the issue of adequate limits—and to the question of what percent of replacement cost should be reflected in the limits. Insuring to 80 to 90 percent of insurable value may not be enough. For one thing, more than the insurable value of the present building is covered. The full value of *the replacement building* must be considered. Also, while many buildings are unlikely to sustain a total loss, the existence of the building ordinance greatly increases the probability that the entire structure will be destroyed—either by the direct loss or by the enforcement of the ordinance.

It is quite possible that an appropriate amount of insurance will exceed 100 percent of the replacement cost value of the building! In fact, the ISO *Commercial Lines Manual* contains an example showing the need for a $630,000 limit of insurance on a building with a current replacement cost of $400,000. This example appears in Exhibit 4-2.

Putting it all together:

- The basic policy, with the replacement cost option activated, covers the replacement cost of the property that sustains the direct damage and the expense of removing that property's debris.
- The building ordinance coverage endorsement covers the value of the undamaged property that must be demolished, the expense of the demolition, and the removal of that property's debris. The endorsement also covers the increased cost of a conforming building.
- Adequate limits of insurance are necessary to cover all aspects of the loss.

It should be apparent that the operation of building codes is a hazard that can create substantial loss exposures—exposures of which the insured might be unaware. Even when the exposure is recognized, it is easy to overlook its potential effect on business income losses, as explained further in Chapter 5. Identification of the ordinance or law exposure requires some research into the building codes that may affect insured property. If this exposure is not identified, insurance or other loss-financing alternatives cannot be planned, and the exposure will unconsciously be retained.

Earth Movement

Earthquake is one of the most catastrophic perils known to humanity. Long periods of time can pass without a single significant earthquake anywhere in the U.S. In 1985, for example, the only

Exhibit 4-2
Building Ordinance*

COVERAGE EXAMPLE

a. Assume the following:

(1) An insured building of masonry construction has a replacement cost value of $400,000.

(2) This building is located in an area now zoned for superior construction. The owner knows that substantial damage to the building—assume 50% destruction—will trigger the local ordinance and the entire building will have to be destroyed.

(3) Estimated cost of demolition of 50% of the structure (the undamaged portion) is $30,000.

(4) The additional cost to replace the building with a new structure to comply with the local ordinance and land use laws is $200,000.

b. For purposes of illustration, the following is a possible way of developing the limit of insurance by attachment of the Building Ordinance Coverage Endorsement:

To provide coverage for:

(1) Replacement cost value of the current building (including loss of value of undamaged portion) $400,000

(2) Additional cost to replace the building to comply with building ordinance and land use laws $200,000

(3) Cost to demolish the undamaged part of the existing building after loss occurs $30,000

The limit of insurance would be $630,000 ($400,000 + $200,000 + $30,000)

---

*Source: ISO Commercial Lines Manual, CF-20, Copyright, ISO Commercial Risk Services, 1983, 1984.

significant earthquake (which occurred near Avenal, CA) caused only slight property damage and minor injuries to six persons. At the other extreme, the 1971 earthquake in San Fernando, CA, resulted in property damage losses of over $550 million.[12]

Despite the potential loss severity, the peril is excluded from the "basic" coverage of all "commercial property" policies, although ensuing fire is covered. The earthquake peril is difficult to insure, for several reasons. First, the geographic areas most likely to have earthquakes are somewhat limited, resulting in a poor spread of risk. Second, predictions regarding potential earthquake frequency and severity have been poor—making it difficult to establish a rating system that reflects loss potential. Third, and perhaps most significant, is the catastrophic loss potential: Many separate buildings and their contents are affected by a single set of quakes. A 1985 report estimated that a major earthquake, of the same intensity as the 1906 San Francisco quake, would have a probable maximum loss of $3.381 billion. A similar quake in the Los Angeles area would have a probable maximum loss of $4.660 billion. These figures relate only to initial shake damage to structures and contents insured as of 1983 and do not include any related exposures such as fire following a quake, workers compensation losses, vehicle losses, or life and health insurance losses on earthquake victims.[13]

The following are excluded in all causes-of-loss forms:

(1) Any earth movement (other than sinkhole collapse), such as an earthquake, landslide or earth sinking, rising or shifting. But if loss or damage by fire or explosion results, we will pay for that resulting loss or damage.

(2) Volcanic eruption, explosion or effusion. But if loss or damage by fire, building glass breakage or volcanic action results, we will pay for that resulting loss or damage.

Note that fire or explosion ensuing from any earth movement or volcanic eruption is covered. This exception can be very important, as fire following earthquake is often a major source of loss, especially in congested metropolitan areas containing many combustible structures.

For those who desire coverage for damage caused by earth movement and volcanic eruption, coverage is available under the *causes of loss—earthquake form.*

Causes of Loss—Earthquake Form As the name suggests, this form extends "commercial property" coverage to cover the peril of earthquake. The closely related peril of volcanic eruption is also covered. Earthquake coverage can be written to supplement any of the causes-of-loss forms—basic, broad, or special.

The endorsement simply adds another peril to the list of covered causes of loss. It does not add an additional dollar amount of coverage.

The term "earthquake" is not defined. However, to clarify the application of the per-occurrence limits and deductibles, the form makes it clear that all earthquake shocks or volcanic eruptions within a specified time period will be considered a single earthquake or volcanic eruption. This means that most aftershocks will be considered part of the original event for insurance purposes.

Among the various exclusions and provisions of the form, perhaps the most significant deals with water damage. Specifically excluded are loss or damage caused by or resulting from landslide, tidal wave, flood, mudslide, or mudflow—even if attributable to an earthquake or volcanic eruption.

Fire and explosion losses are excluded under the earthquake form—for the logical reason that they are covered in the other causes-of-loss forms. Also excluded is damage caused by artificially generated electrical current.

Property Not Normally Susceptible to Damage. As mentioned in Chapter 3, underground foundations, excavations, and similar types of property not normally susceptible to damage by fire or the other basic causes of loss are excluded from coverage in the BPP. That makes sense because, in order to meet coinsurance requirements, it would otherwise be necessary to buy insurance on property that seldom sustains serious damage by a covered peril.

However, these property items are highly susceptible to earthquake damage. When earthquake coverage is purchased, it may be desirable to use the *additional covered property endorsement* to restore coverage on such excluded property items—which would then be insured for damage by any covered peril. When this is done, appropriate adjustments in policy limits should also be made in order to avoid a coinsurance penalty.

Masonry Veneer. Masonry veneer (e.g., brick facing on a frame structure) is particularly susceptible to earthquake damage. The basic approach of the earthquake endorsement excludes coverage for loss to masonry veneer, unless the masonry veneer is limited to 10 percent or less of the exterior wall area.

Masonry veneer coverage may be added by placing the words "including masonry veneer" in the premises description of the declarations and paying an appropriate additional premium.

Earthquake Deductible. A percentage deductible in the earthquake form replaces the dollar deductible in the basic form to which it is attached. The applicable percentage, which would appear in the declarations, is a percentage of the *value* of the property (not the limit of insurance). So, for example, if a policy had a 5 percent earthquake deductible, then a $5,000 deductible would apply to a building valued at $100,000 and insured for $80,000.

The earthquake deductible is applied to the value of the property in order to encourage insurance to value. If the deductible were applied to the limit of insurance, it would discourage insurance to value because a lower limit would result in a lower dollar deductible.

Governmental Action

In some situations, government officials (such as police officers or firefighters) must take control of an insured's property to protect the common good of the community. For example, a governmental agency might confiscate contaminated property, or might destroy property to prevent the spread of further destruction. Since insurers do not intend to cover such intentional actions, the causes-of-loss forms exclude:

Seizure or destruction of property by order of governmental authority

However, the insurer does agree to pay for acts of destruction ordered by governmental authority at the time of a fire in order to prevent its spread in circumstances where fire is a covered peril. This is a carry-over from the days when authorities would dynamite buildings to stop the spread of a conflagration. This is rarely done today.

Different types of property insurance take different approaches to loss by governmental action—a point that will become clearer in later chapters.

Power Failure

This provision essentially eliminates coverage for the peril of off-premises failure of power or other utility services, while preserving coverage for any ensuing damage from other covered perils. Where necessary, coverage can be obtained via the *off-premises overhead transmission lines (direct damage and time element) endorsement.*

War and Military Action

Almost all property and liability insurance contracts covering property on land contain a war exclusion. Losses on land caused by war are so potentially catastrophic that they cannot be handled by the insurance mechanism. (Ocean marine insurers face a more limited problem if the exposure is limited to one or several ships.)

The lengthy war exclusion in all three causes-of-loss forms excludes loss by insurrections, civil wars, and undeclared wars, as well as by formally declared wars.

Unlike some other exclusions, the war exclusion contains no exception for ensuing fire. Fires resulting from war are not covered because of the potential for catastrophic loss. Some of the "fire storms" that resulted from World War II bombing raids wiped out entire cities.

Nuclear Hazard

Most property and liability insurance contracts contain a so-called "nuclear exclusion." The "commercial property" causes-of-loss forms state that no coverage exists for loss or damage caused by:

Nuclear reaction or radiation, or radioactive contamination, however caused.

However, an exception to the exclusion notes that:

if loss or damage by fire results, we will pay for that resulting loss or damage.

(Coverage for fire damage in a nuclear war would still be precluded by the war exclusion.) If a nuclear reactor should go out of control and cause a fire, the fire damage would be covered, although the damage caused by the nuclear reaction—apart from the ensuing fire—would not be covered. If a fire causes the release of radioactive particles, contamination damage from them is not intended to be covered.

Limited insurance is available for organizations facing serious nuclear exposures, as detailed in Chapter 14. Despite the catastrophic nuclear problems caused by power plant disasters such as the incidents at Three Mile Island and Chernobyl, the "nuclear" property exposures of many organizations are relatively small. For some, the radioactive contamination endorsement provides the necessary coverage.

Radioactive Contamination Endorsement This endorsement is available to meet the needs of firms that do not need a nuclear energy property policy, but do have a radioactive contamination exposure. The endorsement provides some coverage that would otherwise be eliminated by the nuclear hazard exclusion.

Exposures are found among hospitals, medical clinics, educational and research institutions, and manufacturers using radioactive materials. Overall, the number of organizations that could benefit from this coverage is much greater than the number needing a nuclear energy property policy.

Radioactive contamination is defined as:

direct physical loss or damage caused by:
a. Sudden and accidental radioactive contamination; or
b. Resultant radiation damage to the described property.

The endorsement, which may be used with any of the causes-of-loss forms, adds coverage for radioactive contamination. Two alternatives are possible—the first treats radioactive contamination as a consequence, and the second as a peril.

- *Limited radioactive contamination* means "Radioactive Contamination that directly results from any other Covered Cause of Loss." For example, if a tornado causes radiation to be released from its container, with resulting contamination, the loss would be covered.

● *Broad radioactive contamination* treats radioactive contamination as a free-standing peril, without the requirement that the contamination results from another covered peril. Contamination caused by the negligence of a laboratory technician would be covered by the broad coverage.

Neither basic nor broad radioactive contamination coverage applies if the described premises contain a nuclear reactor or new or used nuclear fuel. Losses arising from radioactive material off-premises are also excluded.

Water

All three causes-of-loss forms have a long water damage exclusion basically intended to exclude coverage for flood-type losses as carefully defined. Flood is generally considered a peril that is difficult to insure for two reasons: Floods can cause widespread catastrophic loss, and the locations most susceptible to flood are low-lying areas that can be readily identified. This can lead to adverse selection against an insurer, since the organizations most likely to purchase flood coverage are those who are also likely to have a flood.

The exclusion in the "commercial property" causes-of-loss forms states that no coverage exists for loss due to:

(1) Flood, surface water, waves, tides, tidal waves, overflow of any body of water, or their spray, all whether driven by wind or not;
(2) Mudslide or mudflow;
(3) Water that backs up from a sewer or drain; or
(4) Water under the ground surface pressing on, or flowing or seeping through:
    (a) Foundations, walls, floors or paved surfaces;
    (b) Basements, whether paved or not; or
    (c) Doors, windows or other openings.

But if loss or damage by fire, explosion or sprinkler leakage results, we will pay for that resulting loss or damage.

This exclusion does not eliminate coverage for all water damage—in fact, water damage is a peril specifically covered by the broad causes-of-loss form. However, that peril deals essentially with leaky pipes and appliances. While the water exclusion deals with what might be considered naturally occurring water. (The distinction somewhat resembles the distinction between lightning and artificially generated electrical currents, but with the opposite result. Natural electricity [lightning] damage is generally covered, while artificial electricity damage is often excluded.)

The water exclusion applies not only to overflow of rivers but also to situations where underground water pressure causes a basement to flood. Coverage for some types of water damage is available from the National Flood Insurance Program and under so-called *difference in conditions* policies discussed in Chapter 14.

SPECIAL NAMED PERILS CAUSES OF LOSS— EXTENDED FORM

As mentioned earlier in the chapter, ISO Commercial Risk Services, Inc. has drafted a named-perils alternative to the "all-risks" type form. The idea behind this form was to provide the broadest set of specified causes of loss that could be offered to insureds in general, without leaving the door open to "concurrent causation" claims as might be the case with a "covered unless excluded" type of approach.

At the time of this writing, the *special named perils causes of loss—extended form*—hereafter referred to as SNP—has not been filed with state regulators and is not expected to be used in the foreseeable future. However, it will be mentioned briefly in order to describe the concept. It also tends to illustrate the scope of identifiable perils added by the special form, but not included in the broad form.

The causes of loss covered by the SNP form include those specified in the causes of loss—broad form. However, the wording defining or limiting some of the perils differs. For example, there is no vehicle damage exclusion for vehicles owned or operated by the owner of the damaged property.

To the causes of loss of the broad form are added the following:

- *Liquid, powder, or molten material.* This peril deals basically with spillage, leakage, overflow, or accidental discharge.
- *Change in temperature or humidity.* Only real property is covered for this peril.
- *Elevator Collision.* This peril refers to the collision of an elevator or its contents with another part of the elevator or another object.
- *Theft.* This peril is subject to exclusions and limitations resembling those of the special form.

Unlike the causes of loss—special form, the named perils approach of the SNP does not shift the burden of proof to the insurer, and the form does not cover those rare, difficult-to-anticipate perils that can result in real, easy-to-recognize losses.

Chapter Notes

1. Paul I. Thomas and Prentiss B. Reed, Sr., *Adjustment of Property Losses*, Gregg Division/McGraw-Hill Book Company, Fourth Edition, 1977, pp. 182-183. Valuation measures are discussed in greater detail in CPCU 1.
2. Eric A. Wiening, "An End to All-Risks Insurance," *The Risk Report*, International Risk Management Institute, Vol. VI, No. 6, February 1984.
3. Engel v. Redwood County Farmers Mutual Insurance Co., 1979 CCH (Fire and Casualty), 466.
4. *FC&S Bulletins*, Personal Lines Section (Cincinnati OH: The National Underwriter Co., August 1979), Q&A 409.
5. William G. Coppock, "What in Blazes," *Adjuster's Reference Guide*, Fire and Allied-38
6. Philip Gordis, ed., *Property and Casualty Insurance*, 23rd ed. (Indianapolis: The Rough Notes Co., June 1974), p. 75.
7. *F C & S Bulletins*, Fire and Marine Section (Cincinnati, OH: The National Underwriter Co., January 1975), Sc.-5.
8. *F C & S Bulletins*, Fire and Marine Section (Cincinnati, OH: The National Underwriter Co., January 1979), Misc. Fire SC-7.
9. Robert W. Decker and Barbara B. Decker, "Volcanos," *1984 Year Book, Covering the Year 1983* (New York: Macmillan Educational Company, 1983), pp. 10 and 413.
10. Wiening.
11. Thomas W. Mallin, *Pollution and Contamination: How Will Property Insurers Respond*, Tort and Insurance Practice Section, American Bar Association, pp. 78-79.
12. *Insurance Facts 1986-87* (New York: Insurance Information Institute, 1986), p. 72.
13. Robert S. Mendenhall, "Threat of Major Earthquake Shakes Up Insurers," *National Underwriter*, Property-Casualty Edition, 2 May 1986, p. 19. See also Chapter Note 6 of Chapter 1.

CHAPTER 5

Time Element Exposures and Insurance

As noted in Chapter 3, insurance coverages for loss of business income, extra expense, and related exposures are considered "time element" coverages. The term *time element* refers to the fact that the extent of loss is directly related to the passage of time. This chapter deals primarily with the business interruption exposure and other exposures that can be covered by the *business income coverage form* (BIC).[1] Related exposures and coverages are also discussed but in somewhat less detail.

The chapter begins by analyzing the business interruption exposure in some detail, followed by the basic approach to insuring time element losses, as represented by the BIC. Alternatives to the basic approach are then examined. The chapter concludes by highlighting some applications of business income coverage and by noting some noninsurance measures for dealing with time element losses.

GENERAL NATURE OF TIME ELEMENT EXPOSURES

Business Interruption

Chapter 1 characterizes *business interruption* as follows:

When property used for producing or selling goods or providing services is destroyed or rendered unusable, sales may be impaired and business lost. A business slowdown or shutdown, therefore, may cause business income losses in the form of:
1. loss of net income that would have been earned, and

239

2. payments for expenses that necessarily continue when the property is damaged or destroyed. (Even if the property is completely destroyed, there may be continuing expenses, such as taxes on the land, noncancelable contracts for heat, light, and power, interest on debt, and salaries for executives. If no loss occurs, these continuing expenses are offset by continuing income.)

Loss of Net Income   When a firm is partially or totally shut down following direct damage to property, the company may lose income that pays for net profits and operating expenses—that is, income that would otherwise have been earned during the period of the reduced or suspended operations.

A company that is not operating profitably may have a net loss, rather than a net profit. A slowdown or shutdown may increase the net loss—resulting in an additional loss of net income attributable to the interruption. For example, if a $50,000 net loss was projected in one year but a shutdown causes results to instead show an $80,000 loss, then the shutdown has caused a $30,000 loss of net income.

A landlord will sustain *loss of rental income* if rent payments are discontinued because the premises are made untenantable. To the landlord, this represents a loss of net income as well as loss of money with which to pay ongoing expenses.

Loss Due to Continuing Expenses   Even when a business is shut down, many expenses are likely to continue. These expenses are normal, ongoing expenses that do not cease—at least not entirely—even when business operations are totally stopped.

Continuing expenses typically include such things as salaries for officers and other key employees; expenses for heat, light, and power; insurance premiums; and installment payments on debts. A building owner may be required to continue mortgage payments during a period of interruption. A tenant may be required to continue lease payments even when the premises are made untenantable—a loss consequence referred to in Chapter 1 as *loss of rental value.*

These so-called "continuing expenses" must be met even when business operations are interrupted, though payments do not necessarily continue at the same level. Some continuing expenses, such as insurance premiums and expenses for heat, light, and power, may be reduced during interruption.

A business does not suffer a loss from *non*continuing expenses—that is, expenses that are suspended when the company is shut down or partially shut down. The cost of janitorial services, for example, may not be incurred while a plant is being rebuilt. Some payroll expenses also may be eliminated, depending on the type of business and the extent of the shutdown.

Extra Expenses

Extra expenses may be incurred during a partial or total suspension of operations. Extra expenses may also be incurred in order to limit or prevent interruption of operations.

Most businesses would cease to operate for a time following a direct property loss that would disrupt business activities. When a business is shut down by direct property damage, it often incurs some unusual expenses—expenses that it would not have incurred had the organization been operating as usual. For example, it may incur expenses to rent temporary office space, machinery, equipment, or fixtures. Storage space for undamaged property may be needed. Advertising costs, in anticipation of the resumption of business, may increase.

Some businesses—banks and dairies, for instance—cannot, under any circumstances, survive an *interruption* of business activities. Such firms must remain in operation "at all costs." Schools and hospitals and other organizations serving a group of people may be unable simply to drop out of operation without providing some continuity of service. To remain in operation when the building or equipment normally used has been damaged or destroyed, a firm will incur substantial extra expenses.

What Property Damage Leads to Time Element Losses

Business interruptions may result from damage to property in a variety of locations. A company that produces canned orange juice, for example, may suffer a loss of income if:

- fire in the orange-squeezing plant destroys its stock of raw material,
- a can manufacturer's warehouse full of empty orange juice cans is destroyed,
- electrical power to the plant is interrupted, or
- insects damage trees in its orange groves.

Business interruption losses can result when nonowned property is damaged—even if the firm has no business relationship with the owner of damaged property. For example:

- A franchised food restaurant may suffer loss if its primary food supplier's premises are damaged. If food supplies cannot be obtained, some food will not be sold.
- If the restaurant is near a high school, it may also suffer a substantial loss of business if the high school is shut down due

to a school fire. Note that no business relationship is involved between the restaurant and the high school, but the drop-off in revenues is just as real. (A similar decline in revenues could occur without property damage—for example, if the school board decides to close the high school because of shifting population patterns.)

Business interruption exposures arising out of the possibility of loss or damage to nonowned property are referred to as *contingent business interruption exposures,* or *dependent property exposures.* Similar extra expense exposures also exist, as discussed later in this chapter.

IDENTIFYING CRITICAL BUSINESS INTERRUPTION EXPOSURES

One challenge facing risk managers is developing a pre-loss assessment of the business interruption exposures and their loss potential in order to implement appropriate loss financing and control measures. Business income insurance or another type of time element insurance may be a desirable part of that financing.

When purchasing insurance, the specific policy provisions must be carefully noted, but since policy provisions deal primarily with payment for losses that have already occurred, they do not necessarily follow the procedures that are most desirable for analyzing loss possibilities. Furthermore, insurance policies deal only with insurable loss possibilities, while sound risk management also recognizes those possibilities that cannot be insured. Loss of raw materials for orange juice because of insect damage to orange trees, or loss of restaurant income because a school board closes an adjacent school exemplify loss possibilities that are not insurable with standard business income forms—if, indeed, they are insurable at all.

Business income insurance will be given careful attention later in this chapter. For now, the discussion almost completely ignores the existence of insurance in order to provide guidelines for answering the question, "How much could a business interruption cost?"

For risk management purposes, analysis of the business interruption exposure requires recognition of a worst-case scenario—severe direct damage to the most critical item at the worst possible time. An organization that has prepared to deal with such problems is also likely to be able to handle business interruption losses of a less serious nature.

Most (but not all, e.g., school-closing) business interruption losses arise as a consequence of direct property damage. Identifying direct damage property loss exposures also identifies many potential sources of a business interruption loss. The business interruption loss exposure would be easy to deal with if direct property damage losses and business interruption losses always occurred simultaneously and in proportionate amounts. Because they do not, it is especially important to be alert to situations in which relatively small direct damage could cause a large business interruption loss. Such situations occur in operations involving time-consuming production processes, bottlenecks, interdependency exposures, property that requires a long time to replace, or contamination exposures.

Time-Consuming Production Processes

Some manufacturers have production processes that require a long time to complete, perhaps because drying, seasoning, or "aging" processes are involved. The making of some varieties of cheese is one example. When goods in process sustain a direct loss, the severity of the resulting business interruption loss depends on the amount of time required to bring new raw materials to the same stage of production the destroyed goods had reached prior to the direct damage. The longer the production process takes, the greater the exposure.

When identifying loss exposures, it is important to pay special attention to any processes that cannot be rushed but simply depend on the passage of time.

Bottlenecks

Just as blockage in the neck of a catsup bottle can stop the flow of catsup, blockage or "bottlenecks" in a business operation can cause the business process to slow down or stop. The term "bottleneck" is often applied to situations where work from several assembly lines or processes must flow through (or depend upon continued operation at) a single job site or position. A relatively small direct loss at this "bottleneck" position could shut down several assembly lines. Production bottlenecks are easiest to imagine, but bottlenecks can also exist in purchasing and selling.

Some companies manufacture a product assembled in a long series of steps that must be performed in sequence. Autos, for example, are assembled in the sequence dictated by the assembly line, which usually has many bottlenecks. Other companies manufacture a product that can be completed in steps that have no necessary sequence. These companies are less prone to production bottlenecks, because no one position has an extraordinary impact on operations at other positions.

A major bottleneck these days can develop in record keeping and controlling—particularly when computers are used. On-line control of operations, scheduling, locating inventory, and other necessary functions are often dependent on the continued operation of a computer. For example, if "only the computer knows" who has ordered what, when it is to be delivered, or where it is now, a shutdown in one segment of the computer may shut down an entire business.

Flowcharts and critical path analysis (to be discussed later) are often effective ways to identify bottlenecks. However, bottlenecks can be difficult to identify before a loss occurs. For example, suppose a large plant is not permitted to operate without adequate pollution control devices. A small fire in the pollution control system could shut down the entire plant. This is an important exposure, but one that most flowcharts would not identify.

Interdependency Exposures

"Interdependency" arises from the transfer within the same organization of raw materials and intermediate products among plants, processing units, production lines, and other facilities essential to production.[2] Interdependency resembles the bottleneck exposure, but there is a distinction. To illustrate interdependency, consider a typical hospital. Under normal conditions, the hospital has X-ray facilities, a medical laboratory, operating rooms, and an emergency room. These facilities are somewhat interdependent. If the operating room facility is shut down, fewer biopsies will be processed by the laboratory, and fewer X-rays will be taken. Patients needing immediate surgery will not be admitted through the emergency room. Likewise, if the laboratory, X-ray facility, or emergency room is shut down, less surgery may be performed in the operating rooms. For all processes to proceed at a normal rate, all interdependent facilities must be fully operative. Similar situations exist in many industrial organizations.

When such interdependencies exist, measurement of potential loss from interdependency can be very difficult. Flowcharts can be used to help identify interdependency exposures, but careful analysis is necessary because interdependencies are much less obvious than bottlenecks.

Property that Requires a Long Time to Replace

The length of a shutdown depends to a great extent on the amount of time necessary to repair or replace damaged property. Consequently, the most critical property items are those that take the longest time to replace. For example, a giant turbine for an electric generating plant might require a few years to manufacture and deliver. Firms that use highly specialized machinery or equipment or depend on overseas manufacturers for parts or repairs can face long interruption exposures.

This aspect of the business interruption exposure is often susceptible to loss control. Measures can sometimes be taken to reduce the amount of time needed to repair or replace critical items. For example, spare critical parts might be kept in inventory, and replacement machinery might be kept on hand.

Contamination Exposures

Of increasing importance is the contamination exposure. Severe interruptions can result from relatively small direct losses if the direct loss contaminates property or premises. Consider the following examples:

1. A small electrical fire in the basement of an office building created such a contamination problem that the modern 8-story building has not been used in the ensuing 3½ years and there is no firm timetable as to when it will be sufficiently decontaminated for human occupancy. Decontamination costs are expected to exceed $25 million.
2. In 1983, the smoke and fumes from a fire in an outside underground vault entered a fresh air intake duct and infiltrated six floors of an adjacent office building. The affected areas were uninhabitable for 10 months, and the cleanup costs were in excess of $20 million.
3. Fire in a small (30' × 50') electric switchgear building involved three capacitors, each containing three gallons of dielectric fluid. The direct fire damage was $75,000. The decontamination expense is currently estimated at $1,000,000, and hopefully the building can be occupied in nine months.

The primary cause—electrical failure and ensuing fire. The complication—involvement of dielectric fluids containing polycholorinated biphenyls (PCBs). For over 40 years it had been common practice to use PCB fluids as the dielectric in liquid-insulated transformers and capacitors to avoid the fire and explosion hazards associated with mineral-oil-filled equipment.[3]

ANALYZING POTENTIAL BUSINESS INTERRUPTION LOSSES

The financial result of a business interruption is felt through effects on revenues and expenses, as illustrated in Exhibit 5-1. Revenues received from sales of goods and services are here referred to as "gross sales." The figure derived by subtracting the "cost of goods sold" or its equivalent from the "gross sales" is the "gross

Exhibit 5-1
Business Interruption Exposures of Company X

	Normal (1)		Total Shutdown (2)	Reduction due to Total Shutdown (1)-(2)
Gross Sales		$ 21,000	$ 0	$ 21,000
Less Cost of Goods Sold:		10,000	0	10,000
Gross Profit		$ 11,000	0	$ 11,000
Continuing Expenses	$4,000		$4,000	0
Other Expenses	6,000			6,000
Less Total Expenses:		10,000	4,000	6,000
Net Income (Gross Profit minus Total Expenses)		$ 1,000	$-4,000	$ 5,000

profit." The "normal" column in the exhibit illustrates the financial results of normal business operations; the "total shutdown" column shows the results during a period when the business experiences a total cessation of operations. The right-hand column is simply the "normal" column minus the "shutdown" column.

During a total shutdown, gross sales decrease. As illustrated in Exhibit 5-1, they may decrease to zero because no goods are being sold. If no goods are sold, then there is no "cost of goods sold" and no "gross profit."

The business interruption shutdown also has an effect on expenses. Some expenses, characterized in Exhibit 5-1 as "continuing expenses," do not abate—they must be paid despite the shutdown. "Other expenses," the noncontinuing expenses, are discontinued. Net income is negative—that is, the business experiences a financial loss because there are no revenues to offset the continuing expenses.

What is the total business interruption loss in this total shutdown situation? It is not the $11,000 reduction in gross profit before taxes, nor is it the −$4,000 net income. The effect of the interruption is to reduce net income from a normal +$1,000 to −$4,000, a total reduction in net income of $5,000.

Not all business interruptions involve a complete shutdown of operations. Often a slowdown, rather than a shutdown, is involved, in which case the reduction in net income would normally be something less than $5,000. (An exception might occur if the shutdown is avoided by incurring sizable "extra expenses.")

The illustration in Exhibit 5-1 is incomplete in several ways. No explanation has yet been given as to how the continuing and noncontinuing expense figures could be derived before a loss takes place—so as to be useful in risk management planning—and nothing has been mentioned regarding the length of the interruption. These factors will be examined in the following sections of the chapter.

Distinguishing Between Continuing and Noncontinuing Operating Expenses

The following paragraphs describe the degree to which expenses in various categories may continue during a business interruption.

Payroll Expense The extent to which payroll expenses continue during a business interruption depends on the duration of the shutdown, the number of employees who have special value to the company, conditions in the local labor market, severance pay policies, obligations to continue providing employee benefits, and other considerations.

During a short interruption, it is unlikely that any payroll will be abated. If the period of the shutdown is very long, a company would probably discontinue the payroll expense for many employees. Yet, few companies would dismiss all employees even in a prolonged interruption. At a minimum, some employees usually are necessary (or desirable) to assure a smooth transition back to business, and new employees will have to be hired and trained before operations can resume.

During any interruption, management must decide whether stockholder dividends or other income payments will need to be continued to the owners, and which salaries and wages are to be paid. Some personnel are usually required to manage the process of repair and construction, and to prepare for successful operations after reopening. In practice, officers' salaries are usually continued regardless of the duration of an interruption. Salaries may or may not be continued for department managers and supervisors. In some cases, highly skilled employees who would be difficult to replace will also continue to receive an income.

Employees such as some retail clerks and messengers who have no special skills and would be easy to replace usually are not retained, unless the period of interruption is brief. How easily unskilled employees can be replaced varies with local labor market conditions at the time of the loss.

Heat, Light, and Power Expense The cost of heat, light, and power would probably be continued minimally during short periods of shutdown. During longer periods, the expense might be discontinued entirely until shortly before reopening. However, sometimes a minimum charge has to be paid to the utility companies.

Organizations that normally have small utility bills will see little difference in their utility expenses during a period of interruption. However, those that normally use a large amount of electricity or otherwise run up large utility bills will see a substantial drop as the noncontinuing expenses abate.

Expenses for Services Performed by Others   Many companies "farm out" functions or services to other companies. Part of the manufacturing process, for example, may be performed by other organizations. And many retailers, such as hardware, appliance, or jewelry stores have alteration, installation, or repair work performed by outsiders. Restaurants and bars often hire musical groups and other entertainers. These services, performed by others, may be under contract—that is, guaranteed; if so, a company may be obligated to make payments to the other companies even during a business interruption. More often, services performed by outside companies will not be continued and payments will not be required.

Lease or Rental Expense   In any particular situation, whether or not lease or rental expense for buildings and equipment would continue during a business shutdown depends on the terms of the rental or lease agreement. (Continuing rental expense is not necessarily bad. A less desirable long-range outcome might be cancellation of a favorable lease. This exposure can be insured by "leasehold interest coverage," as explained in Chapter 6.) Generally, if the lease agreement provides for abatement of rent, it does so only when the rented property itself is damaged and made unusable. Thus, rent on branch offices, warehouses, and storage facilities normally continues during a business interruption at the main location. Likewise, suspension of business normally does not free a lessee from rental payments for autos and trucks rented on a long-term basis.[4]

Interest Expense   Interest payments generally are a continuing expense, but there are some exceptions. If a building is totally destroyed, the mortgage debt probably will be retired from property insurance proceeds. Since new loans are likely to be used to finance a new building, mortgage interest expense will continue under a new loan. Interest on other loans, and mortgages on property away from the undamaged premises, are not affected by a business suspension, and therefore will necessarily continue.

Taxes   A conservative assumption is that property taxes will be a continuing expense. Depending on the situation, major losses may reduce taxable real property values. However, in many areas taxes are assessed as of a given date, say January 1. If a firm has a loss immediately after that date, it could be a year before any property tax relief is given. If the insured rebuilds before the next January 1, reduction in assessments will usually not be made. Similarly, partial losses may cause a business interruption in which there is only a small reduction in taxable property values.

The same reasoning applies to personal property taxes based on inventory. These taxes may continue at the same level (or at virtually the same level) even though business is suspended.

Employer contributions for social security and unemployment compensation would not continue for employees who would not be paid during the interruption.

Advertising Expense   To determine whether advertising expense would be continued during a business suspension, the company's advertising policy must be considered. Some advertising is intended to stimulate sales in the short run; other advertising is intended to enhance the image of the company, and no short-run benefits are expected.

If advertising has been contracted in advance and cannot be canceled, it would be a continuing expense. Otherwise, advertising to stimulate sales would not be necessary except perhaps shortly before the business reopens. However, companies will often choose to maintain their image-enhancing advertisements even during a long shutdown. Such expenses may help to reduce the residual loss of business income once the business reopens.

Franchise and License Fees, Royalties   If based on sales or production, then payment of royalties, franchise fees, and license fees would cease upon suspension of operations. These expenses may continue, however, if they are a flat fee or must meet a guaranteed minimum level.

Postage and Telephone Expense   Communication expenses would probably continue in full during a short period of suspension. In fact, some extraordinary expenses might be incurred because of the necessity to use long-distance telephone service more extensively than usual. During a prolonged period of suspension, these expenses probably would be discontinued immediately but resumed sometime before the business reopens. As a general rule, communication expenses can be regarded as continuing for one or two months.

Collection Expense   Costs associated with the collection of accounts receivable would continue, at least for the normal collection period (assuming the records of accounts receivable have not been destroyed). New receivables would not develop if no sales are being made. However, collection expenses would increase as customers become reluctant to make payments to a nonfunctioning firm. The company's aging schedule for its accounts receivable shows the percentage of accounts receivable not past due and the percent past due. Exhibit 5-2 is a simple illustration of an accounts receivable aging schedule.

Exhibit 5-2
Accounts Receivable
Aging Schedule

Age	Percent of Total
30 days and less	50
31-60 days	30
61-90 days	15
Over 90 days	5

If a company has the experience indicated in Exhibit 5-2, 95 percent of the accounts are normally collected within ninety days. It might be reasonable to assume that collection expenses would continue for three months after the onset of an interruption, probably at a lower rate each month. When the maximum period of a shutdown is estimated at three months, the above figures suggest that collection expenses should be regarded as a continuing expense. Note, however, that if sales are suspended during those same three months, there may be an offsetting "lag" in receivables collection expenses once the business resumes operations.

Professional Fees Fees for accounting and legal services normally are continuing expenses if paid on a retainer basis. If not on a retainer, it may be reasonable to assume one or two months' expenditure as a continuing expense. Although the need for the usual services may abate, extraordinary legal and accounting services may become necessary as a result of the loss.

Travel Expense Most companies would have no travel expenses if the business shut down. Other companies, however, would incur continuing travel expenses or even extraordinary travel costs. The purposes of the travel need to be ascertained as a guide to estimating this expense.

Insurance Expense Insurance expense should be considered in relation to the type of insurance carried.

- Workers compensation insurance premiums would continue only to the extent that they applied to persons continuing to be paid during the suspension.
- A conservative assumption is that property insurance premiums would continue. In the event of the total destruction of stock, equipment, and buildings, property insurance on these items

could be canceled. However, if only partially damaged, the insurance expense would continue and destroyed property would be replaced with new property that must be insured.

- Liability insurance premiums based on gross receipts would probably be held to a minimum, since there would be no receipts during a shutdown except, perhaps, collections on accounts receivable. If the premium is based on a flat annual amount per location or based on floor area, the premium would probably continue.
- Auto insurance premiums would continue unless the autos were destroyed. If not in use during a shutdown, coverage for liability and collision could perhaps be canceled or suspended.
- Transportation insurance premiums usually would not continue during a total shutdown, except possibly for incoming materials. If subsidiary locations remain in operation, transportation insurance premiums may actually increase.
- Life, pension, and employee benefit insurance would continue to the extent that employees are kept on the payroll. Business life insurance premiums would continue, and there is a growing trend toward continuing health insurance benefits, especially in light of "COBRA" legislation.[5]

Maintenance Expense In most instances, maintenance costs would not continue during a business shutdown. However, if the property consists of more than one building or fire division, the property not affected by the loss would probably require at least a minimum amount of maintenance—even if no operations are taking place.

Delivery Expense The determination of whether delivery expense would continue depends on the method of making deliveries. With total suspension of business, deliveries would cease. In some cases delivery expense might continue because of minimum charges to be paid under an existing delivery contract.

Shipping and Packing Expenses Generally, shipping costs would not continue during a period of interruption. However, if a manufacturer's finished goods are not damaged in a fire or other loss, the cost of shipping would continue for a short period and be absorbed in the selling price, as usual. Packaging includes containers of individual units of production, such as cans, bottles, boxes and cartons, and protective packaging materials. These items are really part of the product, so should be considered raw stock. Shipping containers and crates are generally considered shipping expenses rather than raw stock. Neither packaging nor shipping costs would continue during a total business interruption.

Depreciation Expense Depreciation expense does not reflect a current cash outlay. Rather, depreciation expense is the current amortization of a capital expense, as reflected in an organization's accounting and tax records. Despite the fact that it does not represent a current outflow of cash, depreciation expense does reduce the net profit of an ongoing business. Thus, it is necessary to examine the extent to which depreciation expense is affected by a business interruption resulting from a direct property loss.

First, it must be noted that depreciation ceases with respect to property that has been totally destroyed. The value of the property has suddenly dropped to zero, and no further depreciation is possible. Replacement of destroyed property is a function of building and personal property insurance, and depreciation is taken into account when direct property loss is settled on an actual cash value basis. When replacement cost coverage applies, the loss adjustment is made without regard to depreciation (but replacing a depreciated asset with a new asset is accompanied by tax implications discussed in Chapter 15). At any rate, depreciation of totally destroyed property is addressed by insurance covering the direct property damage.

The situation is different when property that has not been totally destroyed is rendered unusable during a business interruption. In general, depreciation on buildings is largely due to obsolescence, but depreciation on furniture, fixtures, and equipment is largely due to wear and tear. Consequently, if interruption of business is due to other than severe damage to the physical properties, most of the depreciation on buildings will continue, but most of the depreciation on furniture, fixtures, and equipment will cease.[6]

Concluding Observations Regarding Continuing Expenses If anything, the precedindg paragraphs have pointed out the difficulty of precisely distinguishing continuing and noncontinuing expenses in advance of a loss. In any given situation, the distinction depends in part on the exact nature of the organization incurring the loss and the severity and length of the loss that does occur. A conservative assumption would be that all expenses continue during an interruption, but this is obviously not the case in most long shutdowns.

Enough information has been developed here to indicate that there is a rather general relationship between the rate at which normal expenses continue and the length of the business interruption. This relationship is shown in Exhibits 5-3 and 5-4. During long interruptions (Exhibit 5-3), many expenses are abated for a time, but increase again shortly before the business reopens. During short suspensions (Exhibit 5-4), nearly all expenses continue unabated.

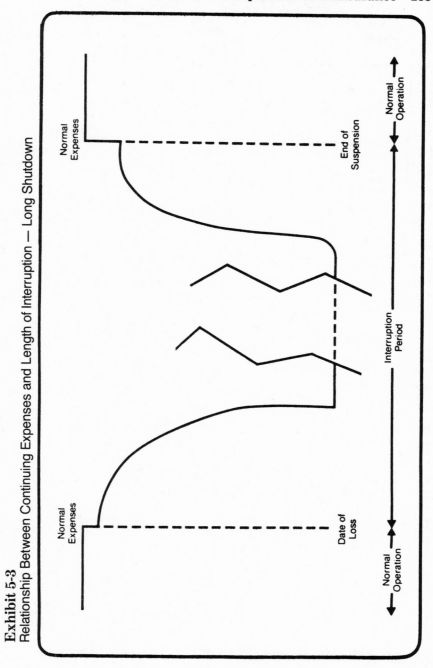

Exhibit 5-3
Relationship Between Continuing Expenses and Length of Interruption — Long Shutdown

Exhibit 5-4
Relationship Between Continuing Expense and Length of Interruption—
Short Shutdown

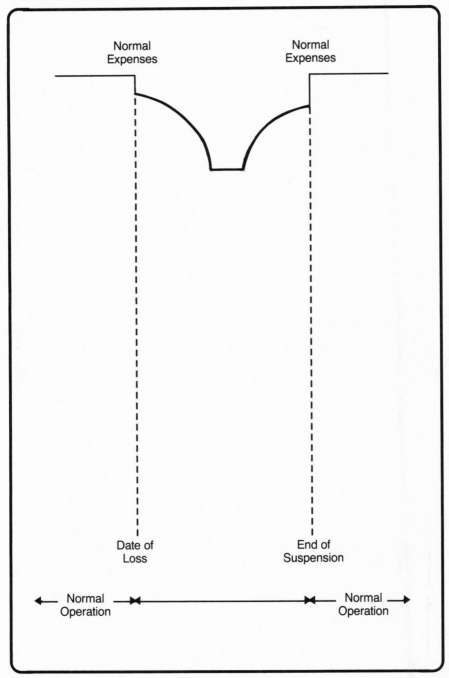

Analyzing the Timing of a Business Interruption

In order to develop a pre-loss assessment of the business interruption exposure and its loss potential, it is necessary to estimate the probable duration of any interruption. The answer to the question, "How much could a business interruption cost?" depends not only on business income figures, but also on:

1. *how long* business income is reduced, and
2. *when* during the year the interruption occurs. After determining how long an interruption could last, it is then necessary to analyze the potential effects of an interruption at the worst possible time of year.

How Long Business Income Is Reduced   The duration of a reduction in business income is directly related to the time required to replace damaged property plus the time that may be required to restore the normal rate of income.

Time Required to Replace Damaged Property.   In analyzing property exposed to loss, it is important to consider not only the probable frequency and severity of the direct loss, but also the amount of time necessary to replace items destroyed. As a practical matter, it is not necessary to determine a replacement period for each and every item. Rather, a conscious effort should be placed on identifying *critical* items—those with a long replacement period.

When critical items are identified, the exposures can be evaluated by contacting a source of the equipment, machinery, or other property to determine how expeditiously a replacement could be obtained under normal circumstances—or, perhaps, under the worst possible circumstances.

In many cases, the time required to resume operations will depend on the time needed to repair or rebuild a building. The most reliable method of estimating the rebuilding time for a building is to obtain an estimate from a reputable contractor. If this is impractical, tables showing average rebuilding time may be useful. Exhibit 5-5 is an example of one such table.

Exhibit 5-5 (do not overlook its footnotes) also provides insights into the effects on time element loss severity of grade of construction, type of occupancy, number of stories, congested conditions, and weather. Note that the construction features that tend to reduce the probable severity of direct losses tend to increase the severity of time element losses. For example, as compared with a frame structure, a fire-resistive building is less likely to sustain severe fire damage, but will take longer to reconstruct if it does.

As noted earlier, the possible length of an interruption is also

Exhibit 5-5
Average Rebuilding Time*

Grade of Construction	Average				Good			
Type of Construction [1]	A	B	C	D	A	B	C	D
Type of Occupancy								
Apartment, 1 story	125	105	90	72	156	131	100	90
Each additional story	15	13	12	10	19	16	15	13
Garages, public, 1 story	63	59	56	48	79	74	70	60
Each additional story	15	14	13	11	19	17	16	14
Hotels, clubs, 1 story	138	110	83	69	180	143	109	90
Each additional story	18	15	12	10	23	20	16	13
Industrial, 1 story [2]	69	66	63	52	86	82	79	65
Each additional story	13	12	11	9	16	15	14	11
Lofts, 1 story [3]	120	100	75	40	150	125	94	50
Each additional story	13	12	10	8	16	15	13	10
Offices, 1 story	130	117	88	79	175	158	119	107
Each additional story	17	16	13	11	23	22	18	15
Schools, 1 story	180	164	155	125	243	222	209	169
Each additional story	36	33	31	28	49	45	42	38
Stores, 1 story	124	104	79	42	155	129	99	52
Each additional story	14	13	11	9	17	16	14	11
Theaters	150	136	110	72	207	182	151	97
Warehouses, 1 story	92	81	66	39	110	97	79	47
Each additional story	13	12	10	8	16	14	12	10

1. A is reinforced concrete floors, roof and masonry walls on steel frame; B is reinforced concrete frame, floors, roof, and masonry walls; C is masonry walls with wood floors and roof (if no basement, grade floor may be concrete); and D is frame, stucco, iron-clad, or all steel.

2. Unfinished interior with very few partitions.

3. Plain interior finish and moderate amount of partitions to enclose space for light manufacturing occupancies.

Each figure represents an estimate of the number of working days it takes to erect a certain building, and it covers the total period from commencement of the plans and specifications to the day when the structure is ready for occupancy. It is assumed that building will be carried on during one shift per day only and that the work would be neither abnormally expedited nor delayed. The construction time is shown for a one-story building, followed by a figure for each additional story above one. Full basements are considered an additional story.

This table presupposes ideal building weather; that is, no time lost due to enforced lay-offs. Increases of 15 percent are suggested in climates where a nominal amount of inclement weather may be expected, and increases up to 35 percent are suggested where uncertain weather is usually the rule or where rigorous winters occur.

The construction time estimates are based upon the location being in a nominally congested district. In highly congested districts or large cities it is necessary to build barricades and a roof over sidewalks, haul materials and refuse through crowded streets, and otherwise operate under adverse conditions. Under such conditions of location, the construction time estimates should be increased about 15 percent. In uncongested localities, the estimates may be reduced by 10 percent.

*Reprinted with permission from E.C. Bardwell, *New Profits — Business Interruption Insurance* (Indianapolis: The Rough Notes Co., 1973), pp. 11-12.

affected by the presence of time-consuming production processes, especially those involving "aging." When such operations exist, the production period must be added to the period to reconstruct a building and replace machinery and equipment.

As suggested in the "expenses" discussion, time is often necessary to train new employees, place merchandise on shelves, and perform similar tasks before resuming normal operations. Allowance must be made for these factors when evaluating the loss exposure.

Time Required to Restore Rate of Income. Many businesses suffer an *extended period of interruption,* because the rate of income does not immediately return to normal as soon as property has been returned to normal. Besides employees, building, equipment, and stock, businesses also need customers. This point is particularly important for some types of businesses. For example, a bowling alley might be entirely restored and ready for business following a shutdown, but might have few customers because all leagues for the season have already formed at other bowling alleys. Special circumstances affect schools and colleges, which may lose tuition for an entire academic year if the campus is unusable at the particular time of year when classes are scheduled to begin. Many other businesses also lose customers during a shutdown, though not necessarily to the same degree. For example, when a restaurant or store is closed, its customers develop the habit of eating or shopping elsewhere, and may not return to their original habitat as soon as it is restored.

Effect of Seasonal Fluctuations Some organizations' earning patterns are not level across the year. For such organizations, it makes a difference when, during the year, the loss occurs. To address this problem, it is necessary to analyze seasonal factors.

Suppose a maximum shutdown of six months is projected. Which six months of the year would the company be shut down? It is impossible to foretell when an interruption will occur, but the question is important unless the company has an earnings pattern that does not vary substantially from month to month. If a seasonal pattern exists, the pattern of fluctuation in earnings must be identified—either by studying the past seasonal figures of the business in question or through the use of figures that show typical seasonal patterns for various types of businesses, as shown in Exhibit 5-6.

Exhibit 5-6 shows ratios of monthly sales in relation to annual sales for a composite of fourteen classes of retail businesses. Notice that 30 percent of the annual sales occur in the peak three months of business activity for the composite of the retail stores in the figure. Certain kinds of businesses, such as custom jewelry manufacturers, retail jewelers, and furriers transact as much as 45 percent of their annual business

Exhibit 5-6

Ratios† of Monthly Sales to Annual Sales of Fourteen Classes of Retail Business*

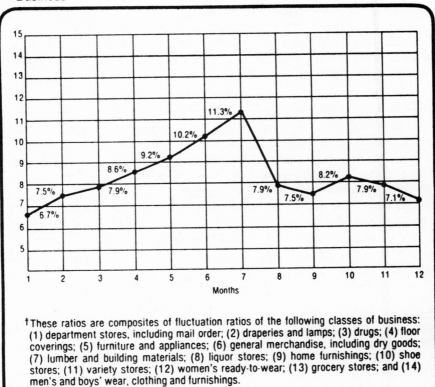

†These ratios are composites of fluctuation ratios of the following classes of business: (1) department stores, including mail order; (2) draperies and lamps; (3) drugs; (4) floor coverings; (5) furniture and appliances; (6) general merchandise, including dry goods; (7) lumber and building materials; (8) liquor stores; (9) home furnishings; (10) shoe stores; (11) variety stores; (12) women's ready-to-wear; (13) grocery stores; and (14) men's and boys' wear, clothing and furnishings.

*Reprinted with permission from E.C. Bardwell, *New Profits—Business Interruption Insurance* (Indianapolis: The Rough Notes Co., 1973), p.14.

during their peak three months, and 60 to 80 percent of their annual business during the six consecutive months of highest business activity. Businesses with an even more seasonal pattern (e.g., vegetable and fruit packers, canneries, and ski resorts) might gain their entire annual income in a three-month period.

Determining the Maximum Possible Business Interruption Loss

For purposes of assessing the business interruption exposure, the most conservative approach would be to assume a complete shutdown at the worst possible time of the year, lasting for the maximum amount of time that can be foreseen to replace a destroyed building, replace critical machinery, and restore inventory and personnel to their pre-loss status. The most conservative approach would also suggest an assumption that *all* expenses will continue throughout the interruption period. However, this is not realistic, and an analysis of conditions affecting each individual organization can lead to some basis for estimating the degree to which expenses will continue. Distinguishing continuing and noncontinuing expenses in advance of a loss is extremely difficult at best, but some assessment can at least be made based on available information and a recognition of the characteristics of various expense types.

Projecting Future Earnings and Expenses

In assessing the business interruption exposure, the objective is to estimate the possible impact of a loss that may occur *in the future*. Past figures must be analyzed and updated in order to project them into the future. How far they must be projected depends on the potential duration of a business interruption.

Projections of earnings and expenses into the future can never be perfectly reliable. However, a simple approach usually provides a usable estimate of the exposure. The approach to be described closely resembles the method for updating loss histories that was introduced in Chapter 2.

If net sales figures for the past several years are known, if the figures seem to indicate a definite trend without too much yearly variation from that trend, and if there is reason to assume that net sales will increase at the same approximate rate in the future, the business interruption exposure can be projected by using a simple trend factor. For example, if the average rate of increase in net sales for the past four years has been 10 percent per year, and there are no unusual circumstances, it is reasonable to assume that net sales next year will increase by 10 percent, and that the year after next will show an increase of 10 percent over next year.

In some instances, more sophisticated methods of projecting sales and income may be desirable. In sizable companies, the accounting or finance department will have made sales and income projections. If available, these projected figures should, of course, be used. Expense projections will seldom, if ever, be available from accounting or finance departments in a form that distinguishes continuing and noncontinuing expenses. However, it will generally be reasonable to apply the sales and income trending factor to any past expense figures, barring information that suggests a significant change in expense relationships.

BUSINESS INCOME INSURANCE

Early time element insurance was known as "use and occupancy" insurance, or simply "U & O." More recently, the term "business interruption insurance" was in vogue. The most common business interruption insurance forms were the "gross earnings" and "earnings" forms. Some practitioners still use these phrases when referring to the general class of coverage now provided by the business income forms.

What Is Insured

The scope of coverage under the business income coverage form can be described in terms of covered events, covered causes of loss, and covered consequences.

Covered Events The basic business income coverage form protects against loss resulting directly from the necessary interruption or partial suspension of business caused by damage to or destruction of real or personal property at the described premises by a covered cause of loss. To be covered, an interruption may be total or partial, but it must be *necessary*—that is, beyond the insured's control. No business income loss occurs unless it is necessary to slow down or to shut down the business following direct damage to property.

The direct damage must be caused by a covered peril. Shutdowns caused by uninsured perils are not covered. Shutdowns caused by damage to property elsewhere than at the described premises are not covered under the basic approach unless the interruption involves an order of civil authority, as detailed later.

Covered Causes of Loss Business income insurance can be written for the same combinations of perils as direct damage policies. Just like the building and personal property coverage form (BPP), the business income coverage form must have an attached causes-of-loss form. Basic, broad, or "all-risks" type coverage is available, and earth movement coverage may be added by endorsement. Perils insured may or may not be the same as those applicable to the insured's building or personal property coverage.

Although business income insurance may be written in conjunction with direct loss property insurance, the limits of insurance are kept separate. That is, it is not usually possible with standard forms to provide blanket coverage with a single amount of insurance for direct and time element losses.

Standard business interruption insurance forms do not cover such perils as flood, landslide, or subsidence. However, coverage is available in some difference in conditions (DIC) contracts, and many insurers are willing to cover such exposures using nonstandard forms or endorsements. Some perils are particularly important as causes of business shutdowns, but are uninsurable under any standard insurance contract. For example, many businesses are shut down when workers go on strike demanding higher wages or other concessions, and loss of business income caused by the strike is not generally insurable. Coverage for a given exposure may be available in some surplus lines markets. If the strike turns into a riot, business interruption attributable to property damaged by rioters would be covered under the riot peril. Otherwise, these exposures must be addressed with risk management techniques other than insurance.

Covered Consequences The bulk of the BIC deals with covered loss consequences. The business income coverage form can be roughly outlined as follows:

I. Business Income Coverage (which might be considered the primary element of the basic approach)
II. Four Additional Coverages (which are automatically included with the basic approach)
   A. Extra Expense
   B. Civil Authority
   C. Alterations and New Buildings
   D. Extended Business Income
III. Coverage Options (preprinted in the form and activated by appropriate entry in the declarations)
   A. Maximum Period of Indemnity
   B. Monthly Limit of Indemnity
   C. Agreed Value
   D. Extended Period of Indemnity

Business Income Coverage

In the basic insuring agreement of the business income coverage form (BIC), the insurer agrees to pay when a business interruption causes a loss of business income. Various constraints on the extent of coverage and the nature of a covered business interruption will be discussed later.

Business Income Defined Business income is defined as:

a. Net Income (Net Profit or Loss before income taxes) that would have been earned or incurred; and
b. Continuing normal operating expenses, including payroll, incurred.

Note that business income is defined as *pre-tax* profit. In order to indemnify the insured, it is necessary to provide funds to replace aftertax profits and also funds with which to pay taxes. Business income recoveries are normally subject to income taxes.

   Actual Loss Sustained   The first words of the insuring agrement are "We will pay for the actual loss of Business Income you sustain." These words emphasize the point that *business income insurance is not a valued contract, but a contract of indemnity.* The insurance company is obligated to pay nothing unless the insured has actually sustained a business income loss, and the extent of the insurer's obligation is limited to the dollar amount of loss actually sustained.

This does not necessarily mean that the insured must have been earning a net income prior to the loss in order to receive any benefit. In fact, one use of business income insurance is to provide coverage for a building under construction. If property damage delays the date on which the building begins to earn rental income or income from operations, the owner is indemnified for the resulting business income loss.

   Period of Restoration   In determining actual loss sustained, the time element is measured by the *period of restoration*—essentially the length of time required to rebuild, repair, or replace the damaged or destroyed property "with reasonable speed and similar quality." This requirement is important. The insured cannot delay the repair or rebuilding process, and he or she must see that all work is reasonably expedited. More precisely, the insured may delay if he or she so chooses, but the insurer will not pay more than if repairs had been expedited. (Courts have held that delays in reconstruction due to acts of persons other than the insured, or even reasonable disputes between the insured and others, are reimbursable.) There can be a large difference between the time *actually* required for repairing or replacing the damaged property and the time required to do the job with *reasonable* speed. In fact, the BIC does not require that the damaged property ever be repaired or replaced. This can be very important to a tenant of a building who has no control over the decision to repair or replace the rented property. If the property is not repaired or replaced, the form would still provide reimbursement for the time it *would have* taken to repair or replace the property.

If unusually severe weather or delay in shipping causes delay in rebuilding, the period of restoration is extended. These latter delays are beyond the insured's control, and it would be "unreasonable" to handle a loss as though construction could have continued during a period when weather conditions made construction impossible.

The restoration period does not cease the instant a damaged or destroyed building is repaired or rebuilt. Time is permitted for the insured to refurnish supplies and restock merchandise. For a manufacturer, time is allowed to bring the production process to the same point where it was before the loss.

An exclusion in the causes-of-loss forms makes it clear that the BIC does not provide coverage for the time required to reproduce *finished* stock. Likewise, the BIC does not cover a manufacturer's loss from damage to or destruction of finished stock. The building and personal property form, and possibly a manufacturer's selling price endorsement—or some other types of personal property coverage—is required to cover the values represented in finished stock in the hands of its manufacturer.

The period of restoration is not terminated by the expiration of the policy. If a fire, for example, damages the property one week before the policy expiration date and causes a three-month suspension, the entire loss is covered—whether or not a renewal premium is paid. (It would still be desirable to carry business income insurance during the period of interruption, in case another direct damage loss during the reconstruction causes a further period of interruption.)

Coinsurance

In order to encourage insurance to value and to simplify ratemaking, the business income coverage form contains a coinsurance clause that operates essentially the same as the coinsurance clause in property insurance policies covering direct damage. Of course, the value of property is not the base against which the coinsurance percentage is applied. Instead, it is one year's net income and operating expenses.

The insured may choose coinsurance of 50, 60, 70, 80, 90, 100, or 125 percent. The chosen percentage generally corresponds roughly to the expected duration of a business interruption—an organization expecting a maximum interruption of six months might purchase coverage with a 50 percent coinsurance clause, since six months is 50 percent of one year. At the other extreme, an organization facing a potential interruption of more than one year might elect coverage with 125 percent coinsurance. However, it would be a gross oversimplification to relate the coinsurance percentage solely to the expected period of interruption. As explained later, the probable maximum loss must be analyzed and compared with business income coverage provisions in order to determine the limit of insurance to purchase. Comparing this limit with projected net income and expenses leads one to select the optimum coinsurance percentage.

Three points about the BIC coinsurance clause must be emphasized:

1. *The amount reflecting the potential business income loss is not the amount of insurance that will meet coinsurance requirements.*
2. *To comply with the coinsurance clause, an insured may be required to purchase more business income insurance than seems necessary.*
3. *What looks like overinsurance is justified, in part, by the additional coverages, which provide for recovery in excess of the loss of business income.* Also, historically, rating factors have always reflected this "overinsurance."

Business Income Exposure Versus Coinsurance Requirement The BIC coinsurance percentage does not apply to the exposure. Business income is defined as net income plus *continuing expenses* incurred during the interruption, but the coinsurance clause applies to net income plus *all operating expenses* that probably would have developed during the twelve-month period following the inception date of the policy. *In determining compliance with the coinsurance provision, both continuing and noncontinuing expenses are taken into account.*

More specifically, the coinsurance clause applies to the net earnings plus expenses as expected to develop during the twelve-month period starting at the beginning of the policy term.

The usual practice when buying insurance is to project figures for one year. The limit of insurance should be reviewed at least once during the policy period to see whether there have been any major changes in earnings or expenses that affect the prediction. As the policy period progresses and earnings and expenses are booked, there is less and less uncertainty over the amount of insurance required to comply with coinsurance provisions. Assuming the insured keeps good records, if a loss occurs on the last day of the policy period, there will be little question as to the net income and expenses during the policy period and little difficulty in determining whether or not coinsurance requirements have been satisfied.

More Insurance than Seems Necessary It might seem most logical for the coinsurance percentage to apply to the subjects insured—net income plus continuing expenses. However, those who drafted the contract language recognized that it is difficult, if not impossible, to distinguish continuing from noncontinuing expenses before any loss occurs. Requiring such a distinction might make it extremely difficult to comply with a coinsurance provision (and even more difficult for an insurer to prove noncompliance).

Another reason for requiring more insurance than seems necessary is that the extra limits may actually be needed, because the BIC covers more than loss of business income, as noted below.

Additional Coverages and Coverage Extension Automatically included in the basic BIC, at no extra cost, are four additional coverages:

1. extra expense,
2. extended business income,
3. alterations and new buildings, and
4. civil authority.

The limit of insurance in the BIC includes these additional coverages, but the related exposures do not affect the amount of insurance necessary to meet coinsurance requirements.

Extra Expense Coverage

Three types of expenses should be considered when evaluating time element exposures:

1. Normal operating expenses that will continue during the interruption—known as *continuing expenses.* Continuing expenses incurred during an interruption are paid by the business income coverage.
2. Normal expenses that will not continue during the interruption—known as *noncontinuing expenses.* Noncontinuing expenses are not incurred. Since no related loss is actually sustained, there is no loss due to noncontinuing expenses and no need for insurance on them.
3. Expenses that would normally not be incurred—known as *extra expenses.* Extra expenses are addressed by the extra expense additional coverage of the BIC.

Extra Expenses Defined In the words of the BIC:

Extra Expense means necessary expenses you incur during the "period of restoration" that you would not have incurred if there had been no direct physical loss or damage to property caused by or resulting from a Covered Cause of Loss.

Several key words appear in that definition.

In order to qualify as extra expenses, certain criteria must be met:

• The expenses must be *actually incurred.*
• They must be incurred *because of the direct loss.*

- They must be *non-normal* expenses.
- The only extra expenses that are covered are those that are *necessary*.
- The only necessary extra expenses that are covered are those incurred *during the "period of restoration"*—the time period beginning with the date of the direct physical loss and ending on the date when the premises are repaired, rebuilt, or replaced with reasonable speed and similar quality.

Covered Expenses Extra expenses, as defined, are covered if they are incurred, following a direct loss, for one of the following four reasons:

1. To continue operations and avoid a suspension of business, if full-scale operations are still feasible.
2. To continue operations and minimize the suspension of business, if full-scale operations are not feasible but some activity is possible.
3. To minimize the suspension of business when operations cannot be continued but the period of shutdown can be shortened by extraordinary measures.
4. To expedite the repair or replacement of property, or the restoration of damaged valuable papers and records, regardless of the extent of the interruption of operations.

Extra expenses to continue operations (items 1 and 2) are covered whether operations are continued at the described premises, at premises that serve as a permanent replacement, or at temporary substitute premises. For example, if the showroom of an auto dealership is destroyed, extra expense insurance might pay the expenses of setting up a tent in the parking lot to serve as a temporary showroom, the expenses of moving to a permanent new location in another suitable building that happens to be available, or the expenses of renting a temporary showroom.

When operations cannot be continued, extra expenses to "minimize the suspension of business"—that is, to keep the interruption period as short as possible—are covered without further qualification or limitation (item 3).

Item 4 seems more to serve as an affirmation of coverage than as an additional item of coverage. As with earlier business interruption insurance forms, the policy clearly covers extra expenses that are cost-effective because they reduce the amount that would otherwise be payable as a business income loss.

Expediting expenses are expenses incurred to repair direct damage. For this reason, coverage of expediting expenses seems not to belong in a time element insurance form. The building and personal property form, or some other type of direct property damage insurance, should normally provide the source of recovery for building and personal property losses. However, the basic coverage of the BPP applies only to the actual cash value of the damaged property, or with the replacement cost option, coverage is extended to cover the amount that is *actually spent* and *necessary* to replace the lost or damaged property. It is doubtful whether the added extra expenses of rushing a repair job would be considered necessary in the context of the BPP.

The extra expense coverage of the BIC affirmatively covers expenses to expedite repair, replacement, or restoration (item 4) to the extent they reduce the amount otherwise payable under the form. For example, the auto dealership might want to complete showroom repair work by the date when new models will be introduced. Perhaps the contractor says it is possible to speed up repairs of the damaged showroom if the dealer is willing to pay the extra cost of overtime work by the construction crew. This extra cost would be covered.

Extra expense coverage applies "to the extent it reduces the amount of loss that otherwise would have been payable *under this Coverage Form.*" [emphasis added] Since the coverage form includes not only business income coverage but also the additional coverages, extra expenses would be covered if they are incurred, for example, in order to reduce loss payable under the additional coverage for extended business income (discussed a bit later). Extra expenses in this category might include expenses incurred in order to advertise a "Grand Reopening."

Some organizations are not likely to sustain a loss of business income because they cannot afford a business interruption but must stay in business "at all costs." Such organizations may prefer to purchase an extra expense coverage form, described later.

Incurring extra expenses, in hopes of reducing a business income loss, can have a dramatic effect on the actual loss sustained. In one case, a manufacturer operating two plants suffered a direct property loss at one of the plants. In cooperation with its insurer, the firm doubled its output at the surviving plant to reduce losses during the period of restoration. The workers from the damaged plant operated as a second shift at the surviving plant. After the damaged plant was back in operation, and the actual business income loss sustained could be measured, it was determined that these measures had resulted in an operation more efficient than the original operation at two separate plants. The expenses to reduce the loss had so effectively reduced the loss that no business income was lost.

Loss Determination Condition Some aspects of extra expense coverage appear to offer the insured a blank check, since many different expenditures could conceivably come under the extra expense umbrella. The loss determination condition states that extra expenses are only those that exceed normal operating expenses that would have been incurred if the loss had not taken place. This at least makes it clear that normal operating expenses are not extra expenses.

Some extra expense dollars might legitimately be spent on the purchase of various property items. For example, an insured might purchase a mobile home to be placed outside the damaged building for use as a temporary office and a command post for reconstruction efforts. The question might then be raised, "What happens to the mobile home when reconstruction is completed? Is it, in effect, a gift from the insurance company—available for use, after it is moved, as the insured's lakeside summer home?" The extra expense form contains a clear answer to this question. The salvage value that remains of any property bought for temporary use during the "period of restoration" will be deducted from the total of extra expenses.

Deduction will also be made for extra expenses that are covered by other insurance.

Extended Business Income Coverage

The extended business income coverage is an addition to the business income coverage. To prevent confusion, the concepts of *extended business income* and *business income* must be distinguished from one another.

Business income coverage replaces income lost during the "period of restoration," which ends when property at the described premises is repaired, rebuilt, or replaced. If the restoration is delayed, the "period of restoration" ends on the date when property should have been restored "with reasonable speed and similar quality." In many cases, this time runs out before the insured's business volume has completely returned to normal. A business that has been shut down for a while does not immediately regain all its customers when its doors reopen. The damaged property may be restored, but business activity may still be depressed.

The *extended business income* additional coverage extends for thirty days the time period for which the insured will be reimbursed for loss of business. The period of extended business income coverage begins on

> the date property (except "finished stock") is actually repaired, rebuilt, or replaced and "operations" are resumed.

Note that this date is not necessarily the same as the date on which the "period of restoration" ends. A gap can occur if the restoration is not completed "with reasonable speed." There could also be a gap between the time business income coverage ends and the time extended business income coverage begins. Business income coverage ends when the property should have been repaired, rebuilt, or replaced—but extended business income coverage does not begin until operations are also resumed.

Extended business income coverage lasts for thirty days if the business could not be completely restored within that time period. However, if the insured could (not "does," but "could") restore the business in a shorter period of time, extended business income coverage ceases. Continued coverage would not be needed anyway.

Thirty days of extended business income coverage is included in the basic BIC. For an additional premium, the *extended period of indemnity* optional coverage of the BIC makes it possible to extend this time frame for as long as 360 days.

"Finished stock" is stock that the named insured has manufactured but not held for sale as a retail outlet "insured under this Coverage Part." A manufacturer's extended business income coverage begins when manufacturing operations resume—not when stock damaged by the direct loss has been remanufactured. The loss of a manufacturer's damaged stock is covered by the BPP or other personal property coverage—it is not the role of business income insurance to pay the cost of remanufacturing damaged stock. However, if a vertically integrated manufacturer also operates a retail outlet, its business income coverage at the outlet applies until the outlet's inventory is replaced, at which point extended business income coverage begins.

Civil Authority Coverage

In most cases, the BIC provides coverage for losses resulting from direct property damage *at the insured premises*. The civil authority coverage extends business income and extra expense coverage to apply when other premises are damaged under a prescribed set of circumstances.

It is not uncommon for a fire or other peril to cause an interruption at a number of adjacent businesses that, themselves, sustain no direct damage. For example, police and fire fighters may deny access to an entire city block when a serious fire occurs.

For *civil authority* coverage to apply, three criteria must be met:

1. Access to the insured's business must be denied *by the order of civil authorities.*
2. The denial of access must be caused *by damage or destruction of property that is not on the described premises.* (Business income loss occasioned by damage to property on the described premises is covered by the basic business income coverage.)
3. The direct property damage must be *from an insured peril.* Hurricane damage, for example, since windstorm is an insured peril, could lead to reimbursement. A hurricane warning that leads businesses to close would not involve direct property damage, and any related interruption would not be covered.

Civil authority coverage applies for a period of up to two consecutive weeks from the date of the civil authority's action.

Alterations and New Buildings Coverage

Some people think business income losses result only from property damage to existing buildings and disruption of operations currently in progress. While most business interruptions fall into this category, business income can also be lost if completion of a new building is delayed because the building sustained some kind of damage during the course of its construction. The same applies to alterations. If alterations to an existing building are not completed on schedule, operations cannot begin and a loss of income may result.

The *alterations and new buildings additional coverage* covers loss of business income sustained due to direct physical loss or damage to:

(1) New buildings or structures, whether complete or under construction;
(2) Alterations or additions to existing buildings or structures; and
(3) Machinery, equipment, supplies or building materials located on or within 100 feet of the described premises and:
  (a) Used in the construction, alterations or additions; or
  (b) Incidental to the occupancy of new buildings.

Coverage applies only if the direct physical loss or damage delays the start of operations. The "period of restoration" begins on the date operations would have begun if the direct physical loss or damage had not occurred.

Newly Acquired Locations Coverage Extension

Unlike the so-called "additional coverages," this "coverage extension" applies only when a coinsurance percentage of 50 or more is shown in the declarations. As a practical matter, this would encompass the majority of policies.

This policy provision extends "Business Income Coverage" but makes no specific mention of extra expense coverage. Since "Business Income Coverage" is the name of the entire form—which encompasses business income and extra expense and other additional coverages—it would seem to extend the additional coverages as well.

This extension is intended to provide thirty days' temporary coverage at a new location, which should give the insured ample time to report the added exposure to the insured company. Coverage under the extension ceases when the policy expires, when the new location is reported to the insurer, or thirty days after the exposure begins, whichever comes first. This is automatic insurance—not free insurance. The insurer is entitled to a premium from the date the exposure begins.

Coverage does not apply to property at fairs and exhibitions. The limit of insurance for this coverage is 10 percent of the business income limit or $100,000—again, whichever is less. The coinsurance provision does not apply to this coverage extension.

Electronic Media and Records Limitation

If a business is interrupted by an insured peril that damages or destroys electronic data processing (EDP) media or programming records, and if no other property has been damaged, then coverage is limited to a period of sixty days. This limitation does not necessarily apply if other property has been damaged along with the EDP media. In such a case, the time limit is the time required to repair or replace the property other than EDP, if longer than sixty days.

The EDP media limitation may be changed, for an additional premium, to ninety days, or eliminated entirely. Alternatively, the exposure may be addressed with an EDP floater policy, described in Chapter 14.

Exclusions

The business income coverage form itself contains no exclusions. However, coverage is subject to the various exclusions of the causes-of-loss forms, as already discussed in Chapter 4. The following "special exclusions" in the causes-of-loss forms apply only to business income losses.

An insurer is not liable for a loss resulting from interference at the described premises by strikers or other persons with rebuilding, repairing, or replacing the property or with the resumption or continuation of business. However, if there is a strike at other locations, such as at a supplier's location, increased time of interruption due to this off-premises strike would be covered. This would affect the time required to return to operations with reasonable speed.

Another special exclusion applies to loss from suspension, lapse, or cancellation of a lease, license, contract, or order. It is not unusual for such privileges or agreements to be canceled when there is physical inability to deliver the contracted material or service. Should a fire or other insured peril trigger such a cancellation, the insured would be covered for such loss during the time required to repair or replace the damaged property with the exercise of reasonable speed. But the insured would not be covered for loss from such cancellation *after* the damaged property has been repaired or replaced.

ALTERNATIVES TO THE BASIC APPROACH

The unmodified business income coverage form (BIC) represents a basic approach to insuring the business interruption and extra expense exposure. Other approaches modify the income and expenses covered, offer alternatives to coinsurance, offer blanket insurance as an alternative to specific insurance, provide contingent business income insurance, cover a school's tuitions and fees, address off-premises utilities exposures, or provide building ordinance coverage. While it is commonly considered appropriate for manufacturers and merchants, the basic business income coverage—with or without modifications—is also highly appropriate for rental exposures and builders risks.

Covered Income and Expenses

Payroll Coverage Options   As noted in the discussion of BIC coverage, necessary payroll expense is reimbursed by the business income coverage. Payroll expense is also included when determining the amount of insurance necessary to meet coinsurance requirements. Earlier in the chapter, when discussing continuing and noncontinuing expenses, it was noted that some payroll expenses do not normally continue during an extended period of interruption. The noncontinuing payroll expenses generally fall within the definition of ordinary payroll. *Ordinary payroll* includes the entire payroll expense (including employee benefits, FICA, union dues, and so forth) for all employees of the named insured, except officers, executives, department managers, and employees under contract. Other important employees may be specifically named or described in the endorsement discussed below.

Ordinary payroll may be insured in one of three ways:

1. Ordinary payroll may be covered in full, to the extent necessary to resume operations (the basic approach).
2. Ordinary payroll may be excluded.
3. Ordinary payroll may be covered for a limited interruption period.

"Full" Coverage. The unmodified BIC covers all necessary ordinary payroll expense. Payroll cost is treated as an operating expense, and this approach affects the amount of insurance necessary to meet the coinsurance requirement. Coverage of ordinary payroll is suitable for many insureds, especially if the maximum duration of a shutdown is brief, if union or other contracts require salary continuation, or if employees generally would be difficult to replace and would not be laid off during a shutdown.

Excluded Coverage. A second approach is to use an *ordinary payroll limitation endorsement* to exclude all ordinary payroll.

Limited Coverage. The third approach—which also uses the *ordinary payroll limitation endorsement*—is to cover ordinary payroll for a limited period of time. Coverage may be provided for 90 or 180 days.

This approach supports the concept that was illustrated in Exhibit 5-4. During a short interruption—which may be the result of minor direct property damage—workers may be kept on the payroll. However, during a longer interruption, workers qualifying as "ordinary payroll" will be laid off until such time as operations are resumed. The limited payroll coverage is intended to mesh with this practice.

When ordinary payroll has a seasonal pattern, it would be wise to determine the highest amount of ordinary payroll anticipated for any consecutive 90- (or 180-) day period. In fact, the ordinary payroll limitation endorsement virtually requires it—the coinsurance requirement with the endorsement is based on payroll for the period of greatest ordinary payroll expenses during the policy year.

Selecting Among Payroll Options. When there is *any* coverage for payroll, payroll expense will be paid only if it is a *necessary* continuing expense. Specific mention of payroll expense does not mean this item is treated differently from any other covered expense. The fact that coverage is provided for a stated period does not mean the entire normal payroll expense *will* be paid for that period. Also, note that payroll coverage is not segregated from coverage for other expenses—there is no separate limit of payroll insurance.

The choice among the three approaches to ordinary payroll depends on the insured's situation, the possible length of an interruption, and the extent to which payroll expenses would continue. However, ordinary payroll should be excluded entirely only after considering the variables that might enter into post-loss handling of ordinary payroll. For example,

- The labor market might be tight in the insured's locale at the time of a loss, and there may be some difficulty in hiring employees—it may be more advisable to retain existing labor.
- There may be more expense than anticipated in training new employees—existing employees are already trained.
- Disputes in loss adjustments may develop over which employees should be classified in the ordinary payroll category—the issue is not raised when the entire payroll expense is covered.

Power, Heat, and Refrigeration Deduction When analyzing continuing and noncontinuing expenses earlier in this chapter, it was noted that power, heat, and refrigeration expenses are relatively large for some manufacturing operations. Yet, if the power, heat, or refrigeration is consumed in the manufacturing process, most such expenses abate when the process is shut down. When these "energy" expenses are noncontinuing expenses, they can create a sizable gap between the business income loss exposure and the amount of BIC coverage that must be purchased to meet coinsurance requirements.

The *power, heat and refrigeration deduction endorsement* provides some relief for manufacturers who have recognized this problem. With the endorsement, the cost of such "energy" used in production operations is not included in either the definition of business income or in coinsurance computations. The result is that a lower limit of insurance may be purchased.

Alternatives to Coinsurance

Maximum Period of Indemnity This optional coverage is preprinted in the BIC and may be activated by an appropriate entry in the declarations. This option is an alternative for businesses that are unlikely to sustain a business interruption of more than four months.

The maximum period of indemnity option is straightforward. The coinsurance condition is not activated. Instead, the insurer promises to pay whatever business income loss is sustained—subject to either a maximum period of 120 days following the direct damage loss or until the limit of insurance is exhausted, whichever comes first.

Premium *rates* are substantially higher with this option, but lower limits of insurance may be chosen to cover the maximum probable loss.

Monthly Limit of Indemnity This option, which is preprinted in the BIC, also suspends the coinsurance clause. With this option, the most the insurer will pay for loss in each period of thirty consecutive days is the limit of insurance times the fraction shown in the declarations. The fractions usually used are 1/3, 1/4, and 1/6. These correspond to expected interruption periods of three, four, and six months, respectively.

After selecting an appropriate percentage limitation, based on the maximum duration of a shutdown, the highest net profit and continuing expense for *any single month* should be determined. This is necessary because no one knows in which month a loss will occur.

The amount of insurance that will cover the maximum anticipated loss is simply the maximum number of months multiplied by the highest monthly exposure.

To illustrate, assume the following facts about the Skey Company:

- It conducts a seasonal business with its best month in December.
- In December, net profits and continuing expense are expected to be $8,000.
- The maximum duration of a shutdown is estimated to be four months.

Based on these facts, the 1/4 monthly limit is selected and the amount of insurance purchased is four times $8,000, or $32,000.

Now, assume that Skey Company is shut down for two weeks and a loss of $5,000 is sustained. The loss will be paid in full because the 1/4 of $32,000, an $8,000 limit, is not allocated evenly over the month. In other words, the $8,000 monthly limit is not further subdivided into $4,000 for two weeks. The full $8,000 is available for any loss lasting less than one month. This is important because it often is not possible to cut continuing expenses quickly or to cut them as much in short shutdowns as in long ones. For example, as noted in the preceding chapter, when the interruption will be short it may be proper to keep on paying "ordinary payroll" to assure the availability of the full workforce at reopening; there is not enough time to find and hire a new set of workers.

Suppose the actual loss turns out to be $6,000 in the first month and $9,000 in the second month (despite the expected maximum of $8,000). The insurer will pay the full $6,000 for the first month, but only $8,000 of the second month's loss. The total reimbursement is $14,000. If the full limit is not used in a month, the "unused" insurance is not added to the limit for future months. *The limit applies to each month separately.*

Suppose Skey Company suffers a four and one-half month business interruption (the four-month maximum estimate was inaccurate) with monthly losses of $6,000, $9,000, $8,000, $8,000, and $4,000. The insurer will pay as shown in Exhibit 5-7. There is no limitation on the number of

Exhibit 5-7
Skey Company Recovery for 4½ Month Loss

Month	Loss	Payment	Basis
1	$ 6,000	$ 6,000	Actual Loss Sustained
2	9,000	8,000	Monthly Maximum
3	8,000	8,000	Actual Loss Sustained
4	8,000	8,000	Actual Loss Sustained
5	4,000	2,000	Limited by $32,000 Policy Limit
Totals	$35,000	$32,000	

months during which losses will be paid, but there are limits on the amount payable (1) in any thirty-day period and (2) for the entire period of interruption.

Sometimes the monthly limits create the impression that the coverage is a valued form. It is not. Subject to the limits, the form still covers the actual loss sustained.

Premium *rates* for the monthly limit of indemnity option are somewhat higher than the rates for the basic BIC. However, there are situations where the *premium* for an appropriate monthly limit of indemnity is less than that for an appropriate unmodified BIC—assuming an "appropriate" form covers the maximum expected loss with no penalty for underinsurance. These situations often develop when the period of restoration is less than six months, the exposure is small, and earnings do not vary month to month. The basic BIC has a 50 percent minimum coinsurance clause, which implicitly assumes a minimum six-month restoration period and an amount of insurance equal to at least half the firm's net income and expenses. By contrast, the 1/3, 1/4, and 1/6 monthly limitation options implicitly assume interruptions of three, four, or six months, respectively.

The monthly limit of indemnity is often appropriate for small firms or for landlords whose primary exposure involves loss of rental income. It is easy to approximate insurance needs by simply calculating (1) how much insurance per month would be required to replace lost business income, and (2) the probable duration of a business interruption. This option also may be appropriate for new businesses without earnings records, or for small businesses for which forecasting is difficult. It has been suggested that this approach also can be appropriate for insureds who are unwilling to share financial information with their agents or insurers, but the logic here is somewhat flawed. If a loss occurs, the books must be opened anyway to effect a loss adjustment.

In many situations involving small businesses or firms with

relatively short periods of interruption, the coverage and cost of both basic and optional approaches must be examined to determine which produces the best insurance value.

Agreed Value Option   The agreed value option of the BIC is comparable to the agreed value option of the BPP. In both cases, the option is preprinted in the form and activated by an entry in the declarations. The coinsurance clause is superseded and the insured and insurer agree to a set of values reported in a written statement. If the limit of insurance agrees with the values in the statement at the time of the loss, the insured's loss will be covered in full, subject to policy limits.

The agreed value option of the BIC differs from that of the BPP in some ways. First, the values reported are not property values, but business income values. A *business income report/work sheet* is made a part of the policy and shows (1) actual financial data for the insured's operations during the past twelve months and (2) projected financial data for the coming twelve months. (A similar worksheet is used in the illustration at the end of this chapter.)

The second difference is that a coinsurance percentage is used, even though the coinsurance provision has been deactivated. For example, if the insured anticipates a maximum interruption of six months, a coinsurance percentage of 50 percent would be shown in the declarations, and the insured would carry a limit of insurance equal to 50 percent of the annual values subject to loss.

A third difference is that a 10 percent premium surcharge is made for this option in the BIC; in the BPP the charge is 5 percent.

Valued Business Interruption Contracts   Most business interruption insurance is written under one of the standard forms described here. These forms are contracts of indemnity, providing reimbursement to the insured on an *actual loss sustained* basis, subject to the policy limits.

Business interruption insurance is also available from a few insurance companies on a nonstandard *valued form*. Although these contracts are less popular than the indemnity contracts, the proponents of valued business interruption policies are enthusiastic about their merits.

The valued approach is simple. (In many ways, the approach is similar to that of disability income insurance, a type of accident and health insurance that pays a predetermined amount for each day, week, or month a person is unable to work due to disability.) In some valued business interruption plans, the insured is paid a specified amount for each day the business is interrupted, up to a specified number of days.

These policies are appropriately called per diem forms. In other plans, the amount of reimbursement may be on a weekly or monthly basis.

Valued policies contain no coinsurance provision. Therefore, it is impossible to have a coinsurance penalty. This does not mean that the insured will necessarily be reimbursed fully for any loss. The amount of insurance may be inadequate either in the daily, weekly, or monthly amount or in terms of the maximum period benefits will be paid.

A business need not be totally shut down to receive valued business interruption benefits. Partial interruptions are also covered according to the percentage that the business is reduced. Suppose, for example, that a company is entitled to receive $50,000 each week it is totally inoperative. If the company is able to operate at 40 percent of capacity, thus suffering a 60 percent loss, the insured will receive $30,000 each week. For manufacturers, the percentage of activity is determined by the percentage reduction in production or output. For merchants, partial suspensions are measured by various methods. The reduction in gross sales probably is most common.

Valued forms have several advantages. One is their simplicity. With no coinsurance and a daily, weekly, or monthly benefit, the coverage is easy to understand. Second, loss adjustments are much simpler and possibly more prompt with the valued forms. It is not necessary to project earnings and expenses for a twelve-month period. With a valued form only two things need to be ascertained: (1) the number of days of the interruption, and (2) the percentage of the shutdown.

Critics of the valued policy approach point out several possible disadvantages. First, the simplicity of the valued form may be an illusion. If the insured does not accurately estimate the amount exposed to loss, the amount of insurance purchased may not be determined with adequate forethought. If the amount purchased is not based on much more than a guess, it is likely to be inadequate. On the other hand, if the amount of insurance is excessive, the insurer may feel a serious moral hazard is involved.

The speed of recovery may not be a genuine advantage of the valued forms. Recovery under a valued policy may be prompt, but even with the other policies, most insurers will advance payments, at least for serious losses.

Another problem with the valued forms, according to critics, is that their cost tends to be higher than that of the other forms. This may or may not be true. From an individual insured's point of view, comparison should be made between two specific appropriate contracts, which also should be evaluated against a given set of needs.

Alternative to a Fixed Limits and Premiums—Premium Adjustment Endorsement

Another alternative is the *business income premium adjustment endorsement*. Although it may also resolve some coinsurance problems, this endorsement does not eliminate the coinsurance provision of the policy to which it is attached.

This endorsement is similar to the value reporting form used with the BPP. Business income is covered subject to a limit of insurance which should be set high enough to cover any anticipated loss. An initial premium is collected based on the limit. A *business income report/work sheet* is submitted to the insurer showing business income values for the past twelve months. This document is the same as the first part of the report used with the agreed value approach. However, the insured is not required to *project* values for the coming year. Instead, another report of business income is submitted at the end of the policy period showing *actual* values for that period, and the actual earned premium is adjusted based on the values in this year-end report.

The penalty may be substantial for an insured who fails to submit any required report, but the approach to arriving at the penalty is extremely simple. In the words of the endorsement, "we will not adjust your premium." In other words, there will be no return premium unless the insured submits a report to indicate what the return premium should be.

Alternative to Specific Insurance—Blanket Insurance

Many companies conduct business operations at more than one location and face the problem of interdependency among locations. If the operations are highly interdependent, it may be inadvisable to insure the various activities in each building or location separately. In such cases, blanket coverage may be preferred. With blanket coverage, several locations are shown as a single item with a single amount of insurance. Blanket coverage is indicated on the declarations page of the policy, and blanket rates are usually used. (Blanket business interruption rates are usually computed on a weighted average based on floor areas at the various locations.)

A major requirement for blanket business interruption insurance is that all premises must be substantially owned, managed, or controlled by the insured. Coverage, of course, is limited to loss resulting from damage to property at a described location.

When functions of the same insured at two or more locations are completely independent, there is no interdependency, and either specific or blanket coverage will do the job. As with blanket direct loss coverage, there is a bit more flexibility in the application of blanket policy limits, and the blanket premium is sometimes lower.

One possible disadvantage of blanket coverage arises during loss adjustments. With a blanket policy, the insured must exhibit all of the books and accounting records (even those relating to locations not involved in the loss) in order to determine whether the coinsurance requirement has been met. The coinsurance requirement is to be met in total, not just at the one location where the loss occurs. When each location is specifically covered, only the books of the damaged or destroyed location have to be checked.

Contingent Business Income Insurance

The standard business income coverage form insures against loss of net profits and continuing expenses when the business is interrupted by an insured peril causing damage or destruction of property *at the premises described in the declarations*—generally, the premises at which the insured conducts operations. Therefore, the basic BIC provides no coverage when the insured's business is interrupted by damage or destruction at other premises not owned, operated, or controlled by the insured. However, coverage is available by endorsement.

The exposures can be explained by examining the relationships of two or three firms illustrated in Exhibits 5-8 and 5-9. In Exhibit 5-8, Contributing Manufacturing Company manufactures goods sold to Recipient Sales Corporation. If Contributing is Recipient's major supplier, a severe fire at Contributing's plant would cause Recipient's operations to be interrupted (assuming no other supplier could conveniently provide the merchandise), even though there was no direct fire damage at Recipient's location. Conversely, if Recipient is a major purchaser of Contributing's products, tornado damage at Recipient's sales outlet might result in interruption of Contributing's business income, even though Contributing's plants are untouched by the windstorm. These exposures, known collectively as *contingent business interruption exposures* (or *dependent property exposures*), arise when the organization's operations may be shut down because damage at premises belonging to someone else interrupts a necessary flow of goods or services.

There are four types of contingent business interruption exposures:

1. When a company is dependent upon one or a few manufacturers or suppliers, the manufacturer or supplier is known as a *contributing location.*

Exhibit 5-8
Contingent Business Interruption

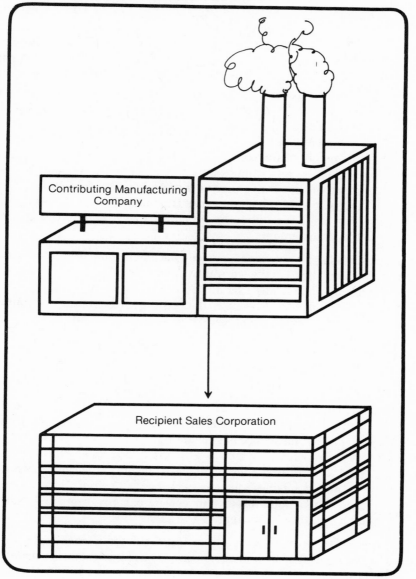

Contributing Manufacturing Company

Recipient Sales Corporation

2. When only one or a few companies purchase all or most of the insured's products or services, each buyer is known as a *recipient location*.

3. When a selling agent derives his or her income from commissions on goods manufactured at one location and shipped directly to the agent's customers, the key location is called a *manufacturing location*. A selling agent does not take title to the goods, but receives a commission for selling the product. This commission income can be lost if the manufacturer is shut down, if the finished goods are destroyed, or if for some other reason the goods that have been sold cannot be delivered. This is a potentially severe loss exposure for many selling agents. (See Exhibit 5-9.)

4. When a company derives all or most of its business as a result of a neighboring company, the latter is known as a *leader location*. As an example, small shops in many shopping centers depend on the traffic drawn to the shopping center by a large chain store. If the chain store is shut down, nearby shops will suffer an interruption in business even though those shops sustain no damage.

Most businesses do not have a major contingent business interruption exposure. Most firms have alternative sources of supply and a large number of customers. The loss of one supplier or buyer usually would not cause a major loss. However, the contingent business interruption exposure may be very important for some organizations, and the exposure is often overlooked.

Coverage against contingent business interruption losses is provided under two insurance forms:

1. *Business income from dependent properties—broad form.* This form is attached to a BIC and extends BIC coverage to apply to losses resulting from damage at contingent properties; the limit of insurance is unchanged.

2. *Business income from dependent properties—limited form.* This form replaces direct business income coverage when only contingent business income coverage is desired. It may also be used when both direct and contingent coverage are desired, with separate limits applying to each.

Contingent business property locations are listed in each form, where each is categorized as a contributing, recipient, manufacturing, or leader location.

Insuring Agreement "Business income from dependent properties" insurance covers only losses resulting from the suspension or destruction *of the insured's operations* caused by damage or destruction of property *at the specified contingent business property locations*. Note that the contingent property must not be owned,

Exhibit 5-9

Contingent Business Interruption Exposure of Selling Agent

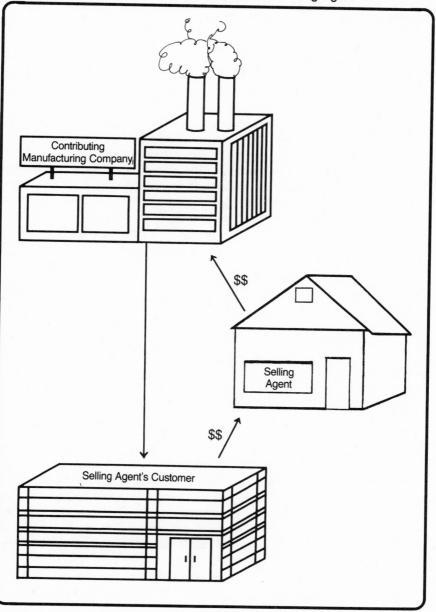

controlled, or operated by the insured. If it is, the standard business income coverage form—perhaps written on a blanket basis—is appropriate.

For coverage to apply, an insured peril must damage contingent business property, causing a shutdown or reduction *of the insured's business operations*. There is no requirement that operations *at the specified location* must be shut down. A peril might destroy finished goods at a contributing property, causing a shutdown of the insured's operations, but not shutting down the other company at all. Conversely, it is possible for a total shutdown at a contributing property not to affect the insured's business. This could happen, for example, if the recipient had a large inventory when the loss occurred.

The form limits compensation to the actual loss of business income necessarily sustained during the period of restoration, and the *period of restoration* is, in effect, the amount of time required, with reasonable speed and similar materials, to repair or replace *the damaged contingent business property*. This provision focuses, not on the insured's resumption of operations, but on conditions at someone else's location. However, the *resumption of operations* provision reduces the insured's recovery to the extent the insured can resume operations by using other sources of materials or other outlets for its products.

Normally, an insured peril must occur at the named contingent business property, but an additional coverage applies to unscheduled locations not operated by the insured. This *miscellaneous locations* coverage is limited to an amount not exceeding 0.03 percent of the sum of all limits for scheduled locations for any one day of interruption of the insured's business. A policy with $200,000 in limits would therefore provide up to $60 per day ($200,000 $\times$ .0003 = $60) for loss arising from a miscellaneous location.

Amount of Insurance to Purchase   The broad form and the limited form differ on this point. The broad form endorsement does not add any additional limits but extends coverage to apply to interruptions resulting from losses at contingent locations. The limited form endorsement requires a scheduled limit of insurance for each contingent location. Limits should be selected based on an analysis of the business income that is dependent on each contributing location—giving due consideration to the possibility of using materials from a substitute source or selling through an alternative outlet.

Tuition and Fees Coverage

Schools and colleges have a business income loss exposure that differs, to some extent, from that of the typical mercantile or manufacturing organization. If school property is damaged during the summer recess, the school may be unable to open its doors at the beginning of the fall session. Even if the school is able to open by October or so, it will find that most students have already enrolled elsewhere. Thus, if property is unusable during a fairly short, but critical, time period, it could cause the school to lose an entire year's tuition. In order to insure this type of exposure, the *tuition and fees endorsement* is added to the basic BIC form. The *tuition and fees endorsement* is designed to define business income in a way that clearly includes a school's sources of revenue and also to address the critical time period issue—basically a matter of providing modified extended business income coverage.

Covered Sources of Revenue The same endorsement may be used to provide either broad or limited coverage. The difference is simply that the broad coverage defines business income in a way that includes more revenue sources.

- *Broad coverage*—business income specifically includes tuition, fees, and other income from educational services and related activities including laboratory fees, bookstores, athletic events, and research grants.
- *Limited coverage*—business income specifically includes tuition and fees from students—including fees from room, board, laboratories, and other similar sources, but does not include income from other sources. (Conspicuous by its absence is income from bookstores, athletic events, and research grants.)

Extended Business Income Whether broad or limited coverage is provided, the extended business income provision of the basic BIC is replaced by a provision in the endorsement. If property is actually repaired, rebuilt, or replaced within thirty days of the scheduled opening of the next school term, the BIC covers the actual loss of business income sustained during that entire school term. "School term" is not defined in the endorsement.

Off-Premises Utilities Coverage

A business interruption usually results when utilities supplying services to the insured's premises are cut off. Interruption of electric power, water supplies, or telephone lines would cause many businesses to quickly grind to a halt—or, at least, to slow down. Even businesses that do not use water in their operations may find it necessary to send employees home if a loss of water makes bathrooms unusable.

The *off-premises services—time element endorsement* was designed to meet the needs of those who face a serious utility exposure. The endorsement modifies the BIC to include loss of business income or extra expense *at the described premises* resulting from an interruption of service *to the described premises*. The interruption must be caused by direct physical loss or damage by a covered peril to off-premises property of one or more of the following types, as indicated in the schedule:

1. *Water supply services*, meaning pumping stations and water mains.
2. *Communications supply services*, such as transmission lines, coaxial cables, and microwave radio relays supplying telephone, radio, microwave, or television services to the described premises. Overhead communication lines (such as telephone wires) and communication satellites are specifically excluded.
3. *Power supply services*, including utility generating plants, switching stations, substations, transformers, and nonoverhead transmission lines supplying electricity, steam, or gas to the described premises.

Although coverage for time element losses caused by damage to overhead transmission lines is excluded in this endorsement, another endorsement can be used to "buy back" the excluded coverage. The buy-back endorsement is called *off-premises overhead transmission lines (direct damage and time element)*, mentioned briefly in Chapter 4.

Although most time element insurance does not involve a deductible, both utility endorsements discussed here include a twelve-hour deductible. (People generally think of deductibles in terms of dollars. However, some insurance policies use time deductibles, also known as waiting periods. Whether dollars or hours is used, the effect is to eliminate coverage for high-frequency, low-severity losses.) Temporary utility outages can be expected on occasion. The role of insurance is to deal with more serious, unexpected losses. The twelve-hour deductible effectively accomplishes this goal.

Building Ordinance Coverage

The building ordinance exclusion of the causes-of-loss forms was discussed in Chapter 4. Coverage is excluded for any extra loss occasioned by the operation of building laws—for instance, when the undamaged portion of a building must be torn down, following an insured loss, in order for the entire building to be reconstructed in compliance with current building codes. The exclusion also applies to business income and extra expense coverage.

Chapter 4 described the steps that must be taken to provide coverage against direct damage to property caused by the operation of building laws. However, the modifications discussed there address only direct damage loss. The operation of building laws can also increase the length of a business interruption to the extent extra time is required to demolish the undamaged structure, remove its debris, and rebuild the entire structure to conform to the code.

The *building ordinance—increased period of restoration endorsement* comes to the rescue in cases such as this. In short, the endorsement extends business income coverage to encompass the increased period of suspension of operations brought about by the operation of building laws. Moreover, the period of restoration is redefined to include the added time necessary to replace damaged property with replacement property that complies with the minimum standards of the law.

As with direct damage coverage, it is important to pay close attention to limits of insurance. The endorsement extends the period during which lost business income will be paid. Since a longer interruption means a greater loss of income, it may be necessary to increase the limit of insurance accordingly.

Coverage for Special Situations

Rental Income   As noted in Chapter 1, the owner of property suffers a loss of rental income if a lessee or tenant is excused from its obligations to pay rent because the rented premises have been damaged by some peril and made untenable. Before the ISO simplification program, separate forms existed to address the exposure to loss of rental income. However, a distinct rental income form is no longer necessary, as the business income coverage form (BIC) adequately addresses the need. Rental income is one form of net income, as covered by the BIC.

Cancellation of a lease because the property has been damaged may have undesirable loss consequences for a tenant, as well. A long-term lease may lock the landlord into a rental rate that is far below current rates for similar property—to the considerable benefit of the tenant. If the lease is terminated, the reconstructed building will be rented once again at normal market rates and the tenant will lose the advantage of the favorable lease. This *leasehold interest exposure* can also be insured, as explained in Chapter 6. On the other hand, if a lease is not canceled when the premises become untenable the tenant may suffer a loss of rental value.

Rental Value If, by terms of the lease, a tenant must continue rental payments during a business interruption, the tenant does not receive the normal value of a usable premises in exchange for the rental payments. Business income coverage applies, since the rental payments are a continuing expense.

When an organization owns and occupies its own building, the situation is similar even though no rental money changes hands. For one thing, interest payments to a mortgage holder represent a continuing expense that is covered. And any extra expense incurred to rent temporary substitute premises or otherwise circumvent the unusability of the normal premises would normally be covered by the BIC, subject to its various terms and conditions.

Builders Risks Most of the discussion to this point has centered on exposures relating to completed buildings and their contents. Builders risk coverage for direct damage to buildings under construction will be discussed in Chapter 6. However, it is worth emphasizing here that "builders risks" are subject to time element losses, as well as to direct damage losses. Damage to a building under construction will normally delay completion of the building, thus delaying its ability to produce rental income for the owner (if a landlord) or to contribute to the owner's income-producing business operations.

The BIC can be written to cover a builders risk, and this application should not be overlooked.

EXTRA EXPENSE COVERAGE FORM

Most businesses would cease to operate for a small time following a direct property loss that would disrupt business activities. For such businesses, the business income coverage form is usually appropriate. Other businesses—dairies and banks, for instance—cannot under any circumstances survive an *interruption* of business activities. The flow of milk and money cannot come to a grinding halt simply because a dairy or bank has been damaged or destroyed. Such firms must remain in operation "at all costs." Schools and hospitals and other organizations serving a community may be unable simply to drop out of operation without providing some continuity of service. Newspapers must publish at all costs, particularly so that public notices may appear at appropriate times, advertising contracts can be fulfilled, and readers' habits can be sustained.

To remain in operation despite property damage to buildings or equipment, these firms will incur substantial extra expenses. Extra expenses are covered as an additional coverage in the BIC, but the primary emphasis of that form is on the replacement of business income. The extra expense coverage is intended for organizations for whom such exposure is incidental. For organizations whose exposure is primarily one of extra expenses rather than lost income, the *extra expense coverage form* was designed. As characterized in the *Commercial Lines Manual*, the extra expense coverage form:

> provides more limited coverage to fit the needs of those insureds who, by the nature of their type of operations, would incur primarily or exclusively extra expenses to resume operatins as quickly as possible in the event of a suspension of operations at the insured premises.

Insuring Provisions

The insuring agreement of the extra expense coverage form is identical to that of the extra expense additional coverage in the BIC. The key distinctions of the extra expense form lie in the *loss conditions* section of the policy in the provision titled *limits on loss payment.*

Insuring Agreement The extra expense insuring agreement was analyzed earlier in connection with the BIC. It reads as follows:

COVERAGE

We will pay the actual and necessary Extra Expense you sustain due to direct physical loss of or damage to property at the premises described in the Declarations, including personal property in the open (or in a vehicle) within 100 feet, caused by or resulting from any Covered Cause of Loss.

1. **Extra Expense**
   Extra Expense means necessary expenses you incur during the "period of restoration" that you would not have incurred if there had been no direct physical loss or damage to property:
   a. To avoid or minimize the suspension of business and to continue "operations":
      (1) At the described premises; or
      (2) At replacement premises or at temporary locations, including:
         (a) Relocation expenses; and
         (b) Costs to equip and operate the replacement or temporary locations;
   b. To minimize the suspension of business if you cannot continue "operations"; or
   c. (1) To repair or replace any property; or
      (2) To research, replace or restore the lost information on damaged valuable papers and records;
      to the extent it reduces the amount of loss that otherwise would have been payable under this Coverage Form.

Limits on Loss Payment Condition This provision might be compared with the coinsurance provision of the BIC and serves essentially the same purpose—encouraging insurance to value. There is no objective measure in advance of a loss of the extra expenses that might be incurred. The actual extra expenses will be subject to the availability of temporary premises, substitute equipment, and so forth. Despite these problems, there remains a need for the insurance contract to encourage the purchase of adequate limits of insurance.

The entire extra expense coverage form is subject to a limit of insurance, which is simply the maximum amount that will be paid for any one occurrence. The declarations page used with the extra expense coverage form also contains a series of percentages that further limit the amount of insurance available to cover losses in any given time period.

The application of these percentages is best clarified by using an illustration. Perhaps the most popular combination of percentages is 40%-80%-100%. With this combination, and a policy with a $100,000 limit of insurance, loss payments would be limited as follows:

- If the period of restoration is thirty days or less, extra expenses up to $40,000 would be covered.
- If the period of restoration is between thirty and sixty days, extra expenses up to $80,000 would be covered.
- If the period of restoration is longer than sixty days, extra expenses up to $100,000 would be covered. These limits of recovery are cumulative. Note that extra expense coverage applies only to the actual loss sustained. The maximum amount payable is based on the length of *the entire period of restoration*, not on the expenses incurred within *each thirty-day period.*

In the example above, suppose an interruption lasted thirty days and the insured incurred only $10,000 of extra expense. The insured would recover only the $10,000 loss actually sustained—this is a contract of indemnity, not a valued coverage. As another example, suppose an interruption lasted forty-five days and the insured actually incurred extra expenses of $50,000 the first month and $10,000 the second month. The full $60,000 would be covered—recovery is *not* limited to $40,000 for the first month because the period of restoration extended into the second month.

The above example contained percentages of 40%-80%-100%, but other percentages are also available. The following options are shown in the *Commercial Lines Manual:*

    100%-100%-100%
    40%-80%-100%
    35%-70%-100%
    30%-60%-90%-100%

25%-50%-75%-100%
20%-40%-80%-100%

Other combinations of percentages are also permitted.

Additional Coverages and Coverage Extension   Like the BIC, the extra expense coverage form includes coverage for (1) alterations and new buildings, (2) civil authority, and (3) newly acquired locations.

Determining the Amount of Extra Expense Insurance to Purchase

There is often little relationship between the normal cost of doing business and the extra expenses necessarily incurred in order to maintain a normal volume of business after loss or damage. This makes it difficult to determine how much insurance to purchase.

Assuming a firm anticipates that it will indeed be able to continue business using emergency measures, consideration should be given to the cost of such emergency measures. There is no principle or rule of thumb on which to base anticipated extra expense of maintaining a normal volume of business during an interruption, but much consideration should be given to an estimate of how long it would take to rebuild or repair the principal building and/or equipment.

By using a work sheet like the one illustrated in Exhibit 5-10, one could tabulate the greatest amount of expense that might reasonably be anticipated. This work sheet shown here is designed to record only the first, second, and third months following a loss. Of course, it could be extended for a longer period, or a computer spreadsheet could be used.

One way to determine the amount of extra expense insurance required is to determine from the work sheet the probable extra expense for *two* periods of restoration: (1) a period of one month, and (2) a period covering the maximum numbers of months that could reasonably be anticipated for resumption of normal operations. The *minimum* amount of insurance that should be carried is determined by dividing the estimated extra expense for the one-month period by the percentage reimbursement when the period of restoration is one month or less. This amount of insurance, however, might not be enough to cover the total extra expense estimated for the maximum possible interruption. In this case, the estimate for the longer period should be used.

For example, using the basic extra expense coverage form with the standard monthly percentage limits (40-80-100), the insured might estimate that extra expense indemnification of $8,000 for a one-month period of restoration would be sufficient. The minimum required

Exhibit 5-10
Work Sheet*

Expenses Necessary to Continue Business	First Month		Second Month		Third Month	
Rent of temporary premises						
Cleaning temporary premises						
Labor equipping temporary premises						
Rent of temporary machinery, equipment, etc.						
Net cost of equipment, etc., purchased						
Expense of moving equipment, etc.						
Light, power, and heat at temporary premises						
Labor at temporary premises						
Insurance expense at temporary premises						
Janitor and watchman at temporary premises						
Other expenses at or because of temporary premises (advertising, telephone, telegraph, legal, etc.)						
Total due to temporary premises						
Add payments to others for manufacturing or processing						
Add necessarily continuing expenses at original location after a loss						
Add bonuses for quick services, etc.						
Total expenses after a loss						
Deduct total of expenses which would have been incurred at the original location for the corresponding period had no loss incurred.						
Extra expense insurance to be carried						

*Reprinted with permission from Henry C. Klein, *Business Interruption Insurance* (Indianapolis: The Rough Notes Co., 1964), p. 253.

insurance is $8,000 divided by 40 percent (0.40), or $20,000. While the $20,000 total amount will assure recovery of up to $8,000 (40 percent) during the first-month period, up to $16,000 (80 percent) during a two-month period, and up to $20,000 (100 percent of the amount of insurance) for any period in excess of two months, the total amount might not be sufficient to cover estimated expenses for a longer period of time. If $30,000 of total coverage is needed, the insured could arrange the coverage for 40 percent recovery for the first month, and so on, as previously described. It is also possible to arrange for an optional combination of cumulative percentages of recovery, such as 35, 70, and 100 percent, or 30, 60, 90, and 100 percent.

The net result is that a generous amount of judgment must be used in determining the amount of insurance for extra expense coverage. The business ultimately will be healthier if it can keep operating. Any shutdown will result in loss of business because some customers will move to the insured's competitors.

Extra Expense Coverage Options

As with business interruption, extra expenses can be incurred due to direct loss or damage at nonowned properties. In cases where an organization can secure materials or services from a different supplier at another location, it could possibly continue business without an interruption or loss of gross revenues. But this may be possible only by using more expensive alternate sources of supply. If so, then there is an exposure to extra expense loss.

Contingent extra expense coverage will indemnify the insured for the extra expense incurred to continue operations with the assistance of a substitute supplier. The contingent extra expense form will cover the cost of materials or services in excess of the price charged by the original supplier, or transportation costs in excess of those normally charged.

The basic extra expense form may be endorsed to provide contingent extra expense insurance. The amount of insurance needed under the contingent extra expense form is based only on the increase in cost to obtain materials or services from other than regular sources. The same approach to periodic limits of liability (e.g., 40, 80, and 100 percent) applies in the contingent form as in the regular extra expense form. The length of time for which the contingent coverage is needed depends on the length of time necessary for restoration of the original supplier's property. Thus, the percentages of apportionments required might change under the contingent form depending on the circumstances and conditions relating to the acquisition and transportation of substitute materials or services.

Two other optional coverages have already been discussed in connection with business interruption coverage. The *building ordinance—increased period of restoration endorsement* and the *off-*

premises coverage endorsement may also be used with the extra expense coverage form.

OTHER VARIATIONS OF TIME ELEMENT INSURANCE

Many variations of time element insurance are available to suit the needs of particular firms. For example, there are special forms and rules to provide coverage on coal mining operations, drive-in theaters, radio and television transmitting stations and studios, and whiskey distilleries and wineries (which have a special "aging" exposure).

Coverage for losses caused by an accident involving boilers or machinery will be discussed in Chapter 6. Business interruptions relating to electronic data processing operations can also be insured in an EDP floater, as explained in Chapter 14.

CONTROLLING TIME ELEMENT LOSS EXPOSURES

For controlling time element losses, two loss control approaches can be used. The first is to prevent the loss from occurring. The second is to reduce the loss that occurs.

Flow Charting—An Aid in Loss Control

As noted in Chapter 1, flow charting is very useful in identifying and analyzing time element loss exposures. By developing a chart of how items flow through a firm's production line, bottlenecks and crucial areas can be identified. If a special type of machine must be used on all products, special attention should be given to spare parts. In some cases, it will pay to keep an extra machine available as a substitute, as is routinely done in power generating plants. Such spare parts of substitute machines should be stored where they would not be destroyed by the same catastrophe that would affect the originals. In many cases, holding idle spare equipment is financially attractive only if other machines cannot be leased and it will take an unacceptably long time for manufacturers to replace the machines. By identifying suppliers of critical items before the loss, the firm should be able to get back to normal sooner.

Of course, the critical item does not have to be equipment. It could be a building. If a warehouse is severely damaged, alternative space will need to be rented. By having some idea of available space before the loss, the firm can restore operations earlier.

Loss Prevention

Most, if not all, of the measures used to prevent direct property loss also prevent time element losses. If a building structure is unlikely to burn because it is made of fire-resistive materials, then it is unlikely that a building fire will cause a business income loss.

The same reasoning applies with respect to the earthquake peril. Fault zones may be rejected as building sites. Chapter 2 discussed a variety of measures that serve the purpose of preventing direct loss. Without direct losses, time element losses cannot occur.

Loss Reduction

For effective reduction of time element losses, the risk manager desires (1) to minimize *the extent of the interruption, by continuing operations in whole or in part,* and (2) *to minimize the length of the period of interruption,* subject to cost constraints. Salvage operations, the critical path method, and reciprocal agreements are approaches that may be used.

Reducing the Period of Restoration Salvage operations can be very important in reducing losses. If partially damaged material can be salvaged and returned to use, the firm will not have to wait while additional material is ordered and shipped. (For example, water-damaged machinery may be salvaged by prompt drying and oiling to prevent rust.) After the emergency is over, loss protective devices should be placed back in operation to prevent or reduce additional losses. Pre-loss planning may establish priorities as to which salvage measures should be taken first. It may be most important to vent smoke before removing water from the floor if materials are stored in racks or on pallets and most of the material would not be in contact with water at floor level. It may also be more important to dry moisture from the racks than to get water off the floor. Materials that are necessary to keep the business running deserve highest priority. Repair of damage to the maintenance shop can perhaps be delayed while production equipment is made operational. In cases when machinery might need special care, manufacturers' representatives should be contacted. These persons should be able to tell the firm how to clean the equipment. The names, addresses, and telephone numbers of these persons should be maintained in a safe location so that they can be reached quickly after a loss.

The firm should be concerned not only with the salvage and restoration process but also with retaining its customers. Sales representatives of the firm need to call on customers and help them stay with the firm. In fact, the marketing department needs a marketing strategy planned for such occasions and should be prepared to put it into action after a loss occurs. It will do a firm little good to restore operations only to find that all customers have taken their business elsewhere. Post-loss marketing—even at extra expense—is usually very important in restoring a company to its pre-loss condition.

Reciprocal Agreements As a loss reduction measure, many organizations enter into reciprocal agreements with other firms. For example, a hospital laundry department can arrange for commercial laundries to handle its needs while the hospital's laundry building is being restored. In some cases, the hospital's laundry staff could operate the commercial laundry plant on a night shift basis. Another area where reciprocal agreements are useful is the printing and/or the newspaper business. Printing firms in different communities can contract with one another to provide temporary services if a loss occurs. Newspapers enter agreements with other printers to print their papers when the newspaper's presses are damaged or are not operating. Use of electronic data processing equipment is a frequent subject of reciprocal agreements.

Normally, such reciprocal agreements do not prevent all financial loss. Circumstances usually cause the damaged firm's operating costs to increase, and some customers may still be lost. A firm may still need extra expense coverage to finance these agreements. Likewise, other control measures are not a substitute for business income insurance or other loss financing measures.

Critical Path Analysis In attempting to reduce a business interruption loss that has occurred, the concept of critical path analysis can be used. Under the critical path method (CPM), one analyzes the steps necessary to restore the business to pre-loss operational levels. The basic idea is to identify the series of events that will take the longest time to restore the business and see if something can be done to shorten that time period.

For instance, after a major loss, the premises must be cleared, repairs made, inventory ordered and stored on the premises, production started, and, finally, output established. Using CPM, the risk manager would make an analysis to see whether expenditures to expedite a certain step would reduce the overall loss. The key question is, "Would the increased cost of performing a given procedure be worthwhile in terms of getting the firm back to normal operations?"

An example is given in Exhibit 5-11. Here, there are three basic paths (A, B, C) from point 1 to point 13. Path A goes 1, 4, 5, 10, 11, 13, and takes forty-nine days. Path B goes 1, 3, 6, 9, 12, 13, and takes fifty-three days; and Path C goes 1, 2, 7, 8, 12, 13, and takes sixty days. Since it is the risk manager's desire to minimize the down time, subject to cost constraints, Path C deserves the first priority. Any reduction along Path C will help until the path time is reduced to forty-eight days at point 12. After a reduction to below forty-eight days along path 1, 2, 7, 8, 12, path 1, 3, 6, 9, and 12 would become critical and then attention would be placed on it. After paths B & C are reduced below forty-nine days, then A becomes critical.

Possible areas of concentration of efforts or changing priorities would include placing more emphasis on the 1-2 path and less on the 1-4 path. It would save the firm four days if 1-2 could be reduced four days even if 1-4 were increased four days. Path A would now be fifty-three days but Path C would be reduced to fifty-six days. Additional resources could be applied along Path C projects. Overtime activities could be authorized. Two cranes instead of one could be used if the Path C steps involved heavy construction. Express freight might be employed as well as using precast material rather than on-site construction.

At the very least, through the use of CPM the risk manager is forced to plot all the activities involved in restoration and see how the various activities fit together. Given a situation like that in Exhibit 5-11, the risk manager can determine that marginal resources should be applied to Path C or even take some resources from A to use on C. By taking this action, the firm could begin operations at an earlier date.

Also by doing the critical path analysis the risk manager would be able to identify any bottlenecks for Path B and Path C, as they both go through that point. However, since point 12 is at the end of the path, it is not as critical as a bottleneck would be at point 6 or 7.[7]

As suggested, CPM enables a risk manager to evaluate the merits of "expense to reduce the loss" measures that are being considered, to channel resources to activities that will, in fact, reduce the loss.

AN ILLUSTRATION

The following case study illustrates many of the principles of this chapter with a hypothetical firm, the Critch Company. After using a business income work sheet to analyze Critch's exposures, the case examines the questions of how much insurance to buy and whether or not to include coverage for ordinary payroll. This case also illustrates the important point that the amount of business income subject to loss does not coincide with the amount of business income insurance that must be purchased to meet coinsurance requirements.

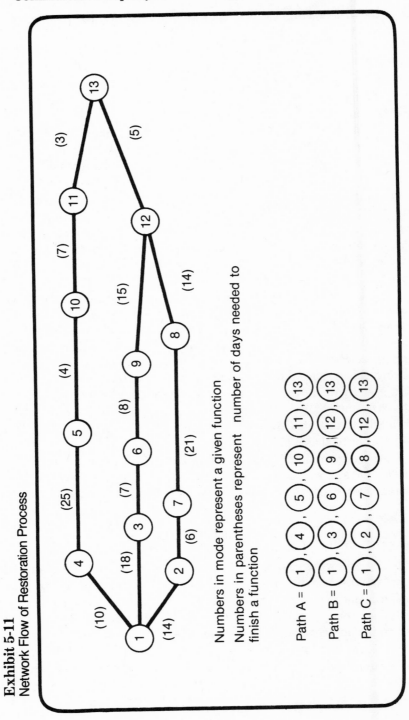

Exhibit 5-11
Network Flow of Restoration Process

Numbers in mode represent a given function

Numbers in parentheses represent number of days needed to finish a function

Path A = 1 , 4 , 5 , 10 , 11 , 13

Path B = 1 , 3 , 6 , 9 , 12 , 13

Path C = 1 , 2 , 7 , 8 , 12 , 13

Analyzing the Exposure

Assume that the exposure for the Critch Company is being evaluated in February 19X3. After identifying what property damage could occur and estimating the effect of such damage on processes and operations, the next step in measuring the exposure is to determine the dollar amounts of revenues and of continuing and noncontinuing expenses that would be affected by damage to processes and operations.

For the sake of this illustration, assume that a careful analysis of available data for 19X2 developed the information shown in items A through L of the left-hand column of Exhibit 5-12.

The figures shown to this point are annual figures, but it is unlikely that Critch would be shut down for exactly one year. Therefore, it is necessary to develop an estimate of the longest period the firm could be out of operation. Generally, this implies a severe direct loss requiring the complete reconstruction of the building.

Assume that the estimate of the time such construction might involve is obtained from a contractor—Critch could reconstruct its entire building in four months. In addition, it appears that another month would be needed to install fixtures. Yet another month would be required to restock and staff the operation with trained employees. The maximum length of the possible shutdown for Critch Company, therefore, is estimated at six months.

Which six months of the year will the company be shut down? It is impossible to foretell when an interruption will occur, but the question is important. For purposes of measuring the business interruption exposure, the safest assumption is that the maximum period of shutdown will occur during the months of greatest earnings. In Critch Company's case, the maximum shutdown period is estimated to be six months. The net profits and continuing expenses during the *highest* consecutive six months of activity should be used.

Suppose Critch's seasonal pattern is as shown in Exhibit 5-13. The numbers for each month represent the percentage of annual earnings. For example, February produces 6.1 percent of Critch Company's annual earnings. For Critch, the highest six months of activity are April through September. In this half year, the company typically produces 62 percent of its total volume.

If Critch Company were shut down from April through September, how much expense would continue during the period? This is a difficult question to answer, but an estimate can be made based on a careful assessment of the various expense types involved in Critch's particular operation and the degree to which each would continue or abate. Assume that such a detailed analysis shows that $205,296 of payroll

Exhibit 5-12
Business Income Report/Work Sheet Financial Analysis*

Income and Expenses	12 Month Period Ending Feb. 19X2		Estimated for 12 Month Period Beginning Feb. 19X3 (19X2 Data X 1.0585)	
	Manufacturing	Non-Manufacturing	Manufacturing	Non-Manufacturing
A. Gross Sales	$	$2,540,863	$	$2,689,503
B. DEDUCT: Finished Stock Inventory (at sales value) at Beginning	-		-	
C. ADD: Finished Stock Inventory (at sales value) at End	+		+	
D. Gross Sales Value of Production	$		$	
E. DEDUCT:				
Prepaid Freight	0			
Returns & Allowances	+143,068			
Discounts	+127,043			
Bad Debts	+362,109			
Collection Expenses	+0			
F. Total	-	- 632,220	-	- 669,204
Net Sales	$	$1,908,643	$	$2,020,299
Net Sales Value of Production				
G. ADD: Other Earnings from your business operations (not investment income or rents from other properties):				
Commissions or Rents				
Cash Discounts Received	+			
Other	+109,534			
Total Other Earnings	+	+ 109,534	+	+ 115,942
H. Total Revenues	$	$2,018,177	$	$2,136,240

continued on next page

	12 Month Period Ending Feb. 19X2	Estimated for 12 Month Period Beginning Feb. 19X3

I. DEDUCT: The cost of the following (net of any cash discounts received):

1. Cost of Goods Sold:

Inventory (including stock in process) at beginning of year $1,000,000

ADD: Cost of the following purchased during the year:

Raw Stock Consumed . . . . +

Factory Supplies Consumed . . . . +

Merchandise Sold . . . . + 885,400

Other Supplies Consumed (including transportation charges) + 107,075

Total Purchase Costs . . . . . . +

Cost of Goods Available for Sale $1,992,475

DEDUCT: Inventory (including stock in process) at end of year . . . . -1,000,000

Cost of Goods Sold . . . .$ 992,475

2. Services purchased from outsiders (not your employees) to resell, that do not continue under contract . . . . + 100,001

Total (Mining Properties — see next page) . . . . -   1,092,476   -   1,156,386

J. Net Income and Expenses (Business Income Basis for Coinsurance if a Coverage Modification does not apply) . . . . $ $ 925,701 $ 979,855

K. Annual Expenses, incl. payroll   - 684,320   - 724,353

L. Annual Net Income   = 241,381   = 255,502

M. Peak Season Factor   x.62   x.62

N. 6 Months' Maximum Net Income   = 149,656   = 158,411

O. Continuing Expenses, incl. payroll   + 205,296   + 217,306

P. Potential Business Income Loss Exposure   = 354,952   = 375,717

*Adapted from Insurance Services Office material with its permission.

Exhibit 5-13
Ratios of Monthly Sales to Annual Sales for Critch Company

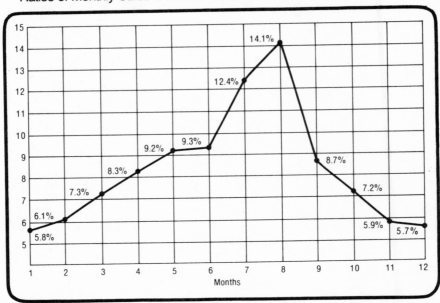

and other normal operating expenses would probably continue during the shutdown.

(Throughout this illustration, figures are rounded to the nearest dollar. This makes it relatively easy for the reader to trace computations. However, it is not meant to imply that business income exposures and losses can actually be projected to the nearest dollar. In practice, figures would probably be rounded to the nearest $1,000 or $10,000—depending on the size of the organization.)

Suppose net sales of Critch Company in recent years have been as shown in Exhibit 5-14. The average annual percentage increase in net sales over this five-year period is 5.85 percent.[8] Furthermore, the deviations from this average have not been large. Barring contrary information, it is assumed that net sales will increase at the same approximate rate in the near future (and the other important relationships will remain about the same). The business interruption exposure for 19X3 can be projected by using a simple updating approach, as indicated in the right-hand column of Exhibit 5-12. At an increase of 5.85 percent, the business interruption exposure will be $375,717 in 19X3.

If Critch Company has no available business income insurance, the available information suggests it could lose as much as $375,717 in 19X3 in the event the company is shut down for a six-month period.

Exhibit 5-14
Critch Company Sales for Past Five Years

Year	Net Sales	Percentage Increase
19W8	$1,520,468	—
19W9	1,610,482	5.9
19X0	1,706,500	5.9
19X1	1,813,210	6.3
19X2	1,908,643	5.3

Determining How Much Insurance to Purchase

Given an estimated six-month maximum business interruption, Critch should probably purchase business income coverage with a 50 percent coinsurance clause. Suppose, after carefully estimating its business income exposures and maximum period of interruption, Critch "did" purchase $375,717 of business income coverage with a 50 percent coinsurance clause. The amount of insurance matches the business income exposure, but according to the BIC coinsurance clause, Critch "should have" purchased $489,928 (50 percent of $979,855)—the "net income and expenses" projected in Exhibit 5-12—to meet minimum coinsurance requirements.

In the event of a loss, Critch would incur a substantial coinsurance penalty. Specifically, Critch would recover no more than 76.7 percent of any loss, calculated as follows (and recalling the " 'did' " over 'should' " coinsurance formula introduced in Chapter 3):

$$\frac{\$375,717 \ (\text{did})}{\$489,928 \ (\text{should})} = 76.7 \text{ percent}$$

In other words, Critch should purchase at least $489,928 of coverage to meet its $375,717 business income loss exposure. While this appears to be $114,211 of excess insurance, it is not coverage that could never be used. As explained earlier, the BIC covers more than loss of business income during the period of restoration. Extra expense coverage is also provided, as are thirty days' extended business income, civil authority, alterations and new buildings, and newly acquired locations. (In fact, if substantial claims under these additional coverages are foreseen, a larger limit of insurance might be advisable, and possibly a higher coinsurance percentage. For example, if claims for extra expenses and extended business income could run as high as

$225,000, Critch might purchase, say, $600,000 of coverage with a 60 percent coinsurance clause.)

Payroll or Utility Coverage Options

The amount of insurance that will meet minimum coinsurance requirements of the BIC can be reduced if Critch chooses to limit or exclude coverage for ordinary payroll. Likewise, power, heat, and refrigeration expenses may be deducted.

Assume that Critch has no extensive noncontinuing-expense-type exposure to power, heat, and refrigeration expenses. However, Critch did have $212,000 of payroll during 19X2 that would qualify as "ordinary payroll." Although Critch's revenues have peak seasons, payroll figures are nearly constant through the entire year. That is, one-quarter of the year's payroll expense, or $53,000, is incurred in any given ninety-day period.

The calculations used to arrive at Critch's options are shown in Exhibit 5-15.

- With full coverage of ordinary payroll, Critch should purchase at least $489,928 of business income coverage.
- With no coverage of ordinary payroll, Critch should purchase at least $377,727 of coverage.
- With ninety days' ordinary payroll coverage, Critch should purchase at least $405,777 of coverage.

In deciding whether or not to insure ordinary payroll expense, Critch needs to consider what will probably happen to those employees who would fall into the "ordinary payroll" category. Suppose Critch feels that all employees would need to be kept on the payroll during a brief interruption of, say, a month or two. On the other hand, "ordinary" employees would be laid off for an interruption of six months' duration. In that case, Critch would have no need to purchase full coverage for ordinary payroll expenses, and the ninety-day option would appear to be the most logical choice.

Before making a final decision, Critch needs to consider the relative cost of the alternatives. According to the *Commercial Lines Manual*, the ninety-day payroll limitation increases the premium rate by 6 percent, and the complete payroll exclusion increases the rate by 12 percent.

Premium differentials for the various coverage alternatives are not emphasized in this text. However, this example underscores the fact that many coverage decisions can best be made only after considering the cost of the various coverage alternatives.

Exhibit 5-15
Business Income Report/Work Sheet Coverage Modification*

	12 Month Period Ending...19X2		Estimated for 12 Month Period Beginning...19X3	
NET INCOME and EXPENSES (item J.1. or J.2.)..	$ 925,701		$ 979,855	
x 50% =		$ 462,850		$ 489,928
If Ordinary Payroll Limitation form is attached:				
DEDUCT: All Ordinary Payroll Expenses......	- 212,000		- 224,402	
	713,701		755,453	
x 50% =		$ 356,851		$ 377,727
If "90 days" is indicated for Ordinary Payroll Limitation:				
ADD: The largest amount of Ordinary Payroll Expense incurred during any 90 day period	+ 53,000		+ 56,101	
	766,701		811,553	
TOTAL..........		$ 383,351		
x 50% =				$ 405,777

* Adapted from Insurance Services Office material with its permission, 1983.

Chapter Notes

---

1. This form also includes extra expense coverage, although "extra expense" is not in the form's name. An ISO committee is working on the development of a "business income only" form that will not also include extra expense. It is possible that the name of the business income coverage form (BIC) will be revised when these changes are made.
2. John A. Krembs and James G. Perkins, "Business Interruption Interdependency: The Hidden Exposure," *Risk Management,* November 1981, pp. 12-24.
3. Industrial Risk Insurers, "PCB Contamination: Shutdown Facilities, Expensive Cleanup, A Lingering Threat," *The Sentinel,* Vol. 16, No. 4, 4th Quarter, 1984.
4. For considerably more detail, see *Insuring the Lease Exposure,* a research project of The Society of Chartered Property and Casualty Underwriters, Cincinnati Chapter (Cincinnati OH: The National Underwriter Company, 1981).
5. Consolidated Omnibus Budget Reconciliation Act of 1985.
6. Bardwell, E.C., *New Profits—Business Interruption Insurance* (Indianapolis: Rough Notes Co., 1973), p. 26.
7. For more information on the Critical Path Method, see K. Roscoe Davis and Patrick G. McKeown, *Quantitative Models for Management* (Boston: Kent Publishing Company, 1981), pp. 265-267.
8. This figure reflects the effect of compounding and is calculated as follows:

$$\$1{,}520{,}468 \ x^4 = \$1{,}908{,}643$$
$$x^4 = 1{,}908{,}643/1{,}520{,}468$$
$$x = 1.0585$$

In this case, 5.85 is also the average of the figures in the right-hand column of Exhibit 5-14 but it will not necessarily work out that way in other situations.

CHAPTER 6

Miscellaneous "Commercial Property," Boiler and Machinery Exposures and Insurance

Chapters 3, 4, and 5 dealt primarily with the building and personal property coverage form (BPP), the business income coverage form (BIC) and other time element forms, and the related causes-of-loss forms of the ISO "commercial property" program. This chapter completes the analysis of "commercial property" insurance by examining several other forms.

The "commercial property" forms discussed here are the following:

- condominium association coverage form,
- condominium unit-owners coverage form,
- builders risk coverage form,
- builders risk reporting form,
- leasehold interest coverage form,
- legal liability coverage form,
- standard property policy, and
- glass coverage form.

The chapter then discusses another line of coverage: boiler and machinery insurance.

The ISO condominium and builders risk coverage forms can be considered variations on the BPP tailored for exposures with some distinctive characteristics. Most of the provisions in all three forms are the same, and each of the three forms is collated with a causes-of-loss form and other documents to form a complete contract. Discussion in this chapter emphasizes the distinctive coverage characteristics and does not dwell upon policy provisions shared with the BPP.

The leasehold interest and legal liability coverage forms deal with loss exposures that result from damage to property but are not entirely related to the value of property or income derived from property. Although these forms are not commonly purchased, they address exposures that are significant for some organizations. These forms are also combined with other simplified ISO forms to make up a complete policy.

The standard property policy stands on its own and may not be combined with other coverage forms. Designed for "high-risk" properties, it is basically a no-frills, stripped down version of the BPP covering basic causes of loss, and its provisions closely resemble those of other forms—except where the frills have been stripped.

Glass exposures are given limited coverage in most "commercial property" forms. The glass coverage form can be used to add specific coverage for glass, picking up where the BPP and other forms leave off. Glass coverage can be included with other coverages in a commercial package policy.

Boiler and machinery exposures are covered to some extent by "commercial property" forms, but boiler-and-machinery-related "accidents" are not covered. A separate set of boiler and machinery coverage forms addresses the loss exposures faced by many types of property because of potential "accidents" to boilers, machinery, and other objects.

CONDOMINIUM PROPERTY EXPOSURES

Condominiums involve a system of separate ownership of individual units in a multiple-unit building or buildings. In a condominium, each purchaser, or "unit owner," (1) becomes the owner of that condominium unit and (2) acquires an undivided interest with all other unit owners in the jointly owned "common elements" of the building. A *condominium association* is formed by unit owners to manage the condominium, and also to form an entity that can own real property (the common elements). The ISO "commercial property" program has a form designed specifically to provide the coverages needed by condominium associations.

A *condominium unit* is generally the "box of air" enclosed by the unfinished surfaces of perimeter walls, floors, and ceilings. Property of any kind within the condominium unit, except (1) common building elements and (2) pipes, wires, conduits, and other utilities specified in "easements," are considered as solely owned by the condominium unit owner. Note that the unit owner *may* be the sole owner of some property normally considered as "building" (e.g., a wall) which is located within the unit but is not a common building element or building utility.

The *common elements*, which are jointly owned by all unit owners, generally include the foundations; exterior walls; interior walls except those contained within individual units; structural columns and beams; roofs; corridors; lobbies; stairs; parking and storage areas; central power, light, heating, and air conditioning systems; and often other property items. Note that some of these items may be located within, or may pass through, the unit owner's "box of air."

Unit owners in residential condominiums may insure their personal property, liability, and related exposures with a homeowners form HO-6 policy discussed in CPCU 2. Not all condominiums are residential. Some are used for offices, stores, or other business activities. The ISO "commercial property" program has forms to provide the coverages needed by unit owners in such commercial condominiums.

Documents Clarifying Status

All fifty states, Puerto Rico, and the District of Columbia have enabling legislation or statutory law for condominiums. There is substantial variety among jurisdictions. In many cases, the law has some provisions relating to ownership interests and the purchase of insurance. In any event, producers, underwriters, and persons with risk management responsibility for condominium exposures will find it necessary to familiarize themselves with applicable state law.

The other essential document for evaluating the exposures of any particular condominium is the *condominium association agreement*, also referred to as the *master deed, declarations, or bylaws*. This formidable document, which is prepared by the developer who first establishes the condominium association, usually describes what each unit owner has purchased and clarifies unit owners' rights and responsibilities. The master deed should describe the land, the building, and the common elements and identify each individual unit. It should establish a method of collecting and paying for such expenses as maintenance, upkeep of common areas, and insurance. The master deed should also specify the governing procedures, the powers of the association land, and the procedures for modifying the bylaws.

Under condominium statutes or master deeds, the condominium association is usually obliged to maintain insurance coverage for the benefit of unit owners. Unit owners are also permitted to purchase insurance at their own expense for their own benefit.

Barewall Concept Versus Single Entity Concept

When dealing with condominium exposures, one critical issue involves the dividing line between the unit owners' property interests and the association's property interests. There are two general approaches appearing in law or in a master deed or declaration:

1. *Barewall concept*—under this approach, the association has no ownership interest within the unit owner's bare walls. All paint and wall coverings, carpet and floor coverings, drapes, cabinets, appliances, non-load-bearing interior walls, doors, plumbing, and electrical fixtures are considered to be owned by the individual unit owner, who is also the party to obtain insurance on these items. When required to insure these elements on behalf of the individual unit owners (by statute, declarations, or bylaws) the association's insurable interest is that of a trustee.

2. *Single entity or "all in" concept*—in this approach, the condominium association is considered as the owner of all values contained in the unit as it was sold to the original purchaser. Normally, at the time of sale, carpets, cabinets, electrical fixtures, and appliances have been installed. Consequently, the association would be responsible for insuring these items under this concept.

In practice, the master deed is not necessarily clear with respect to all items exposed to loss. To illustrate the problems of applying these concepts, consider the exterior doors, the windows, air conditioner compressors, sinks, or balcony railings associated with individual units of a residential condominium building. Should they be insured by the unit owners or by the association? In any areas where there is doubt, the problem *can* be addressed by having the association obtain insurance with the broadest possible description of covered property, with a policy limit set accordingly—but unnecessary insurance is expensive and wasteful. If unit owners adopt a similar strategy and insure as broadly as possible, they may be obtaining expensive and unnecessary duplicate coverage. If the wrong entity insures a given property item, it may be discovered after a loss that the insured entity cannot collect due to lack of an insurable interest and that the entity with an insurable interest cannot collect because it has no insurance. If neither the association nor the unit owner insures some property items, there may be no outside source of recovery following a loss.

The problem is not merely one of describing covered property. More difficult is the problem of measuring insurable values and purchasing appropriate amounts of insurance. It can be especially difficult for the directors of a condominium association to value items located within the various units, particularly as they are modified by the unit owners. Failure to properly evaluate property items exposed to loss could leave a commercial unit owner or a condominium association with a coinsurance penalty following a partial loss, or with inadequate coverage to pay for a substantial loss.

The valuation problem becomes even more complex when the interest of mortgagees is considered. Each unit owner typically obtains a mortgage for as much as 90 percent or more of the price of purchasing the condominium unit. A considerable portion of this sales price may be derived from the demand for a "box of air" *at that particular location*—with an ocean view, for example. The selling price of condominium units is not necessarily proportionate to the insurable value of the building. Collectively, the amounts outstanding in all condominium mortgages will, in some locales, be much greater than the amount of property insurance needed by the association. Yet, it is the association's property policy that is expected to protect the values in all mortgages. This problem will not be discussed further here because a good overall solution seems to be lacking. Although mortgagees often accept the situation, it is questionable whether all interests are completely protected when the total of mortgages exceeds the total amount of insurance.

Insurance Requirements

Faced with the aforementioned obstacles, one would hope the condominium association agreement in any individual case, if not the statutes, would be clear enough to indicate what insurance should be carried by the association. Unfortunately, these documents are often drafted by attorneys who have little understanding of insurance terminology. For an example of the results, consider the following excerpt from a master deed:

> [The association is required to keep in force] broad form insurance against loss by fire and against loss by lightning, windstorm and other risks normally included within all risk extended coverage, including vandalism and malicious mischief....

Given the lack of precision of this typical perils requirement, it is not surprising that other insurance specifications of a master deed are often lacking in clarity.

When evaluating condominium loss exposures, it is important to analyze the particular situation in question. The situation varies substantially from one jurisdiction to another, and even from one association to another. It is essential, in any case, to examine the condominium association agreement.

CONDOMINIUM PROPERTY INSURANCE

In general, oversimplified terms, the insurance needs of a condominium association are analogous to the building insurance needs of a building owner/landlord, while the needs of a condominium unit owner are analogous to the personal property insurance needs of a tenant. Two ISO property forms have been designed especially for condominium exposures:

- *condominium association coverage form,* and
- *condominium commercial unit owners coverage form.*

Like the BPP, each of these simplified forms can be combined with causes-of-loss forms and other component documents to form a monoline policy or a commercial package policy.

The condominium "commercial property" forms resemble the BPP in many ways. Discussion here emphasizes the distinctive features of the condominium forms rather than repeating points of similarity that have already been discussed in previous chapters.

Condominium Association Coverage Form

Like the BPP, the condominium association coverage form provides coverage for property in three categories:

1. building,
2. business personal property of the named insured, and
3. personal property of others.

Each coverage applies only if a limit of insurance for that coverage is shown in the declarations.

Like the BPP, the condominium association coverage form also contains the following *additional coverages:*

- debris removal, and
- preservation of property.

The following *coverage extensions,* which are identical to those of the BPP, apply when a coinsurance clause of 80 percent or higher is indicated in the declarations:

- newly acquired or constructed property,
- personal effects and property of others,
- valuable papers and records—cost of research,
- property off-premises, and
- outdoor property.

Building Coverage The building coverage of the condominium association coverage form closely resembles the building coverage of the BPP.

A significant difference relates to fixtures, improvements and alterations, and appliances (for refrigerating, ventilating, cooking, dishwashing, laundry, or housekeeping) contained within individual units—even if they are owned by the unit owner:

- If the condominium association agreement requires the association to insure them, such property items are included in the condominium *building* coverage.
- Otherwise, such property items are not included in the association's building coverage. (As explained later, the unit owner's coverage picks up where the association's coverage leaves off, and vice versa.)

This provision clearly affects the amount of insurance required to comply with the form's coinsurance provision and underscores the importance of examining the condominium association agreement when establishing insurance requirements.

Coverage for the Named Insured's Business Personal Property A condominium association might need personal property insurance to cover furniture in common areas or to cover any other personal property that does not already fall within the scope of building coverage. Here, again, the condominium association coverage form clarifies the dividing line between personal property insured by the association and that insured by individual unit owners.

- Business personal property is covered if it is owned by the association or if it is indivisibly owned by all unit owners.
- Business personal property is not covered if it is owned only by a unit owner.

Coverage for Personal Property of Others The condominium association coverage form's coverage for personal property of others is the same as that of the BPP. Provided an 80 percent or higher coinsurance clause is in effect, the form automatically includes a *coverage extension* for property of others up to $2,500 at each described premises. If this extension is not adequate to meet exposures, separate coverage may be purchased.

This coverage may take on special significance in some condominiums where individual unit owners allow their personal property to be used in the building's common areas for decorative purposes or for specific building maintenance and repair projects. Subject to other terms of the policy, the condominium association coverage form would cover such items, provided a limit for this coverage is shown in the declarations.

Loss Payment Provision If the association has designated an *insurance trustee*, the insurer may make any loss adjustment payable to the insurance trustee. The board of trustees of a condominium generally serves in this capacity. The board receives all loss proceeds "in trust" for the individual unit owners. The board then acts on behalf of all unit owners.

Unit-Owners Insurance Provision If the unit owner also has coverage applying to the same property, the association's policy is primary.

Waiver of Rights of Recovery The insurance company agrees not to subrogate against any unit owner of an insured condominium.

Condominium Unit-Owners Coverage Form

While association coverage applies to either residential or nonresidential condominiums, discussion now turns to the coverage needs of nonresidential condominium unit owners. A complete monoline policy is created by combining the condominium unit-owners coverage form with a declarations form, a causes-of-loss form, the common policy conditions form, and the condominium property conditions. With additional documents, a condominium package policy may be created.

Covered Property A condominium unit owner generally has no need for building insurance in its own name, so the form includes coverage only for business personal property of the named insured and personal property of others. Coverage generally tracks with the BPP.

Fixtures, improvements, and alterations that make up part of the building, but are owned by the unit owner, are covered by the unit owner's insurance. (Recall from Chapter 3 that the BPP covers only a tenant's *use interest* in improvements and betterments. The limited duration of a lease imposes a limit on the tenant's interest, but an ownership interest is not so limited.)

Coordination with Association Coverage A unique exclusion serves to dovetail unit-owners coverage with condominium association coverage: Fixtures, improvements, alterations, and appliances (used for refrigerating, ventilating, cooking, dishwashing, laundering, security, or housekeeping) are not covered by the unit-owners form if the condominium association agreement requires the association to insure them.

Another policy provision makes unit-owners coverage excess over the coverage of any association insurance covering the same property.

Condominium Commercial Unit-Owners Optional Coverages Two optional coverages often required by condominium unit owners are available in a single endorsement that may be attached to the condominium unit-owners coverage form. Either or both of these optional coverages may be purchased; they are included in a single endorsement as a matter of convenience.

Loss Assessment Coverage. The optional loss assessment coverage requires the insurance company to pay the unit-owner's share of any assessment charged to all unit owners by the condominium association when the assessment is made as a result of direct physical loss or damage caused by an insured peril to property in which each unit owner has an undivided interest.

The form allows payment for each assessment up to the limit of insurance shown for the endorsement, subject to a $250 deductible. However, coverage is limited to $1,000 per scheduled unit for assessments that are a direct result of a deductible in the insurance purchased by the condominium association. For example, suppose that a fifty-unit condominium association selects a $100,000 property insurance deductible on its condominium association coverage form and subsequently sustains a serious fire. Each unit owner is assessed $2,000 to cover its share of the association deductible. A unit owner who purchased the optional loss assessment coverage will recover $1,000 of this loss assessment from its own insurer. If the unit-owner's loss assessment coverage applied on an "all-risks" basis, the association had coverage for the basic causes of loss, and the $200,000 damage was caused when a roof collapsed due to the weight of snow, then the unit-owner's coverage would pay the entire assessment, subject to the $250 deductible ($2,000 − $250 = $1,750), assuming the limit of insurance is at least $2,000. As illustrated by this example, a unit owner might purchase loss assessment coverage to protect against assessments that develop because the association's property insurance is not sufficiently broad. In a sense, the unit-owner's loss assessment coverage would then deal with losses arising out of the so-called "difference in conditions" between the association's coverage and the unit owner's coverage.

Miscellaneous Real Property Coverage. The unit-owners coverage form normally covers only personal property, fixtures, improvements, and alterations. The *miscellaneous real property coverage* expands the form to include real property items when:

1. the property pertains to the named insured's condominium unit only, or
2. the named insured has a duty to insure the real property according to the condominium association agreement.

Should the condominium association have other insurance covering the same property, the unit-owner's insurance will provide excess coverage.

A wide variety of situations may suggest a need for this coverage. Examples include:

- a storage building erected by a condominium unit-owner for use in its business operations,
- a separate garage structure owned by the association but used solely by the unit owner,
- an attached addition to the external walls, such as a balcony which, while part of the realty, solely benefits the unit owner.

BUILDERS RISK PROPERTY EXPOSURES

Structures under construction—referred to in insurance jargon as "builders risks"—present a special problem of changing values. A building's value varies from nearly zero at the time construction begins to the full completed value when the building is finished. In addition, the variety of interests involved—including owner(s), contractor(s), and subcontractor(s)—creates a need for some different approaches to interests insured.

Buildings under construction face special hazards. Building materials are susceptible to loss by theft, especially since it is usually difficult to secure a building under construction. Also, because fire protection (sprinkler systems, standpipes, and so on) may not be fully installed or operational and fire walls may not be in place, builders risks can be especially susceptible to fire damage. These hazards require no special policy treatment but are reflected in the premium rates.

Because builders risk insurance forms are designed to cover buildings or structures *under construction*, they attempt to clearly specify the point at which construction is deemed to be completed and coverage to cease. At that point, to cover the completed structure, a BPP or other comparable form replaces the builders risk form.

BUILDERS RISK INSURANCE

Some builders risks are insured on an inland marine form, as discussed in Chapter 10. Inland marine forms can be manuscripted to create elaborate, complex insurance contracts for large or complex projects. Inland marine forms are also used to provide installation floater coverages and special protection for machinery, equipment, and supplies used in the construction industry.

The basic approach to insuring buildings in the course of construction is "commercial property" coverage, using the builders risk coverage form.

Builders Risk Coverage Form

The ISO builders risk coverage form is a simplified "commercial property" form that is combined with the common policy declarations, common policy conditions, commercial property declarations, commercial property conditions, a basic, broad, or special (and possibly also an earthquake) causes-of-loss form, and any necessary endorsements to form a complete monoline policy. If other coverage parts are added, the builders risk coverage form may be part of a builders package policy.

Eligible Property Most properties covered by builders risk coverage are those that will become eligible for BPP coverage. The builders risk coverage form may be used to insure buildings such as condominiums, farm buildings, and individual dwelling property that will not be eligible for coverage under the building and personal property coverage form (BPP) when construction is completed. The builders risk coverage form is also suitable for additions or alterations to existing buildings. Rules in the *Commercial Lines Manual* explain how to go about (1) excluding the value of the existing property from the builders risk coverage form, using the *builders risk renovations endorsement,* and (2) excluding the value of the renovation from the BPP or other insurance form covering existing property.

Eligible Insureds The builders risk coverage form may be used to insure:

- the interest of the building owner,
- the interest of the contractor, or
- the owner and the contractor jointly, as their interests may appear.

Where necessary, subcontractors' interests may be excluded or specifically insured:

- The interest of separate contractors or subcontractors may be excluded by using the *builders risk—separate or subcontractor's exclusion endorsement.*
- Specific insurance for the interest of separate contractors or subcontractors may be written by adding the *builders' risk— separate or subcontractor's coverage endorsement.*

Covered Property Builders risk coverage is logically directed toward buildings, rather than contents. However, it is necessary to address the exposures of many loose, unattached items (such as windows, doors, sinks, and furnaces) that will eventually become part of the building.

The builders risk coverage form deals with only one category of covered property—*buildings under construction.* The only covered "buildings under construction" are those described in the declarations. Nonbuilding "structures" under construction may also be covered if they are described in the declarations.

Coverage is specifically included for:

1. *foundations*—whether above or below-ground.
2. *scaffolding, cribbing, construction forms, and other temporary structures built or assembled on the construction site*—so long as they are not covered by other insurance (the contractor is likely to have coverage under a contractors equipment floater).
3. *fixtures, machinery, and equipment used to service the building*—so long as they are in the building, on the building, or within 100 feet of the premises, and are intended to become a part of the building.
4. *the named insured's building materials and supplies*—so long as they are in the building, on the building, or within 100 feet of the premises, and are intended to become a part of the building. A *coverage extension* also provides up to $2,500 coverage for similar items owned by others but in the insured's care, custody, or control.

The list of "property not covered" is short. As in the BPP, there is no intention of covering land, and an exclusion emphasizes that intent. The only other excluded types of property are outdoor (1) lawns, trees, shrubs, or plants; (2) antennas; and (3) detached signs.

When Coverage Ceases As noted, the builders risk coverage form is intended to cover only buildings in the course of construction; when they are completed, another form such as the BPP or the condominium association coverage form should be used. It is necessary, therefore, to specify the circumstances under which builders risk coverage comes to an end.

The builders risk coverage form states that, unless the insurer specifies otherwise, coverage ceases when an insured building is occupied, in whole or in part, or put to its intended use (some buildings or structures—water towers, for example—are not literally "occupied"). If no occupancy or use takes place—as, for example, if the building remains vacant while the owner tries to sell it—coverage ceases ninety days after the construction is completed. As might be expected, coverage also ceases if the policy expires or is canceled, if the named insured's interest in the property ceases, or if the property is accepted by a purchaser.

Despite the apparent precision of these policy provisions, it should be recognized that the date and time that one of these conditions occurs is sometimes difficult to determine. Specific cases may involve questions of fact that ultimately need to be resolved in the courts.

Need for Adequate Insurance A policy condition titled "need for adequate insurance" is, in effect, a 100 percent coinsurance clause where the amount of insurance that "should" be carried is based on the value of the completed building on the date it will be completed. The formula is as follows:

$$\left(\frac{\text{Limit of Insurance}}{\text{Building's Completed Value}} \times \text{Loss}\right) - \text{Deductible} = \frac{\text{Amount Payable}}{\text{by Insurer}}$$

No underinsurance penalty is involved if, at the time of the loss, the limit of insurance equals or exceeds the building's completed value. While it might seem to be a simple matter to comply with this requirement, the completed value of a building is not necessarily firmly fixed before construction begins. Often, design changes during the course of construction increase the final cost of the building—and result in a potential penalty for underinsurance if there is a loss. To avoid this problem, it is important to review the builders risk limit of insurance every time there is a change that will increase the completed value of the building above the original contract price.

Completed Value Approach and Premium Computation The builders risk coverage form contains a standard valuation condition, providing coverage on the basis of actual cash value. There is usually little practical difference between the actual cash value and the replacement cost of a building under construction.

The inception date of a builders risk policy should be no later than the date construction starts above the lowest level of the basement floor or, if there is no basement, the date construction starts. At that point, the dollar values exposed to loss are little higher than zero, and they progressively increase until the building reaches its full completed value.

Although policies are issued for a minimum term of one year, many buildings are completed in a shorter period of time. When "coverage ceases," the insured is given a pro-rata refund of the unearned premium.

Builders Risk Reporting Form

The *builders risk reporting form endorsement* may be used to change from a completed value approach to a reporting approach. When this is done, the insured selects a day of the month (e.g., the tenth) and gives monthly reports as to the actual cash value of covered property on that date. As with the *value reporting form* used with the BPP, serious penalties apply if reports are absent, tardy, or wrong:

- If no report has been filed, the insurer will not pay more than the actual cash value as of the inception date.
- If the last required report is overdue, the insurer will not pay more than the value stated in the last report actually filed.
- If actual values at the time of the last report were greater than the values reported, loss adjustment is prorated by what resembles a 100 percent coinsurance clause (amount insured did report divided by amount insured should have reported, times the loss).

An initial premium is collected and premiums are adjusted during the policy term based on the values shown in the reports.

Business Income Coverage for Builders Risks

As mentioned in Chapter 5, builders risks face time element exposures as well as exposures to direct physical loss or damage. If direct loss delays the completion date of a building or structure, it also delays the time at which it can be occupied or put to use. Net income losses resulting from this delay can be insured using a business income coverage form.

For example, suppose Edwin's Overshoe Emporium, a retail store, was scheduled to open for business at a new location on February 1 and had agreed to vacate its present business location by that date. On January 1 a fire destroyed part of the building under construction to house Edwin's store, causing a two-month delay in completing the structure. Edwin's Overshoes will have to wait until April 1 to begin operations. In this example, if business income coverage had been purchased, Edwin's Overshoes would be able to collect the loss of income for the two months during which it sustained a business interruption. Extra expenses might also be incurred that could be covered by the business income coverage form.

A similar exposure is faced by owners of rental property. If a loss delays the date on which property can be rented, the owner sustains a loss of rental income—which can be covered with the business income coverage form.

LEASEHOLD INTEREST EXPOSURES AND COVERAGE

A lessee (tenant) may suffer a financial loss beyond loss of rental value if the lease is canceled. One of the principal reasons for cancellation of a lease is substantial damage or destruction of the building occupied by the tenant. Most leases contain a *fire clause* which describes the conditions that would permit the owner to cancel. A typical fire clause in a lease reads as follows:

> If the building or premises are damaged by fire or other cause to the extent of 25 percent of the value thereof, the lease may be terminated by the lessor. If the building or premises are rendered untenantable due to damage by fire or other cause, the lessee is relieved of the payments of rents during the term that the premises are untenantable whether the lease is cancelled or not.

Some leases may have cancellation options based on, say, 50 percent damage or upon a certain amount of time required to repair or replace damaged property. When the lease is silent on terms of cancellation, general law applies.

There are a number of circumstances when cancellation of a lease may cause a tenant to suffer financial loss. For example:

1. *A lessee who has a favorable lease at a rental rate much lower than the current rental value of the premises.* Such a lessee would not be able to obtain as favorable a lease upon cancellation. (The "loss" would be the additional cost to rent equivalent premises for the duration of the current lease.)

2. *A lessee who has sublet the premises to another at a profit.* (The loss would be the loss of profit margin for the duration of the lease.)

3. *A lessee who has paid a bonus to acquire a lease.* (The loss would be the unamortized value of the bonus. In some leases, however, there is a provision for the return of the pro-rata unearned portion of a bonus if the lease is canceled.)

4. *A lessee who has installed expensive improvements and betterments.* (The use value of these would be lost as a result of the cancellation of the lease. Note the distinction between this exposure and the improvements and betterments exposure covered by the BPP. In the BPP, the proximate cause of the loss is direct damage to the building, and the improvements can be replaced. A leasehold interest loss is caused by cancellation of the lease, and the improvement normally cannot be replaced.)

5. *A lessee who has paid advance rent that is not recoverable under the terms of the lease in the event of cancellation.* (The lessee loses the value of the advance rent.)

In all the above circumstances, the tenant will suffer a loss if the lease is canceled. The amount of the loss depends on the unfulfilled portion of the lease, so the values exposed will continue to decline as the lease runs. There is a resemblance between this declining loss exposure and the exposures covered with some form of decreasing term life insurance (e.g., "mortgage life" or "credit life").

The leasehold interest policy is written for the total amount of *net leasehold interest* of the insured for the unexpired months of the lease at the inception of the policy. It is a condition of the policy that the amount of insurance is automatically reduced from month to month. The type of leasehold interest described in 1 and 2 is discounted and subject to modification, as set forth in a net leasehold interest table in the policy. The remaining types (3, 4, and 5) are "amortized" for the term of the lease.

Leasehold interest insurance may be used to treat the loss exposures in the five examples just cited. For some organizations, leasehold interest insurance fills a valuable need. As a practical matter, however, little insurance of this type is sold. This may be due to the fact that many risk managers and insurer personnel are unaware of its existence. It is also likely that this is usually a relatively small exposure that most organizations can retain without threatening their success in meeting risk management objectives.

LEGAL LIABILITY EXPOSURES AND COVERAGE

The legal liability coverage form is an unusual "commercial property" form providing liability coverage.

Exposures

A person or organization may be held liable when that person or organization negligently causes damage to personal or real property of others. The commercial general liability coverage form (CGL), which is used to insure most organizations' general liability exposures, excludes coverage for damage to property of others in the insured's care, custody, or control. However, it provides limited coverage for liability arising out of damage to real property owned, rented, or occupied by the insured. The so-called "fire legal liability 'coverage'" of the CGL provides coverage for property damage liability arising out of fire damage (but not damage by other perils) to rented property for which the insured may be held liable. A minimum of $25,000 fire legal liability coverage is provided by the standard CGL, and this amount may be increased.

Various property coverages are available to insure the personal property of others. For example, the building and personal property coverage form (BPP) can be used to provide coverage for the personal property of others in an insured's care, custody, or control. Many bailee exposures can also be covered by an inland marine policy.

Sometimes the lease agreement requires the tenant to purchase property insurance on a building, protecting the interests of both landlord and tenant. In such cases, the tenant arranges for property insurance covering the full building value.

It is also possible for a tenant to protect itself against liability claims for damage to a rented building by purchasing full property insurance coverage on the landlord's building. In such cases, the tenant has an insurable interest in the building because of the potential for a liability claim. Although a standard "commercial property" policy such as the BPP could be used, the tenant would be required to pay the full cost of insuring the building against all losses by any covered peril. However, unless the lease contract specifies otherwise, the tenant would be legally liable only for those losses caused by the tenant's negligence. In cases not involving the tenant's negligence, and where the tenant had no contractual obligation to obtain insurance for the owner's interest, the tenant would have no insurable interest in the building loss and the tenant's BPP would provide no coverage.

Legal Liability Coverage Form

The legal liability coverage of the "commercial property" program is designed to address this situation by covering the insured's legal liability for damage to specified property when that damage arises out of an insured peril. Since only legal liability losses are caused, the premium is reduced. A basic, broad, or special causes-of-loss form indicates the applicable perils.

Coverage The insuring agreement of the legal liability coverage form states that the insurer agrees to pay sums that the named insured becomes legally obligated to pay as damages because of direct physical loss or damage, including loss of use, to covered property caused by accident and arising out of any covered cause of loss. The fact that "loss of use" is included means that the insurer would pay for time element losses, as well as for the cost of repairing or replacing damaged property.

Besides paying for damages up to policy limits, the contract includes defense costs and certain other supplementary benefits similar to those in other liability insurance policies.

Four conditions must be met for coverage to apply:

1. The named insured must become legally obligated to pay damages.
2. The damage must be accidental.
3. The damages must be due to direct physical loss or damage to covered property.
4. The direct damage must be caused by a covered cause of loss.

Because basic, broad, or special causes-of-loss forms are used, coverage can be much broader than the *fire* liability coverage of the CGL.

As is typical of liability insurance, the form contains no deductible.

Premium Rates Legal liability coverage is much less costly than direct property insurance. The rate for real property is 25 percent of the 80 percent coinsurance rate that would otherwise apply. For personal property, the rate is 50 percent of the usual 80 percent contents rate. The legal liability rate is lower because the insurer pays only when the insured is responsible for the damage.

Insurance to Value There is no coinsurance clause in the legal liability coverage form. However, insurance buyers should carefully examine the extent of the exposure when establishing insurance limits. The maximum possible loss that could be sustained under this form would include loss of all property of others described in the form and in the care, custody, and control of the insured—including damages for loss of use—that might be sustained in a single loss. For a tenant occupying an entire building, the entire building might be in the tenant's care, custody, and control. A tenant occupying a portion of a multiple-occupancy building would need only to consider the value of that portion of the building. Damage to other portions of the building, if caused by the insured's negligence, would normally be covered by property damage liability insurance of the insured's CGL.

Other Approaches

Insurance is by no means the only way to treat a tenant's fire legal liability exposure. Obviously, the exposure can also be retained. Three alternative approaches are also possible:

1. *Revise the lease agreement.* A tenant could revise the lease agreement with the landlord to state that the tenant will not be held liable for loss by fire and other perils. A major problem with this approach is getting the landlord to accept it. Further,

if a loss is caused by perils not included in the agreement, the tenant could still be held responsible. It would also be important to address the potential loss of use of rented property.

2. *Name tenant as additional insured.* The tenant can be added to the property owner's "commercial property" insurance as an additional named insured. This approach should prevent the property owner's fire insurance company from subrogating against the tenant, but it creates at least three other problems. First, the landlord may not desire to take this approach. Second, there may be several tenants, and it is difficult to add everyone to the policy. When tenants are transient, continuous updating of the policy becomes necessary. Moreover, violation of a policy condition by one insured may have an undesirable effect for all insureds. A third problem is that the limit of insurance on the building and contents might be inadequate. If it is, the owner would still have the right to recover from the tenant for the uncovered damages.

3. *Waiver of subrogation.* The most attractive noninsurance approach is to have the landlord and tenant sign an agreement releasing each other from any liability for loss negligently caused by either party to the property of the other. The landlord will not hold the tenant liable for any damage to the building, and the tenant will not hold the landlord liable for damages to the tenant's personal property.

There are problems with this approach as well. First, of course, the landlord might object. Second, the landlord might wish to retain the rights to pursue any claim that exceeds policy limits or arises out of perils not covered. Third, the tenant may still be unprotected against damages for loss of use.

STANDARD PROPERTY POLICY

The building and personal property coverage form (BPP) and other simplified commercial property forms go well beyond basic fire insurance. However, there remains a small market for a bare-bones "commercial property" policy, suitable for use in the FAIR plans and in other "high-risk" situations in which insurers are reluctant to grant coverage. The standard property policy was designed for this segment of the commercial property insurance market.

The standard property policy (SPP) is a self-contained monoline policy containing all necessary coverages, conditions, exclusions, and causes-of-loss descriptions in a single document. Only a completed declarations page is needed to complete the contract. Because it stands on its own, the SPP cannot be included in a commercial package policy. Separate monoline policies, or a separate commercial package, can be written to handle an insured's other coverage needs, but they stand completely separate from the SPP. One effect of this approach is that the SPP is not eligible for a package discount.

In most respects, the SPP is similar or identical to the BPP. In recognition of the coverage reductions, premiums are subject to a 2 percent discount, as compared with the BPP. Discussion here will summarize the differences, which are also illustrated in Exhibit 6-1.

Covered Property

The declarations indicate what limits of insurance, if any, apply to buildings, business personal property, or property of others. The additional coverages and coverage extensions are the same as those of the BPP. However, the coverage extensions (newly acquired or constructed property, personal effects and property of others, valuable papers and records—cost of research, property off-premises, and outdoor property) apply only to property located in the same state as the described premises.

Coverage applies on an actual cash value basis. There is no replacement cost option; neither are the inflation guard and agreed value options offered.

Covered Perils

Recall from Chapter 4 that the *causes of loss—basic form* automatically includes a long list of perils. Although it is not usually done, rules permit the exclusion of (1) windstorm or hail, (2) vandalism, and/or (3) sprinkler leakage. A major difference of the SPP is that it may be used to provide coverage for only fire, lightning, and explosion.

1. Fire, lightning, and explosion coverage is mandatory.
2. An "X" appears in the appropriate place of the declarations if the policy includes coverage for the packaged perils of windstorm or hail, smoke, aircraft or vehicles, riot or civil commotion, sinkhole collapse, and volcanic action (the windstorm or hail peril can be excluded).
3. Vandalism is covered only if another "X" appears in the declarations.
4. Sprinkler leakage is covered only if an "X" appears in the declarations.

The above perils may be covered in the following combinations: 1 only;

Exhibit 6-1

Comparison of Standard Property Policy and Building and Personal Property Coverage Form*

Standard Property Policy	Building and Personal Property Coverage Form
Policy is self-contained. Form includes:	Separate forms must be attached to provide these.
● Common policy conditions ● Commercial property conditions ● Causes of loss (and exclusions)	
Coverage may be purchased separately for the following incremental groupings of causes of loss:	All perils included automatically in basic causes-of-loss form, with options to exclude:
● Fire, lightning, & explosion (mandatory) ● Windstorm or hail (may be excluded), smoke, aircraft or vehicles, riot or civil commotion, sinkhole collapse, Volcanic action ● Vandalism and/or sprinkler leakage	● Windstorm or hail ● Vandalism ● Sprinkler leakage
Coverage extensions apply only in the state where the described premises are located.	No such limitation.
5 days' notice of cancellation permitted—10 days for mortgage holders	30 days' notice of cancellation, except 10 days for nonpayment of premium.
No coverage for buildings vacant or unoccupied after:	Unlimited unoccupancy permitted. No coverage for vacancy after 60 days for losses due to:
● 30 days for vandalism ● 60 days for any other peril	● Vandalism ● Sprinkler leakage ● Building glass breakage ● Water damage ● Theft
No replacement cost coverage.	$2500 replacement cost coverage built in for building losses if coinsurance is complied with. Option exists for full replacement cost coverage.
Coverage is suspended during any increase in hazard.	No such condition.
No optional coverages.	Optional coverages available in form for: ● Inflation guard ● Agreed value

*Adapted from ISO handout at Commercial Lines Simplification Seminar, 1986.

1 and 2 only; 1, 2, and 3; 1, 2, and 4; 1, 2, 3, and 4. As noted, windstorm or hail can be excluded from perils package 2.

Conditions

Three conditions in the SPP are more restrictive than those of the BPP.

Vacancy   The insurer will not pay for loss or damage by any peril if the building has been vacant or unoccupied for more than sixty days. After thirty days' vacancy or unoccupancy, coverage for vandalism ceases.

Increase in Hazard   Coverage is suspended during any period in which the hazard has been increased by means within the knowledge and control of the named insured.

Cancellation   The insurer may cancel the policy by providing only five days' advance notice to the insured. (Some state laws require longer notification periods.)

Condominium Association Coverage Endorsement

A *condominium association coverage endorsement* is available to make the standard property policy suitable for use when insuring condominium association property. The endorsement makes essentially the same changes to the SPP as the condominium association coverage form makes to the BPP—such as revising the "building" and "your business personal property" coverages to track with the requirements of a condominium association agreement and to dovetail with the coverage of a condominium unit owner's policy.

GLASS EXPOSURES

Exterior glass is normally considered part of the building. Glass may also be part of the contents of a building—for example, glass in movable showcases or merchandise made of glass or contained in glass bottles. In still other cases, glass may be considered improvements and betterments, such as glass office partitions of a tenant.

Glass of many different types is subject to loss by a variety of causes. The frequency and severity of glass losses depend on several factors. While glass exposures represent a relatively minor portion of property values for most insureds, some buildings have exterior walls comprised almost entirely of glass, with glass values in the millions of dollars.

Types of Glass Property

There are literally dozens of varieties of glass. Some are tempered so that they absorb heat or resist breakage. Glass may be laminated with a plastic material to make it highly resistant to breakage, as in safety glass and "bullet-proof" glass. Glass may be colored or molded into various shapes. Various types of plastic may be used as glass substitutes and are eligible for glass insurance.

The settings required to hold plate glass windows and other structural applications of glass may be expensive. Signs and decorations commonly are placed upon the glass, particularly in show windows and similar applications. Loss of the glass will also entail loss of lettering, ornamentation, or settings. The lettering and decorations usually are less expensive than the glass itself, but the additional cost of the lettering and decorations may substantially increase the total loss.

Perils and Loss Consequences

Many perils may result in damage to glass. The three general types of damage are breakage, abrasion, and chemical damage.

The brittle nature of glass results in obvious loss due to breakage. Many glass losses involve cracking or breaking without an identifiable blow from an outside source. This is why glass breakage is considered a peril, even though it is technically the outcome of a peril damaging property. The following list identifies nineteen common causes of glass breakage.

1. Wind
2. Contraction or expansion of glass
3. Poor store-front construction
4. Large crowds
5. Slamming of doors
6. Falling of goods on display
7. Window dressing and cleaning
8. Settling of building
9. Burglars
10. Riots and civil commotion
11. Explosions
12. Stones or other missiles thrown by vandals
13. Heat from radiators placed too near the glass

14. Window frames warped
15. Persons leaning or falling against windows or showcases
16. Articles dropped on showcases
17. Racketeers and malicious breaking of glass
18. Tripping or falling against inside glass
19. Use of stepladders, tools, etc., inside of store[1]

Glass is also subject to abrasion. Windblown sand or dust, such as may occur in a dust storm or sandstorm, may damage the glass and decrease its transparency. A plate glass show window that is so damaged may no longer be suitable for its purpose. Certain acids also damage glass.

Frequency and Severity of Glass Losses

Several factors influence the severity and frequency of glass losses—size, type of glass, its location in the building, and the location of the building itself. Large panes of glass are more susceptible to loss than small panes, and of course will sustain more severe losses. Different types of glass vary in their susceptibility to breakage. Glass inside a building or at the upper levels of the exterior is not exposed to many of the perils affecting exterior glass or glass at the street level. Logically, glass exposed to heavy traffic or in areas with heavy crime or vandalism also faces increased loss exposures.

The potential loss from glass breakage or other damage usually is not catastrophic to the same extent that a fire loss or windstorm loss may be. The cost of replacing a large plate glass window may amount to several hundred or even a few thousand dollars, as contrasted to the many thousands of dollars that could be lost when a building is destroyed by fire or tornado. However, any building with plate glass windows may face a serious loss if many windows are broken as a result of a storm or riot or a major incident of vandalism.

A comparatively new exposure to additional loss results from laws and ordinances in some geographical areas that require "safety glazing material" in some parts of structures. A merchant whose windows are of ordinary glass may find it necessary to install the more expensive safety glazing materials in case the windows are broken.

Glass in windows or other applications may be installed in such a way that removal of other fixtures would be necessary in order to replace the glass. This, too, is a loss exposure that could be substantial for the owner of the glass.

Immediate replacement of damaged glass is essential for show windows and similar situations. Many stores depend on show window displays to generate sales. Broken glass also affects a building's security. A tornado, riot, or other occurrence that results in many breakages in a particular neighborhood may make if difficult for a store proprietor to get immediate replacement or even to get a storefront protected by boarding up. Substantial additional damage or business interruption may result if the property owner does not have some arrangement for prompt replacement. The need for immediate replacement of broken glass is a factor which the property owner must consider in connection with potential glass losses.

THE GLASS COVERAGE FORM

In short, the glass coverage form may be used to cover building glass exposures that are not covered by other "commercial property" forms (such as the building and personal property form—BPP) when combined with the "commercial property" causes-of-loss forms. Although the BPP, condominium coverage form, and builders risk coverage form do not list glass as "property not covered" or otherwise exclude it, the causes-of-loss forms impose substantial coverage restrictions.

The basic causes-of-loss form does not include the *peril* of glass breakage, though it does provide coverage when glass is damaged by one of the other specified perils. Broad and special causes-of-loss forms do cover glass breakage—subject, however, to dollar limitations. As noted in Chapter 4, when discussing the broad causes-of-loss form:

> The broad form causes-of-loss form covers only glass that is part of a building or structure. Furthermore, coverage is limited by both a $100 "per-item" type limit and a $500 "per occurrence" limit. To be more specific, the $100 limit applies to "each pane, multiple plate insulating unit, radiant or solar heating panel, jalousie, louver, or shutter."
>
> Coverage would apply to property cut or otherwise damaged by breaking glass. Coverage would also apply to the pane of glass itself, even if the glass simply breaks for no obvious reason. However, the main effect of this [breakage of glass] peril is to cover nominal amounts of glass breakage by vandalism. (Remember, glass breakage is excluded by the vandalism peril.) The $100/$500 limits would have no effect when glass is broken by perils such as fire or windstorm, since there is no restriction on glass coverage under those perils.
>
> In connection with glass breakage, it should also be noted that there is no glass breakage coverage after the building has been vacant for more than sixty consecutive days. . . .

A complete monoline policy is formed by combining the glass coverage form with a declarations, common policy conditions, and commercial property conditions. A separate causes-of-loss form is not needed, because causes of loss and exclusions are included in the glass coverage form. Of course, glass coverage may also be written as part of a commercial package policy.

Eligible Property

Certain types of glass that are artistic in nature are ineligible for the glass coverage form—art glass, half tone screens, lenses, memorial windows, mosaic art, rotogravure screens, stained glass, and stained glass in leaded sections. Virtually all other "glass" is eligible, including such diversified categories as barber poles, burglar alarm foil, glass blocks, lucite, mirrors, and Plexiglas.

The glass that is to be covered is described in the policy. The location of the building is listed, along with individual descriptions of covered glass or wording such as "all glass of the type described." Specifics are handled either by a description in the declarations or by a glass coverage schedule that describes the kind of glass and its size, along with a description of any lettering, ornamentation, or other covered decorations.

Property Covered

The insurer agrees to pay for the direct physical loss of or damage to glass, as described in the declarations or a glass coverage schedule. Glass that is broken or cracked at the inception of the glass policy can be covered by using a *broken or cracked glass exclusion endorsement* which describes the current extent of the damage and excludes coverage for any extension of current breaks or cracks. This approach might be feasible when, for example, a large plate glass window has a rock chip, a small bullet hole, or a cracked corner which, by itself, does not justify replacement of the window.

Covered Perils

Two "causes of loss" are covered in the glass coverage form:

1. breakage of glass, and
2. chemicals accidentally or maliciously applied to glass.

Other than scratches or abrasions, these two "perils" encompass virtually everything that can result in damage to or destruction of glass.

Three causes of loss are excluded. The ubiquitous "nuclear hazard" and "war and military action" exclusions are present. However, the "fire" exclusion may come as a surprise. As noted in the section of Chapter 4 quoted above, the BPP and other similar property forms, combined with the basic causes-of-loss form, provide full coverage on glass damage by fire and other perils. Since glass damage by fire is (or should be) covered by another form, there is no logical reason to provide "duplicate" coverage under the glass coverage form. (It would not lead to duplicate recovery because of the "insurance under two or more coverage provisions" condition of the *commercial policy conditions.*)

One might then ask why glass breakage by other basic causes of loss is not also excluded. Long before commercial policy simplification, "glass" and "fire" were separate, free-standing policies, and "glass" insurance stayed out of the province of "fire" insurance. Glass insurance policies always had a fire exclusion. While the exclusion no longer serves a useful purpose, it is carried into the new form as a vestige of more embryonic forms and as a reminder that there is no change to coverage intent. It would be harmless to also exclude other basic perils from the glass coverage form, but the page or so of text required to describe the excluded perils would not be in keeping with policy simplification.

When combined with another property form covering glass against basic, broad, or special causes of loss, the glass coverage form provides the broadest coverage available to any type of property under the "commercial property" program. In effect, the other form covers the basics and the glass coverage form covers the "difference in conditions" between the basics and "full" coverage. Not even flood or earthquake is excluded.

Vacancy Exclusion

The insurer will not pay for loss or damage if the building has been vacant for a specified time period (thirty or sixty days) prior to the loss. *Coverage for vacant buildings* may be added for an additional premium—subject, of course, to the insurer's approval.

Additional Coverages

The glass coverage form includes four additional coverages.

Debris Removal As with other "commercial property" forms, this additional coverage pays for expenses to remove debris of covered property following damage by a covered peril. When glass breaks, its debris may be blown into the street or sidewalks or get enmeshed into carpets, furniture, and other personal property. The glass must be removed. Sidewalks and streets can be swept clean, as well as adjacent entrances or foyers. Furniture, clothing, stock, and the like may have to be professionally cleaned. In short, debris removal can involve significant costs over and above the value of the glass itself.

Temporary Plates The insurer agrees to pay the cost of installing temporary plates in, or boarding up, openings containing insured glass when necessary because of unavoidable delay in repairing or replacing such damaged glass.

Frames The insurer agrees to pay the necessary cost of repairing or replacing frames encasing the damaged glass.

Removal of Obstructions Also covered is the cost incurred to remove or replace any obstructions, other than window displays, when repairing or replacing covered glass. A certain amount of clear space is required to maneuver a large pane of glass. Since glass is not necessarily the last thing installed when a building is constructed, it may be necessary to remove pillars, partitions, equipment, or even walls in order to repair or replace glass. In some cases, obstructions might also include such things as autos, building parts, and dead or wounded animals that have crashed into the glass.

Coverage Extension—Newly Acquired Glass

An extension similar to the newly acquired property extension of the BPP provides sixty days' automatic coverage for newly acquired glass at the described location or glass at newly acquired locations. Within sixty days the insured is expected to report the new location to the insurer and pay a premium from the date the exposure was originally acquired. This is automatic insurance—not free insurance.

Limits of Insurance

An unusual feature of the glass coverage form is that it usually has no dollar limit of coverage on glass. Premiums are calculated based on the type, size, and location of the glass, and the insurer simply agrees to repair or replace glass meeting that description (and to pay for related debris removal, temporary plates, frames, and removal of obstructions).

The glass coverage form contains no coinsurance provision, since it would be difficult to underinsure (except, perhaps, by underreporting the dimensions of covered glass).

A dollar limit is usually specified in the glass coverage schedule for lettering and ornamentation. Some types of glass in special installations may also be insured for a specified dollar limit.

Deductible

Either glass is broken or it is not broken. Therefore, a glass deductible serves no useful purpose in eliminating claims for small losses—except, perhaps, in cases where many panes of glass are subject to a single deductible. On that basis, one might argue against the logic of having a deductible in a glass policy. However, deductibles also serve another purpose—they involve insureds in the loss and therefore encourage insureds to be somewhat more careful to prevent loss than if the entire loss is covered by insurance. The glass coverage form can be written with no deductible or with a "per occurrence" deductible—not a "per item" deductible—and manual rules show a minimum deductible of $50 when the option is selected.

Valuation and Loss Payment Provisions

For purposes of the glass coverage form, glass is valued at its actual cash value, unless applicable statutes, ordinances, or building codes require that the glass be replaced with safety glazing material. In such a case, the glass is valued at the minimum cost required to replace it with glass that complies with the code. (This provision might be compared with the building ordinance coverage endorsement discussed in Chapter 4.)

In the event of loss or damage, the insurer has the choice of paying to the insured the value of lost or damaged property, or the cost of repairing or replacing it. Alternatively, the insurer may actually repair, rebuild, or replace the property.

Replacement Service In many glass losses, the replacement is arranged directly by the insurance company. This practice is so well established that one important reason for the purchase of glass insurance is to secure the replacement service of the insurer. Replacement service can be especially important when a storm results in heavy breakage in a neighborhood. The volume of business an insurance company gives to a glass dealer may secure preferred service for insurance-company-initiated replacements.

Loss Payment for Large Plates An "optional coverage" preprinted in the policy is actually an optional reduction in coverage in exchange for a premium credit. Large plates of glass over 100 square feet are costly to repair or replace. The *loss payment for large plates* option gives the insurer the right to replace such large plates with two or more smaller plates of glass and to pay for the necessary alterations to accomplish this.

BOILERS AND MACHINERY

Any organization using power equipment is exposed to loss from explosion of pressurized equipment and breakdown of electrical and mechanical devices. Failure to recognize and treat these exposures may result in the retention of potentially severe losses.

- Boiler and machinery exposures are obvious for many large firms—such as papermills, electric utilities, chemical plants, steel mills, and refineries.
- Many medium-sized firms have substantial exposures to breakdown loss as well. Food processors, textile manufacturers, electronics manufacturers, high-rise offices and stores, newspapers, cold storage firms, breweries, wineries, dairies, and hotels are examples.
- Less obvious are the exposures of small businesses—including dry cleaners and laundries (these always have boilers), stores (with boilers and air conditioning equipment), auto repair and service operations (which generally use boilers for heating and have air compressing equipment), churches, theaters, small offices, schools, bowling alleys, and others.

Many boiler and machinery losses are severe, running into the millions of dollars. At least one loss has reached the $80 million range, including both direct and business interruption losses. Often the direct damage property loss is minor when compared with the attendant business interruption.

Loss Exposures—Property and Perils

Accidents to boilers and machinery are, in most instances, directly related to the energy inherent in their operation: heat, pressure, electrical energy, centrifugal force, and reciprocating motion.

Boilers and fired pressure vessels are subject to several different perils:

- Explosion, due to internal pressure of steam or water;
- Burning (overheating), caused by continued firing after the water drops below a safe level;
- Cracking of cast iron sections, due to such things as expansion and contraction stresses, rust growth between sections, porous castings, and tie rods that are too tight;
- Bulging or bagging, usually caused by improper heat transfer due to buildup of scale or sediment, and

● Collapse (of the cylindrical furnace of a Scotch marine boiler), generally due to "low water."

Unfired pressure vessels, such as air tanks, electric water heaters, steam cookers, hydropneumatic tanks, and process vessels, are subject to the perils of explosion, bulging, cracking, and collapse (implosion).

The vessels, coils, and piping that form part of *refrigerating systems* can explode, collapse, or crack. The most common type of failure is cracking, which is often caused (oddly enough) by freezing due to control failure. An additional hazard is encountered in the operation of ammonia refrigerating systems. Ammonia that is released by an accident (such as breaking a pipe) can cause heavy contamination losses, especially to foodstuffs.

Mechanical equipment—compressors, pumps, blowers, fans, engines, turbines, and the like—is subject to a variety of hazards. Among the more common causes of failure are metal fatigue, loss of lubrication, overspeed, mechanical stress, and shock loads.

Electrical equipment can also be damaged in many ways. The most common hazards are burnouts caused by such things as overload, brittle insulation, line surge, lightning, and moisture.

Many of the objects insurable under a boiler and machinery policy are actually combinations of two or more components. They are therefore subject to a wider range of hazards than those of individual pieces of equipment. Several such units are noteworthy.

● Air conditioning units, 50 hp or less, and small refrigerating units, 15 hp or less (consisting of refrigerating vessels, coils and piping, motors, compressors, fans, pumps, and electrical control).
● Small air-compressing units, 15 hp or less (consisting of motors, compressors, air tanks, and electrical controls).
● Steam, water, or gas turbine units (each consisting of the driving turbine and the driven generator, compressor, pump, fan, or blower).

Controlling Boiler and Machinery Loss Exposures

Forty-three states currently have laws requiring periodic inspection of boilers and/or pressure vessels by a licensed inspector. In most states and provinces, boiler insurers' loss control representatives are licensed as deputy inspectors for the state, and their inspections meet the requirements of the law. State, county, and municipal inspectors may also conduct inspections which assure compliance with statutory codes.

A key purpose of boiler inspection is to detect dangerous conditions before trouble occurs. To accomplish this, an inspector may do such things as make sure the equipment is suited for the job, oversee the testing of controls and safety devices, check equipment maintenance, and review operators' logs.

A boiler that has passed an inspection is less likely to have a major breakdown than one that has not been inspected. This is why inspections are required by so many states. It is also why approximately 30 cents out of every insurance premium dollar is expended in loss control services. In addition to helping their insureds prevent losses, insurance company boiler inspectors keep underwriters informed so that rates and coverages can be kept in line with the exposures.

Because boiler inspections are mandatory in many jurisdictions throughout the world, the decision usually is not *whether* to inspect, but *who* will inspect. Any organization subject to inspection laws has to decide whether to obtain the necessary inspections from the authority's inspector or to have the inspection service as a part of an insurance program. (Machinery inspections are not generally required by statute, but they still reduce both loss frequency and severity.) Of course, with insurance, any covered losses that are not prevented are paid for by the insurer.

Other Policies Insuring Boiler and Machinery Losses

"Commercial property" forms cover losses to boilers and machinery, as well as to other property, when caused by perils insured against. However, these forms do not cover damage to boilers and machinery or anything else when the loss is caused by uninsured or excluded perils. Among these other perils are explosions and other sudden breakdowns in boilers and machinery in general. Losses from these are subject to boiler and machinery insurance.

A logical first step in examining insurance on boiler and machinery losses is to look at the explosion coverage of "commercial property" forms. Exhibit 6-2 contains the wording that relates to these exposures. While this is the wording of a specified perils form, similar provisions are found in the special ("all-risks") form.

Note that the "commercial property" policy covers explosion of gases or fuel in the furnace or flues of a fired vessel. This peril is generally referred to as "furnace explosion." Another type of boiler explosion, however, is usually much more violent than a furnace explosion. An explosion caused by pressure of steam or water within the boiler can be devastating. Note that the "explosion" provisions of the "commercial property" form specifically exclude loss from the explosion of *steam boilers, steam pipes, steam engines,* and *steam*

Exhibit 6-2
Excerpts from Causes of Loss — Basic Form*

Covered Causes of Loss means the following:

Explosion, including the explosion of gases or fuel within the furnace of any fired vessel or within the flues or passages through which the gases of combustion pass. This cause of loss does not incude loss or damage by:

a. rupture, bursting or operation of pressure relief devices: or

b. rupture or bursting due to expansion or swelling of the contents of any building or structure, caused by or resulting from water.

We will not pay for loss or damage caused by or resulting from:

a. artificially generated electrical current, including electric arcing, that disturbs electrical devices, appliances or wires.

   But if loss or damage by fire results, we will pay for that resulting loss or damage.

b. rupture or bursting of water pipes (other than Automatic Sprinkler Systems) unless caused by a Covered Cause of Loss.

c. leakage or discharge of water or steam resulting from the breaking or cracking of any part of a system or appliance containing water or steam (other than an Automatic Sprinkler System), unless the system or appliance is damaged by a Covered Cause of Loss.

d. explosion of steam boilers, steam pipes, steam engines or steam turbines owned or leased by you, or operated under your control.

   But if loss or damage by fire or combustion explosion results, we will pay for that resulting loss or damage.

e. mechanical breakdown, including rupture or bursting caused by centrifugal force.

   But if loss or damage by a Covered Cause of Loss results, we will pay for that resulting loss or damage.

*Includes copyrighted material of Insurance Services Office, Inc., with its permission.

turbines that are owned or leased by the insured or operated under the insured's control.

Since the "commercial property" form makes no exclusionary mention of the explosion of *hot water boilers* and *pressure vessels*, such an occurrence is generally accepted as being covered. Some "accidents" that frequently happen to this equipment are not covered by "commercial property" forms:

- *"burning"* (overheating) of boilers or fired vessels due to a lack of water;
- *cracking* of sections of cast iron boilers, due to a variety of causes;

- *bulging or bagging,* usually the result of the buildup of scale or sediment.

Note also the *electric arcing* exclusion in "commercial property" forms. The electrical burnout of motors, generators, circuit breakers, electrical distribution boards, cables, and transformers—from such causes as short circuits and line surges—is not covered. (Damage caused directly by lightning is covered under the lightning peril).

Note also that the "commercial property" form specifically excludes *mechanical breakdown* and explosion of equipment due to *centrifugal force.* These are the types of accidents that happen to a wide range of machinery. Thus, the property insurance forms described earlier in this text provide very limited protection against the most common boiler and machinery losses.

BOILER AND MACHINERY INSURANCE

In general, boiler and machinery insurance provides coverage for many of the loss exposures discussed in the previous pages that are excluded by other property forms. High and low pressure boilers, including both steam and hot water boilers, piping, air conditioning and refrigerating systems, pumps, compressors, deep well pumps, turbines, engines, wheels, gears, shaft drives, electrical distribution equipment, transformers—in fact, almost anything that can control, transmit, transform, or use mechanical or electrical power—can be insured with a boiler and machinery policy.

Boiler and machinery insurance is considered a somewhat specialized line, requiring special technical expertise—especially among boiler and machinery inspectors and underwriters. A limited number of insurance companies write boiler and machinery insurance. A number of insurance companies include a boiler and machinery coverage form as part of their commercial package policy, but they reinsure the entire boiler and machinery exposure with an insurer that specializes in that line. A number of insurers use their own boiler and machinery coverage forms, but many use the ISO forms discussed here.

ISO Policy Format

Like "commercial property" insurance, boiler and machinery coverage is available on simplified ISO forms that either serve as the foundation of a monoline policy or can be combined with other coverages to form a commercial package policy. As illustrated in Exhibit 6-3, a complete monoline policy is formed by combining the following:

Exhibit 6-3
Boiler and Machinery Policy Structure*

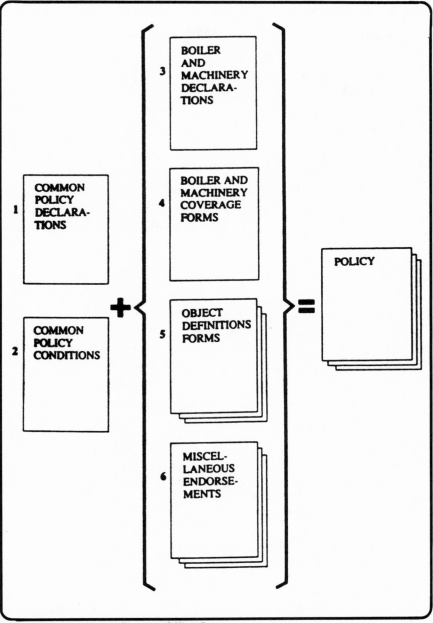

- common policy declarations,
- common policy conditions,
- boiler and machinery declarations,
- boiler and machinery coverage forms,
- object definitions forms, and
- miscellaneous endorsements.

(Object definitions forms are not used with the small business form, described later.) Boiler and machinery coverage applies to an "'accident' to an 'object.'" An "object definitions form" clarifies in considerable detail exactly what boiler or other item is a covered object.

Scope of Coverage—Accident to an Object

Boiler and machinery insurance applies only when there is an "accident" to an "object."

Object   When coverage is written under the standard boiler and machinery coverage form, four different "object definitions forms" are used, singly or in combination, depending on the subjects of insurance in any given case:

- Pressure and refrigeration objects
- Mechanical objects
- Electrical objects
- Turbine objects[2]

The content of these forms is discussed later. The idea of these "object definitions" is to provide coverage for all objects of a certain type included within the object group definition—all pressure and refrigeration objects, for example.

The actual "objects" insured in any given policy are described (specifically or in blanket manner) in the policy declarations. The object definition serves the function of "tailoring" the policy provisions to assure that the definition of "object" includes the type of machinery or equipment actually insured with the policy. The purpose of four separate endorsements is to reduce the actual number of object definitions required in a given policy by permitting definitions of objects *not* covered by the policy to be kept out of the policy.

Note that the objects themselves are not the only items of covered property—other property and liability losses are covered as well. However, coverage applies only when there is an accident to an object, as defined. Further, the object must be in use, or connected ready for use.

Coverage for objects being dismantled, reassembled, transported, or in storage, may be added by endorsement—but even then coverage does not apply if an accident is a direct result of the object being worked upon.

Accident   "Accident" is defined as:

a sudden and accidental breakdown of the "object" or a part of the "object." At the time the breakdown occurs, it must manifest itself by physical damage to the "object" that necessitates repair or replacement.

This is a very broad definition. However, it is restricted a little by a list of events that are not considered "accidents." Since any of the following is not an "accident" and therefore does not trigger coverage, this list serves, in effect, as a series of exclusions.

None of the following is an "accident;"
a. Depletion, deterioration, corrosion or erosion;
b. Wear and tear;
c. Leakage at any valve, fitting, shaft seal, gland packing, joint or connection;
d. Breakdown of any vacuum tube, glass tube or brush;
e. Breakdown of any electronic computer or electronic data processing equipment;
f. Breakdown of any structure or foundation supporting the "object" or any of its parts; nor
g. The functioning of any safety or protective device.

These exceptions reinforce the idea that covered accidents are only to include sudden and accidental incidents—as opposed to losses that are almost certain to occur over the life of a mechanical device, such as its components' wearing out with the passage of time. "Accidents" resulting from strikes, riots, civil commotion, acts of sabotage, or vandalism are not excluded.

An accident to an object occurs, for example, when an insured flywheel suddenly and accidentally breaks apart during its operation, resulting in damage that necessitates its repair or replacement. An accident does not occur when a routine inspection of another flywheel reveals that the flywheel has suffered metal fatigue as a result of normal wear and tear, necessitating its replacement.

Limited Coverage.   Insurers sometimes require the limited coverage approach when providing coverage for old or obsolete objects. The *boilers, fired vessels and electric steam generators—limited coverage endorsement* amends the definition of "accident" to include only losses arising from a sudden and accidental tearing asunder of the object or part of the object. This tearing asunder must be caused by pressure of water or steam within the object.

Covered Property

Covered property includes *any property owned by the named insured.* Property owned by the named insured can be either real or personal property, and is *not* limited to the actual objects scheduled in the policy. The purpose of boiler and machinery insurance is not merely to insure damage to the scheduled objects, but also to cover damage to other property that results from accidents involving the scheduled objects. The breadth of this insuring agreement is narrowed a bit by a provision in the valuation condition which eliminates coverage for loss or damage to property that is obsolete or useless to the named insured. So, for example, if a boiler explosion damages a junked truck that happens to be next to the insured's building, the insurer would have no obligation to pay for repair or replacement of this obsolete and useless vehicle.

Coverage also applies to *other property in the insured's care, custody, or control for which the insured is legally liable.* Although most insureds have commercial general liability (CGL) coverage, the CGL excludes liability for damage to property in the insured's care, custody, or control. The boiler and machinery form plugs this gap when the liability arises out of an accident to an insured object. In connection with this legal liability coverage, the form also states that the insurer will defend the insured against any claim or suit alleging liability for damage to the property of others. Note that this coverage does not apply to all property of others that is damaged by an accident to an object, but only to property in the insured's care, custody, or control. If an insured object explodes causing damage to a neighboring firm's building, the boiler and machinery coverage form would provide no coverage. However, such a loss would be within the scope of commercial general liability (CGL) coverage.

Bodily Injury Liability Coverage Long before general liability insurance was widely used, boiler and machinery policies covered bodily injury liability arising out of boiler explosions. At one time, the potential for a boiler explosion might have been considered one of the most serious liability exposures facing businesses. Bodily injury liability coverage is still available, via the *bodily injury liability endorsement.* This coverage amends the boiler and machinery coverage form to include coverage for liability for bodily injury to third parties injured because of an accident to an object. Coverage is excess over any other valid and collectible insurance. This coverage is now used only under unusual circumstances.

Coverage Extensions

Four extensions appear in the boiler and machinery coverage form.

Expediting Expenses Expediting expenses are made to speed up temporary or permanent repairs or to hasten the permanent replacement of destroyed boilers or other objects. The boiler and machinery form will pay expediting expenses up to:

- $5000, or
- whatever is left of the limit of insurance after covered property losses have been paid,

whichever is less. In other words, the expediting expenses extension does not provide coverage in addition to policy limits.

Automatic Coverage for Newly Acquired Locations Accidents to objects at newly acquired property are covered for up to ninety days after the date of acquisition, during which time the insured is expected to report the new location and pay the appropriate premium.

The *object group condition* makes it clear that additional premiums will be charged for objects in newly acquired structures and structural additions. Conversely, a return premium will be allowed for structures and additions that are removed during the policy term.

Defense Like the *legal liability coverage form* discussed earlier in this chapter, the boiler and machinery coverage form is a type of property insurance that includes an element of liability coverage. Like other liability insurance forms, the boiler and machinery gives the insurer the right to defend or settle the claim or suit.

Supplementary Payments Like other liability forms, the boiler and machinery coverage form includes coverage for all defense and investigative expenses incurred by the insurance company, the cost of bonds to release attachments, up to $100 per day in lost wages, all costs incurred when defending a legal action, pre-judgment interest, and all interest on the full amount of any judgment that accrues after the entry of the judgment and before the insurance company pays the claim.

Exclusions

The boiler and machinery coverage form contains the ubiquitous nuclear and war exclusions and also the ordinance or law exclusion which precludes coverage for any increase in loss brought about by the operation of building codes or other similar ordinances. More significant, for purposes of this discussion, are the eleven exclusions under the heading "other exclusions."

Explosion- and Fire-Related Exclusions   The boiler and machinery coverage form exclusions begin by removing all explosion coverage. They then restore coverage for explosion of any:

- steam boiler,
- electric steam generator,
- steam piping,
- steam turbine,
- steam engine,
- gas turbine, or
- moving or rotating machinery, if the explosion is caused by centrifugal force or mechanical breakdown.

The boiler and machinery coverage form excludes coverage for:

1. fires, or
2. explosions outside the object

that occur at the same time as an accident or that ensue from an accident. (For electrical equipment, fire is excluded only if it occurs outside the object.) Conversely, the form also excludes coverage for "accidents" that result from combustion explosions or fires. Also excluded is loss caused by water or other means used to extinguish a fire.

Furnace Explosion Coverage.   The basic boiler and machinery coverage form excludes explosions caused by unconsumed fuel or gas within the furnace of a boiler or fired vessel, because such losses are generally covered under "commercial property" insurance. However, this peril may be added to the boiler and machinery policy by using the *furnace explosion coverage* endorsement.

Explosion Exclusion.   Coverage for accidents resulting from explosion of a specified object or kind of objects may be excluded by using an *explosion elimination endorsement.*

Chemical Recovery Boiler Exclusion.   When a chemical recovery boiler is located on the premises, the insurer may wish to exclude coverage for related explosions. The *chemical recovery boiler exclusion* excludes coverage, not only for explosions within the furnace of a chemical type boiler, but also for explosions in the passage from the furnace to the atmosphere, as well as any "accident" that results from the explosion.

Flood Exclusion   Loss resulting directly *from flood* is excluded. However, if an "accident" results from a flood, the insurer will pay for direct damage to covered property caused by the "accident." For example, if a heating boiler is damaged by a flood occurring in the summer when the boiler is not in use, the boiler and machinery coverage form will not cover the loss—the boiler did not suffer an "accident." However, if flood waters damage the operating boiler in January, causing the boiler to crack, the damages from this "accident" would be covered.

Earthquake Exclusions Loss resulting from an "accident" caused directly or indirectly by earthquake, landslide, mudslide, subsidence, or volcanic eruption is excluded. Only "commercial property" coverage for earthquake will cover this exposure.

Testing Exclusions Loss resulting from any "accident" to any "object" while being tested is excluded. The boiler and machinery coverage form is designed for objects that have been installed and are ready for use. Testing is, in a way, a part of the installation process and is accompanied by serious hazards. During testing, objects are strained to their highest limits to see if they will fail. Not only testing on installation, but also routine seasonal testing, is excluded.

Indirect Loss Exclusions The boiler and machinery coverage form is designed to cover direct losses to property arising out of accidents to objects. Three exclusions reinforce that intention:

We will not pay for . . . loss caused by or resulting from . . .

A delay in, or an interruption of, any business, manufacturing or processing activity;

Lack of power, light, heat, steam or refrigeration; or

Any other indirect result of an "accident" to an "object."

Some of these excluded exposures can be insured separately, as noted later.

Limits of Insurance

The boiler and machinery declarations page shows the limit of insurance purchased. Limits can range from $25,000 to as high as $10,000,000 or more. The limit is payable for any "one accident" (as defined), meaning that all objects, vessels, and other property damaged or destroyed in an accident are collectively subject to the limit. Both liability coverage for damage to property of others and property coverage for damage to the insured's property are subject to this same limit. (As respects liability claims, defense costs and supplementary payments are covered in addition to policy limits.)

As reflected in "coverage limitations," four types of expenses are each subject to a $5,000 sublimit. These sublimits do not increase the limit of insurance available to pay for direct damage losses. Stated differently, the insurance covers losses within each of the following four categories but will pay no more than $5,000 in each category.

- *Expediting Expenses*—As noted earlier, the insurer will pay no more than $5,000 for expenses covered by the "expediting expenses" coverage limitation. The $5,000 limit may be increased by endorsement.
- *Hazardous Substance Limitation*—The insurer will pay up to $5,000 for any additional expenses incurred by the insured for cleanup, repair, or replacement, or disposal of property that is declared by a governmental agency to be damaged, contaminated, or polluted by a substance presenting health hazards. For example, if an accident causes an electrical transformer using PCB-based oil to leak, the insurer would pay up to $5,000 to have the transformer cleaned and the building decontaminated.
- *Ammonia Contamination Limitation*—Many refrigeration systems use ammonia as a coolant. When such systems are damaged by an accident, the ammonia can contaminate the objects and other property of the insured. A food-processing plant, for example, might face this type of loss, which would be covered up to $5,000. This limit may be increased by endorsement.
- *Water Damage Limitation*—If property is damaged by water from an accident caused by refrigerating or air conditioning equipment or its piping, the boiler policy will cover the loss up to $5,000. This limit may be increased by endorsement.

The boiler and machinery coverage form contains no coinsurance clause or other insurance-to-value provision.

Deductible   A deductible shown in the declarations applies to all damage in any one accident, regardless of the number of objects involved.

Conditions

Most conditions of the boiler and machinery coverage form are those expected to be found in any property insurance policy. They require no discussion here. However, several conditions that have not already been examined deserve special mention.

Suspension   The suspension provision is unique to boiler and machinery insurance but is reasonable when one considers the dangerous instrumentalities involved. Whenever an object is found to be in, or exposed to, a dangerous condition, any of the insurance company's representatives can immediately suspend the insurance on losses arising from accident to that object. Suspension is accomplished by delivering or mailing a written notice of coverage suspension to the named insured. Once coverage has been suspended, it can be reinstated only by endorsing the policy.

The suspension provision allows a boiler inspector or other representative of the insurer to take action when there is imminent danger of an accident. The purpose of an inspection is to detect dangerous conditions so that corrective actions can be taken before an accident occurs. Most insureds want a loss-free operation and willingly cooperate when a dangerous situation is discovered.

The suspension provision seldom has to be invoked. Usually it is applied only when the condition is "life-threatening." Yet, it serves as a last resort that can be used when the insured or its personnel will not cooperate.

Valuation "Covered property" includes both the named insured's property and property of others in the insured's care, custody, or control, and for which the insured is legally liable. However, the form's valuation condition applies only to property of the named insured.

In the case of a legal liability loss, the extent of the insurer's obligation is determined by the extent of the insured's legal liability—which is determined by legal considerations rather than the terms of the insurance contract. According to the insuring agreement the insurer is obligated to pay only direct damage losses—any legal liability for loss of income or other indirect losses would presumably not be covered by the boiler and machinery coverage form.

As respects property of the named insured, the boiler and machinery coverage form provides *replacement cost coverage* on the basis of the actual loss sustained by the insured, subject to policy limits. No payment will be made unless and until the damaged property is actually repaired or replaced within eighteen months of the accident.

Actual Cash Value Coverage. As noted, the boiler and machinery coverage form provides replacement cost coverage. The *actual cash value endorsement* may be required by the insurer when covered property is old, in poor condition, or otherwise badly depreciated.

Other Insurance (Joint Loss) A *joint loss* occurs when other insurance applies to a loss also insured by the boiler and machinery coverage form. Before explaining the boiler and machinery form's "other insurance" provision, it will be helpful to examine a few principles that apply to "other insurance" clauses, in general.

Some "other insurance" provisions make it clear that only one policy will apply when two policies cover the same loss. More often, the "other insurance" provision specifies a method of sharing the loss among two or more insurers. Provisions of this type are sometimes referred to as "proportional sharing provisions." Three different approaches to proportional sharing are possible:

1. Insurers pay equal shares until the loss is paid in full or one insurer's limits run out, at which point the insurer whose limits have not run out continues to pay.
2. Each insurer's obligation is prorated *based on limits of insurance.*
3. Each insurer's obligation is prorated *based on amounts that would be payable in the absence of other insurance.*

The boiler and machinery coverage form's "other insurance" clause compares the second and third approaches and agrees to pay whichever result is less.

Object Definitions Endorsements

"Object" in the boiler and machinery coverage form is simply the equipment described in the declarations. However, full descriptions of specific object categories are found in the object definitions endorsement(s) attached to the coverage form.[3]

One or more of the four object definitions endorsement(s) must be attached to the basic boiler and machinery coverage form. The names of the four endorsements are listed below, along with the more specific categories of objects found under each endorsement.

Object Definitions No. 1—Pressure and Refrigeration Objects
1. Boilers, Fired Vessels, and Electric Steam Generators
2. Unfired Vessels
3. Refrigerating and Air Conditioning Vessels and Piping
4. Auxiliary Piping
5. Small Compressing and Refrigerating Units
6. Air Conditioning Units

Object Definitions No. 2—Mechanical Objects
1. Deep-Well Pump Units
2. Miscellaneous Machines, Gear Wheels, and Enclosed Gear Sets
3. Engines, Pumps, Compressors, Fans, and Blowers
4. Wheels and Shafting

Object Definitions No. 3—Electrical Objects
1. Rotating Electrical Machines, Transformers, and Induction Feeder Regulators
2. Miscellaneous Electrical Apparatus
3. Solid State Rectifier Units
Object Definitions No. 4—Turbine Objects

The object definitions go into considerable detail—more than can be discussed here—as to what an "object" includes and what it does not include. As one example, the object definition for small compressing and refrigerating units states that "object" means any small compressing or refrigerating unit shown in the declarations whose maximum nameplate rating is not over fifteen horsepower, but does *not* include any wiring or piping leading to or from the unit. The significance of the exception to the definition is that if an accident occurs in the wiring or piping leading to the unit, it is not an accident to an object and therefore is not an insured event. However, the exception does not eliminate coverage for the wiring in the event that an accident occurs within the object as defined. Remember that boiler and machinery insurance is intended to cover damage to any property of the named insured as long as a "covered cause of loss" is responsible.

Time Element Coverages

Chapter 5 discussed in detail the need for business income and extra expense coverage and the "commercial property" coverage forms and endorsements that address those needs. As noted, "commercial property" time element coverage is available for the perils covered by the standard causes-of-loss forms. A similar need exists for time element coverage in connection with boilers and machinery. If covered property is damaged by an accident to a covered boiler or other insured object, the insured can suffer a shutdown just as if the property had been damaged by a cause of loss covered under its business income coverage form (BIC). Similarly, if the insured's business is of a sort that requires extra expense insurance (i.e., operations must continue with minimal or no interruption following a loss), the need will be just as acute with respect to losses resulting from accidents to insured objects.

Business interruption and extra expense coverage can be added to the boiler and machinery coverage form by various *endorsements*, discussed here. The endorsement approach is different from that of the "commercial property" forms, where time element coverage is provided on separate forms which are not endorsements to the BPP or other form covering direct damage to property.

Business Interruption—Actual Loss Sustained The "actual loss sustained" endorsement represents the most popular type of time element coverage for boiler and machinery exposures. The general idea is to provide coverage similar to that of the "commercial property" business income coverage form for business interruptions resulting from an accident to an object. However, the construction and language of the "business interruption—actual loss sustained coverage" form are quite different from those of the BIC, with resulting differences in coverage. Readers are warned not to assume that the boiler and machinery form merely substitutes "accident to an object" in place of the covered perils of the BIC—the differences go much deeper than that and are discussed here only in summary fashion.

Coverage. When an accident to a covered object occurs during the policy period, the insurer agrees to pay (1) the "actual loss" due to a resulting slowdown or shutdown and (2) extra expenses *that reduce or avert the interruption.*

The definition of *actual loss* generally resembles that of the BIC, providing replacement of unearned net profits and continuing expenses.

Unlike the BIC, ordinary payroll expense is not covered unless it is specifically indicated in the declarations or added by endorsement. Also, the boiler and machinery business interruption—actual loss sustained endorsement—does not provide full extra expense coverage but covers only extra expenses that reduce the business interruption loss.

Limit of Loss. The endorsement contains a *limit of loss* which is, in effect, a separate limit of insurance applicable only to business interruption coverage, apart from the limit of insurance in the boiler and machinery form to which it is attached. A single limit of loss is chosen to apply to all losses at any one premises.

Deductibles. One of three types of deductibles may be chosen when the policy is set up. Which approach applies is indicated in the declarations.

- *Dollar Deductible*—This is the familiar fixed dollar deductible. The insurer pays covered losses in excess of the deductible, up to the endorsement's "limit of loss."
- *Time Deductible*—The insurer pays only when the interruption exceeds a certain specified time period. The time deductible chosen may range from twelve hours to twenty-five days, or longer.
- *Multiple of Daily Value Deductible*—The insurer determines the "daily value"—the amount that would have been earned each working day if the accident had not occurred. If, for example, the selected "multiple of daily value deductible" is 5, and if the "daily value" is $1,000, then $5,000 would be

subtracted from the covered loss. The effect can be significantly different from that of a five-day deductible in the event of a partial interruption of business.

Insurance-to-Value, Reporting Provisions. The approach used for boiler and machinery exposures is similar to that of the "commercial property" *business income premium adjustment endorsement* discussed in Chapter 5. The insured submits annual reports of its "Business Interruption Annual Value" for the past year on an "Approved Report Form" furnished by the insurer. Premiums are adjusted for the past policy term based on those reports.

A provision titled *coinsurance* (which really is not quite the same as a typical coinsurance provision) provides that if it is discovered at the time of a loss that the last report understated the actual "Business Interruption Annual Value," then the insurer's payment will be prorated by the amount of the understatement:

$$\left(\frac{\text{Did Report}}{\text{Should Have Reported}} \times \text{Loss}\right) - \text{Deductible} = \begin{array}{c}\text{Amount Insurer Pays}\\ \text{(Subject to Limits)}\end{array}$$

Business Income Coverage—Agreed Value Approach The coinsurance provision in the actual loss sustained form can be suspended with the use of a *conditional suspension of coinsurance endorsement* which is attached to a business interruption report of values. The coinsurance provision is reinstated if the next report is not sent to the insurer on schedule.

This approach ensures that the insurer will not make a coinsurance deduction from a future loss based on inaccuracies in the past report. In effect, it indicates that the insurer agrees that the values in the report were accurate. For that reason, the effect is nearly the same as the agreed value option of the BIC.

Business Interruption—Valued Coverage The *business interruption—valued coverage endorsement* is not a contract of indemnity, intended to indemnify the insured for the actual loss sustained. Rather, it is a valued contract in which the insurer agrees to pay the named insured a specified dollar *daily limit* for each day of total interruption.

A business interruption does not necessarily involve a complete shutdown, so the form also specifies how partial interruptions will be handled:

We will compare each "day's" "business" after the "accident" with the average daily "business" you had for the 30 "days" just before the accident. In computing this average, we will use only those "days" on which there was any "business" at the location. To determine how much we will pay you, the Daily Limit will be multiplied by the percentage of reduction in "business"....

Reasonable extra expenses incurred to reduce the payment otherwise made for total or partial interruption are also paid by the insurer. Extra expenses might be incurred to reduce either the duration of the interruption or the degree of partial interruption.

Coverage is subject to a *limit of loss*, which represents the total amount payable under the endorsement for any single accident. The form includes a time deductible and a dollar deductible, either of which may be selected and indicated in the declarations. Since this is a "valued" coverage, no reports are required and there is no coinsurance provision.

Extra Expense Coverage The boiler and machinery *extra expense endorsement* meets the same need as the extra expense coverage of the BIC or the "commercial property" extra expense coverage form, except, of course, that coverage applies only when the extra expense is caused by an accident to a covered object. Coverage is limited to a stated percentage of the *limit of extra expense*, depending on the length of the period of restoration. For example, the endorsement might limit coverage to:

- 40 percent of the limit for a restoration period of less than one month,
- 70 percent of the limit for a restoration period of one to two months,
- 90 percent of the limit for a restoration period of two to three months, and
- 100 percent of the limit for a restoration period of more than three months.

A dollar deductible specified in the form is subtracted from the amount the insurer would otherwise pay.

Combined Business Interruption and Extra Expense The boiler and machinery *combined business interruption and extra expense endorsement* gives the insured one limit of coverage to apply to both business interruption and extra expense losses. This approach, which generally combines the provisions of the separate business interruption and separate extra expense endorsements, resembles that of the "commercial property" business income coverage form (BIC).

Consequential Damage Coverage Consequential damage coverage is unique to the boiler and machinery program but covers an important exposure of many organizations. The boiler and machinery *consequential damage endorsement* defines the covered exposure as follows:

"Consequential damage" means loss due to spoilage from lack of power, light, heat, steam or refrigeration resulting from an accident.

Spoilage losses can be substantial for food processors, cold storage warehouses, dairies, restaurants, meat packers, florists, greenhouses, schools, canneries, and other organizations dealing with perishable commodities or other products that might be damaged by temperature changes.

Naturally, an insured's potential loss is not necessarily related to total building or personal property values but is limited by the amount of spoilable property exposed to loss. "Specified property" is described by a manuscript entry in the endorsement, and the insuring agreement states:

We will pay you for "Consequential Damage" to "Specified Property" that is caused solely by an "accident" to an "object". . . .

A coinsurance provision reduces the insured's loss recovery proportionately if the endorsement's *limit of loss* does not equal at least the stated coinsurance percentage times the actual cash value of all specified property at the location of the accident. In other words, assuming a 25 percent coinsurance clause:

$$\left(\frac{\text{Limit of Loss}}{25\% \times \text{ACV of Specified Property}} \times \text{Loss}\right) - \text{Deductible} = \frac{\text{Most Insurer}}{\text{Will Pay}}$$

Manual rules show rating factors for coinsurance percentages of 25, 50, and 80. Choice of a coinsurance percentage should take into account the specified property's susceptibility to spoilage. Coverage is also available on a "no coinsurance" basis.

Small Business Boiler and Machinery Forms

The small business boiler and machinery forms are designed to provide the property, business interruption, and extra expense boiler and machinery coverages needed by many insureds with no processing equipment and simple, unsophisticated exposures limited to heating and cooling equipment, and air compressors. These forms are widely used. Discussion here is brief, not because the forms are unimportant, but because the most significant features of boiler and machinery insurance have already been mentioned in this chapter.

The small business forms are generally intended for groups with less significant boiler and machinery exposures, many of whom might easily overlook the need for boiler and machinery coverage. Eligibility in the ISO program is limited to apartment buildings, churches, hotels, motels, office buildings, schools, retail stores, medical buildings, garages, service stations, banks, restaurants, nursing homes, funeral homes, theaters, clubs, and similar small organizations with a replacement value of insurable property of no more than $5 million. A simple rating approach makes this form much easier to handle than the standard boiler and machinery forms.

Two small business boiler and machinery forms are available:

- *small business boiler and machinery coverage form*, and
- *small business boiler and machinery coverage broad form.*

For purposes of this discussion, we will refer to them as the "basic form" and the "broad form." The principal difference between the basic and the broad form is that the broad form may be used to cover more objects. As shown in Exhibit 6-4, the broad form contains a shorter "objects definition" that actually includes a wider range of objects. Because the broad form includes coverage on electrical equipment, it is the more likely choice for businesses that depend heavily on electrical supply.

Both forms are designed to be combined with common policy declarations and common policy conditions to form either a monoline policy or part of a commercial package policy. Unlike the regular boiler and machinery coverage form, the "small business" forms require no separate "objects definition forms" because the covered objects are defined in the coverage form itself.

The basic form covers only two types of objects:

- boilers and pressure vessels, and
- air conditioning and air compressing units.

The broad form includes protection for boilers, pressure vessels, process boilers, air conditioning, and air compressing units. The broad form can also be extended to cover consequential (spoilage) losses.

Coverage is essentially the same as that of the standard boiler and machinery coverage form. That is, the insurer agrees to pay for direct damage to covered property caused by an accident to an object indicated in the declarations. Covered property includes both property owned by the insured and property of others in the insured's care, custody, or control for which the insured is legally liable. Coverage for expediting expenses is included.

Business interruption and extra expense coverage are automatically included in both small business forms. The limit available to pay time element claims is 25 percent of the limit of insurance and will be paid *in addition to* the limit of insurance. In other words, an insured with a $100,000 limit of insurance could collect as much as $125,000 for a single accident:

- $100,000 to cover the loss to covered property, including no more than $5,000 of expediting expenses, plus

Exhibit 6-4
Small Business Boiler and Machinery Coverage Forms Object Definitions*

Basic Form

"Object" means the equipment shown in the Declarations. Full description of specific "object" categories are as follows:

a. "Object" means any of the following equipment owned or leased by you or operated under your control:

(1) Boiler and Pressure Vessels

(a) Steam heating boiler and condensate return tanks used with it;

(b) Hot water heating boiler and expansion tanks used with it;

(c) Hot water supply boiler;

(d) Other fired or unfired vessels used for maintenance or service of the premises where it is located but not used for process or manufacturing. Any unfired vessel will be considered as connected ready for use if that "object" is:

(i) Periodically filled, moved, emptied and refilled in the course of its normal service; and

(ii) Used for storage of gases or liquid;

(e) Steam heating boiler piping, valves, fittings, traps and separators, but only if they:

(i) Are on your premises or between parts of your premises;

(ii) Contain steam or condensate of steam; and

(iii) Are not part of any other vessel or apparatus.

(2) Air Conditioning Units

(a) Any air conditioning unit which has a capacity of 60,000 Btu per hour (5 hp — minimum nameplate rating) or more;

(b) Any air compressing unit that has a capacity of 15 hp (maximum nameplate rating) or less.

b. However, "object" does not mean with respect to:

(1) Boiler and Pressure Vessels

(a) Equipment that is not under internal vacuum or internal pressure other than weight of contents;

(b) Boiler setting;

(c) Insulating or refactory material;

(d) Radiator, inductor or convector;

(e) Electrical apparatus;

(f) Coil or vessel connected to or used with a refrigerating or air conditioning system; or

(g) Buried vessels or piping.

(2) Air Conditioning Units

(a) Steam boiler, steam piping or hot water boiler;

(b) Vessel, cooling tower, reservoir or other source of cooling water for a condenser or compressor, or any water piping leading to or from that source;

(c) Wiring or piping leading to or from the unit; or

(d) Electronic computer or electronic data processing equipment; or

(e) Buried vessels or piping.

Broad Form

"Object" means any of the following equipment owned or leased by you or operated under your control:

a. Any boiler;

b. Any fired or unfired vessel subject to vacuum or internal pressure other than weight of contents;

c. Any refrigerating or air conditioning system;

d. Any piping and its accessory equipment;

e. Any compressor, pump, engine, turbine, motor, generator, gear, gear set, fan or blower, including any shaft forming a part of the "object," together with any coupling, clutch, wheel or bearing on that shaft;

f. Any transformer or electrical distribution equipment; and

g. Any other mechanical or electrical equipment used for maintenance or service of the premises, but not used for processing or manufacturing.

However, "object" does not mean any:

(1) Oven, or stove or furnace;

(2) Structure, foundation or setting supporting or housing an "object;"

(3) Insulating or refractory material;

(4) Computer or data processing equipment (unless used only to control or operate another "object" covered by this Coverage Part);

(5) Equipment for communication, lighting, advertising, display, testing, experimental, research, diagnostic, therapeutic, surgical, dental, or pathological purposes;

(6) Sewer piping;

(7) Underground gas piping;

(8) Piping forming part of sprinkler system;

(9) Water piping other than boiler feed-water piping, boiler condensate return piping or water piping forming part of a refrigerating or air conditioning system used for cooling, humidifying or space heating;

(10) "Object" that is being, or has been, manufactured for sale;

(11) Vehicle, elevator, escalator, conveyor, hoist or crane; or

(12) Other mechanical or electrical equipment used for processing or manufacturing.

- another $25,000 to cover the business interruption and extra expense loss.

In the basic form, business interruption and extra expense coverage applies to air conditioning and air compressing units only if it is so indicated in the declarations. There is no coinsurance clause, percentage limitation, or other insurance-to-value provision applicable to the time element coverage.

Chapter Notes

1. Aetna Life and Casualty Commercial Lines Casualty & Surety Division, Educational Course Group II, Lesson 6, December 1967.
2. Although the initial filing has four object definitions, ISO has developed numbers five and six, which had not yet been filed at the time this text was being written. The additional definitions are expected to be very commonly used, as they were widely used in presimplified forms. The two new definitions provide a form of coverage known as "comprehensive," in lieu of coverage under a combination of object groups. "Comprehensive" definitions are manuscript definitions designed to include all object groups. "Comprehensive" coverage can be written without production machinery (Object Definition #5) or with (Object Definition #6).
3. See note 2, above.

CHAPTER 7

Crime Exposures and Controls

Most of the insurance coverages examined in previous chapters exclude or severely restrict coverage for one type of property—money and securities. Also, most of the named-perils property forms for merchandise, equipment, and other types of property do not provide coverage against any form of theft. In broad terms, these are the province of "crime" insurance.

In pure risk management terms, this characterization of "crime" creates an artificial category of loss exposures. It is obvious that money and securities can be destroyed by fire and other perils that involve no criminal action. Likewise, the loss exposures of other types of property involve a wide range of criminal and noncriminal perils. We acknowledge that insurers' "crime" category is somewhat artificial and that analysis along these artificial lines represents an overt departure from a pure risk management approach. (A pure risk management approach would ignore insurance in order to identify all types of property and perils that could cause loss. Much further along in the risk management process, insurance would be considered as one means of addressing some of the identified exposures.) However, this chapter concentrates on the set of exposures circumscribed by crime insurance, in order to set the stage for the discussion of crime insurance coverages in Chapter 8.

Crime insurance can cover *money and securities* against burglary, robbery, theft, destruction, disappearance, and employee dishonesty. Crime insurance can also cover *property other than money and securities* against loss due to specified crime perils such as burglary, robbery, theft, computer fraud, extortion, and employee dishonesty. (As might be expected, these perils are carefully defined in each policy.)

The crime exposure is highly susceptible to control, and crime control measures should always be considered, whether or not the exposure is insured. Many loss control measures (such as locks and safes) prevent crime losses by making it difficult for an outsider or an employee to steal the protected property. Other measures (such as burglar alarms and hidden cameras) are primarily loss reduction measures that increase the likelihood that a criminal will be apprehended and the stolen property recovered. Risk managers who retain crime loss exposures have a direct incentive to exercise loss control. Insurers quite often insist on loss control measures before they will provide insurance. A further incentive is the fact that insurers often grant discounts if loss control measures are used. Thus, whether crime losses are retained or insured, loss control measures play a very important role in treating the crime loss exposure.

Crime exposures are generally analyzed in two broad categories:

1. crimes committed by outsiders (the usual burglars or robbers), and
2. crimes committed by employees (such as bookkeepers embezzling money or clerks stealing merchandise).

There are many similarities between the two categories of exposures: They are subject to many of the same control measures; and they have the same result—stolen property is missing whether it was stolen by an employee, by an outsider, or by an employee in collusion with an outsider. Furthermore, when a theft obviously has been committed, it is sometimes impossible to learn whether or not it was an "inside job."

Despite the similarities and overlaps, there are distinct differences between the employee dishonesty loss exposures and other crime loss exposures. Among them, employees generally have more access to money, securities, and other property; they can more readily engage in a series of thefts over a long period of time; and there are a variety of loss control considerations unique to the employee dishonesty exposures. A less important reason for distinguishing employee dishonesty from other dishonesty lies in the fact that two distinct types of insurance coverage have evolved to meet the variations in exposures to loss.

Chapter 7 begins with a discussion of crime exposures, with emphasis on property and perils unique to crime insurance coverage. Techniques for controlling crime exposures are also examined. In both cases, the initial discussion emphasizes crimes by nonemployees. This sequence is not intended to suggest that employee dishonesty exposures are of lower priority—indeed, they usually represent the most significant exposures. Rather, this approach recognizes that most of the crimes that can be committed by nonemployees can also be committed by employees, and employees are involved in additional criminal losses, as well.

CRIME EXPOSURES THAT CAN BE TREATED BY INSURANCE

Crime exposures involve almost any type of property and a variety of perils that result in loss consequences of several kinds. Discussion under this heading explores the general nature of crime exposures and introduces some of the approaches used in commercial crime forms and the crime general provisions form. Specific crime coverages will be examined in Chapter 8.

Property Exposed to Crime Loss

Crime insurance generally covers money and securities, other personal property, and property damaged (but not stolen) by burglars or robbers. Although these are primarily on-premises exposures, some property off-premises is also exposed to losses that can be covered with crime insurance.

Money and Securities The meaning of the word "money" may seem obvious. Certainly "money" includes coins and paper currency. But does it also include coin collections? What about checks? What about the following?

- credit cards
- debit cards
- electronic fund transfer cards
- travelers checks
- money orders
- the carbon (or no-carbon-required) copies of a credit card sales slip that a merchant eventually exchanges for cash
- stamps
- stamp collections
- tokens
- vouchers

Stocks and bonds are not exactly "money," but they are certainly "securities" that may need insurance protection. To clarify these points, the *crime general provisions form* contains the following definitions:

"Money" means:
a. Currency, coins and bank notes in current use and having a face value; and
b. Travelers checks, register checks and money orders held for sale to the public.

"Securities" means negotiable and non-negotiable instruments or contracts representing either "money" or other property and includes:

a. Tokens, tickets, revenue and other stamps (whether represented by actual stamps or unused value in a meter) in current use; and

b. Evidences of debt issued in connection with credit or charge cards, which cards are not issued by you:

but does not include "money."

While this definition answers many questions, it leaves others unresolved—especially as regards numismatic (coin) collections. Is a coin collection "in current use"? And what relation does the requirement that it have a face value have to the actual value of the coin collection? Also, "money" means those types of items listed, but "securities" includes items on the list. One wonders what other items, not on the list, might also qualify as securities.

Some crime policies cover both money and securities; some cover only money; some cover only securities; some cover only a specific type of security. And some cover neither money nor securities.

Other Property Subject to Theft Many items of personal property have loss exposure characteristics similar to money. Items like diamonds or gold bullion are small, high in value, and attractive to thieves. Such items tend to receive handling similar to money and securities. When not in use, they are kept in a safe or vault or other protected location, and they are transported only under closely controlled conditions.

According to the *crime general provisions form:*

"Property other than Money and Securities" means any tangible property other than "money" and "securities" that has intrinsic value but does not include any property listed in any Coverage Form as Property Not Covered.

This description applies to property weighing several tons, as well as to property weighing less than a gram. However, limitations on the location of covered property sometimes effectively restrict coverage to small valuable items. For example, some policies cover only loss of property stolen from a designated safe. It is unlikely that such safe burglary coverage would be called upon to pay for the loss of, say, a forklift truck. Other crime insurance policies would, however, pay for the loss of large items, depending on policy provisions.

In any case, the definition clearly limits coverage to tangible property with an intrinsic value, and would not include such intangibles as ideas, formulas, or the combination to a safe. Items such as these are clearly subject to theft, even though they are not readily insurable. This observation underscores the deficiencies in any insurance-oriented approach to risk management. Even when insurance is the primary risk management technique chosen to address a set of exposures, it is important to analyze *all* policy provisions—including those not labeled as exclusions—in order to recognize those exposures that remain uninsured.

Property Damaged by Burglars or Robbers but Not Stolen Burglary involves *breaking* and entering, as well as taking. While the focus of crime insurance is on the taking of personal property, many crime insurance policies also cover damage caused by the breaking which involves damage to real or personal property. Sometimes there is only minor damage to a door frame when a door is jimmied; in other cases, there is major damage to floors, walls, safes, and vaults drilled, blown, or forced open to gain access. Fires set to cover up a burglary may also cause major building damage, but as noted later, fire loss is not covered by crime insurance.

Like burglars, robbers are not characterized by a high regard for their victims' property. Some robberies involve property damage— bullets and blood damage mirrors and carpets in real life, as well as in cowboy movies. However, property damage by robberies is rarely severe.

Even property unlikely to be stolen may be exposed to loss in either a burglary or a robbery. Crime insurance policies generally cover property damage caused by burglars and robbers (including damage to real property) but prevent overlapping coverage by excluding fire and vandalism losses.

Property Off-Premises Money, securities, and other property may be stolen when in transit whether carried by a businessowner or employee or transported by messenger service, mail, parcel service, or other means. When not literally in transit, property may be stolen from the car or residence of a businessowner, employee, or other carrier. Some property may be more or less permanently located off-premises— securities in a bank safe deposit box, for example. Separate crime insurance coverages apply to property inside the premises, property outside the premises, and property in a safe depository.

Crime Insurance Perils

The major causes of loss covered by crime insurance fall into six broad, overlapping categories:

1. *Destruction or Disappearance of Money and Securities*— Money and securities, like other property, have tangible substance (generally paper or metal) susceptible to damage by

fire and other perils; however, they may also disappear without evidence of physical destruction.

2. *Burglary*—Property can be stolen by someone who forcibly enters the place where the property is kept. Burglaries at a place of business occur outside of normal business hours. Burglaries are usually discovered *after* they have been committed.

3. *Robbery*—a "hold-up" in the broadest sense, robbery involves the use of force (or threat of force) against the person or persons from whom the property is taken. Under most circumstances, victims are immediately aware that a robbery is taking place, but are unable to halt it without increasing the likelihood of bodily harm.

4. *Theft*—A broad term, theft encompasses burglary and robbery, as well as stealing when there is no forcible entry, threat of bodily harm, or immediate awareness. Shoplifting is a type of theft.

5. *Employee Dishonesty*—In a very general sense, employee dishonesty is theft by an employee. However, employee dishonesty may be much more subtle, may take place over a much longer period of time than most thefts, and may include actions that are not truly thefts.

6. *Forgery or Alteration*—Employees or others may sign someone else's name to a document or alter the document—for example, by changing a "$100" check to a "$1,000" check.

These are general definitions. Sharper definitions are developed next, with particular attention to the ways in which insurance policies define covered causes of loss.

It should be emphasized that the insurance definitions discussed here are by no means the only definitions that are used to describe these various criminal activities. Legal definitions are found in statutes and common law and in legal dictionaries. Common everyday usage tends to be somewhat less precise and is generally reflected in English language dictionaries. A distinct sequence applies in interpreting the words in insurance contracts (and other contracts as well). Of highest importance are definitions contained in the contract. Legal definitions are secondary. Common definitions are in last place, though it must be noted that common everyday usage governs in the absence of a more stringent standard.

The insurance contract definitions discussed here will generally apply where insurance coverage is involved. Of course, in any case, the language of the specific policy in question must be considered.

Many insurance policy causes-of-loss provisions, such as those described in Chapter 4, tend to develop an insurance definition that is more restrictive than the everyday definition. For example, "smoke" in insurance contracts does not include smoke from agricultural smudging operations—even though everybody knows that the particulate matter emanating from such operations is a form of smoke. As far as crime perils are concerned, the opposite tends to be the case: Policy provisions relating to specific crime perils tend to include more causes of loss than would be expected based on the everyday meaning of the word. Watch for this as the insurance definitions of these various crime perils are analyzed in the discussion which follows.

Destruction or Disappearance of Money and Securities Some crime policies insure against *theft, disappearance, or destruction* of money and securities, subject to stated exclusions, notably an exclusion for loss by employee dishonesty. Although not actually "all-risks" in form (covered causes of loss are specified), this coverage is "all-risks" in effect. If the property has not been destroyed (*destruction*) and is still present (it has not *disappeared* or been stolen), there has been no physical loss.

The situation with *destruction or disappearance* is somewhat comparable to that of *collapse* or *glass breakage* as mentioned in earlier chapters. Although sometimes treated as perils, destruction and disappearance might more accurately be recognized as the *result* of some peril. The catch, of course, is that the other peril may not be identifiable. For example, when property has mysteriously disappeared, the proximate cause may or may not be a theft. An error in taking inventory may be involved, the item may have been misplaced, or the item may have been carried away by an animal.

An interesting quality of money and securities is that partial damage is generally impossible. In the absence of any special numismatic value or problems relating to international exchange rates, money can either be negotiated for its full face value or it is worthless. The same applies to some types of securities.

Reduction in value of money and securities does not require physical loss or damage. It can result from many other causes—such as stock market fluctuations or variations in international currency exchange rates. Reduction in value from such causes is not within the scope of crime insurance.

On the other hand, if money or securities have been stolen, burned, shredded, blown away, or just disappeared for no known reason, the loss is within the scope of destruction or disappearance coverage, barring an applicable exclusion. Naturally, such broad coverage is rather expensive. Moreover, because of the moral hazards involved, underwriters do not freely offer such broad coverage to all insureds.

Less expensive and more readily obtainable policies cover less broadly defined causes of loss, described under subsequent headings.

Burglary When burglary is covered, it is necessary to specify what must be burgled if coverage is to apply. Some policies cover only burglary from a safe or vault (*safe burglary*). Others cover against loss by burglary from within the insured's premises (*premises burglary*). Premises burglary deals basically with forcible entry into insured premises. Sometimes a thief gets around the entry problem by hiding inside a store until it is locked at night. Then, after everybody else has left, he or she selects property to steal and, from the inside, "breaks out" carrying the stolen property. Is this any less of a burglary than the loss caused by someone breaking in? Different opinions may exist, but there is no need to rely on opinion. Premises burglary policies resolve the dilemma by defining burglary in a way that specifically includes both *forcible entry* (breaking in) and *forcible exit* (breaking out). Note, however, that one or the other must be by force. If entrance occurs while the premises are open, and exit is accomplished by turning a knob or pushing a panic bar to unlock a door, the insurance definition of burglary is not met.

Note that the typical armed robbery would not be covered by burglary insurance because there is no forcible entry or exit. Neither would the typical commercial burglary coverage apply to loss of property removed from an off-premises vehicle or residence, even if the loss involves forcible entry into the vehicle or residence.

Robbery Upon returning to an unoccupied office that has been ransacked, many people, using the wrong term, exclaim: "We've been robbed!" Although not as easy to say, the correct statement would be: "Our office has been burglarized!" A robbery cannot take place when there are no people around except the crooks—at least in the sense that the term "robbery" is used in insurance policies.

In its most restrictive form, *robbery* means taking property by violence or threat of violence against a person. It is not necessary that the person actually be harmed. A mean-looking person who brandishes a gun, or even a large fist, and demands money would certainly be considered a robber.

In other situations, it may be difficult to determine whether any violence is involved. Suppose a tall, hefty lumberjack enters a store staffed by a lone clerk, grabs a chain saw from the display, and departs from the store. Suppose the clerk takes no action to prevent the lumberjack from leaving with the saw, and suppose also that the lumberjack has not actually threatened the clerk. Did a covered robbery occur? Yes, because crime policies define robbery to include any obviously unlawful act witnessed by the person who had care and custody of the property.

Unlike burglaries, which can be covered at a given location (the one that may be broken and entered), robberies may occur both at and away from the premises. Separate insuring agreements are used to insure against "robbery inside the premises" and "robbery outside the premises." Separate terms are also used in insurance policies to designate the person from whom property is taken. According to insurance contract definitions:

- A *custodian* has care and custody of insured property on premises.
- A *messenger* has care and custody of insured property off premises.

A messenger or custodian may be the insured, a partner of the insured, or an employee. In this peculiar use of terms, a janitor is *not* a "custodian." And an outside messenger service employee is not a "messenger." The insurance policy definition of "custodian" also explicitly excludes a watchperson even though *watchperson* is defined as any person retained by the insured *solely* to have care and custody of property inside the premises.

Robbery insurance does not include coverage for burglary, and vice versa. But what about the following situation which, strictly speaking, is neither a burglary nor an inside or outside robbery as defined so far? Suppose a merchant has just locked his store at night and is beginning to walk away when someone pokes a gun into his back and forces him to unlock the door or to turn over his keys. After the door is unlocked, the villain "cleans out" the store. Is this a "robbery inside the premises"? The holdup took place outside. Is it a "robbery outside the premises"? No forcible entry or exit was involved since the key was used. If the merchant had both burglary and robbery coverage, would he have suffered a loss that was not covered? Not necessarily, because crime insurance is often broad enough to cover such incidents. One way of doing this is to cover *robbery of a custodian* as a separate peril. Other policies have defined the peril of *kidnapping* to refer to this type of situation, although this usage does not reflect the common understanding of kidnapping.

A similar situation occurs when a thief gains entry to closed premises by threatening or injuring a watchperson. Remember, a "watchperson" is not a "custodian." The solution? *Robbery of a watchperson* is covered as a specified peril in some crime policies.

The peril of *extortion* is most readily illustrated by an example. The wife of an insurance company president is taken by force and held hostage until a ransom is paid by the insurance company. This is not a robbery in the usual sense, since the person who pays the ransom is not the person who is threatened with bodily harm. However, it is an example of the peril of extortion, a peril specifically covered in some crime insurance forms. Again, terminology is tricky. Although the word "kidnap" is commonly used when describing such a scenario, in the language of crime insurance "kidnapping" sometimes means robbery of a custodian, as noted above. Therefore, holding a person for ransom falls within the extortion peril for insurance purposes.

Theft The term *theft* refers to any act of stealing. Thus, theft includes burglary, robbery, and also such things as shoplifting, sneaking a typewriter out of an office when no employees are looking, removing candlesticks from an unlocked church, and tiptoeing out of a greenhouse with some valuable hybrid tulips while the guard is asleep. Theft also includes removal of property by entering premises with a key or through an unlocked door or window. Making off with property from a safe opened by manipulating the combination lock is also theft.

To control the moral hazard, insurance policies covering theft usually require the insured to provide some evidence that missing property was actually stolen, and they usually exclude coverage for mere inventory shortages. Inventory shortages may be caused by careless record keeping and other factors and are not necessarily evidence that a theft has been committed.

Employee Dishonesty Probably the most significant crime peril for most businesses is the peril of employee dishonesty. When employee dishonesty losses are mentioned, most people envision thefts of money, jewelry, securities, or other property combining high value with low bulk. While such property is a popular target of criminals, employee dishonesty may involve any kind of property. For example, a pickle manufacturer was forced into bankruptcy by several employees who, acting in collusion, stole $600,000 worth of sugar.

Employee dishonesty losses pose a particularly serious threat to employers because there is no reliable way to make an advance estimate of the maximum possible loss. There have been instances in which the total loss over a prolonged period of time exceeded the assets of the firm at any one point in time. While such instances are unusual, they do illustrate the potential severity of the employee dishonesty exposure.

Losses to a business organization from employee dishonesty can take several forms, but embezzlement is the principal cause of such losses. *Embezzlement* is a form of theft in which a person in a position of trust takes for his or her own benefit property belonging to another. Therefore, embezzlement can be perpetrated against anyone whose property may be entrusted to the custody or control of the embezzler.

Employees are in a particularly favorable position to embezzle because of their frequent and convenient access to their employer's property.

An embezzler is not necessarily an employee. Embezzlement can be perpetrated by a trustee of an estate, by a public official who has money or securities in his or her custody, or, in fact, by anyone who is in control of property belonging to someone else. However, this discussion is concerned primarily with embezzlement and other forms of dishonesty loss that may be caused by employees.

Dishonesty should be distinguished from actions that are the result of poor judgment and not of intent to appropriate property for the employee's own use. This distinction was brought out a few years ago in an Oklahoma case involving policy wording that is no longer used. An organization interested in community development set up a corporation to help increase local industry and expand the job market. The development corporation became indebted to the parent organization and eventually defaulted on loans. All of this was arranged by an employee who was later accused of dishonesty because of the loss. The court held that the employee had not been dishonest and noted that no funds had been appropriated to his own use. All of his actions, while later shown to be unwise, had been approved or ratified by the interested parties. The court pointed out that bad or unwise judgment does not constitute dishonesty if there is not intent by the person involved to profit personally. The court made the interesting observation that an attempt was made to prove the manager dishonest because of the losses, although he would have been a hero if the project had succeeded.

Who Steals from an Employer?   An attempt sometimes is made to profile the "typical" dishonest employee, but this has not been possible. An embezzling employee may be male or female, of almost any age, married or unmarried, of any level of wealth from penniless to extremely rich, and from any type of background.

The dishonest employee characteristically operates alone, although there have been cases where two or more employees were involved in a theft scheme. One study of thefts from savings and loan associations showed that only three out of seventy-five losses involved more than one person, and in none of the seventy-five cases were more than two acting in collusion. So losses involving more than one employee are relatively rare, but they do occur and the possibility must be recognized. In one such instance, members of an employer's van pool who worked in different departments but commuted in the same van jointly concocted a scheme to embezzle funds.

Motives.   The following have been cited as the five principal motives for theft by employees:

1. *Compulsive gambling.* A typical case involved a man who "borrowed" $5,000 to bet on a "sure thing" at the race track. He lost and continued to lose over a period of several years during which he embezzled several hundred thousand dollars. He covered up the thefts by manipulating the employer's accounts until an audit revealed his activities.
2. *The desire to live far beyond one's means.* The maintenance of an expensive apartment, car, mistress, or boyfriend has been the cause of embezzlement in many cases.
3. *Alcoholism and drug addiction.* The costs of the habit to be supported and the fear of losing a job, which often accompany addiction, both contribute to the decision to embezzle.
4. *The astronomical increase in health care costs.* An employee may see embezzlement as the only way to meet extremely high medical expenses.
5. *The effect of example.* Stealing by bosses has led many workers to believe that theft will be condoned. A perception develops that corporate executives make questionable use of slush funds and maintain high expense accounts at corporate expense. Lower level employees rationalize that they also deserve some "extras."

An additional reason, sometimes encountered, arises from an overactive ego. There have been cases where an embezzler has used the employer's funds for contributions to charities, church organizations, and other projects from which the embezzler did not get any personal financial benefit. The motive behind some of these embezzlements has been to enhance the embezzler's prestige and standing in the community.

Often embezzlers contend that they intended only to borrow the money and expected to pay it back. The availability of the money, and the ever-increasing amount to be paid back, prevent the embezzler from making good.

Characteristics of Employee Dishonesty Losses. In an embezzlement loss, money or any other type of property (1) is taken physically, or (2) is credited to the embezzler or someone else designated by the embezzler to receive the money or property.

Money is always an attractive target and may be pilfered in many ways. In one case, which also involved forgery, the culprit was the woman who served as secretary to a lawyer-real estate agent. The principal of the firm delegated the entire financial operation of the office to the secretary. She took checks out of the checkbook, forged the employer's signature, and deposited the checks to her own account in another bank. The employer eventually was startled to find that his bank balance was much less than he knew it should be, and an investigation revealed defalcations that ran to many thousands of dollars. While this case involved physically taking and forging the checks, many large money losses have involved manipulations of computer records.

Other property that is embezzled is usually (though not necessarily) property with high value and low volume and weight. The higher the value in relation to volume and weight, the greater the chance of property being pilfered. Another important factor is the degree of control present. Lax inventory control encourages theft of property by employees. One manufacturer and wholesale distributor found to its surprise that two of its warehouses were nearly empty. A salesman and an assistant warehouse manager had taken advantage of some weaknesses in the computer system. By using another computer, they had sent shipping instructions to the warehouses. Because the company relied on its central computer to keep shipping records, it had been unaware of its losses. Damage to property may also accompany employee dishonesty losses, just as damage to doors and windows often accompanies a burglary.

Forgery or Alteration Checks, drafts, promissory notes, "IOUs," and other demands to pay money can be forged or altered. If the instrument is converted to cash before the forgery or alteration is discovered, it may be difficult or impossible to recover the funds. If an instrument is not honored on the basis that it has been forged or altered, legal expenses may be incurred in defending that position.

Forgery or alteration may be committed by employees or outsiders. When committed by employees, it is included, for insurance purposes, within the category of employee dishonesty and is excluded from coverage in the forgery category.

Other Crime Insurance Perils In addition to those mentioned above, other causes of loss, described in the following paragraphs, are frequently covered by crime insurance. Discussion here is intended to outline the general nature of the exposures. Applicable coverages, together with relevant extensions, limitations, and options, will be discussed in Chapter 8.

Computer Fraud. Along with the growing use of computer systems has come a new opportunity for criminal loss. Many thousands of homes and offices contain all the equipment needed to gain entry into a business computer system and probe for weaknesses in its defenses. Once a weakness has been discovered, perhaps simply by guessing the right password, it may be possible to obtain and copy sensitive data or to transfer money or merchandise without leaving a record of the transaction. Sometimes even worse, stored data or programs may be erased, rendered meaningless, or subtly but significantly altered. The computer fraud peril includes theft of money, securities, and other property directly related to the use of the computer.

Liability for Property of Others. In some cases, one party is held responsible for loss to other people's money, securities, or other property. This may be the case for a hotel that is held responsible for property in guests' rooms or valuables in the safe-deposit boxes of a hotel or other organization. Money, securities, and other compact, valuable property are generally involved and the major exposure is to theft loss. Some crime insurance forms (discussed in Chapter 8) address exposures of this nature.

Crimes Covered by Other Types of Property Insurance

Conspicuous by their absence among the perils discussed thus far are vandalism and arson—both of which constitute criminal activity. Money and securities are not covered by property policies in general, but the disappearance and destruction perils noted earlier are broad enough to include fire, vandalism, and most other causes of loss to money and securities. Vandalism and arson losses to buildings and other property are usually covered by other forms of property insurance (unless it is proved that the insured conspired to cause the "loss.")

A point of potential overlap involves criminals who damage property in the course of committing a crime. Some damage usually is done by burglars in the process of forcibly entering a building or safe. Additional damage, bordering on vandalism, may be done out of meanness or spite. Even worse, thieves often set fires to cover their tracks. Crime insurance policies and other insurance policies often define covered causes of loss and/or covered property in a way intended to omit overlapping coverage. When the definitions overlap, the crime general provisions form and the commercial property conditions form preclude coverage for the same loss under more than one coverage of the same policy.

Sometimes employees damage the property of their employers for revenge or malice. This is not embezzlement (and is not covered by employee dishonesty coverage) because it does not involve conversion of the property to the personal use of the thief. However, it can be very expensive. Destructive behavior by employees is a threat in many industrial and mercantile operations, particularly where employee morale is low. Many acts of revenge or malice are done with no intent of receiving a financial benefit. One case involved an employee who disabled the computer operation whenever he wanted to take time off.

Vandalism or arson may also be committed in an attempt to cover up an employee's theft on the premises. It is often impossible to distinguish arson or vandalism by outsiders from that perpetrated by employees.

Consequences of Crime Losses in General

Crimes against property involve not only loss of the property taken or a reduction in value of damaged property but other consequences as well.

Loss or Reduction in Value of the Property Taken or Damaged The obvious consequence of a crime is the direct loss of the property that is taken. Ownership rights might remain, but unless stolen property can be recovered and identified, its absence effectively reduces the value of the ownership rights to zero.

Stolen property generally consists of money or other tangible property, although industrial espionage may involve the theft of ideas, formulas, or information. (Only tangible property is insured.)

The value of lost money is easily measured, provided business records permit ready calculation of the amount stolen. This may not be possible under circumstances where a day's receipts are stolen before they can be counted, as, for example, when the offering is stolen from a church. Securities of some types have a fluctuating value that makes loss valuation particularly difficult.

Damage to Other Property In addition to the value of the property that is taken, other property loss often results from a crime. The breaking and entering by a burglar usually causes some damage to the premises. A frequent type of crime is the smash-and-run theft from show windows. The object of such a theft usually is a high-value item in the show window, but the value of the smashed window sometimes exceeds the value of any property that is taken.

A successful safe burglary almost always results in serious damage to the safe. In many cases, the safe is so badly damaged that it is no longer useful for securing valuable property. On occasion, the entire safe is taken by the crooks. The building containing the safe, as well as fixtures adjacent to the safe, may be damaged if a safe is opened with the aid of explosives.

As noted earlier, some criminals express their resentment to society or to a business organization by vandalizing the premises in addition to taking property. Thus, both crime perils and the vandalism peril may be involved in a single incident. Another serious type of damage that may accompany a burglary involves a fire set in an effort (sometimes successful) to conceal the crime. The resulting arson loss may involve only a portion of the premises, contents, or stock—or it may ultimately involve destruction of the entire property.

Business Interruption One of the most important consequences of some crimes is the loss from disruption of business. A store that handles high-value merchandise, such as jewelry, may have a substantial portion of its stock taken in a burglary and may lose sales until the stock can be replenished. The profit that would have been made on the lost sales constitutes an important part of the loss to the business. Depending on the nature of the stock and the length of time required for replacement, a business could lose its entire trade to competitors for a time. Tools or equipment taken may be difficult or impossible to replace, necessitating a cutback or cessation of all or part of a manufacturing or service business.

A burglary or robbery almost always interferes with normal operations. Employees may spend a considerable amount of time in answering the questions of police. They will also be involved in determining the amount and nature of the property taken for purposes of preparing insurance claims.

Crime insurance forms do little to cover business income losses. However, commercial property business income coverage on an "all-risks" (special causes of loss) basis would cover some of the losses just described. Also, except for the effect of market fluctuations, there is little "time element" with money and securities losses.

Unfavorable Publicity Loss of business may also result from unfavorable publicity from crime. Repeated robberies during business hours may frighten customers away and make it difficult to hire new employees.

Lowered Morale An important indirect cost is the effect upon employee morale when an embezzlement is discovered. Discovery of an embezzlement perpetrated by a top official of an organization may cause other employees to feel that theft is acceptable. The discovery that one lower-echelon employee was stealing from the company may cause other employees to feel that they could get away with a similar theft if they were more careful. Even when incidents like these do not lead other employees to steal, they can have a demoralizing effect.

Consequences of Employee Dishonesty Losses

For most organizations, the most significant crime exposure involves loss by employee dishonesty. Thefts committed by employees are behind at least 60 percent of crime-related losses.[1] The yearly cost of embezzlement and employee pilferage reportedly exceeds by several billion dollars the losses sustained from burglary and robbery throughout the nation.[2] While the most frequent employee thefts involve petty pilferage that can be absorbed as a business expense, the exposure is not properly characterized as "low severity." Losses often involve sums that exceed the employer's ability to absorb. In fact, employee theft and embezzlement are considered to be the direct cause of 30 to 40 percent of all business failures.[3]

Given an exposure of this importance, one might suppose that coverage against such losses would be purchased by all by the smallest organizations. However, fewer than 25 percent of mercantile establishments protect themselves with fidelity coverage. Failure to obtain such protection is concentrated primarily in nonfinancial organizations; most financial institutions are covered.[4] And, while annual employee dishonesty losses are in the billions, annual claims payments under these coverages have been running only a little in excess of $100 million per year.

While the above information is a bit shocking, it underscores the importance of this topic in any discussion of crime exposures. The employee dishonesty exposure is much more significant than many risk managers realize. In fact, the exposure is often unidentified or underevaluated. For these reasons, the employee dishonesty exposure deserves special attention.

Several "rule-of-thumb" formulas have been devised to guide business organizations in estimating their probable or possible losses. Unfortunately, these formulas do not give much help to smaller business organizations, and they are indicative only of the exposure of a large organization with no unusual characteristics.

The factors taken into account in estimating the exposure to embezzlement loss are generally:

1. the firm's assets,
2. current inventory of physical goods on hand,
3. the annual income or gross sales of the organization,
4. the nature of the business and the nature of the product or goods handled,
5. the size of the organization (determined in various ways), and
6. the number of employees.

The current assets of the organization are perhaps the most important indication of exposure. Current assets include cash, bank deposits, securities, accounts receivable, and inventory. Everything else being equal, the larger the current assets, the greater the exposure.

Ordinary bookkeeping audits are not the tool for uncovering embezzlement and fraud. Auditing firms generally do not claim an ability to detect embezzlement. Many auditing firms require their clients to acknowledge that the audit is merely a check of bookkeeping procedures and of assets on hand.

TECHNIQUES FOR CONTROLLING CRIME LOSS EXPOSURES

In most cases, the probable severity of a crime loss is less than that from other property exposures. A fire may destroy an entire building and its contents, but a thief is likely to steal only a small percentage of the total contents. Likewise, theft of cash in any one occurrence is limited to the amount of cash on hand. (This suggests some obvious avoidance or loss reduction measures: Eliminate or limit the cash!) Despite the lower severity of crime exposures, the overall frequency of crime loss may be greater than the frequency of fire losses (which suggests that loss prevention can be very useful).

Avoidance

Some crime exposures can be avoided, thus eliminating any possibility of loss. For example, if no furs are carried in inventory by a clothier, there is no exposure to burglary of fur garments while the premises are closed—that specific exposure has been avoided. And if no employees are hired, none will be dishonest.

When one specific exposure is avoided, it is important to recognize that other exposures still exist and may even become more serious. For example, if money is removed from the premises overnight, that does not avoid crime exposures due to theft of money during business hours. Moreover, this measure requires that a messenger will take money to a bank or residence every night at closing time—a practice that may increase the possibility of "outside robbery." Likewise, if *independent contractors* are used instead of *employees*, perhaps it is technically possible to avoid the employee dishonesty exposure—but the practical effect will usually be to increase the probability of theft by nonemployees.

Loss Control

Protective measures against crime loss may be divided roughly into five groups:

1. physical protection to premises in order to delay access by the criminal;

2. installation of alarm systems and other devices or the use of guards or security patrols that will indicate when access to the premises has been gained by an outsider;
3. use of automatic cameras or closed circuit television systems to help identify criminals in order to facilitate their arrest and conviction;
4. various protective *procedures,* including procedures for handling money and securities that will reduce the likelihood of theft or reduce the amount of property accessible to a thief; and
5. management and personnel measures directed specifically toward the employee dishonesty exposure, e.g., the use of polygraph tests.

Physical Protection A businessowner can install passive restraints to entry. The type of lock used on doorways can make a difference of several minutes in the entry time needed by a thief. The ordinary snap lock can be manipulated in a matter of seconds. A deadbolt lock cannot be manipulated in the same way as a snap lock, but usually requires the picking of the tumblers or the use of force. Lockpicking requires tools and skills that many ordinary burglars do not possess.

The rear doors in a store or office can be barred from the inside so that access is difficult. Bars, gates, and grills can be put across windows or doorways. An "unbreakable" glazing material can be used for doors or windows where the proprietor wishes to maintain a clearly visible window display. (It is worth noting that any measure that impedes entry or exit by burglars may also serve to impede entry by firefighters or emergency exit by members of the public.)

Many burglaries involve breaking a show window and grabbing valuable items. Ordinary plate glass is easily broken. Varieties of breakage-resistant glass and plastic materials often improve protection, particularly for smaller windows. In jewelry display windows, another device effectively impedes the access of a burglar to a show window display. This is a sheet of breakage-resistant glass suspended behind the show window glass. This second sheet is hung on chains from the top of the show window so that it swings backward when struck. The show window can be broken but this second sheet of glass is difficult to break—because of its composition and, particularly, because it swings. It is difficult for a thief to reach around such a glass when it is properly installed.

The installation of good locks, gates, bars, breakage-resistant glass, and similar devices may provide satisfactory protection for mercantile stocks of low value. This may be particularly true if the premises are under frequent surveillance by police and in a low crime area. However, such passive restraints merely delay the entrance of a burglar and do not guarantee that a burglary will not occur. The adequacy of such measures also must be considered in light of the values involved and whether small volume and weight plus high value would make the merchandise attractive to a burglar.

Safes are another type of physical protective device. Safes vary in their vulnerability to burglary. Many safes are basically fire protection devices, referred to as *record safes*, and offer little resistance to the burglar. Designed to protect money and valuable records from fire damage, *fire resistive safes* generally have square doors, and are mounted on wheels.

Money safes are designed to be burglar resistive. Money safes generally have round doors and are not mounted on wheels (However, some modern money safes have been designed with square doors to facilitate their use with cash register trays.)

Within each category, the safes offer degrees of resistance to fire and/or burglary. Exhibit 7-1 lists the classifications used in rating some crime policies and will give some idea of the different degrees of protection afforded by the various types of safes.

Safes can be most readily classified by reference to the *Underwriters Laboratories label* found inside the door of most quality safes. (In older safes the label was located on the outside of the door, but it is now deemed undesirable to tell burglars how much difficulty they might have.) One safe label is shown in Exhibit 7-2.

Safes, like other physical protective devices, do not eliminate the possibility of a loss. However, they reduce the likelihood of loss in proportion to the quality of the safe and the skill of the thief.

Alarm Systems   Unlike some physical protection devices, alarm systems do not prevent the entry of a burglar. Except to the extent that they serve as a deterrent, the function of an alarm system is to indicate when an intruder has entered the premises.

Some alarm systems use simple electrical circuits that give an alarm when an electrical connection is made or broken, depending on the nature of the system. Other systems use more sophisticated electronic devices. These may give alarms when a foreign object, such as the body of a burglar, is present within the premises. Some use invisible light rays which, when broken, give an alarm signal. The principal varieties of these devices will be described here.

A simple alarm system consists of electrical contacts or metal tapes on each door, window, or other opening into the building. Usually, the system is wired so that an electrical current is passing through the system constantly. Opening a door or window interrupts the electrical current, which activates an alarm system. This is a *perimeter system;*

Exhibit 7-1
Safe and Vault Classification*

Safe, Chest, Cabinet or Vault Classification	Doors	CONSTRUCTION WALLS	
		Safe, Chest or Cabinet	Vault
B (Fire-resistive)	Steel less than 1" thick, or iron	Body of steel less than ½" thick, or iron	Brick, concrete, stone, tile, iron or steel
	Any iron or steel safe or chest having a slot through which money can be deposited		Not Applicable
C (Burglar-resistive)	Steel at least 1" thick	Body of steel at least ½" thick	Steel at least ½" thick; or reinforced concrete or stone at least 9" thick, or non-reinforced concrete or stone at least 12" thick
	Safe or chest bearing following label: "Underwriters' Laboratories, Inc. Inspected Keylocked Safe KL Burglary"		Not Applicable
E (Burglar-resistive)	Steel at least 1½" thick	Body of steel at least 1" thick	Same as for C
ER (Burglar-resistive)	Safe or chest bearing the following label: "Underwriters' Laboratories, Inc., Inspected Tool Resisting Safe TL-15 Burglary"		Not Applicable
F (Burglar-resistive)	Safe or chest bearing one of the following labels: 1. "Underwriters' Laboratories, Inc. Inspected Tool Resisting Safe TL-30 Burglary" 2. "Underwriters' Laboratories, Inc. Inspected Torch Resisting Safe TR-30 Burglary" 3. "Underwriters' Laboratories, Inc. Inspected Explosive Resisting Safe with Relocking Device X-60 Burglary"		Not Applicable

Class			
G (Burglar-resistive)	One or more steel doors (one in front of the other) each at least 1½" thick and aggregating at least 3" thickness	Not Applicable	Steel at least ½" thick; or reinforced concrete or stone at least 12" thick; or non-reinforced concrete or stone at least 18" thick
H (Burglar-resistive)		Safe or chest bearing one of the following labels: 1. "Underwriters' Laboratories, Inc. Inspected Torch and Explosive Resisting Safe TX-60 Burglary" 2. "Underwriters' Laboratories, Inc. Inspected Torch Resisting Safe TR-60 Burglary" 3. "Underwriters' Laboratories, Inc. Inspected Torch and Tool Resisting Safe TRTL-30 Burglary"	Not Applicable
I (Burglar-resistive)		Safe or chest bearing one of the following labels: 1. "Underwriters' Laboratories, Inc. Inspected Torch and Tool Resisting Safe TRTL-60 Burglary" 2. "Underwriters' Laboratories, Inc. Inspected Torch, Explosive and Tool Resisting Safe TXTL-60 Burglary"	Not Applicable
J (Burglar-resistive)		Safe or chest bearing the following label: "Underwriters' Laboratories, Inc. Inspected Torch and Tool Resisting Safe TRTL-30×6 Burglary"	Not Applicable
K (Burglar-resistive)		Safe or chest bearing one of the following labels: 1. "Underwriters' Laboratories, Inc. Inspected Torch and Tool Resisting Safe TRTL-60 Burglary" 2. "Underwriters' Laboratories, Inc. Inspected Torch Explosive and Tool Resisting Safe TXTL-60 Burglary"	Not Applicable
Vaults meeting these specifications or better.	Steel at least 3½" thick		Steel at least 1" thick or 18" of reinforced concrete or 36" of non-reinforced concrete

Exhibit 7-2
Underwriters Laboratories, Inc., Safe Label*

*Reprinted with permission from Mosler, Inc., Hamilton, OH.

the intent is to give an alarm whenever entry is made into the building through a door, a window, or other opening that is protected by the system.

A perimeter system protecting all doors, windows, and other openings still gives no protection against entry through a roof or a wall. A more complete system will be activated if entry is made through a roof or wall. This may require the installation of wires or other devices that protect the areas of wall or roof accessible from neighboring buildings. Various sensing devices are illustrated in Exhibit 7-3. Sensing devices usually are connected to either local or central station alarms.

Alarms are not limited to burglary prevention. Alarm systems may also be used to reduce the robbery exposure. Holdup buttons or foot pedals may be situated so they can be triggered by a bank teller or store clerk, sending a "silent alarm" to a central station company or to the police. (The "silent" alarm is silent at the location being robbed.) If rapid response is possible, the police may arrive while a robber is still on the premises.

Local Alarms. Many simple alarm systems are connected to an interior gong or alarm and also to a gong on the outside of the premises. An interior alarm system may be effective in a store with security personnel on duty at all times, and where the alarm system would alert such security personnel to entry by a burglar. However, the outside alarm may be almost completely useless in an industrial or mercantile district where few people are present during the night. The local alarms often ring for hours before anyone pays any attention to them. Sometimes neighbors call the police only because the noise eventually interferes with their sleep. In the meantime, the burglars have left with the stolen goods.

Central Station Alarms. A more effective type of alarm system is connected directly to a central station of an alarm company. The central

Exhibit 7-3
Burglar Alarm System Design*

Door Switches (Contacts) These devices are usually magnet-operated switches. They are affixed to a door or window in such a way that opening the door or window removes the magnetic field. This, in turn, activates the switch causing an alarm.

These devices may be surface-mounted or recessed, exposed or concealed. A variety of switches exists for every kind of door or window and for all levels of security.

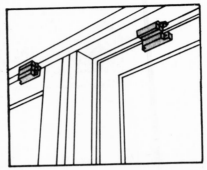

Metallic Foil (Window Tape) Metallic foil is the traditional means for detecting glass-breakage. Strips of thin foil are affixed to a glass surface. Breaking glass ruptures the foil and interrupts the detection circuit to signal an alarm.

Thin foil, however, is easily damaged by people or objects accidentally touching the glass surface. Also, bonds at the corners and between multiple-foil strips deteriorate with time. Metallic foil, therefore, requires frequent maintenance, especially on glass doors.

Wooden Screens Openings such as air-duct passages and skylights can provide paths for an intruder. These can be secured by a cage-like frame of wooden rods. An intruder breaks the wire embedded within the frame which triggers an alarm.

Wood screens are custom-built for each application. They can be mounted permanently or removed when the alarm system is turned

Continued on next page

off. Wooden screens require little maintenance. They are suitable for protecting openings where aesthetics are not important.

Lacing (Paneling) Lacing can protect walls, doors and safes against penetration. Lacing is a closely woven pattern of metallic foil or fine brittle wire on the surface of the protected area. An intruder can enter only by breaking the foil or wire. This activates the alarm. A panel over the lacing protects it from accidental damage.

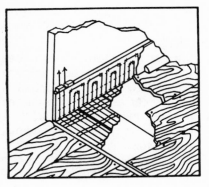

Photoelectric (Eyes, Beams) Photoelectric devices transmit a beam across a protected area. When an intruder interrupts this beam, the photoelectric circuit is disrupted. This starts an alarm.

Modern photoelectric devices are a great improvement over their predecessors. Today's photoelectric devices use diodes that emit infrared light. These make the beam invisible to the naked eye. The beam usually pulses rapidly to prevent compromise by substitution.

Photoelectric devices are effective and reliable. Some have ranges of more than 1,000 feet for large buildings and hallways. These devices provide excellent protection for relatively low-risk areas.

Ultrasonic Detectors These devices also sense movement. Ultrasonic means "above the range of hearing." An intruder disrupting the ultrasonic wave pattern initiates the alarm.

Ultrasonic devices can be mounted on the ceiling or wall. They protect three-dimensional areas with an invisible pattern. However, they are

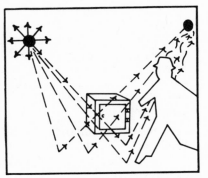

Continued on next page

prone to false alarms, due to excessive air currents or ultrasonic noises from mechanical equipment. Again, proper application is important.

Infrared Detectors These devices are part of the motion-detection group. They sense the body heat of an intruder as he or she passes through the protected area. A change from the area's normal heat profile triggers an alarm. Infrared detectors are relatively free of false alarms. They provide relatively inexpensive protection for confined areas.

Microwave Detectors This kind of motion detector uses high-frequency radio waves, or microwaves, to detect movement. Microwave devices have greater range than ultrasonic. Since microwave devices do not use sound, or air, they are not prone to false alarms from air currents. However, they can cause false alarms, because they penetrate materials such as glass, and metal objects reflect them. This means microwaves can detect motion outside the protected area if the detectors are not properly installed.

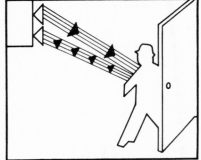

Object Protection

Object protection provides direct security for individual items. It often is the final stage of an in-depth protection system with perimeter and area-protection devices. The objects most frequently protected are safes, filing cabinets, display cabinets, models and expensive equipment.

Proximity (Capacitance or Electrostatic) With this system, the object itself becomes an antenna, electronically linked to the alarm

Continued on next page

control. When a person approaches or touches the object, its electrostatic field becomes unbalanced. This initiates the alarm. Only metal objects isolated from the ground can be protected this way.

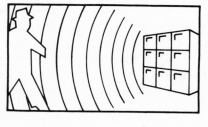

Vibration Detectors (Seismic) These sensing devices use a highly sensitive piezoelectric crystal or microphone to detect the sound pattern that a hammer-like impact on a rigid surface would generate. These devices are attached directly to safes and filing cabinets or walls and floors.

The devices instantly detect a vibration an intruder makes. Some vibration detectors are adjustable. They can be adjusted to detect a sledge-hammer attack on concrete or the delicate penetration of a glass surface.

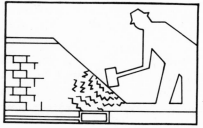

This kind of protection generally is for securing the perimeter surfaces of a vault. The correct number, spacing and location of these sensors is important for suitable detection.

*Reprinted with permission from *Alarm Handbook for the Security Manager,* Honeywell, Inc. 1984, pp. 8-11.

station of an alarm company is monitored at all hours. Electrical or electronic monitoring of all circuits is performed from the central station. An alarm to the central station usually results in an alarm company guard being sent to the premises, and also a notification to police that an alarm has been received from those premises.

Selection of Alarm Systems. Alarm systems vary as to their quality and extent of protection. Insurance rate manuals generally give credits only for *approved alarm systems.* An approved system is one installed by an approved burglar alarm company named in the rating manual. Underwriters Laboratories, Inc., issues alarm certificates which indicate the grade, type, and extent of the alarm system, and these certificates are considered in granting insurance rate credits. An Underwriters Laboratories certificate is shown in Exhibit 7-4. No matter how expensive, an alarm system without a U.L. certificate may receive no premium reduction, a fact too often discovered only after money has been spent on an alarm.

Burglar alarms should not be confused with fire alarms. Each type of alarm is designed to accomplish a different purpose. A fire hose is not much more effective against a burglar than an armed police officer is against a fire.

Deficiencies of Alarm Systems. There are many problems with burglar alarm systems. One of the most difficult problems is false alarms caused by accidental triggering. One survey indicated that more than half of the major police emergency calls in a large city were actually false alarms. As a result, police in some cities assign a low priority to calls that come in from burglar alarm systems.

Another deficiency is that an alarm system does not stop burglaries from occurring—it merely shortens the burglar's operating time. There is always a delay of five to fifteen minutes or more from the time an alarm is given until a guard or police officer can reach the premises. This may be enough time for the burglars to complete their work. The response time is a vital consideration in determining whether the expense of a sophisticated burglary or robbery alarm system is worthwhile.

Central station contracts with merchants ordinarily require that the central station guard remain on the premises for up to two hours after the alarm has been received in order to give the proprietor time to arrive and arrange for securing the premises. There have been cases where the proprietor failed to arrive within the specified two hours and the alarm company left the premises at the end of the two-hour period, after which burglars re-entered the premises at leisure and made off with the property they originally intended to steal.

One alarm device for use where a central station service is not available is an automatic device that dials the police telephone number and transmits a recorded message to the police department when the alarm is activated. Such a system can be arranged to send a robbery alarm when a button is pushed, or it can be arranged to indicate a burglary when the premises are entered. Unfortunately, there are ways to deactivate such a system by placing other telephone calls from nearby phones or by disconnecting the telephone lines. In fact, a major problem is that telephone circuits generally are used to transmit signals from the premises to the central station or police department. A sophisticated burglar may be familiar enough with telephone lines in general that the security can be breached at some point where the lines are accessible. This may be in the basement of a multiple-occupancy

Exhibit 7-4
Underwriters Laboratories, Inc., Certificate*

CENTRAL STATION BURGLAR ALARM CERTIFICATE   No. **BC** 1031954

UNDERWRITERS LABORATORIES INC.
333 PFINGSTEN ROAD · NORTHBROOK, ILLINOIS 60062   ®

an independent, not-for-profit organization testing for public safety

_____ Property Name and Address _____

File No._____ Service Loc. No. _____

System Grade	Type of System	Extent of Protection

System Grade:
☐ A ☐ AA
☐ B ☐ BB
☐ C ☐ CC

Type of System:
☐ Premises
☐ Stockroom
- - - - - - - -
☐ Safe
☐ Vault
☐ Night Depository
☐ Automated Teller Machine

Extent of Protection:
☐ Extent 1
☐ Extent 2
☐ Extent 3
- - - - - -
☐ Partial
☐ Complete

THIS CERTIFIES that the Alarm Service Company Whose Name Appears Hereon is included by Underwriters Laboratories Inc. in its Directory as furnishing the burglar alarm system described hereon and is authorized to issue this certificate for the equipment described hereon as its representation that such equipment and all connected wiring and devices is in compliance with requirements established by Underwriters Laboratories Inc. This certificate does not apply in any way to the installation of any additional alerting systems, such as; fire, smoke, holdup, or otherwise, that may be connected to or installed along with the burglar alarm system described hereon.

Alarm Transmission To Central Station

☐ Derived Channel   ☐ Digital Communicator
☐ Direct Wire   ☐ McCulloh
☐ Multiplex   ☐ Radio

LIMITATION OF LIABILITY Underwriters Laboratories Inc. makes no representations or warranties, express or implied, that the alarm system will prevent any loss by burglary, hold-up or otherwise, or that the system will in all cases provide the protection for which it is installed or intended. This certificate only evidences that UL conducts countercheck field inspections of representative installations of the alarm service company. UL does not assume or undertake to discharge any liability of the alarm service company or any other party. UL is not an insurer and assumes no liability for any loss which may result from failure of the equipment, incorrect certification, non-conformity with requirements, cancellation of the certificate or withdrawal of the alarm service company from inclusion in UL's Directory prior to the expiration date appearing on this certificate. If an installation is found not in conformity with requirements, it shall be corrected by the alarm service company or the certificate is subject to cancellation.

Keys	Bell	Response Time Category

Keys:
☐ Yes
☐ No

Bell:
☐ Yes
☐ No

Response Time Category:
☐ 15 min.
☐ 20 min.
☐ 30 min.

Issued Date _____

Expiration Date_____
    (Not to be Issued for a Term of More than 5 Years)

[ ] New Certificate
[ ] Renewal

Alarm Service Company _____

By _____
           Authorized Signature

Central Station Location_____
                              (City, State)

The undersigned, representing the property named in this Certificate acknowledges he has read and understands the terms and conditions of this certificate.

Representative of Property Named Above

_____

_____
Authorized Signature

Dated _____, 19 __

CERTIFICATE HOLDER COPY

*Reprinted with permission from *The Alarm Handbook for the Security Manager,* Honeywell, Inc.

building, in the overhead lines, or in a telephone line on a pole or box outside the building.

An alarm system may have what is called a shunt switch, which gives the store operator a few seconds to get out of the store when the premises are closed for the night, or get into the store upon entering in the morning, without giving an alarm. This is particulary likely in the case of a local alarm where the proprietor does not wish to activate the outside gong when leaving or entering the premises. It is a simple matter for the sophisticated burglar to determine in advance exactly what the proprietor does in using the shunt switch. The burglar then does the same thing.

Watchman or Security Patrols Many organizations find it worthwhile to maintain watchman service on the premises. A watchman goes through the building at periodic intervals (typically hourly) to see that everything is in good order. This, of course, protects against fire and, to a degree, against other catastrophes such as burglary. It is considered necessary to use some device to make certain that the watchman does patrol at the required intervals. One frequently used system uses a special clock carried by the watchman that records the visits to stations throughout the building. A key is fastened to each location, and inserting the key into the special clock records the time when the watchman visited that particular station. By checking the records, the employer can be sure the watchman completed all rounds. The weakness of this system is that when a watchman is overpowered during the night, no one knows about it until the premises are reopened the next morning. The presence of the watchman is a deterrent as far as burglars are concerned, but it by no means eliminates loss possibilities.

Central station alarm companies also maintain a *supervised system* under which the watchman signals to the central station upon visiting each station throughout the premises. These systems are arranged so that a guard is sent to the premises by the central station alarm company if the watchman at the premises fails to signal as required. Sometimes burglars or robbers will force a watchman to continue making rounds while a theft is being carried out. Most signaling systems contain an arrangement whereby the watchman can secretly signal for help even while making rounds under the burglar's scrutiny.

Large organizations may contain a complete security system with a central station on the premises for the supervision of one or more watchmen. The expense of such a system to protect against crimes would be justified only if large values were involved or if the supervision of watchmen were needed for other reasons.

Surveillance Cameras   Banks and other firms with high robbery exposure frequently install automatic cameras to photograph criminals in the process of committing a crime. Such installations are effective in two ways:

1. They facilitate the identification and conviction of criminals after the offense has been committed, making the offenders unavailable for future offenses, at least for a short time.
2. The increased probability of identification and conviction discourages robbery.

Protective Procedures   A property owner can institute many procedures in addition to using the devices just described. One simple procedure used by many merchants is to have the safe or other particularly valuable property located where it can be observed by police patrols from outside the building. A light is installed to keep the inside of the premises illuminated.

Another common procedure is for some businesses to accept only credit cards and/or exact change and to immediately deposit all money into a burglar-resistant safe, making deposits through a one-way slot or chute. Robbers tend to "hit" isolated businesses with large amounts of money or "stealable" property and limited personnel. Steps that reduce isolation, reduce the amount of money or other attractive property on hand, and increase the number of people on duty tend to reduce the likelihood of a robbery.

Controlling the Employee Dishonesty Exposure   Other loss control measures directly address the employee dishonesty exposure, and should be used by every organization with employees.

- *Loss prevention* measures decrease the probability that an employee theft will be committed.
- *Loss reduction* measures reduce probable loss severity by increasing the probability that employee thefts will be discovered or by limiting the amount that can be taken without discovery.

The lines of demarcation are not rigid, and some measures serve both to prevent and to reduce losses. For example, an employee who is aware that any theft will probably be discovered quickly is less likely to attempt a theft. Therefore, measures that reduce severity often present a threat that also helps to prevent losses.

Exhibit 7-5 presents one method of categorizing internal theft prevention systems. The top half of the chart depicts measures that increase the probability of quick discovery. These are labeled "low trust measures," because they are based on the assumption that it is not wise to trust all employees fully. However, which employees should not be fully trusted cannot be determined in advance.

- Stringent *accounting controls*, to keep track of cash flows and detect any improprieties, limit loss caused by manipulating a firm's records. Examples of such controls include internal auditing, patrolling, observing, leaving audit trails, and enforcing the use of standardized procedures.
- Stringent *access controls* reduce losses of merchandise and other property (including currency and coins, confidential documents, and trade secrets) by limiting access to target property to a limited number of key employees. For extremely valuable property and information, locked entrances, armed guards, and identification badges may be among the devices used to limit access. Keys and safe combinations are usually given to only a limited number of employees. Authority to sign checks, purchase orders, and contracts is given to only selected employees who cannot operate without this access.

Following this philosophy, employee theft can best be controlled by assuming nobody is to be trusted and then setting up a system that is very hard to beat. This is the traditional approach to controlling the employee dishonesty exposure, and there is much to recommend it.

Yet, it appears that some organizations with tight controls experience high theft rates, while others in an environment with loose controls have few problems. Why this paradox? Jack Bologna suggests that there are practical limits on the effectiveness of conventional accounting and access controls.[5] Cost is a major constraint, especially when one considers the cost of "watchers" and the added cost of people to "watch the watchers." Bologna also suggests that a "police state mentality" among employees may, in fact, invite theft by way of retaliation.

According to a different management theory, a high level of trust between the laboring and managerial employee groups reduces the need for accounting and access controls. An environment built on trust and ethical behavior is less conducive to dishonesty than an environment that assumes employees will steal if given half a chance.

Unfortunately, a favorable environment does not remove all dishonesty. Therefore, control measures are still needed for those who do not respond to the good attitudes around them. These are the measures previously discussed.

Personnel Screening. Motivation, leadership, and management controls are dealt with in a much broader context in CPCU 7— Management. However, one management strategy is so important that

Exhibit 7-5
An Internal Theft Prevention System*

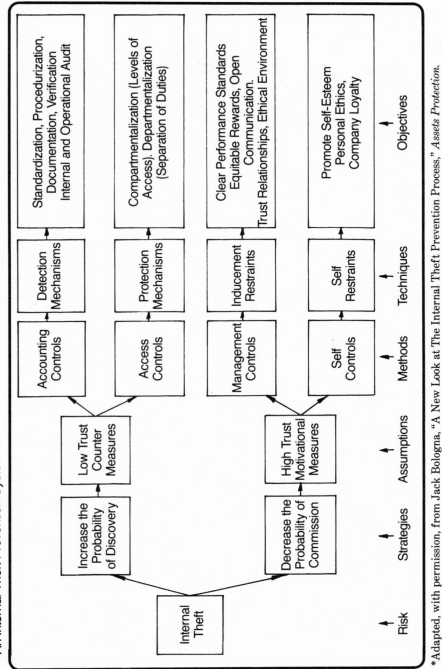

*Adapted, with permission, from Jack Bologna, "A New Look at The Internal Theft Prevention Process," *Assets Protection.* Sept./Oct. 1980, 33.

it will be emphasized here—proper personnel screening decreases the probability of employee theft, because employees who are likely to steal are not hired if they are screened out. Separation of duties is another important strategy in many programs to control employee theft. An additional strategy suggests the use of particular types of employee benefit programs to reduce incentives to steal caused by employee hardship. And, of course, the measures that serve to control theft by outsiders also tend to control employee thefts.

One of the objectives of personnel screening is to prevent employee dishonesty losses by not employing dishonest people. How can this be done? A key ingredient is gathering information about job applicants and checking references before hiring. In order to be effective, information regarding a prospective employee's background should be supplied by sources other than the applicant. Although there are many legal restrictions on hiring practices, these restrictions do not prohibit the use of background investigations.[6]

Separation of Duties. The majority of employee thefts involve one employee acting alone. Proper separation of duties makes it difficult for any one employee to steal (or to steal a great deal) without the collaboration or cooperation of at least one other employee.

The handbook on *White Collar Crime* describes this approach and also illustrates the practical limitations on controls.

1. No individual should have total control over every phase of any significant transaction or sensitive job. (For example, those who maintain inventory records do not participate in physical counts of inventory.)
2. Work flows should proceed from one person to another so that, without duplication, the work of the second acts as a check upon that of the first. (Merchandise for shipment is picked by one employee, taken to the loading dock by another, and checked onto a truck by a third—all of whose tallies should agree.)
3. Those who authorize the use of assets should not also be responsible for their custody. (The inventory clerk releases materials only upon receipt of an authorization from a department head.)
4. Record keeping and bookkeeping activities should be separated from the handling and custody of assets. (The accounts receivable clerk should not also open mail containing incoming payments.)

If a business is so small that there are not enough employees among whom to divide responsibilities in a manner that would otherwise be desirable, job rotation might be considered. Or assignment of dual responsibility for a given task could achieve the same purpose.

As with any control, the application of separation-of-duties could be carried to such lengths that it creates a counterproductive atmosphere of mutual distrust among employees or generates such a labyrinth of procedural red tape that various informal shortcuts are devised over which no controls exist.[7]

Employee Benefit Programs. At first glance, there may seem to be little relationship between employee thefts and employee benefits (except, perhaps, that the undetected thief receives unintended benefits). Recall, however, that one prominent motive for embezzlement is "the astronomical increase in health care costs." Employees sometimes steal in order to pay for essential medical treatment for themselves or their loved ones. When the employer provides a sound group health insurance program for employees and their dependents, this motive is substantially reduced.

Noninsurance Transfers

Organizations that handle large quantities of money or securities may arrange for frequent deposits at a bank in order to keep the amount of money or securities at a minimum. This results in a smaller value on the premises at any one time and also means that messengers carrying property to the bank carry smaller quantities. While these are loss reduction effects, there is also a noninsurance transfer, because most exposures are transferred to the bank once the bank obtains custody of the deposited money.

Another procedure followed by many organizations is to transport money and securities by an armored car messenger service. In such situations, when money, securities, or other valuable property are entrusted to another entity who assumes responsibility for its safekeeping, a portion of the crime exposure is transferred along with custody of the property.

The use of an outside security service or alarm company may provide some recourse if a guard, watchman, or alarm system fails to perform properly. The extent of the transfer depends in part on provisions in the contract with the service company. Generally, alarm companies use noninsurance transfers to protect themselves by requiring their customers to waive any claim against the alarm company.

There are limitations on the use of noninsurance transfers as a method of controlling employee dishonesty. If some operations are transferred to another entity, the other entity's employees may steal. However, such a transfer might still be desirable if the transferee is in the better position to exercise control.

Noninsurance transfers can be effective in some instances. For example, by depositing cash in a bank, an organization transfers to the bank responsibility for some losses of that cash. If employees of the bank steal the cash, or if the bank is robbed or burglarized, the bank will generally bear the consequences of the crime without loss to the depositor.

CONCLUDING REMARKS

Many types of property are subject to criminal loss by a variety of perils. For most businesses, the most significant cause of criminal loss is employee dishonesty.

Crime loss is susceptible to a variety of control measures, and crime control measures should always be considered once the exposure to crime loss has been identified. However, losses do occur despite the best control measures, and those losses need to be paid for, or "financed." Retention is the financing technique that is often most appropriate for nonemployee crime exposures. Employee dishonesty, on the other hand, usually presents a potentially severe loss exposure best handled by employee dishonesty insurance. Chapter 8 will deal with employee dishonesty insurance and other coverages that fall within the broad category of "crime insurance."

Chapter Notes

1. *Crime in Service Industries* (Washington, DC: U.S. Department of Commerce, 1977), p. 101.
2. *White Collar Crime* (Washington, DC: U.S. Chamber of Commerce, 1974), p. 4.
3. *Practical Risk Management,* March 1978 issue, as reprinted by permission in *Readings in Risk Management* (Malvern, PA: Insurance Institute of America, 1980), p. 267.
4. *Insurance Facts* (New York: Insurance Information Institute, 1981-82), p. 27.
5. Jack Bologna, "A New Look at the Internal Theft Prevention Process," *Assets Protection,* Sept./Oct., 1980, pp. 32-33.
6. Carole Sewell, "Preventing Pilferage—Screening Potential Employees Thwarts Theft," *Business Insurance,* 11 May 1981, p. 41.
7. *White Collar Crime,* p. 60.

CHAPTER 8

Commercial Crime Insurance

As Chapter 7 emphasized, organizations can sustain financial loss by many types of crimes, in a variety of ways. Nothing short of avoidance—which usually is not feasible—can eliminate the possibility of crime loss. However, a variety of crime insurance coverages can complement the control measures taken by every prudent business. A sound crime insurance program can reduce the chances that a loss will cripple an organization's financial well-being.

Fifteen *commercial crime coverage forms* are available on Insurance Services Office (ISO) forms, and any of these coverages can be written by itself. Also, some of the coverage forms can be combined into so-called *coverage plans*. This chapter explains the various crime coverages that are available and the intended scope of each coverage. Once the individual coverages are understood, it is relatively easy to combine an appropriate set of forms, using one of the coverage plans, if desired, to meet an organization's set of crime insurance needs. Absent from the present discussion are financial institution coverages which are discussed in Chapter 14.

Since all "simplified" crime policies follow essentially the same format and most include the same basic conditions, it is best to begin by explaining how the policies are structured.

POLICY STRUCTURE

Like other coverages of the simplification program, commercial crime insurance can be written in a *monoline policy* or it can be combined with other coverages in a *commercial package policy*. The structure of a typical monoline crime policy is shown in Exhibit 8-1. An alternative approach would be to combine the commercial crime

Exhibit 8-1
Commercial Crime Policy Structure*

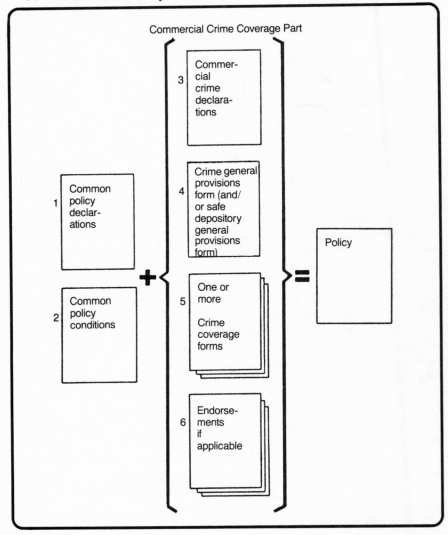

declarations (item 1 in the exhibit) and the common policy declarations (item 3) into a single document.

Crime coverage can be combined with other coverages simply by inserting the appropriate documents (items 3, 4, 5, and 6 in the exhibit) into a policy that already contains the common policy declarations (item 1) and the common policy conditions (item 2).

The common policy declarations and conditions were discussed in previous chapters and will not be re-examined here. This chapter focuses on the various crime coverage parts. A *crime coverage part* comprises items 3, 4, 5, and 6 of the exhibit—the commercial crime declarations, crime general provisions (for most coverages), one or more crime coverage forms, and any applicable endorsements.

Fifteen *crime coverage forms* are available:

Form A— Employee Dishonesty (Blanket)
Form A— Employee Dishonesty (Scheduled)
Form B— Forgery or Alteration
Form C— Theft, Disappearance and Destruction
Form D— Robbery and Safe Burglary
Form E— Premises Burglary
Form F— Computer Fraud
Form G— Extortion
Form H— Premises Theft and Robbery Outside the Premises
Form I— Lessees of Safe Deposit Boxes
Form J— Securities Deposited with Others
Form K— Liability for Guests' Property—Safe Deposit Box
Form L— Liability for Guests' Property—Premises
Form M— Safe Depository Liability
Form N— Safe Depository Direct Loss

Forms A and B are "under the jurisdiction of" the Surety Association of America (SAA)—meaning the SAA develops and maintains coverage forms, rules, and rates on these lines for its member companies. The remaining forms are under the jurisdiction of Insurance Services Office (ISO). These two advisory organizations cooperated to develop a coordinated set of forms that could be combined with the same common conditions.

The various "coverage plans" will be detailed later, but two examples will illustrate the concept:

- Plan 1—*combination crime separate limits option*—offers any combination of Coverage Forms A through J, with each coverage subject to a separate limit.
- Plan 4—*storekeepers burglary and robbery coverage*—requires Coverage Forms D and E.

A complete crime insurance policy includes an appropriate declarations page, crime general provisions (in most cases), and one or more coverage forms.

CRIME DECLARATIONS PAGES

Two types of crime declarations pages were developed as part of the simplification program. The first type is designed for use with a monoline crime policy, eliminating the need for a separate common policy declarations form. The second type supplements a common declarations page, including only those items of information that relate to the crime coverage(s). Either type of crime policy declarations lists the coverage forms, limits of insurance, deductibles, and endorsements that apply. The first type also contains information to identify the named insured, the insured's address, the policy period, and the producer.

CRIME GENERAL PROVISIONS FORM

The *crime general provisions form* combines in one document all the exclusions, conditions, and definitions that are common to forms A through J. (Coverage forms K through M themselves contain all applicable provisions not found in the *common policy conditions.*)

The first sentence in the crime general provisions form contains the instruction to read the policy carefully and warns that various provisions restrict coverage. While that is good advice, it is unlikely to be read by somebody who is not already heeding it.

General Exclusions

Six exclusions, sequenced in alphabetical order in the form, apply to coverage forms A through J. In the following discussion, they are taken up in an order that facilitates logical explanation. Remember, these exclusions apply to all crime forms except K through M.

Acts of Named Insured or Partners Excluded from coverage under all attached crime coverage forms is any loss resulting from a dishonest or criminal act committed *by the named insured or its partners,* whether they acted alone or in collusion with others. This exclusion eliminates coverage for losses that are intentional from the standpoint of the named insured.

Notice that the general exclusions do not eliminate coverage for a loss resulting from the dishonesty of corporate officers or other employees. However, this does not mean that all crime insurance forms cover losses caused by employee dishonesty. Crime coverage forms B through J contain their own exclusions for loss by employee dishonesty. Thus, the primary effect of this exclusion is to narrow the coverage of

Form A—employee dishonesty—so that it covers only the dishonesty of employees and not the dishonest or criminal acts of the named insured or partners.

Indirect Loss The so-called "indirect loss" exclusion attempts to make it clear that the policy covers only direct losses. However, there has never been widespread agreement as to what losses are not "direct." The intent here is probably to cover only one type of loss consequence—the reduction in value of covered property.

The indirect loss provision excludes "loss that is an indirect result of any act or 'occurrence' covered by this insurance." "Occurrence" is not defined in the common provisions form, but is defined in the various crime coverage forms that use that term. The most common definition of occurrence is as follows:

"Occurrence" means an:
(1) act or series of related acts involving one or more persons; or
(2) act or event, or a series of related acts or events not involving any person.

The common provisions form contains three categories of "indirect losses" that would not be covered. These are only examples and are not intended to be exhaustive. The types of losses given in these examples are as follows:

- *Loss of income.* For example, an insured store loses sales because a substantial portion of its stock was stolen and a period of time elapses before the stock can be replenished. *Business income coverage* with the *causes of loss—special form* would cover this type of loss.
- *Liability for punitive damages.* The party having crime coverage might be held liable for damages if property belonging to a third party is stolen or damaged by thieves while in the named insured's case. Compensatory damages to replace or repair the property might be covered, but other damages would not. This exclusion is intended to preclude coverage for punitive damages.
- *Costs of proving the loss.* The burden of proof is on the insured, and the costs of bearing that burden cannot be shifted to the insurer.

Legal Expenses Further strengthening the intention of covering only direct losses, this exclusion precludes coverage for expenses related to any legal action.

Governmental Action Also excluded is loss resulting from the seizure or destruction of property by order of governmental authority. Some other types of property insurance do provide limited coverage for the governmental action exposure. For example, a provision in the "commercial property" causes-of-loss forms specifically covers acts of destruction ordered by governmental authority and taken at the time of a fire to prevent its spread. However, the crime general exclusion makes it clear that crime coverage for such governmental action losses would not apply to money, securities, or other covered property—even when fire ensues.

This exclusion would be effective, for example, if money is confiscated in a "drug bust" or a "sting operation" and the owners of the money present a claim for the lost money under their crime coverage.

Other General Exclusions   Other general exclusions concern:

- loss from nuclear reaction, radioactive contamination, or any related act or incident; and
- loss resulting from war and related acts or incidents.

General Conditions

The crime general provisions form contains eighteen conditions, arranged alphabetically in the form but grouped here to facilitate discussion.

Conditions Relating to Property and Interests Insured

Ownership of Property; Interests Covered.   Crime insurance is a first-party coverage, as underscored by this provision, which states that the insurance applies only to property owned or held by the named insured or for which the named insured is legally liable. The provision further stipulates that the insurance is for the named insured's benefit only. In other words, it is not intended to provide rights or benefits to any person or organization other than the named insured.

Joint Insured.   In some cases, more than one insured is named on a policy. This is common when two or more entities have the same management—for example, a parent corporation and its subsidiaries. In these cases, the first named insured acts not only for itself but also for all other insureds. If it should happen that the first named insured ceases to be covered, then the next named insured becomes the first named insured.

In addition, if any insured, partner, or officer of that insured knows any information relevant to this insurance, that knowledge is considered to be knowledge of every insured. For example, coverage is not intended to apply to an employee from the time that *any* insured learns that the employee has committed a fraudulent or dishonest act. It does not matter whether the act was committed in the service of the insured or otherwise, or even whether the act was committed before or after the insured employed the dishonest person.

The major effects of this provision are to give *every* insured "employee dishonesty" coverage with respect to employees of *any* insured, when employee dishonesty coverage is provided. This provision also prevents duplicate coverage. When employee dishonesty coverage is excluded, dishonesty by employees of all insureds is excluded.

If the policy or any of its coverages is canceled or terminated as to any insured, loss sustained by that particular insured is covered only if the loss is discovered no later than one year after the cancellation or termination.

Consolidation-Merger. If the covered organization consolidates or merges with another organization or purchases additional facilities, the insurer must be notified within thirty days of the consolidation or merger and pay the additional premium.

The insured must be especially careful about this thirty-day limitation when commercial crime coverage is part of a commercial package policy (CPP), because the commercial general liability coverage form (CGL) gives the insured up to *ninety* days to notify the insurer of a consolidation or merger. These differing periods should not be confused. The best rule of thumb is to notify the insurance company as promptly as possible of any consolidation or merger.

Conditions Relating to Covered Time Periods

Policy Period. This condition points out that the policy period is as shown in the declarations. The insurer will pay only for loss that the named insured sustains through acts committed or events *occurring* during the policy period (subject to the *loss sustained during prior insurance provision,* to be discussed shortly). It is not necessary that the loss be *discovered* during the policy period.

Discovery Period for Loss. The insurer is not obligated to pay a loss that is discovered later than one year from the end of the policy period. This provision is designed especially for employee dishonesty coverage. Employee dishonesty losses can go undetected for long periods and sometimes are not discovered until after coverage has terminated and not been replaced. If a commercial crime policy were to be canceled or nonrenewed but replaced, the potential severity of this provision is diluted by the condition discussed next.

Conditions Relating to Other Insurance

Loss Sustained During Prior Insurance. This provision is sometimes referred to as a *superseded suretyship provision*—especially when it applies to employee dishonesty coverage (which was traditionally considered a form of suretyship). The effect of this provision is to extend coverage for a loss *discovered* during the *current* policy's coverage period, and after the discovery period of the prior policy has run out, for a loss that *occurred* during the coverage period of an *earlier* policy which would have been covered by that policy. Certain conditions apply:

- First, the current insurance must have become effective at the same time the prior policy was canceled or terminated. Any discontinuity of coverage between the past policy and the current policy eliminates coverage under this provision.
- Second, the loss must be within the scope of the earlier policy, but also would have been covered by the *current* insurance had it been in effect at the time when the acts or events causing the loss during a prior policy period were committed.

It is further stipulated that the prior insurance is part of, rather than in addition to, the limits of insurance of the current policy. Payment is limited to the lesser of the amount recoverable under (1) the current policy as of its effective date (any subsequent endorsement that increased policy limits would have no effect) or (2) the prior insurance, had it remained in effect.

This provision addresses a complication that arises in cases where an insured changes insurance companies. The terminated coverage covers only those losses that (1) occurred while the insurance was in effect and (2) are discovered before the expiration of its discovery period. In other words, the insurer whose policy has terminated provides no coverage for an act discovered after the expiration of that policy's discovery period. *If* the new policy did not cover any losses that occurred prior to its effective date, then the insured would have no coverage under either policy for any loss that *occurred* while the old policy was in force but *is discovered* after the old policy's discovery period has run out. Superseded suretyship prevents this problem.

Superseded suretyship can seem like a difficult, unnecessarily complex concept if the reasoning behind it is not recognized. To illustrate, consider the dilemma of Insurance Company B that wants to sell employee dishonesty coverage to an employer already covered by Insurance Company A. If the employer continues to renew the coverage with A, coverage will continue to exist for any losses that have occurred since the original inception date of A's policy. If a replacement policy is purchased from B, the employer's coverage for prior losses will cease after A's discovery period elapses—*unless* B's policy has a superseded suretyship provision.

Simply stated, without superseded suretyship, it would be difficult to sell employee dishonesty coverage to anyone already covered.

Exhibit 8-2

Discovery Periods and Superseded Suretyship Illustrated

Policy A in Force	Policy B in Force		No Coverage in Force	
Period 1	Period 2	Period 3	Period 4	Period 5

19X0   19X2   19X3   19X4   19X5   19X6

Policies A and B have a one-year discovery clause and
a superseded suretyship provision

Loss Occurs	Loss Discovered	Policy Providing Coverage
Period 1	Period 1	Policy A
Period 1	Period 2	Policy A
Period 1	Period 3	Policy B[1]
Period 1	Period 4	Policy B[1]
Period 2	Period 2	Policy B
Period 3	Period 3	Policy B
Period 3	Period 4	Policy B
Period 3	Period 5	None[2]
Period 4	Period 4	None

[1]Loss paid due to Policy B's superseded suretyship provision. Amount payable is the *lesser* of:

a. Amount payable under Policy A if A had remained in force, or

b. Amount payable under Policy B.

[2]Policy B's discovery period has expired and no superseding policy is in force.

Superseded suretyship eliminates the penalties for changing insurance companies.

Discovery periods and superseded suretyship are illustrated in Exhibit 8-2.

Non-Cumulation of Limit of Insurance. This provision precludes the stacking of coverage limits from year to year. No matter how many years the insurance remains in force or how often the premium is paid, the limit of insurance does not cumulate from year to year or from period to period.

This provision is especially important with employee dishonesty coverage, because losses can develop over a period of years. For example, an employee might embezzle $5,000 every month—$60,000 per year—during a five-year period before the loss is discovered. Suppose the employer has kept $50,000 of employee dishonesty coverage in force throughout these five years. While the employer has sustained a total loss of $300,000, the most it can collect—because of this provision—is $50,000.

Loss Covered by This Insurance and Prior Insurance Issued by Us or Any Affiliate. If any loss is covered partly by this insurance and partly by any prior canceled or terminated insurance provided by the same insurance company (or an affiliated company), the most the insurer will pay for any loss is the *larger* of the amount recoverable under the current or prior policies.

Loss Covered Under More Than One Coverage of This Insurance. If two or more commercial crime insurance coverages apply to the same loss, the insurer is obligated to pay no more than the sum of the limits of insurance applicable to those coverages. Of course, the insurer will not pay more than the actual amount of the loss.

The purpose of this provision is to uphold the principle of indemnity in cases where two or more crime coverage forms might apply to a loss. The same principle is represented in the common policy provisions in the condition titled *insurance under two or more coverages,* which is designed to handle duplication of coverage under various combinations of coverages—such as the situation that might occur when both the "commercial property" coverage and commercial crime coverage of a commercial package policy apply to the same loss.

Other Insurance. This provision is designed to make insurance of the crime coverages apply as excess when the limit of other insurance is insufficient to cover the entire loss.

Conditions Relating to Post-Loss Procedures

Records. The named insured is required to keep records of all covered property so that the insurer can verify the amount of any loss.

Duties in the Event of Loss. After the named insured discovers a loss or a situation that may result in loss to covered property, the named insured is required to:

1. notify the insurer as soon as possible,
2. submit to an examination under oath if so requested by the insurer and provide a signed statement,
3. provide the insurer with a detailed, sworn proof of loss within 120 days, and
4. cooperate with the insurer in the investigation and settlement of any claim.

A provision in the crime coverage forms, except Forms A and B, also imposes on the insured a duty to notify the police if a crime has been committed.

Transfer of Your Rights of Recovery Against Others to Us. Like most other coverages, commercial crime insurance contains a *subrogation provision* stating that, once the insurer has paid any loss to the named insured or settled any loss on its behalf, the named insured agrees to transfer its rights of recovery against any other person or organization to the insurer. The named insured must make sure those rights are not impaired.

Recoveries. If, after paying a loss, the insurer is successful in making any recoveries, the amounts recovered—less the costs of obtaining the recovery—will be distributed in the following sequence:

- First, to the named insured until he or she is reimbursed for any retained loss that exceeded the limit of insurance plus any deductible amount. The named insured does not recover the deductible, at this point.
- Next, any remaining amount is taken by the insurer until it is reimbursed for the settlement that was made.
- Finally, if any amount remains, it is payable to the named insured until he or she is reimbursed for the amount of loss that was retained because of the deductible.

Some recoveries that might result in a duplicate benefit are not subject to this provision: (1) recovery from insurance, suretyship, reinsurance, security, or indemnity taken for the insurer's benefit, and (2) securities that are recovered after duplicate securities have been issued.

Legal Action Against Us. This so-called "suit provision" specifies the conditions under which the named insured may bring an action against the insurer. The conditions precedent to such action are that the named insured:

- has complied with all terms of this insurance,
- has waited at least ninety days after filing proof of loss with the insurer, and
- brings suit against the insurer within two years from the date the named insured discovered the loss.

Condition Relating to Property Valuation and Loss Settlement The *valuation—settlement* condition addresses the manner by which money, securities, and other property are valued, as well as the way in which losses are to be settled. Note that this condition tends to favor the insurer.

- *Money.* When a loss involves "money," as defined, the insurer will pay no more than its face value. Furthermore, at the insurer's option, loss of money issued by any country other than the United States of America may be paid (a) at face value in the money issued by the country in question, or (b) in the USA dollar equivalent determined by the rate of exchange on the day the loss in question was discovered.

- *Securities.* When loss involves "securities," as defined, the insurer will pay no more than the value of such securities at the close of business on the day the loss in question was discovered. At the insurer's option, loss may be settled by paying the value of such securities or replacing them in kind. In either case, the named insured is required to assign all of its rights, title, and interest in the lost securities to the insurer.

  Another option available to the insurer is that the loss may be settled by paying the cost of any *lost securities bond* that is required when issuing duplicates of lost securities.

- *Property Other than Money and Securities.* When a covered crime loss includes "property other than money and securities," or loss from damage to the "premises" (as both terms are defined), the insurer does not have to pay any more than (1) the actual cash value of the property on the day the loss in question was discovered, (2) the cost to repair the property or premises, or (3) the cost to replace the property with property of like kind and quality. At the insurer's option, it may instead pay the actual cash value of the property or make the repairs or replacement. If there is disagreement between insurer and named insured as to the cost of repair or replacement, the matter will be settled by arbitration.

Loss settlement can be complicated when foreign exchange rates are involved. The manner in which non-USA money losses will be settled was described above. The form also addresses the problem of international losses of securities or "other property." The insurer has the option to pay for loss (1) in the money of the country in which the loss occurred or (2) in the United States of America dollar equivalent of the money of the country in which the loss in question took place as determined by the rate of exchange on the date the loss was discovered.

Whatever valuation or settlement option is exercised, property paid for or replaced by the insurer becomes the insurer's property. Suppose, for example, the insurer pays a claim following theft of a stolen jewel. If the jewel is later recovered, it belongs to the insurer.

Miscellaneous Conditions

Territory. The territorial scope of commercial crime insurance is not the same as that of "commercial property" coverage. Commercial crime insurance is limited to acts committed or events occurring within the United States of America, U.S. Virgin Islands, Puerto Rico, Canal

Zone, or Canal. (The coverage territory for "commercial property" does not include the Virgin Islands or the Canal Zone.)

Coverage Extensions. This provision makes it clear that, unless otherwise provided in the coverage forms, extensions of coverage are considered to be part of the form's limit of insurance, rather than providing additional limits.

Here again there is a difference among coverage parts, as the coverage extensions of the building and personal property form (BPP) do provide additional insurance.

EMPLOYEE DISHONESTY COVERAGE—FORM A

If an organization is interested in coverage against loss of money, securities, and other property *by employees*, it may purchase some form of employee dishonesty insurance. Virtually all other forms of property insurance eliminate coverage for the kinds of losses within the scope of dishonesty insurance. For example, neither the basic nor broad causes-of-loss forms, as used with "commercial property" insurance, covers theft losses—whether committed by an employee or a nonemployee. Although the causes-of-loss special form covers theft losses, it specifically excludes loss or damage caused by or resulting from dishonest or criminal acts by the named insured, employees, directors, trustees, authorized representatives, or anyone to whom the named insured entrusts property regardless of purpose.

Schedule Versus Blanket Coverage

Employee dishonesty insurance can be written as either schedule coverage or blanket coverage. The differences between these two approaches are summarized in Exhibit 8-3. Schedule coverage, in turn, can be either on a name schedule basis or a position schedule basis.

Schedule Coverage Schedule coverage applies only to some employees—as identified in a "schedule" on the form. When employee dishonesty insurance is written on a schedule coverage basis, the insured has the option of either scheduling the *names* of covered *employees* or of scheduling the *titles* of covered *positions* and indicating the number of persons who occupy each scheduled position.

- On a *name schedule* basis, the additional definition of "employee" found in the coverage form serves to restrict coverage to the person(s) named in the schedule.
- On a *position schedule* basis, all that is required to effect coverage is designation by title of the covered positions, the

Exhibit 8-3
A Comparison of Employee Dishonesty Forms

	Form A Schedule	Form A Blanket
Form number	CR 00 02	CR 00 01
Definition of "employee"	Part of Form	Part of General Provisions Form
Dishonest employee must be identified	Yes	No
Coverage basis	Each employee	Per loss
Employee collusion amount payable	Each identified employee times limit	Per loss

location of the positions (e.g. at the main office and branch office), and the number of employees occupying each designated position. For example, a position schedule form might list the positions of "messenger," "receiving clerk," "shipping clerk," and "bookkeeper."

In either case, the amount of coverage for each named person or each unnamed person in a scheduled position may vary depending on the employer's estimate of the amount that could be stolen by a person occupying that position.

As compared with the name schedule approach, the position schedule has some advantages to the employer, because no changes are necessary as employees leave and are replaced. It is well suited to a situation where employees tend to move from one position to another based on work demands. The position schedule also permits continuous coverage even though persons holding those positions may change.

On the other hand, as noted later, the employer could be penalized under the position schedule if there are more employees occupying a given position than the number actually declared in the schedule.

Blanket Coverage Generally speaking, the blanket approach provides broader coverage than the schedule approach with no sacrifice in flexibility.

With blanket employee dishonesty coverage, there is no need to name either covered employees or covered positions. *All* "employees," as that term is defined, are subject to coverage. The definition of "employee" must be studied carefully to determine whether any given individual is within the scope of insurance. If an employer, for example, hires temporary help from time to time, the definition in the crime general provisions form would encompass such persons, but not while these temporaries have care and custody of property outside the premises.

If one or more persons do not fit within any category of the "employee" definition, it is still possible to add such persons by endorsement. Among the additional persons who can be included as employees are:

1. the spouse and children of any building manager, superinten-dent, or janitor;
2. the chairman, directors, trustees, and/or members of specified committees;
3. volunteer workers; and
4. designated agents.

Likewise, certain designated persons or classes of persons can be deleted from the definition of "employee."

If higher limits are desired for certain individuals or positions, the blanket form can be endorsed accordingly.

Coverage Characteristics

Two different employee dishonesty coverage forms are used:

● Form A—Schedule, and
● Form A—Blanket.

The schedule form is used for either name schedule coverage or position schedule coverage.

While the formats of the schedule and blanket employee dishones-ty coverage forms are identical, some provisions differ. Both forms contain provisions dealing with the coverage agreement, limit of insurance, deductible, and additional exclusions, conditions, and definitions. Similarities and differences in the two forms are noted below.

Coverage Agreement Whether employee dishonesty insurance applies on a schedule or blanket basis, the employer is protected for loss of, and damage to, covered property resulting directly from the covered cause of loss.

● The *covered* property consists of "money," "securities," and "property other than money and securities," as those terms are defined in the crime general provisions form.

- The *covered cause of loss* includes only one peril—"employee dishonesty," as defined in the form.

Here there is an important difference between the two forms:

- When coverage is written on a *schedule basis,* "employee dishonesty" requires that a dishonest act be committed by *an identified employee.*
- When coverage applies on a *blanket basis,* the definition of "employee dishonesty" requires only that the dishonest acts be committed by *an employee,* whether identified or not.

In either case, coverage applies whether the employee was acting alone or in collusion with other persons (except for collusion with the named insured or a partner).

In both coverage forms, the term "employee dishonesty" also requires that such dishonest acts be with the manifest intent of causing the named insured to sustain loss *and* to obtain financial benefit for the employee or any person or organization intended by the employee to receive that benefit.

Blanket employee dishonesty insurance, unlike schedule coverage, contains a coverage extension to cover loss caused by an "employee" while temporarily outside the specified territory for not more than ninety days. Specifying such a specific time period should leave little or no room for argument.

Limit of Insurance The most the insurer will pay under either form in any one "occurrence" is affected by the definition of occurrence in both coverage forms and the additional "limit of insurance" provisions in the schedule coverage form.

In both employee dishonesty forms, the term *occurrence* is defined to mean "all loss caused by, or involving, one or more 'employees,' whether the result of a single act or a series of acts."

- With *blanket* coverage, the most the insurer will pay in any one occurrence is the amount designated in the declarations.
- With *schedule* coverage, the most the insurer is obligated to pay in any one occurrence is the sum of the limits that apply to each "employee" who is involved in the defalcation and is designated by name or position in the schedule.

Say, for example, that the limit designated in the schedule opposite each of the named covered employees is $25,000 and that two covered employees are identified as being involved in one "occurrence." The most the insurer would be obligated to pay is the amount of loss less the applicable deductible, subject to a maximum amount of $50,000. If, instead, employee dishonesty coverage is written on a blanket basis with a $25,000 limit of insurance, the most the insurer would be required to pay is $25,000.

The schedule form also clarifies that the policy limit is not cumulative from year to year. It does not matter how long the insurance remains in effect with respect to each employee.

If coverage is written on a *position schedule* basis, two additional provisions apply. The first deals with the situation where an employee occupies more than one position, the second with the situation where more employees than are scheduled occupy a given position.

The most the insurer is obligated to pay for loss by an "employee" (i.e., a person engaged to perform the duties of a position shown in the schedule) who serves in more than one position is the largest limit of insurance in effect and applicable to any one of those positions at the time the loss is discovered. Say, for example, that a dishonest employee worked part-time in the position of assistant bookkeeper, which is subject to a $50,000 scheduled limit, and also served as a receiving clerk, which is subject to a $25,000 scheduled limit. The maximum amount payable for any one occurrence involving this identified person would be $50,000 (the higher of the two limits).

If, at the time of loss, more employees are serving in a covered position than the number of employees listed opposite that position in the schedule, then the limit of insurance will be prorated among the employees according to the following formula (which closely resembles the familiar coinsurance formula):

$$\frac{\text{Number of employees shown in the position}}{\text{Actual number of employees in the position}} \times \text{Limit of Insurance}$$

$$= \text{Adjusted limit of insurance}$$

Assume, for example, that two employees are designated in the cashier's position for a limit of $50,000 each. At the time a $150,000 loss is discovered, there are actually three persons employed as cashiers. Based on the above formula, and assuming all three employees caused the loss, the insurance company will pay $33,333 on each employee, for a total of $100,000. Had the employer notified the insurer of the additional person and paid the premium, the entire loss could have been recovered.

The position schedule coverage form is advantageous to the employer whose organization has only a few employees and is relatively stable with the different positions clearly defined. It is less well suited to a situation with several employees or where employees tend to move from one position to another based on workload demands.

For insureds with many employees, a blanket bond will generally also be less expensive. Some further comments on selecting among these approaches appear at the end of the chapter.

Deductible The deductible provisions of both coverage forms are identical. No loss in any one "occurrence" is payable by the insurer unless the amount exceeds the deductible amount. The minimum deductible is $100, but higher deductibles of $250, $500, $1,000, or higher are available subject to appropriate premium reductions.

Although no coverage applies to losses below the deductible amount, the employer must notify the insurer, as soon as possible, of any loss of the type subject to coverage—even though the loss falls entirely within the deductible amount. On request, the insured may also be required by the insurer to give a statement that describes the loss. This notification is more important than first meets the eye. As explained below, coverage is automatically canceled on any employee who is known to have committed a dishonest act, and no deductible applies to the size of the dishonest act that triggers cancellation. Once the insured gives notice of a loss within the deductible, both parties should be aware that further coverage on the guilty employee has terminated.

Additional Exclusions. The blanket and schedule coverage forms are subject to two special exclusions, in addition to the exclusions that appear in the crime general provisions form.

Employee Canceled under Prior Insurance. The insurer will not pay for loss, under either the schedule or blanket form, caused by an employee in any circumstance whereby insurance on that employee was canceled under any similar prior insurance and not reinstated since that last time of cancellation. Whether the cancellation was prompted by a loss or by questionable characteristics of the employee, this provision serves as a safeguard in those cases where such employees are technically subject to the insurance because of oversight, rather than intent.

Inventory Shortages. The insurer is not obligated to pay for a loss, or part of a loss, if the only evidence of employee dishonesty—or the amount of dishonesty—is an inventory shortage or a profit and loss computation.

The fact that a shortage exists does not necessarily mean that there has been a theft, and it certainly is not a sure sign of employee dishonesty. "Shrinkage" of inventory can result from spoilage and breakage—both of which may result in the disposal of property without properly deleting it from inventory records.

Inventory and record-keeping errors abound in even the most carefully controlled systems. Often, it is ultimately discovered that a missing inventory item has been properly sold and paid for, but a record-keeping error did not remove the item from inventory or credit the payment to the right account. There is also a substantial likelihood of inventory shrinkage from shoplifting in many mercantile operations, as well as other forms of theft by nonemployees.

For these and other reasons, shortage simply is not a clear indication of employee dishonesty, and even when dishonesty has been proven, the extent of any shortage is not an accurate measure of the extent of the dishonesty. The purpose of employee dishonesty insurance is to cover employee dishonesty, not inadequacies or inaccuracies in the insured's record-keeping system.

The courts have upheld the intent that inventory or profit and loss computations are inadmissible as evidence in *establishing* loss by employee dishonesty. However, there have been cases in which the courts permitted inventories or profit and loss computations to be used to establish the amount of the loss once employee dishonesty was established without relying on inventory computations.

Additional Conditions Both blanket and schedule forms are subject to an important condition that explains the cancellation of coverage on specific employees. Only the schedule form contains a provision relating to consolidations and mergers.

Cancellation for Dishonest Employee When the named insured or any partner, officer, or director learns that an employee has committed a dishonest act, coverage ceases with respect to future acts by that employee. This provision applies whether the dishonesty occurred in connection with present employment or otherwise. (It may have been in connection with previous employment, or totally outside employment—defalcation as a church officer, for example.) It applies whether or not a claim was submitted for the dishonest act, and whether or not the amount involved was within a deductible. However, this provision does not apply to knowledge held by partners, officers, or directors who are in collusion with the dishonest employee.

This provision can present some difficult problems for an unwary employer.

Some employers hesitate to discharge a valuable employee even though the employee has been discovered to have acted dishonestly. One salesperson for a corporation was found to have stolen $100,000 worth of merchandise from his employer. The corporation would neither discharge the employee nor take legal action against him, because the salesperson was responsible for generating about $1 million of profit per year. The salesperson's manager said that when the theft of this employee exceeded the profit he made for the organization, then the manager would discharge the employee and proceed against him. This situation is not unusual. Some employers are quite willing to overlook employee dishonesty as long as the employee has other valuable assets for the organization. Others are hesitant to confront an employee if the evidence is not unquestionably solid. But an insurance company cannot afford to continue coverage automatically on an employee who has already been discovered in a dishonest act.

When the employer discovers the dishonesty, coverage ceases immediately. If it is the insurer who learns of the employee's dishonesty, then another provision may be invoked, as explained below.

It should also be noted that nothing in the policy language limits the nature of the dishonest act that cause coverage to be canceled. The form refers simply to "any dishonest act"—a phrase that could be subject to rather broad interpretation.

Cancellation for Employee by Insurer   The insurer may cancel coverage for any employee on the date specified in a notice mailed to the named insured. When this option is exercised, the insurer must give at least thirty days' advance notice of the cancellation.

Consolidation and Mergers   An additional condition found only in the schedule coverage form stipulates that the consolidation-merger general condition does not apply to this coverage form. It stands to reason that coverage cannot apply automatically with the acquisition or merger of another firm if it is necessary that employees either be named or their positions declared before coverage can apply. This is not a condition of the blanket coverage form because neither employees nor their positions have to be designated. Of course, the employer with the blanket coverage form is still obligated to notify the insurer within the permitted time limit, because the number of employees has an effect on insurance cost and the insurer also may want the background of new employees to be checked.

FORGERY OR ALTERATION COVERAGE—FORM B

Forgery or alteration coverage Form B, under the jurisdiction of the Surety Association of America, is designed to cover loss sustained by an insured because of forgery or alteration of, or on, any covered instrument. The instruments covered by this form are defined to mean:

> checks, drafts, promissory notes, or similar written promises, order or directions to pay a sum certain in "money" that are:
> a. made or drawn by or drawn upon you;
> b. made or drawn by one acting as your agent;
> or, that are purported to have been so made or drawn.

Neither forgery nor alteration is defined in the form. However, forgery is generally understood to mean the making or altering of any writing with the intent to defraud. So, when an instrument is not changed from the way its maker drew it up, there is not a forgery. An example occurs when a check is made payable "to the order of John Jones or bearer." Anyone who gets hold of the check becomes a bearer and may endorse and cash it. If the check is endorsed with the bearer's own name it is not a forgery—even if the check was illegally obtained. It may be a crime, but it is not a forgery.

In the event the named insured is sued for refusing to pay on any covered instrument because it may have been forged or altered, and the insurer gives its written consent to defend against the suit, then the insurer will pay the reasonable legal expenses incurred. Such expenses are payable in addition to the policy limit.

An exclusion for loss stemming from acts of employees, directors, and trustees appears in the form. This supplements the exclusions of the crime general provisions form to which this coverage form must be attached.

THEFT, DISAPPEARANCE, AND DESTRUCTION— FORM C

The theft, disappearance, and destruction coverage of Form C is one of the least restricted coverages available. It is directed at the loss of:

- money and securities both inside and outside the premises (the covered property)
- resulting directly from the covered causes of loss of "theft," disappearance, and destruction (the covered perils).

The fact that "theft" is defined in the form as "any act of stealing" means that there is no limitation on the way covered property can be stolen. Loss, for example, can arise from burglary, robbery, larceny, swindling, or any other wrongful taking of property without the consent of its owner. (Some earlier policies attempted to clarify this broad meaning of "theft" by saying that it meant "any felonious abstraction," although it is questionable whether that phrase added much in the way of clarification.) Despite the broad definition, as noted below, covered causes of loss are narrowed down in the form—largely in order to prevent overlap with other forms.

Neither "disappearance" nor "destruction" is defined by this form. The insured should have proof that property has been destroyed if that is the cause of loss alleged in the claim. Disappearance would be covered whether it is mysterious or not, and whether or not there is a presumption that theft was the root cause of the disappearance.

Inside the Premises

The word "premises" is a favorite of the crime insurance policy drafters; unfortunately, it is not necessarily the clearest word to deal with. The dictionary defines "premises" as "a piece of real estate; house or building and its land," but crime insurance policies use their own definition. In some situations, the word seems to denote a place with no physical substance; in others, the word seems to refer to a building—or to a portion of a building.

Coverage for loss of money and securities from inside the "premises" includes such property lost from within "banking premises." As defined in Form C and other crime forms, "premises" means "the interior of that portion of any building 'you' occupy in conducting 'your' business," and "banking premises" means "the interior of that portion of any building occupied by a banking institution or similar safe depository." The words *inside* and *interior* make it quite clear that no coverage applies for loss of money or securities outside—for example, loss by a robbery in the parking lot. The outside coverage is provided elsewhere in this coverage form, as discussed below.

Two coverage extensions in this coverage section apply to (1) containers of covered property and (2) "premises damage." Both deal with property of a certain specified kind other than money and securities.

Containers of Covered Property The first extension deals with locked containers that hold money and securities. The insurer agrees to pay for the loss of, and loss from damage to, a locked safe, vault, cash register, cash box, or cash drawer located in the "premises" (the interior of that part of any building the named insured occupies in conducting its business—here "premises" is a place). Such loss or damage must result directly from an actual or attempted (a) "theft" of the container, or (b) unlawful entry into the container.

What this means is that the insured will be indemnified if, say, a safe is damaged by burglars—whether the entry into the container is successful or not. Coverage will also apply if the entire container is carted away and recovered in damaged condition, with or without contents.

Premises Damage The insurer also agrees to pay for loss from damage to the "premises," as defined above, or to their exterior, which results directly from an actual or attempted "theft." (Here "premises" have damageable physical substance. Moreover, premises are "the interior . . ." but they also have an exterior, according to this provision.) The intent seems to be to cover burglars' or robbers' damage to the inside or the outside of a building, presumably including damage to contents. The only qualification is that the named insured must be the owner of the "premises" or liable for damage to them.

This is an especially important extension because of the limitations on vandalism coverage under the basic and broad causes-of-loss "commercial property" forms. It is often difficult to prove whether damage to the interior of property was caused by vandals who decided to steal something or by burglars who decided to vandalize something. This problem is discussed further below, in connection with the vandalism exclusion.

Outside the Premises

Coverage outside the "premises" applies to loss by "theft," disappearance, or destruction of money and securities in the care or custody of a "messenger." For purposes of this coverage form, "messenger" is defined as the named insured or any of the named insured's partners or employees while having care and custody of the property outside the premises. If an employee, for example, while conveying money to the bank for deposit, is robbed in the firm's parking lot, this coverage should indemnify the employer. Coverage would also apply if the robbery took place inside the building occupied by the insured, so long as it was outside the portion of the building occupied by the named insured.

Conveyance of Property by Armored Motor Vehicle Company Only one extension of coverage deals with money and securities outside the premises, and that relates to the use of armored car services.

Generally, armored car services carry insurance covering loss to money and securities of others in their care and custody. A business that purchases armored car services should request evidence that insurance is being provided for the benefit of the purchaser of such services. However, if it turns out that the insurance carried by an armored car service was not sufficient to fully compensate for a loss— or if the named insured is not otherwise able to obtain reimbursement from the armored car service, then the insurer under this extension will pay for the loss (subject, of course, to policy limits).

Limit of Insurance—Deductible

The insurer is not obligated to pay for any loss that does not exceed the deductible. For larger losses, the most the insurer is obligated to pay for any one "occurrence" is the limit of insurance shown in the declarations.

Additional Exclusions

Given the broad nature of the insuring agreements, it should come as no surprise that Form C contains many exclusions. Most of these exclusions also appear in other crime coverage forms.

The approach that will be taken is to discuss the exclusions in some detail here and to simply refer to them as they appear in the other coverage forms discussed later. Exhibit 8-4 contains a tabular summary showing which exclusions are found in which forms.

Accounting or Arithmetic Errors or Omissions As the name of this exclusion suggests, it precludes coverage for accounting or arithmetical errors or omissions. While many losses of this nature are within the policy deductible, there could be some sizable ones as well.

Although accounting or arithmetical errors are not crimes, they may result in loss of money. This exposure falls within the general category of "business risks" that can most appropriately be addressed by loss control measures, with any losses retained by the business.

Acts of Employees, Directors, Trustees, or Representatives Again, the title is self-explanatory. No coverage is provided for dishonest or criminal acts by the classes of persons specified in this exclusion. Employee dishonesty coverage is designed to cover such exposures.

Exchanges or Purchases No coverage applies for loss due to giving or surrendering property in an exchange or purchase. Thus, a fraudulent transaction or confidence scam that involves the loss of money or securities is not covered. Like other excluded exposures, this one is—or should be—within the control of the named insured to a high degree.

Fire The fire exclusion makes it clear that this crime coverage does not apply to the destruction of the premises by fire, however the fire may be caused. For example, suppose burglars break into a building, steal the safe, and set fire to the interior of the building. Even such burglar-caused damage or destruction by fire is not covered.

It is expected that an insured would have "commercial property" insurance covering the premises and other property against loss by fire. Criminal loss by fire is not excluded in the "commercial property" forms, while a fire exclusion is found in all crime coverage forms other than F, G, and H.

Exhibit 8-4
Special Exclusions of Commercial Crime Forms
Forms C to J

Special Exclusions	Commercial Crime Forms							
	C	D	E	F	G	H	I	J
Accounting or arithmetical errors or omissions	Yes	No	No	No	No	No	No	No
Acts of employees, directors, trustees or representatives	Yes	Yes	Yes	Yes	Yes	Yes	Yes	Yes
Exchanges or purchases	Yes	No	No	No	No	Yes	Yes	Yes
Fire	Yes	Yes	Yes	No	No	Yes	Yes*	No
Money operated devices	Yes	No	No	No	No	No	No	No
Transfer or surrender of property	Yes	Yes	No	No	No	Yes	Yes	Yes
Vandalism	Yes	Yes	Yes	No	No	Yes	No	No
Voluntary parting of title to or possession of property	Yes	No	No	No	No	Yes	Yes	Yes
Changes in conditions	No	No	Yes	No	No	Yes	No	No
Inventory shortages	No	No	No	Yes	No	No	No	No
Non-notification of authorities	No	No	No	No	Yes	No	No	No
Property owned by or held by a depository as collateral or in trust	No	No	No	No	No	No	Yes	No
Locations you occupy	No	No	No	No	No	No	No	Yes
Property owned or held in trust	No	No	No	No	No	No	No	Yes

* Section 2 only.

Money Operated Devices This exclusion relates to the theft of money and securities (for example, tokens or tickets) from vending machines, amusement devices, and coinchanging machines. No coverage applies unless an internal continuous recording instrument keeps track of the amount of money deposited. In the absence of a recording device, it could be difficult or impossible to establish the amount of the loss attributable to theft.

Transfer or Surrender of Property This exclusion addresses two important exposures that may require special coverage. Both excluded exposures involve giving property to someone outside the premises or banking premises.

- The first involves giving property to someone on the basis of unauthorized instructions. (This exposure is also excluded under "commercial property" causes of loss—special form.)
- The second involves giving property as the result of a threat to do bodily harm to a person or damage to property.

Many "unauthorized instructions" losses involve computer fraud, which may be insured under crime coverage Form F. Apart from computer fraud, it is possible to sustain a loss by voluntarily parting with property under the mistaken assumption that delivery was proper. If the unauthorized instructions were designed to defraud the employer, then the loss of property should be covered by employee dishonesty insurance. Many "unauthorized instruction" losses can be prevented with the use of proper safeguards, and the exposure to unprevented losses might be considered a "business risk."

There is some overlap between this exclusion and the "exchanges or purchases" exclusion discussed earlier, as well as with the "voluntary parting of title" exclusion discussed later. These overlaps are not particularly relevant. A loss that is excluded once is as excluded as if it were excluded twice or three times. If one exclusion applies, the loss is not covered.

Vandalism As noted earlier, Form C includes a coverage extension for damage to the interior and exterior of the premises *resulting directly from actual or attempted "theft"* of money and securities, as well as damage to containers of covered property *from actual or attempted "theft" or unlawful entry*. At the same time, however, the vandalism exclusion makes it clear that damage to the interior or exterior of the premises—as well as containers—*by vandalism or malicious mischief* is not covered. "Commercial property" insurance with the basic or broad causes-of-loss forms includes coverage for damage to the described property by vandalism, including building damage caused by the breaking in or exiting of burglars, but provides no coverage when the damage is caused by or results from theft.

To illustrate the dilemma, assume that an owner of business property discovers that a break-in occurred over a long holiday weekend. A window and its wood trim are found damaged as a result of the break-in. Some of the appliances, such as sinks and water heaters, along with piping, have been removed from the property. The vault containing securities is also heavily damaged, but the burglars did not gain entry into it. Much of the remaining personal property within the business premises appears to have been purposely damaged by the burglars. The businessowner carries crime coverage Form C with Insurance Company C and has "commercial property" insurance with Insurance Company P. The question is: How much of this loss is going to be paid by each insurer, assuming the limits of insurance are sufficient and no deductible applies?

Based on the provisions in both policies:

1. Damage to the exterior of the building caused by entry of the burglars should be covered under both policies.
2. Theft of the appliances would be insured by coverage Form C because the appliances were attached to the realty and therefore were considered part of the premises. Damage to the premises resulting from theft of appliances is also covered here. Theft is not a covered cause of loss under the "commercial property" basic and broad causes-of-loss forms, but is under the special form.
3. Damage to the vault should come under coverage Form C, since damage resulting from attempted unlawful entry is covered. Note, however, that if such damage is inflicted by vandals rather than burglars, coverage Form C would not apply.
4. Malicious damage to the personal property within the premises should be covered by the "commercial property" insurance form, whether the damage is inflicted by burglars or vandals.

A more serious question can arise if the cause of the event is unknown—that is, no one knows for sure whether the intruders were burglars or vandals. When both the crime coverage form and the building and personal property coverage are with the same insurance company, this question is less likely to develop. However, a variety of constraints often inhibit such coverage combinations.

Voluntary Parting of Title to or Possession of Property This exclusion relates to what is sometimes called the *trick or device loss*. Its purpose is to preclude payment of loss when the named insured, or someone acting on the express or implied authority of the named

Exhibit 8-5
Form C — Theft, Disappearance, and Destruction Coverage Form*

	Inside the Premises	Outside the Premises
Covered Property	Money and securities inside the premises or a banking premises	Money and securities outside the premises in the care and custody of a messenger
Covered Causes of Loss	(1) Theft (2) Disappearance (3) Destruction	(1) Theft (2) Disappearance (3) Destruction

*Reprinted with permission from *ISO Commercial Lines Policy and Rating Simplification Project Workshop Leader's Guide*, Insurance Services Office, Inc., 1985.

insured, is induced by a dishonest act to part voluntarily with possession or title to a property. This same exclusion is also found in the causes of loss—special form. Under Form C, of course, the only property involved would be money or securities.

For example, suppose a businessowner posts instructions to the effect that a bank messenger is to pick up currency, subject to a certain maximum, at a given time each day. One day somebody impersonates the messenger and is given the money. Because of this exclusion, the loss is not covered.

Additional Condition

One condition that applies to coverage Form C—and to a number of other crime forms as well—concerns the insured's duties in the event of loss. If the named insured has reason to believe that any loss of, or damage to, covered property involves a violation of law, the named insured must notify the police. By their nature, most crime coverage losses involve crimes which, by definition, are violations of the law. (Exceptions involve such things as the accidental destruction of money and securities.) Failure to observe these policy provisions can release the insurer from liability as certainly as when coverage is otherwise excluded by the policy.

The coverage of Form C is summarized in Exhibit 8-5.

ROBBERY AND SAFE BURGLARY COVERAGE— FORM D

In general, the basic provisions of this form cover loss of, and loss from damage to:

- "property other than money and securities," from within the premises (covered property) because of robbery of a custodian or safe burglary (covered perils); and "property other than money and securities" outside the premises (covered property) by actual or attempted robbery (covered peril).

Inside and outside coverages can be purchased separately, or both coverages may be combined.

Robbery Inside the Premises

Covered property, which can also include money and securities by endorsement, must not only be stolen from within the premises but also must be in the care and custody of a "custodian." As in Form C, "premises" is defined to mean "the interior of that portion of any building you occupy in conducting your business." Note again that if the insured rents only a portion of a building for its business, it is only that *portion* that falls within the scope of coverage—not the entire building or the land on which the building rests. Note also that the property must be in the care of a "custodian"—meaning the named insured, any partners of the named insured, or any employee while having care and custody of the property inside the premises, but not including any janitor or "watchperson." A "watchperson" is a watchman of any gender who is retained by the insured to have care of and custody of property inside the premises and has no other duties.

Coverage is provided for loss of covered property, as described above, only against loss by actual or attempted "robbery," which is defined to mean:

The taking of property from the care or custody of a person by one who has:
(1) Caused or threatened to cause that person bodily harm; or
(2) Committed an obviously unlawful act witnessed by that person.

Note the criterion of a robbery: Property must be taken by a person who:

1. causes the custodian bodily harm,
2. places the custodian in the fear of violence, or

3. commits any other unlawful act in the presence of such custodian—as, for example, when a person enters the premises, breaks a showcase, takes property, and leaves without otherwise showing force or saying a word.

There must be no doubt about how the loss has happened. If property is taken while the custodian is napping, no coverage applies under this form.

Of course, the stolen property must also be of a kind that is covered. This particular form encompasses virtually all kinds of tangible property other than motor vehicles and trailers.

Under an extension of coverage, the insurer will also pay for loss from damage to the "premises," as well as to their exterior, if the named insured is the owner of the premises or is liable for damage to them. The intent appears to be to cover damage by robbers to building and contents to the extent of the named insured's insurable interest.

Safe Burglary

Safe burglary coverage might be most appropriate for businesses that have valuable merchandise or raw materials kept in a safe or vault. Those requiring coverage for money and securities could add coverage for such property, as well.

The insured property is covered against loss by actual or attempted "safe burglary," defined to mean:

1. *taking property from within a locked safe or vault by a person who unlawfully enters such safe or vault (as evidenced by marks of forcible entry on the exterior).* It is not a requirement of this coverage that there be forcible entry *into the premises.* The burglar might have hidden within the premises or might have entered the premises leaving no trace of force or violence—but that has no bearing as long as there is a forcible entry *into the safe or vault.* However, the insurer may restrict coverage by endorsement to require forcible entry into the premises.
2. *taking a safe or vault from inside the premises.*

Although complete removal of a safe or vault from the premises is covered, there is no coverage while the on-premises safe or vault remains intact but is entered by manipulation of the combination or when the safe or vault is left unlocked.

An extension of coverage applies to damage to the "premises" and also to a locked safe or vault (assuming the named insured is the owner of the property or is liable for damage to it).

Robbery Outside the Premises

Coverage under this section applies for loss to

- property other than money and securities,
- outside the premises,
- in the care and custody of a messenger,
- by actual or attempted robbery.

The definitions of covered property, property not covered, premises, and robbery are the same for both parts of this form. However, while the inside coverage deals with a "custodian," the outside robbery coverage is concerned with property in the care of a "messenger."

A "messenger," like a "custodian," can include the named insured ("you"), any of the named insured's partners, or any employee having care and custody of the property outside the premises. Unlike a custodian, a messenger may also be a "watchperson" or janitor or any other person who is entrusted with covered property and is outside the premises.

A coverage extension also covers loss resulting from robbery of property in the care and custody of an armored motor vehicle company. Except for the covered property and perils, this extension is the same as the armored car extension discussed under Form C.

Limit of Insurance—Deductible

The insurer is not obligated to pay for any loss that does not exceed the deductible. For larger losses, the most the insurer is obligated to pay in any one "occurrence" is the limit of insurance shown in the Declarations. These provisions are identical to those of Form C.

Additional Exclusions

Form D contains the same exclusions as Form C, but does not contain those exclusions dealing with generally nonviolent acts:

- accounting or arithmetical errors or omissions,
- loss by exchanges or purchases,
- money operated devices, and
- voluntary parting of title to or possession of property.

There is no reason to exclude exposures that are not covered by an insuring agreement. This form covers robbery, safe burglary, and crimes with violent characteristics. It should be obvious why these exclusions are not needed.

Exhibit 8-6
Form D — Robbery and Safe Burglary Coverage Form*

	Inside the Premises		Outside the Premises
	Robbery of a Custodian	Safe Burglary	
Covered Property	Property other than money and securities inside the premises in the care and custody of a custodian	Property other than money and securities inside the premises in a safe or vault	Property other than money and securities outside the premises in the care and custody of a messenger
Covered Causes of Loss	Actual or attempted robbery	Actual or attempted safe burglary	Actual or attempted robbery

Other Information

- Coverage for money and securities can be provided by endorsement.
- If the insured wishes, coverage under this form can apply to both robbery *and* safe burglary, or can be limited to either robbery *or* safe burglary.

*Reprinted with permission from *ISO Commercial Lines Policy and Rating Simplification Project Workshop Leader's Guide*, Insurance Services Office, Inc., 1985.

Additional Conditions

Like Form C, Form D requires the insured to notify the police if there is reason to believe that loss or damage to covered property involves a violation of law.

Form D also contains a condition titled *special limit of insurance for specified property*. This condition places a $1,000 *per occurrence* limit on losses of or damage to:

> precious metals, precious or semi-precious stones, pearls, furs, completed or partially completed articles made of or containing such materials that constitute the principal value of such articles; or manuscripts, drawings, or records of any kind or the cost of reconstructing them or reproducing any information contained in them.

This $1,000 limit can be increased by endorsement.

The coverage of Form D is summarized in Exhibit 8-6.

PREMISES BURGLARY COVERAGE—FORM E

This coverage form is designed to pay the insured for loss of, and loss from damage to:

- property other than money and securities inside the premises (the covered property)

● caused by actual or attempted (1) robbery of a watchperson or (2) burglary (the covered perils).

This form may be suitable for businesses whose exposure to loss is greatest when the premises are not open for business and when the property susceptible to loss is not enclosed in a safe or vault.

Money and securities are not covered property. Motor vehicles and trailers are the only other types of property that are specifically not covered. Of course, there are practical limitations on the types of property that can be burglarized.

Robbery of a Watchperson

With one exception, the scope of robbery coverage is virtually identical to that of coverage Form D. The exception is that loss by robbery under Form E is limited to property that is in the care and custody of a "watchperson"—meaning any person whom the named insured retains specifically to have care and custody of the property within the premises and who has no other duties. Coverage can be broadened, by endorsement, to include eligible property while in the care and custody of a janitor.

Burglary

Coverage applies only when property is taken from within the interior of the premises by a person who unlawfully enters or leaves the premises and leaves marks of forcible entry or exit. As is usual, coverage also applies for loss because of damage to the interior or exterior of the "premises" resulting directly from robbery of the watchperson or burglary, but only if the named insured is the owner of the premises or is liable for damage to it.

Premises burglary exposures are affected to a high degree by the presence or absence of various loss control measures. Several provisions in Form E, discussed below, emphasize the importance of maintaining protective safeguards.

Limit of Insurance—Deductible

The provisions of this form actually dealing with the limit of insurance and the deductible are identical to those of the preceding coverage forms. However, buried within the section of Form E titled *limit of insurance* is an important policy condition: If a covered loss occurs, coverage is suspended until the premises are restored to the same condition, from the standpoint of security, as existed before the

Exhibit 8-7
Form E — Premises Burglary Coverage Form*

	Inside the Premises
Covered Property	Property other than money and securities inside the premises
Covered Causes of Loss	(1) Actual or attempted robbery of a watchperson (2) Actual or attempted burglary

*Reprinted with permission from *ISO Commercial Lines Policy and Rating Simplification Project Workshop Leader's Guide,* Insurance Services Office, Inc., 1985.

loss—unless the named insured maintains at least one "watchperson" while the premises are closed for business.

Additional Exclusions

With one exception, the exclusions of Form E are similar to those applicable to crime Form D. An additional exclusion, labeled *changes in conditions,* precludes coverage for loss when there is an increase in hazard that is within the control of the named insured.

As suggested above, a burglary or robbery may create a condition that involves an increase in hazard. However, coverage may be maintained in force by using a watchman as a substitute for the usual security devices that have been impaired by robbers.

Increase in hazard may also occur when a business owner forgets to activate a burglar alarm at closing time or when the owner fails to have an alarm system promptly repaired when a problem is discovered. If property is taken in a burglary and either of these conditions exists, the insured does not receive the protection that would otherwise apply.

Additional Conditions

Two conditions in Form E that are identical to those of Form D concern

- duties in the event of loss and
- special limit of insurance for specified property.

Additionally, the fire exclusion has been modified to provide that loss occurring *during* a fire is not covered.

The coverage of Form E is summarized in Exhibit 8-7.

PREMISES THEFT AND ROBBERY OUTSIDE THE PREMISES COVERAGE—FORM H

Coverage Form H may wisely be substituted for Form D or Form E when a business is concerned about:

- property other than money and securities, inside the premises, subject to
- loss not only by burglary and robbery, but also by other types of actual or attempted theft.

As suggested by its name, Form H also covers loss to property outside the premises in the care and custody of a messenger, but coverage for such property is limited to actual or attempted robbery.

Aside from the premises theft feature, coverage Form H is quite similar to Forms D and E, including the restrictions concerning property not covered—such as motor vehicles and trailers.

Separate limits apply to premises theft and outside robbery coverages. As with the other forms, the most the insurer will pay in any one occurrence is the limit shown in the policy declarations. Like Form E, Form H also suspends coverage until the premises are restored to the same level of security that existed before a loss, unless a "watchperson" is substituted.

Additional Exclusions, Conditions, and Definitions

Form H contains the following exclusions, which have already been discussed under previous forms:

- Acts of employees, directors, trustees, or representatives
- Changes in conditions
- Exchanges or purchases
- Fire
- Inventory shortages
- Transfer or surrender of property
- Vandalism
- Voluntary parting of title to or possession of property

Conditions and definitions are likewise similar to those in other forms. The coverage of Form H is summarized in Exhibit 8-8.

COVERAGE FOR PROPERTY IN SAFEKEEPING

Banks and other organizations maintain safe deposit boxes for the

Exhibit 8-8
Form H — Premises Theft and Robbery Outside the Premises Coverage Form*

	Inside the Premises	Outside the Premises
Covered Property	Property other than money and securities inside the premises	Property other than money and securities outside the premises in the care and custody of a messenger
Covered Causes of Loss	Actual or attempted theft	Actual or attempted robbery

*Reprinted with permission from *ISO Commercial Lines Policy and Rating Simplification Project Workshop Leader's Guide,* Insurance Services Office, Inc., 1985.

use of their customers. People place valuable property in safe deposit boxes in order to prevent loss from theft, damage, or destruction. However, this loss control measure is not foolproof, and losses do occasionally occur. For example, the depository building can be damaged by fire, tornado, or other perils. The contents of safe deposit boxes may be lost by burglary, robbery, misappropriation by bank employees, access and theft by unauthorized persons and, of course, loss by the negligence of the box renter.

Crime coverage Forms I and J are available to cover the depositor and the depository against crime losses to property in safe deposit boxes.

Lessees of Safe Deposit Boxes Coverage—Form I

Section 1 of this form is designed to cover:

- "securities," as defined, against
- "theft," disappearance, or destruction.

Section 2 is designed to cover:

- property other than money and securities, against
- actual or attempted "burglary" or "robbery," or vandalism.

Both sections provide coverage for property inside a safe deposit box or during the course of deposit or removal from a safe deposit box. In either case, the loss must occur inside the "depository premises," meaning the interior of that portion of any building at the location shown in the form and occupied by the depository named in the form or its safe depository affiliate in conducting a banking or safe deposit business.

Exhibit 8-9
Form I — Lessees of Safe Deposit Boxes Coverage Form*

	Theft, Disappearance or Destruction of Securities	Burglary or Robbery of Property Other Than Money and Securities
Covered Property	Securities inside (1) Insured's safe deposit box in a vault in a depository premises (2) A depository premises during the course of deposit or removal from insured's safe deposit box	Property other than money and securities inside (1) Insured's safe deposit box in a vault in a depository premises (2) A depository premises during the course of deposit or removal from insured's safe deposit box
Covered Causes of Loss	(1) Theft (2) Disappearance (3) Destruction	(1) Actual or attempted burglary or robbery (2) Vandalism

Other Information:
● The Lessees of Safe Deposit Boxes Coverage Form includes a schedule that is used to identify the locations of the depositories at which coverage will apply.

*Reprinted with permission from *ISO Commercial Lines Policy and Rating Simplification Project Workshop Leader's Guide*, Insurance Services Office, Inc., 1985.

In this form, "burglary" is defined to mean "the taking of property from within a locked safe deposit box in a locked vault in a depository premises by a person unlawfully entering the box and vault as evidenced by marks of forcible entry upon the exterior of the box and vault." The definition of "robbery" is identical to that found in other forms already discussed.

Most of the exclusions in Form I are also found in other forms:

● Acts of employees, directors, trustees, or representatives
● Exchanges or purchases
● Fire (applicable under section 2 only)
● Transfer or surrender of property
● Voluntary parting of title to or possession of property

An exclusion unique to this form precludes coverage for loss of property owned by the depository or held by it as collateral or held by the depository in trust for more than thirty days. This exclusion can be modified, by endorsement, under Section 1 coverage, to provide coverage for loss of securities held by the bank or depository in trust— but not as collateral—while the described boxes are under the dual control of the depository and a co-fiduciary.

The coverage of Form I is summarized in Exhibit 8-9.

Securities Deposited With Others Coverage—Form J

Form J covers securities at certain covered locations (covered property):

- inside the "custodian's" premises,
- being conveyed outside the "custodian's" premises by the "custodian" or an employee of the "custodian," or
- on deposit by the "custodian" for safekeeping in a depository

against loss by the covered perils of:

- theft,
- disappearance, or
- destruction.

The name of the custodian and the name of the depository are entered into the coverage form. If a depository specified in the schedule is changed by the custodian, the insurance will apply to the new depository if the insured gives notice within thirty days of the change.

As indicated in Exhibit 8-4, Form J is subject to the same exclusions as Form I, with four exceptions:

1. Unlike Form I, Form J *does not* exclude loss of property owned by or held by a depository as collateral.
2. Unlike Form I, Form J *does* exclude loss to securities at any location that the named insured occupies. This simply reinforces the intent that coverage is meant to apply while the securities are in the possession of the designated custodian and at a declared depository—not at the insured's own business location.
3. Also, Form J *does* exclude coverage for loss to property owned by the custodian or depository or when the securities are held by the custodian or depository in trust for over thirty days. The difference between the Form I wording and the Form J wording reflects the difference in covered property and the nature of the losses to which it is subject.
4. While Form I contains a fire exclusion, applicable to Section 2 of that policy, no similar exclusion appears in Form J.

The most the insurer will pay under Forms I and J in any one occurrence is the amount designated in the schedule over the applicable per occurrence deductible. Both forms also are subject to the crime general provisions form.

The coverage of Form J is summarized in Exhibit 8-10.

Exhibit 8-10

Form J — Securities Deposited with Others Coverage Form*

Covered Property	Securities while inside the custodian's premises, while being transported by the custodian, or while on deposit in a depository
Covered Causes of Loss	(1) Theft (2) Disappearance (3) Destruction

*Reprinted with permission from *ISO Commercial Lines Policy and Rating Simplification Project Workshop Leader's Guide*, Insurance Services Office, Inc., 1985.

Safe Depository Liability Coverage—Form M

Businesses that rent safe deposit boxes for use of their customers are involved with a bailment that is guided not only by common law but also by statute. Despite their obvious safety, losses from safe deposit boxes do occasionally occur. Two crime forms are available for organizations *other than financial institutions* that offer safe deposit boxes.

- Form M offers coverage on a liability basis.
- Form N pays for direct loss because of certain types of loss.

These forms are used with *safe depository general provisions* rather than crime general provisions. Of course, the common policy conditions are also applicable.

With Form M, the insurer agrees to pay those sums which the depository becomes legally obligated to pay by reason of liability for loss of customer's property. The property of customers can consist of money, securities, and tangible property other than money and securities that has intrinsic value. Coverage applies only to loss or destruction of or damage to customers' property while:

1. inside the customers' safe deposit boxes in vaults in the premises, i.e., the interior of that portion of any building at a location shown in the declarations that the named insured occupies in conducting its business;
2. stored in the vaults in the premises; or
3. temporarily elsewhere in the premises while in the course of deposit or removal from the boxes or vaults.

The exclusions of the safe depository general provisions form deal with liability stemming from:

- acts committed by the insured or its partners,
- governmental action,

Exhibit 8-11
Form M — Safe Depository Liability Coverage Form*

Coverage	The sums that the insured becomes legally obligated to pay as damages because of loss or destruction of, or damage to, customers' property while the property is
	a. Inside the customers' safe deposit boxes in vaults in the premises b. Stored in such vaults in the premises c. Temporarily elsewhere in the premises while in the course of deposit in or removal from the boxes or vaults

Other information:
- This coverage form is subject to the Safe Depository General Provisions Form rather than the Crime General Provisions Form. The Safe Depository General Form contains General Exclusions, Conditions, and Definitions specifically tailored to Safe Depository Coverage.

*Reprinted with permission from *ISO Commercial Lines Policy and Rating Simplification Project Workshop Leader's Guide,* Insurance Services Office, Inc., 1985.

- nuclear reaction, radiation, and kindred exposures, and
- war and similar actions.

The only exclusion in the form itself concerns liability that the named insured may assume under any written agreement.

The coverage of Form M is summarized in Exhibit 8-11.

Safe Depository Direct Loss—Form N

This form is written to cover the lessee of a safe deposit box against loss from actual or attempted robbery or burglary, as well as damage or destruction from the same locations as specified in the liability form. However, unlike Form M, this form applies to securities and other property, but not to money.

The property covered, therefore, includes any type of tangible property other than money that might be placed in the box—such as securities, jewelry, or other valuable articles. Property may include that held in trust or for safekeeping by the insured, or property held by the insured as a bailee or in any capacity that would make the insured liable to the owner for loss.

As an extension, coverage also applies for loss from damage to the premises and all furnishings, fixtures, fittings, equipment, safes, and vaults in the premises by actual or attempted burglary, robbery, or vandalism, if the named insured owns such property or is legally liable for the damage.

In addition to the general exclusions, direct loss Form N specifically precludes coverage for loss by fire, any indirect loss that results as the consequence of an occurrence, and inherent vice.

Exhibit 8-12
Form N — Safe Depository Direct Loss Coverage Form*

Covered Property	Customers' property while the property is a. Inside the customers' safe deposit boxes in vaults in the premises b. Stored in such vaults in the premises c. Temporarily elsewhere in the premises while in the course of deposit or removal from the boxes or vaults
Covered Causes of Loss	a. Actual or attempted robbery or burglary b. Destruction c. Damage

Other information:
● This coverage form is subject to the Safe Depository General Provisions Form rather than the Crime General Provisions Form. The Safe Depository General Form contains General Exclusions, Conditions, and Definitions specifically tailored to Safe Depository Coverage.

*Reprinted with permission from *ISO Commercial Lines Policy and Rating Simplification Project Workshop Leader's Guide,* Insurance Services Office, Inc., 1985.

The coverage of Form N is summarized in Exhibit 8-12.

LIABILITY FOR GUESTS' PROPERTY

Two crime forms protect an innkeeper against liability because of property loss sustained by guests of hotels and other lodging facilities. Although theft is a major source of loss, these forms provide broad coverage against noncriminal losses, as well.

- Form K is designed to cover the legal liability of innkeepers for loss of valuables belonging to guests while the valuables are *in a safe deposit box on the premises.*
- Form L is designed to cover the legal liability of innkeepers for loss of covered property belonging to guests while the property is *on the premises or in the innkeeper's possession.* Property covered under Form L does not have to be in a safe deposit box.

Both forms address exposures that are excluded by standard property and liability insurance forms.

- The commercial general liability coverage form (CGL) excludes liability for personal property (which includes money and securities) in the insured's care, custody, or control.
- "Commercial property" policies exclude from coverage accounts, bills, currency, deeds, and evidences of debt.
- The building and personal property coverage form (BPP) covers other personal property belonging to others as an extension of

coverage, but coverage depends on the "commercial property" causes of loss to which the policy applies. Additionally, an amount of insurance may be specified for property of others as the covered property.

Both Forms K and L are autonomous in the sense that neither is subject to the crime general provisions form applicable to most other crime forms. Many of the same conditions appear in Forms K and L. Since all applicable provisions—insuring agreements, exclusions, conditions, and definitions—are contained within the forms, they are more in the nature of self-contained policies. However, besides needing a declarations page, the policy is not complete without at least one other document—the separate common policy conditions.

Liability for Guests' Property—Safe Deposit Box Coverage—Form K

With Form K the insurer agrees to pay, on behalf of the named insured, damages that the insured becomes legally obligated to pay because of loss or destruction of or damage to *any* property belonging to guests, so long as the property, at the time of loss, was in a safe deposit box at the "premises" described in the policy.

No covered causes of loss are listed in the policy, since it is the named insured's liability that triggers coverage. As a practical matter, however, it seems most likely that the named insured will become liable for property lost by the perils of fire, burglary, or robbery. Therefore, it is noteworthy that fire losses are excluded.

Because this form provides liability coverage, the insurer also agrees to pay the costs of any defense that may be required, as well as payment for other legal costs and expenses that may be incurred at the insurer's request.

Coverage is subject to a number of exclusions. Exclusions needing no explanation here concern:

- acts committed by the named insured or its partners,
- loss caused by governmental action,
- inherent vice,
- nuclear reaction, radiation, contamination, and the like, and
- war and similar actions.

As noted, fire damage is also excluded. In this respect, Form K is consistent with other crime coverage forms. However, the exclusion may leave a noteworthy coverage gap, which is not completely filled by standard "commercial property" or general liability insurance.

Insureds must be very careful not to assume liability for loss of

Exhibit 8-13

Form K — Liability for Guests' Property — Safe Deposit Box Coverage Form*

Covered Property	Any property belonging to the insured's guest while the property is in a safe deposit box in the premises
Coverage	The sums that the insured becomes legally obligated to pay as damages because of loss or destruction of, or damage to, covered property

Other information:
● This coverage form contains all exclusions, conditions, and definitions that relate to it except for the Common Policy Conditions. Therefore, the Crime General Provisions Form is not used with this coverage form.

*Reprinted with permission from *ISO Commercial Lines Policy and Rating Simplification Project Workshop Leader's Guide,* Insurance Services Office, Inc., 1985.

property, because liability assumed under any written agreement is expressly excluded. Another exclusion applies if the insured releases any other person or organization from legal liability; the exclusion preserves the insurer's right of subrogation.

The coverage of Form K is summarized in Exhibit 8-13.

Liability for Guests' Property—Form L

Form L is commonly referred to as *innkeepers' liability insurance.* Its purpose is to protect an innkeeper or hotel operator from legal liability because of damage stemming from:

● loss, damage, or destruction to nearly any kind of guests' property while it is within the "premises" or possession of the insured innkeeper.

No coverage applies unless there is liability on behalf of the insured's business establishment. However, the insured would receive the benefit of any legal and defense coverage so long as a complaint alleges a situation that would potentially be covered by the policy.

Any kind of property will qualify for coverage under the policy, but property is not covered in some situations. Not covered are samples or articles carried or held for sale or for delivery after sale, and vehicles—including their equipment and accessories. Also not covered is any property contained in or on a vehicle. Thus, this form will not cover theft of property from an auto or truck that is parked on the insured's premises by guests or others for business or personal reasons.

The exclusions of Form L are virtually identical to those of Form K, with two exceptions. The first exception concerns assumed liability.

Exhibit 8-14

Form L — Liability for Guests' Property — Premises Coverage Form*

Covered Property	Any property, other than that specified as Property Not Covered, belonging to the insured's guests while the property is in a. The premises b. The insured's possession
Coverage	The sums that the insured becomes legally obligated to pay as damages because of loss or destruction of, or damage to, covered property

Other information:
* This coverage form contains all exclusions, conditions, and definitions that relate to it except for the Common Policy Conditions. Therefore, the Crime General Provisions Form is not used with this coverage form.

*Reprinted with permission from *ISO Commercial Lines Policy and Rating Simplification Project Workshop Leader's Guide*, Insurance Services Office, Inc., 1985.

Form L covers liability assumed by the insured under a contract written before an occurrence of loss, damage, or destruction, that increases by $1,000 or less the amount for which the insured may otherwise be held liable. This provision may be desirable because some state statutes specifically limit an innkeeper's liability for loss of guests' property. Thus, for example, if such a limit were $100 and the insured were to agree, in writing, to be accountable up to $500 for any future loss, the extra $400 liability of this written assumption would be covered by Form L.

The second difference, as compared with Form K, is that Form L also excludes loss, damage, or destruction caused by the spilling, upsetting, or leaking of food or liquid. This exclusion appears because Form L is concerned with all kinds of property (except samples and vehicles, as noted earlier). In the absence of this exclusion, the form might even be called upon to cover damages when a clumsy waiter spills wine onto a guest's evening gown.

Unlike Form K, Form L also excludes loss for property while in the named insured's care and custody for purposes of laundering or cleaning. Inland marine forms are available to specifically cover this bailment exposure.

The coverage of Form L is summarized in Exhibit 8-14.

EXTORTION COVERAGE—FORM G

Extortion is the cause of loss involved when a businessperson or a member of his or her family is kidnapped and held for ransom. In Coverage Form G, "extortion" is defined as:

> the surrender of property away from the "premises" as a result of a threat communicated to you or an "employee," or to a relative or invitee of either, who is, or allegedly is, being held captive.

It is worth emphasizing that the threat must be bodily harm rather than threats to property, and surrender of the property must be *away* from the interior of that portion of the building that the named insured occupies in conducting its business.

Covered property under this form can consist of money, securities, and property other than money and securities—all of which are defined in the general crime provisions.

The coverage form requires the person receiving the threat to attempt to report the threat to an associate, to the Federal Bureau of Investigation (FBI), and to local law enforcement authorities. In fact, any loss because of property surrendered before reasonable effort has been made to report an extortionist's demands will negate coverage under this form. Also, the perpetrator cannot be an employee, director, trustee, or authorized representative of the insured.

Insurance under this form can be purchased with or without a *loss participation clause* under which the insured agrees to bear a portion of every loss. When a loss participation clause is chosen, the most the insurer will pay under the policy in each occurrence over the applicable deductible is the percentage of loss specified as that of the insurance company's—or the limit of insurance, whichever is less. In absence of the participation clause, the amount payable is the limit of insurance per occurrence over the applicable deductible. The loss participation clause is intended to make the insured more loss control conscious. It should also reduce the cost of insurance.

In light of the fact that extortion is a worldwide problem, the coverage territory of this form is noteworthy. In the standard ISO form, loss is covered only if the actual or alleged captivity takes place within the United States of America, U.S. Virgin Islands, Puerto Rico, Canal Zone, or Canada. A corporation that desires coverage on a worldwide basis would need to seek insurance in an excess and surplus lines market.

The coverage of Form G is summarized in Exhibit 8-15.

COMPUTER FRAUD COVERAGE—FORM F

As noted in Chapter 7, the growing use of electronic data processing systems has enhanced the opportunities for fraud and other criminal loss. Markets for computer fraud coverage, though limited, are

Exhibit 8-15
Form G — Extortion Coverage Form*

Covered Property	(1) Money (2) Securities (3) Property other than money and securities
Covered Causes of Loss	Extortion

*Reprinted with permission from *ISO Commercial Lines Policy and Rating Simplification Project Workshop Leader's Guide*, Insurance Services Office, Inc., 1985.

Exhibit 8-16
Form F — Computer Fraud Coverage Form*

Covered Property	(1) Money (2) Securities (3) Property other than money and securities
Covered Causes of Loss	Computer Fraud

*Reprinted with permission from *ISO Commercial Lines Policy and Rating Simplification Project Workshop Leader's Guide*, Insurance Services Office, Inc., 1985.

located in the United States as well as London. Some insurers cater only to banks, while others will consider any business establishment that uses computers.

If a business otherwise qualifies, it may be possible to purchase protection under coverage Form F of the commercial crime insurance program. This coverage will pay for loss of, and loss from damage to:

- covered property consisting of money, securities, and property other than money and securities, by computer fraud.

"Computer fraud" is defined in the form to mean:

> "theft" of property following and directly related to the use of any computer to fraudulently cause a transfer of that property from inside the "premises" or "banking premises" to a person (other than a "messenger") outside those "premises" or to a place outside those "premises."

Not covered is loss caused by acts of employees, directors, trustees, or representatives while acting alone or in collusion with other persons, as well as loss by authorized representatives while performing services for the named insured. And, in common with Forms A and H, no coverage applies for loss or that part of a loss in which the proof depends on an inventory or profit and loss computation.

The coverage of Form F is summarized in Exhibit 8-16.

Exhibit 8-17
Crime Coverage Plans*

Plan Number	Title	Old Crime Policy Equivalent	Coverage Forms Included
Plan 1	Combination Crime—Separate Limits Option	Comprehensive Dishonesty, Disappearance, and Destruction Policy	A—J (any combination)
Plan 2	Combination Crime—Single Limits Option	Blanket Crime Policy	A—D (mandatory) E—J (optional)
Plan 3	Storekeepers' Broad Form	Broad Form Storekeepers' Form	A—E (mandatory)
Plan 4	Storekeepers' Burglary and Robbery	Storekeepers' Burglary and Robbery Form	D and E (mandatory)
Plan 5	Office Burglary and Robbery Form	Office Burglary and Robbery Form	D and H (mandatory)
Plan 6	Guests' Property—Safe Deposit Box	Hotel Safe Depository Form	K (mandatory)
Plan 7	Guests' Property—Premises	Innkeepers' Liability Policy	L (mandatory)
Plan 8	Safe Depository	Combination Safe Depository Policy	M—N (either one or both)
Plan 9	Excess Bank Burglary and Robbery	Bank Excess Burglary and Robbery Form	D (mandatory)
Plan 10	Bank Excess Securities	Bank Excess Securities Form	C (mandatory)

* Adapted from Insurance Services Office, Inc., material with its permission.

CRIME COVERAGE PLANS

Ten "crime coverage plans" combine the various coverage forms into particular combinations available to organizations that qualify. The main function of these plans is to approximate the coverages of earlier crime coverage packages offered by the ISO and SAA, thus easing the process of converting to simplified forms (see Exhibit 8-17).

As the various coverage forms have already been described, only brief discussion of the combination plan is necessary.

Plan 1—Combination Crime Form—Separate Limits Option

Any combination of coverage forms A through J, each subject to a separate limit, can be purchased under this plan. This plan provides results very similar to the old comprehensive dishonesty, disappearance, and destruction policy, the so called "3-D."

Subject to individual coverage form exceptions, any entity is eligible for this plan except an insured eligible for a financial institution blanket bond (discussed in Chapter 14). Additionally, endowment funds, foundations, and mutual funds having nonemployee sales representatives, though eligible for financial institutions bonds, are eligible for coverage under Plan 1.

Plan 2—Combination Crime Form—Single Limits Option

Under this plan, coverage forms A (blanket), B, C, and D are mandatory with the same single limit of insurance applicable to each. Premiums for Forms C and D are based on values exposed to loss rather than the limit of insurance. Coverage forms E through J are optional, each subject to a separate limit of insurance. Under prior programs, this type of combination was known as a blanket crime policy.

Any entity is eligible for this plan except insureds eligible for a financial institution bond, armored motor vehicle companies, and insureds eligible for a public official or public employee blanket bond. State universities, colleges, and schools are also eligible if:

1. faithful performance of duty coverage is not required,
2. the insured is not a state department or state board,
3. the officials or employees are not required by law to be bonded.

Plan 3—Storekeepers Broad Form

To write this plan, coverage forms A (blanket), B, C, D, and E are mandatory, with the same limit of insurance applying separately to each such coverage. The limit of insurance may be $1,000, $1,500, $2,000, or $2,500—no other limits may be written. Coverage of this plan applies to money, securities, and property other than money and securities. Any business establishment with a single location and not more than four employees is eligible for this plan. Not eligible, however, is anyone who qualifies for a public official or public employee blanket bond.

Plan 4—Storekeepers Burglary and Robbery Coverage

This plan provides coverage for money, securities, and property other than money and securities against burglary and robbery. Coverage forms D and E are mandatory. The money coverage is provided by the attachment of an endorsement to coverage Forms D and E. The same range of limits apply here as with Plan 3. No restriction applies on insureds eligible for this combination of coverages.

Plan 5—Office Burglary and Robbery Coverage

This plan requires the combination of coverage Forms D and H. The effect is to cover loss of money, securities, and property other than money and securities pertaining to an office because of burglary and robbery. No eligibility restrictions apply and coverage is subject to a minimum limit of $1,000, but no maximum limit.

Plan 6—Guests' Property—Safe Deposit Box

Since Coverage Form K is mandatory, the protection provided under this plan is the equivalent of the coverage form that provides liability coverage against loss of guests' property from safe deposit boxes. Any insured that provides lodging facilities is eligible for this coverage plan.

Plan 7—Guests' Property—Premises

Coverage L is mandatory under this plan. The product is the equivalent of the old innkeepers liability policy. Any insured providing lodging facilities is eligible. Coverage under this plan can be modified by endorsement to add loss by

- fire damage,
- food or liquid damage,
- property in the custody of a laundry or cleaner,
- property of others occupying leased lodging accommodations, and
- samples and articles held for sale or delivery.

Plan 8—Safe Depository Coverage

This plan is comprised of either or both of two coverage forms:

- Coverage Form M provides liability protection to a depository for loss of customers' property.
- Coverage Form N covers customers' property against direct loss or damage.

Separate limits apply to each coverage form, and both are subject to the safe depository general provisions form. All insureds providing safe deposit box facilities, other than financial institutions, are eligible for this plan.

Plan 9—Excess Bank Burglary and Robbery

Robbery and safe burglary coverage form D is mandatory under this plan. It applies to all premises of the insured and provides coverage for loss involving money, securities, and property other than money and securities. Any institution authorized by federal or state government to conduct a banking or trust company business is eligible for this plan.

Plan 10—Bank Excess Securities

Section 1 of Form C is mandatory under this plan. The result is coverage for loss involving securities against theft, disappearance, and destruction. Eligibility is the same as for Plan 9.

THE FEDERAL CRIME INSURANCE PROGRAM

The Federal Crime Insurance Program was initiated because Congress decided that insurance against losses from crime was not available at affordable rates in some parts of the United States. The program has many times been slated for elimination but has received numerous last-minute reprieves. At the time of this writing, it is still in operation.

The program is operational in twenty-eight states, the District of Columbia, Puerto Rico, and the Virgin Islands. For organizations in eligible territories, the federal program provides a source of coverage that might otherwise be unavailable from normal sources. The program is administered by the Federal Emergency Management Agency (FEMA). The Federal Crime Insurance Program uses its own policy forms, and is not based on the standard forms previously described.

Perils and Property Covered

The property covered by the policy under this program includes merchandise, furniture, fixtures, and equipment. Also, money and securities are covered against robbery or safe burglary.

The perils covered under this program are essentially burglary and robbery, with some minor extensions to other crime perils. Definitions of perils are similar to those in the currently available crime insurance coverage forms and plans previously described.

- Burglary, and larceny incident to burglary, is the stealing of property from within premises that have been forcibly entered, with visible marks of such forcible entry at the place of entry.

- Robbery means the stealing of business personal property from the insured in the insured's presence and with the insured's knowledge either inside or outside the premises.

Coverage also applies for damage to the premises committed during the actual or attempted course of a burglary or robbery. By extension, coverage also applies for loss by theft from a night depository or from safe burglary.

Mysterious disappearance is not a covered peril. There must be an actual incident of breaking or entering or of robbery for a loss to be covered. This insurance does not cover inventory shortages.

Limits and Deductibles

Only a limited amount of insurance can be purchased under the federal program. Insurance may be purchased in amounts from a minimum of $1,000 to a maximum of $15,000 per occurrence. When compared with values exposed to loss, this is a modest amount of coverage for many businesses. However, the program is intended primarily to provide a degree of crime insurance coverage for smaller inner city merchants who are unable to secure any amount of crime insurance or find it extremely difficult or expensive to obtain.

All policies are subject to a per loss deductible that varies in amount according to the annual gross receipts of the insured, subject to a minimum of 5 percent of the gross amount of loss. For example, the deductible is $50 for a business whose gross receipts are less than $100,000 annually. It ranges upward to a $200 deductible for businesses with annual gross receipts of $500,000 or more. This variation in the deductible amounts according to gross receipts is different from the usual approach offered by insurance companies.

Protection Requirement

The program requires that certain protective devices be in place before a firm is eligible for federal crime insurance. In general, a business must have its doors, windows, and other accessible openings adequately protected against burglary during nonbusiness hours. This protection requirement may include certain types of locks on doors, bars on windows and doors of glass, and other bars or protective devices that would impede entry by a burglar. Payment of loss is dependent on the maintenance of the protective devices by the insured during the policy term.

CRIME LOSS FINANCING ALTERNATIVES

In terms of loss financing alternatives, most crime loss exposures are not substantially different from other property exposures. However, some unique characteristics of the employee dishonesty exposure bear special mention.

A key question in financing the employee dishonesty exposure is to determine what exposures, if any, to insure. This question goes beyond merely asking whether or not to purchase employee dishonesty insurance. No employee dishonesty insurance will cover all possible losses, and the insurance invariably has a limit that may be lower than an organization's maximum possible loss, since the loss potential from dishonesty is virtually open-ended. Furthermore, employee dishonesty insurance is available in a number of different forms that also require study and careful selection.

Blanket Versus Scheduled Coverage

When considering the purchase of employee dishonesty insurance, a risk manager must decide whether to purchase coverage on a schedule basis (individual or position) or a blanket basis.

Presumably, a decision to purchase blanket coverage is based on the principle that all employees are potential thieves. Conversely, a decision to purchase insurance on certain employees suggests that certain nondesignated employees are prohibited from embezzling by morality or circumstances, while others are highly suspect.

The major distinction between employee dishonesty insurance written on a blanket and schedule basis deals with their treatment of collusive theft involving more than one employee. A logical basis for deciding between the two approaches would be the likelihood of a collusive embezzlement within a particular organization. However, even though the possibility of collusion always exists, most employee thefts do not involve collusion. Moreover, the cost for the two coverage types reflects the fact that the schedule position insurance may have a higher loss payout if more than one employee is involved in a loss. In comparing two forms, it is necessary to recognize that comparable coverage does not mean two employee dishonesty insurance policies subject to the same limits. Assuming both forms are available, the only rational bases on which to make a decision are an assessment of the probability of collusive behavior by employees, some determination of whether the guilty parties can be identified, and an analysis of the amount of coverage of each type that can be purchased for a comparable cost.

Determining Amounts of Coverage to Purchase

Various formulas have been published, but it is important to remember that any rule of thumb is only a guideline. As with other loss exposures, risk managers should rely heavily on experience and informed judgment.

One important factor that might be considered in making such judgment is the length of time during which an employee might steal before being apprehended. In the short run, consideration could be given to the frequency of physical inventories or other checkpoints. In the long run, it may be necessary to consider such things as employee turnover.

Recognizing the Application of Limits

It is important to remember that policy limits apply to the accumulated amount of loss at the time of discovery. Thus, when an employee has been discovered to have taken $20,000 a year over the past five years, a $100,000 limit is needed (at the time of discovery) to cover the full $100,000 of loss.

Use of Excess Coverage

As noted, most organizations face the possibility that almost any employee could steal. The existence of this possibility argues strongly in favor of a blanket, rather than a schedule, position form. Yet, it is not necessarily true that all employees have an equal opportunity to steal large amounts. A receptionist usually will not be able to steal as much as a financial officer. Excess protection is often desirable on those key employees who are clearly in a position that provides the opportunity to steal large amounts. Of course, it is extremely difficult to make a decision on who might embezzle funds and the ultimate amount.

Retention as an Alternative

The majority of businesses do not insure against employee dishonesty. This makes sense, to a degree, since most employee dishonesty losses are relatively minor. Most incidents of petty pilferage of inventory or cash go undetected. Those that are discovered are well within the typical organization's ability to absorb loss. To the extent regular, low-level pilferage occurs, it is entirely appropriate to treat losses as normal business expenses. There is no need to insure such losses.

But not all losses are minor, and it should be obvious by now that employee dishonesty can result in losses so severe that they threaten the survival of the organization.

Importance of Record Keeping

Whether or not an organization purchases crime insurance, careful record-keeping practices are virtually essential. Records are important to prove a loss for tax purposes, as well as to help establish the amount of an insured loss.

Index

C

Fixtures, trade, *160*
Flame and oxidation, *206*
Flammable (explosive) range, *100*
Flash point, *90*
Flat insurance, *188*
Flood, *22, 76*
Flood exclusion, *346*
Flood and high water losses, *126*
Flow chart analysis, *38*
Flow chart technique, applying, *38*
Flow charting, loss control and, *294*
Forcible entry, *368*
Forcible exit, *368*
Forgery, *366*
Forgery or alteration, *373*
Forgery or alteration coverage—
  Form B, *418*
Form, value reporting, *191*
Frame construction, *92, 93*
Frames, glass, *334*
Franchise and license fees,
  royalties, *249*
Fraud, computer, *373*
Freezing exclusion, *218*
Frequency, loss, *59*
Frequency and severity by peril, *74*
Friendly fire, *105, 206*
Friendly versus hostile fire, *206*
Fuel, building contents as, *91*
  buildings as, *92*
  removing, *101*
Fuels, *90*
"Full" coverage, *273*
Full reporting clause, *193*
Functional replacement cost
  endorsement, *186*
Furnace explosion coverage
  endorsement, *346*
Furnace firebox explosions, *210*
Furniture, equipment, and supplies,
  10
Future earnings and expenses,
  projecting, *259*

G

General Standard Fire Policy, *135*
Generally noninsurable perils, *22*
Generic classification system, *15*
Glass, *212*
  breakage of, *20, 216*
  perils and loss consequences, *329*
Glass coverage, limits of insurance
  in, *334*
Glass coverage form, *331*
  additional coverages in, *333*
  deductible in, *335*
  vacancy exclusion in, *333*
  valuation and loss payment
    provisions in, *335*
Glass exposures, *328*
Glass losses, frequency and
  severity of, *330*
Glass property, types of, *329*
Governmental action, *403*
Governmental action exclusion, *232*
Growth, continued, *4*
Guests' property, liability for, *439*
*Guiding Principles—Casualty,
  Fidelity, Inland Marine—
  First-Party Property Losses
  and Claims, 150*

H

Hail, *76*
Halogens, *103*
Halon, *103*
Hazard, *15*
Hazardous substance limitation, *348*
Heat, excessive, *206*
  removing, *101*
Heat as a by-product, *105*
Heat, light, and power expense, *247*
Heat sources, *89*
  controlling, *104*
  fixed versus mobile, *90*
  planned versus unplanned, *90*
  unplanned, *106*

M

U

V

Vandalism or malicious mischief
(VMM), *202*
Vault, fire resistive, *111*
Vehicles, *12, 209*
Vertical fire spread, limiting, *107*
Vibration detector, *387*
VMM (vandalism or malicious
mischief), *202, 211*
Volcanic action, *19, 215*
Volcanic eruption, *215*
Volcanic explosion, *211*
Voluntary insurance, *86*
Voluntary parting of title to or
possession of property, *425*

W

Wall, fire, *109*

War and military action, *233*
War perils, *22*
Watchman or security patrols, *390*
Watchperson, *369*
  robbery of, *431*
Water, fire control and, *102*
Water damage, *20, 77, 210, 217*
  controlling, *121*
Water damage exclusion, *235*
Water damage limitation, *348*
Weight of snow, ice, or sleet, *20,
217*
Wet pipe system, *116*
Windstorm, *75, 207*
Windstorm damage, control of, *126*
Windstorm and hail, *18*
Wooden screens, *384*
Working layer, *64*